Arthur Middleton Reeves

The Finding of Wineland the Good

The history of the Icelandic discovery of America, edited and translated from the earliest records

Arthur Middleton Reeves

The Finding of Wineland the Good
The history of the Icelandic discovery of America, edited and translated from the earliest records

ISBN/EAN: 9783337317713

Printed in Europe, USA, Canada, Australia, Japan

Cover: Foto ©ninafisch / pixelio.de

THE FINDING OF WINELAND THE GOOD

The History of the Icelandic Discovery of America

EDITED AND TRANSLATED FROM THE EARLIEST RECORDS

BY

ARTHUR MIDDLETON REEVES

WITH PHOTOTYPE PLATES OF THE VELLUM MSS. OF THE SAGAS

London
HENRY FROWDE
OXFORD UNIVERSITY PRESS WAREHOUSE
AMEN CORNER, E.C.
1890

PREFACE.

A CHAPTER title in the Codex Frisianus, 'Fundit Vínland góða' [Wineland the Good found], which has been reproduced in enlarged facsimile on the cover, has suggested the title for this book. The chapter which this title heads will be found on page 14. The Icelandic text there cited has been copied directly from the original, and this method has also been pursued in the other cases where citations of strictly historical matter have been made. In printing these citations, accents, punctuation and capital letters have been added, and supplied contractions have been printed in italics. Passages which have not been regarded as clearly historical have also been given in the original, but in this case it has been deemed sufficient to print after the best published texts. Icelandic proper names, where they occur in the translations, have been somewhat altered from their correct form, to the end that they might appear less strange to the English reader. This liberty has been taken with less hesitancy since it has been possible to give these names in their proper forms in the Index.

To the kindness of Dr. Bruun, Librarian of the Royal Library of Copenhagen, I am indebted for the privilege which has made the photographic reproduction of the Wineland History of the Flatey Book possible. I am under like obligation to the Arna-Magnæan Legation for the use, for a similar purpose, of the manuscripts AM.[1] 557 4to and 544 4to. To one member of the Arna-Magnæan Legation, Dr. Kristian Kålund, I am under still further obligation for very many favours, which his profound acquaintance with

[1] This contraction is used throughout to describe the manuscripts belonging to the Arna-Magnæan Collection.

Icelandic manuscripts, and especially with those in his charge as Librarian of the Arna-Magnæan Library, have rendered particularly valuable. To Professor Gustav Storm I feel myself peculiarly indebted for the kindly help, which he so freely tendered me at a time when the courtesy was extended at the expense of his own personal engagements. My thanks are also due to Dr. Finnur Jónsson, for his supervision of the photographing of the Arna-Magnæan manuscripts, and for other friendly acts. I am likewise under obligation to Captain Holm, of the Danish Navy, and Captain Phythian, of the United States Navy, for help, which finds more particular mention elsewhere. Finally and especially, I owe to Dr. Valtýr Guðmundsson an expression of the appreciation I feel for his frequent and ever ready assistance, and particularly for his review of the proofs of the Icelandic texts.

The kindness which these friends have shown me has contributed in no small degree to the pleasure which the making of these pages has afforded.

A. M. R.

BERLIN, *July*, 1890.

TABLE OF CONTENTS.

THE FINDING OF WINELAND THE GOOD.

INTRODUCTORY.

THE Icelandic discovery of America was first announced, in print, more than two centuries and a half ago. Within the past fifty years of this period, the discovery has attracted more general attention than during all of the interval preceding,—a fact, which is no doubt traceable to the publication, in 1837, of a comprehensive work upon the subject prepared by the Danish scholar, Carl Christian Rafn. Although it is now more than half a century since this book was published, Rafn is still very generally regarded as the standard authority upon the subject of which he treats. But his zeal in promulgating the discovery seriously prejudiced his judgment. His chief fault was the heedless confusing of all of the material bearing directly or indirectly upon his theme,—the failure to winnow the sound historical material from that which is unsubstantiated. Rafn offered numerous explanations of the texts which his work contained, and propounded many dubious theories and hazardous conjectures. With these the authors, who have founded their investigations upon his work, have more concerned themselves than with the texts of the original documents. If less effort had been applied to the dissemination and defence of fantastic speculations, and more to the determination of the exact nature of the facts which have been preserved in the Icelandic records, the discovery should not have failed to be accepted as clearly established by sound historical data. Upon any other hypothesis than this it is difficult to account for the disposition American historians have shown to treat the Icelandic discovery as possible, from conjectural causes, rather than as determined by the historical records preserved by the fellow-countrymen of the discoverers.

Bancroft, in his History of the United States, gave form to this tendency many years ago, when he stated, that:

'The story of the colonization of America by Northmen rests on narratives mythological in form, and obscure in meaning, ancient yet not contemporary[1]. The intrepid mariners who colonized Greenland could easily have extended their voyages to Labrador, and have explored the coasts to the south of it. No clear historic evidence establishes the natural probability that they accomplished the passage, and no vestige of their presence on our continent has been found[2].'

The latest historian of America, traversing the same field, virtually iterates this conclusion, when he says:

'The extremely probable and almost necessary pre-Columbian knowledge of the north-eastern parts of America follows from the venturesome spirit of the mariners of those seas for fish and traffic, and from the easy transitions from coast to coast by which they would have been lured to meet more southerly climes. The chances from such natural causes are quite as strong an argument in favor of the early Northmen venturings as the somewhat questionable representations of the Sagas[3].'

The same writer states, elsewhere, in this connection, that:

'Everywhere else where the Northmen went they left proofs of this occupation on the soil, but nowhere in America, except on an island on the east shore of Baffin's Bay, has any authentic runic inscription been found outside of Greenland[4].'

If the authenticity of the Icelandic discovery of America is to be determined by runic inscriptions or other archæological remains left by the discoverers, it is altogether probable that the discovery will never be confirmed. The application of this same test, however, would render the discovery of Iceland very problematical. The testimony is the same in both cases, the essential difference between the two discoveries being, after all, that the one led to practical results, while the other, apparently, did not (1). The absence of any Icelandic remains south of Baffin's Bay makes neither for nor against the credibility of the Icelandic discovery,—although it may be said, that it is hardly reasonable to expect that, in the brief period of their sojourn, the explorers would have left any buildings or implements behind them, which would be likely to survive the ravages of the nine centuries that have elapsed since the discovery.

[1] If by colonization is meant the permanent settlement or continuous occupation of the country for a long series of years, it should be noted that its story rests on the fertile imaginations of comparatively recent editors, not upon the original Icelandic records.

[2] Bancroft, History of the United States, vol. i. ch. i. of the earlier editions.

[3] Narrative and Critical History of America, edited by Justin Winsor, vol. ii. p. 33.

[4] Winsor, loc. cit., vol. i. pp. 66, 67.

The really important issue, which is raised by the paragraphs quoted, is the broader one of the credibility of the Icelandic records[1]. These records, in so far as they relate to the discovery, disentangled from wild theories and vague assumptions, would seem to speak best for themselves. It is true that Icelandic historical sagas do differ from the historical works of other lands, but this difference is one of form. The Icelandic saga is peculiarly distinguished for the presentation of events in a simple, straightforward manner, without embellishment or commentary by the author. Fabulous sagas there are in Icelandic literature, but this literature is by no means unique in the possession of works both of history and romance, nor has it been customary to regard works of fiction as discrediting the historical narratives of a people which has created both. It is possible to discriminate these two varieties of literary creation in other languages, it is no less possible in Icelandic. There is, indeed, no clear reason why the statements of an historical saga should be called in question, where these statements are logically consistent and collaterally confirmed.

The information contained in Icelandic literature relative to the discovery of America by the Icelanders, has been brought together here, and an attempt has been made to trace the history of each of the elder manuscripts containing this information. Inconsistencies have been noted, and discriminations made in the material, so far as the facts have seemed to warrant, and especially has an effort been made to avoid any possibility of confusion between expressions of opinion and the facts.

It is not altogether consistent with the plan of this book, to suggest what seems to be established by the documents which it presents, these documents being offered to bear witness for themselves; but a brief recapitulation of the conclusions to which a study of the documents has led, may not be amiss, since these conclusions differ radically, in many respects, from the views advanced by Rafn and his followers, and are offered with a view to point further enquiry, rather than to supplant it.

The eldest surviving manuscript containing an account of the discovery of Wineland the Good, as the southernmost land reached by the Icelandic discoverers was called, was written not later than 1334. This, and a more recent manuscript containing virtually the same saga, present the most cogent and consistent account of the discovery which has been preserved. Many of the important incidents therein

[1] Thus formulated by Winsor, l. c., vol. i. p. 87: 'In regard to the credibility of the sagas, the northern writers recognize the change which came over the oral traditionary chronicles when the romancing spirit was introduced from the more southern countries, at a time while the copies of the sagas which we now have were making, after having been for so long a time orally handed down; but they are not so successful in making plain what influence this imported spirit had on particular sagas, which we are asked to receive as historical records.'

set forth are confirmed by other Icelandic records of contemporary events, and the information which this saga affords is simply, naturally and intelligibly detailed. This information is of such a character, that it is natural to suppose that it was derived from the statements of those who had themselves visited the lands described: it is not conceivable from what other source it could have been obtained, and, except its author was gifted with unparalleled prescience, it could not have been a fabrication. According to this history, for such it clearly is, Wineland was discovered by a son of Eric Thorvaldsson, called the Red, the first Icelandic explorer and colonist of Greenland. This son, whose name was Leif, returning from a voyage to Norway, probably not later than the year 1000, was driven out of the direct track to Greenland, and came upon a country of which he had previously had no knowledge. He returned thence to Greenland, and reported what he had found, and an ineffectual attempt was made soon after to reach this strange land again. A few years later one Thorfinn Thordarson, called Karlsefni, an Icelander, who had recently arrived in Greenland, determined to renew the effort to find and explore the unknown country which Leif had seen. He organized an expedition and sailed away from Greenland toward the south-west. He first sighted a barren land, which, because of the large flat stones that lay strewn upon its surface, received the name of Helluland. Continuing thence, with winds from the north, the explorers next found a wooded land, to which they gave the name of Markland, from its trees, which, to these inhabitants of a treeless land, were a sufficiently distinguishing characteristic. Proceeding thence, they next descried a coast-land, along which they sailed, having the land upon their starboard side. The first portion of this land-fall proved to be a long, sandy shore, but when they had followed it for some time, they found it indented with bays and creeks, and in one of these they stopped, and sent two of their company inland to explore the country. These explorers, when they returned, brought with them, the one a bunch of grapes, the other an ear of wild ['self-sown'] grain. They hoisted anchor then, and sailed on until they came to a bay, at the mouth of which was an island with strong currents flowing about it. They laid their course into the bay, and, being pleased with the country thereabouts, decided to remain there the first winter, which proved to be a severe one. In the following year, Karlsefni, with the greater portion of his company, continued the advance southward, halting finally at a river, which flowed down from the land into a lake and thence into the sea. About the mouth of this river was shoal water, and it could only be entered at flood-tide; they proceeded up the river with their ship, and established themselves not far from the sea, and remained here throughout the second winter. There were woods here, and in the low-lands fields of wild 'wheat,' and on the ridges grapes growing wild. Here for the first time they encountered the inhabitants of the country, to whom they gave the name of Skrellings (Skrælingjar), a name which seems to bear evidence of their opprobrium. In the spring after their arrival at this spot, they were visited for the second time by the Skrellings, with whom they now engaged in barter; their visitors, however, becoming alarmed at the bellowing of a bull, which Karlsefni had brought with him, fled to their skin-canoes and rowed away. For three weeks after this, nothing was seen of the natives; but, at the end of this interval, they returned in great numbers and gave battle to Karlsefni and his companions. The Skrellings finally withdrew, having lost several of their number, while two of Karlsefni's men had fallen in the affray. The explorers, although they were well content with the country, decided, after this experience, that it would be unwise for them to attempt to remain in that region longer, and they accordingly returned to the neighbourhood in which they had passed the first winter, where they remained throughout the third winter, and in the following spring set sail for Greenland.

In a manuscript written probably between 1370 and 1390, but certainly before the close of the fourteenth century, are two detached narratives which, considered together, form another version of the history of the discovery and exploration of Wineland. In this account the discovery is ascribed to one Biarni Heriulfsson, and the date assigned to this event is fixed several years anterior to that of Leif Ericsson's voyage; indeed, according to this account, Leif's voyage to Wineland is not treated as accidental, but as the direct result of Biarni's description of the land which he had found. This version differs further, from that already described, in recounting three voyages besides that undertaken by Leif, making in all four voyages of exploration—the first headed by Leif, the second by Leif's brother, Thorvald, the third by Karlsefni, and the fourth and last led by Freydis, a natural daughter of Eric the Red. This account of the discovery is treated at length, and certain of its inconsistencies pointed out in another place, and it is, therefore, not necessary to examine it more particularly here. The statement concerning the discovery of Wineland by Biarni Heriulfsson is not confirmed by any existing collateral evidence, while that which would assign the honour to Leif Ericsson is; moreover, beyond the testimony of this, the Flatey Book, version, there is no reason to believe that more than a single voyage of exploration took place, namely, that of Thorfinn Karlsefni. So far as the statements of this second version coincide with that of the first, there seems to be no good reason for calling them in question; where they do not, they may well receive more particular scrutiny than has been directed to them, hitherto, since the Flatey Book narrative is that which has generally been treated as the more important, and its details have, in consequence, received the greater publicity.

Especially has one of the statements, which appears in this second version, claimed the attention of writers, who have sought to determine from it the site of Wineland.

Rafn, by the ingenious application of a subtile theory, succeeded in computing from this statement the exact latitude, to the second, of the southernmost winter-quarters of the explorers, and for nearly fifty years after its publication Rafn's method of interpretation remained essentially unassailed. In 1883, however, Professor Gustav Storm, of Christiania, propounded a novel, but withal a simple and scientific interpretation of this passage [1], which can hardly fail to appeal to the discernment of any reader who may not in advance have formed his conclusions as to where Wineland ought to have been. Professor Storm's method of interpretation does not seek to determine from the passage the exact spot which the explorers reached (for which, it may be remarked, the passage does not afford sufficiently accurate data), but he is enabled by his process of reasoning to determine a limit, north of which Wineland could not have been, and this limit is approximately 49°. A region not far removed to the southward of this latitude conforms sufficiently well to the descriptions of the country, given in the narratives of the exploration, to serve to confirm Professor Storm's result, and also the relative accuracy of the mooted passage itself. It will be apparent from an examination of this author's treatise that it is not necessarily proven that Wineland may not have been situated to the southward of latitude 49°, but it would seem to be wellnigh certain that thus far south it must have been.

There is no suggestion in Icelandic writings of a permanent occupation of the country, and after the exploration at the beginning of the eleventh century, it is not known that Wineland was ever again visited by Icelanders, although it would appear that a voyage thither was attempted in the year 1121, but with what result is not known. That portion of the discovery known as Markland was revisited however, in 1347, by certain seamen from the Icelandic colony in Greenland.

It will be seen from this summary that the Wineland history is of the briefest, but brief as it is, it has been put in jeopardy no less by those who would prove too much, than by those who would deny all. It may not be unprofitable in the present aspect of the question to appeal to the records themselves.

[1] Published in Arkiv for Nordisk Filologi, November, 1885, under the title 'Om Betydningen af "Eyktarstaðr" i Flatøbogens Beretning om Vinlandsreiserne.'

CHAPTER I.

EARLY FRAGMENTARY REFERENCES TO WINELAND.

WINELAND the Good is first mentioned in Icelandic literature by the Priest Ari Thorgilsson [Þorgilsson], in a passage contained in his so-called Íslendingabók [Icelanders' Book]. Ari, commonly called the Learned [fróði], an agnomen which he received after his death[1], was born in Iceland in the year 1067[2], and lived to the ripe age of eighty-one[3], acquiring a positive claim to the appellation 'hinn gamli' [the Old, the Elder], which is once given him[4]; in this instance, however, to distinguish him from another of the same name[5]. Of Ari, the father of Icelandic historiography, the author of Heimskringla[6], the most comprehensive of Icelandic histories, says in the prologue to his work:

'The priest Ari Thorgilsson the Learned, Gelli's grandson, was the first of men here in the land [Iceland] to write ancient and modern lore in the Northern tongue; he wrote chiefly in the beginning of his book, concerning Iceland's colonization and legislation, then of the law-speakers (2), how long each was in office[7], down to the introduction of Christianity into Iceland, and then on to his own day. Therein he also treats of much other old lore, both of the lives of the kings of Norway and Denmark, as well as of those of England, as likewise of the important events, which have befallen here in the land, and all of his narrations seem to me most trustworthy. . . . It is not strange that Ari should have been well-informed in the ancient lore, both here and abroad, since he had both acquired it from old men and wise, and was himself eager to learn and gifted with a good memory[8].'

[1] Íslendingabóc, ed. Finnur Jónsson, Copenhagen, 1887, p. vi.

[2] Or, 1068. Cf. Maurer, 'Über Ari Thorgilsson und sein Isländerbuch,' Germania, xv. p. 293; Möbius, Are's Isländerbuch, Leipzig, 1869, p. iv. n. 4. The date of Ari's birth is twice assigned, in the Icelandic Annals, to 1066, but this date is without collateral support. Cf. Islandske Annaler, ed. Storm, Christiania, 1888, pp. 58, 471.

[3] Chr. Worm says '91;' an obvious blunder, as is the explanation of 'hinn gamli' immediately following. Vide, Aræ Multiscii Schedæ de Islandia, Oxford, 1716, p. 184.

[4] Kristni-Saga, Copenh. 1773, p. 104.

[5] Cf. Werlauff, De Ario Multiscio, Copenh. 1808, p. 13.

[6] By this name the great historical work, 'The Lives of the Kings of Norway,' is generally known. The name is derived from the introductory words of the history, '*Kringla heimsins* sú er mannfólkit byggir,' i.e. '*the world's orb*, which is inhabited by mankind.'

[7] Lit. 'how long each spoke.'

[8] Heimskringla, ed. Unger, Christiania, 1868, pp. 2, 3.

In the introduction to the Íslendingabók, Ari says:

'I first composed an Íslendingabók for our Bishops Thorlak [Þorlákr] and Ketil [Ketill], and showed it to them, as well as to Sæmund (Sæmundr) the Priest. And forasmuch as they were pleased [either] to have it thus, or augmented, I accordingly wrote this [the "libellus"[1]], similar in character, with the exception of the genealogy and lives of the kings, and have added that of which I have since acquired closer knowledge, and which is now more accurately set forth in this [the "libellus"] than in that[2].'

These words conjoined with the quoted statement concerning the character of the historian's work, and supplemented by references to Ari in other Icelandic writings[3], have given rise to a controversy as to the probable scope of Ari's literary activity. Whether the conclusion be reached that Ari was the author of several books, as has been claimed, or that the Íslendingabók, which has perished, to which he refers in the words above quoted, was a much larger and more comprehensive work than the so-called Íslendingabók which has been preserved to us, there seems to be abundant reason for the belief that all of Ari's historical material was by no means comprised in the only book of his now existing, about whose authorship there can be no room for dispute[4]. Of this book, the so-called Íslendingabók, the oldest manuscripts are two paper copies, of a lost parchment manuscript, belonging to the Arna-Magnæan Collection in the University Library of Copenhagen, which are known as 113 *a* and 113 *b* fol. At the end of 113 *a*, the scribe has written as follows:

'These "Schedæ" and narratives of the priest Ari the Learned are copied from a vellum in his own hand, as men believe, at Villingaholt, by the priest John Ellindsson [Jón Erlendsson], Anno domini 1651, the next Monday after the third Sunday after Easter.'

This John Erlendsson is known to have made transcripts of many of the sagas

[1] Ari, himself (?), heads the introduction to the so-called Íslendingabók with a Latin title, 'Incipit libellus Islandorum,' wherefore the Icelandic title of the later composition should be Íslendinga-bæklingr, rather than Íslendingabók. Cf. Maurer, Über Ari Thorgilsson, ubi sup., p. 312.

[2] The proper interpretation of the passage, which is by no means as obvious as could be wished, is critically considered by Björn M. Ólsen in an article entitled 'Om Forholdet mellem de to Bearbejdelser af Are's Islændingebog,' contained in Aarbøger for Nordisk Oldkyndighed og Historie, Copenh. 1885, p. 341 et seq.

[3] As in Landnámabók [Book of Settlement: the Domesday Book of Iceland]: 'So Ari Thorgilsson says, that twenty-five ships sailed to Greenland that summer,' &c., ch. 14, pt. 2; and again, ch. 15, pt. 5: 'Now we have considered briefly the settlement of Iceland, according to that which learned men have written, first, the priest Ari Thorgilsson the Learned,' &c.

[4] The various views concerning the scope of Ari's authorship will be found in Maurer's and Ólsen's articles, loc. cit., and in the latter author's admirable treatise, 'Ari Þorgilsson hinn fróði,' in Tímarit hins ísl. bókmenntafjelags, Reykjavík, 1889, pp. 214–40. Further, in the introduction to the 'Isländerbuch' of Möbius, ubi sup., and in 'Bemerkninger om Are frodes Forfattervirksomhed,' contained in Pt. I. of Undersøgelse af Kongesagaens Fremvæxt by A. Gjessing, Christiania, 1873.

for Bryniolf [Brynjólfr] Sveinsson, Bishop of Skálholt[1]. To this worthy bishop's[2] literary ardour, and zeal in collecting the neglected treasures of his language, we owe the preservation of many manuscripts, which would, but for him, doubtless, have perished before the coming of the indefatigable collector, Arni Magnusson.

Bishop Bryniolf, unfortunately, left no heir, interested in the preservation of his library, and his books were soon scattered. When Arni Magnusson visited Iceland, thirty years after the Bishop's death, and ransacked the island for surviving manuscripts, the vellum of the Íslendingabók, doubtless one of the oldest of Icelandic manuscripts, had entirely disappeared[3]. Concerning the two paper copies of this vellum, which he succeeded in obtaining, Arni has inserted the following memorandum in the manuscript described as 113 *b.* fol.:

'The various different readings noted here throughout in my hand, are taken from another copy [113 *a.* fol.] written by the Rev. John Erlendsson in 1651. This was formerly the property of the Rev. Torfi Jonsson [Jónsson] of Bær, who inherited it from Bishop Bryniolf Sveinsson; I obtained it, however, from Thorlak, son of Bishop Thord [Þorlákr Þórðarson]; it formed originally a portion of a large book, which I took apart, separating the treatises. This copy I have called "Codex B," signifying either "Baiensis[4]," or the second, from the order of the letters of the alphabet. Concerning 'Codex B,' it is my conjecture that the Rev. John copied it first from the vellum; that Bishop Bryniolf did not like the copy [for this Codex is less exact than Codex A, as may be seen by comparing them].... wherefore the Rev. John made a new copy of the parchment manuscript, taking greater care to follow the original literally, whence it is probable that this Codex A was both the later and the better copy.'

Both of the paper manuscripts 'A' and 'B' were written, it is believed, within the same year, and in each of them the paragraphs containing the reference to Wineland are almost identical; the Icelandic name in 'A' being spelt Winland, in 'B' Vinland, a clerical variation, devoid of significance. This paragraph, which is the sixth in Ari's history, is as follows:

'That country which is called Greenland, was discovered and colonized from Iceland. Eric the Red [Eirekr enn Rauþi] was the name of the man, an inhabitant of Breidafirth

[1] At that time an episcopal seat in southern Iceland.

[2] A brief but entertaining account of this remarkable man is contained in the Introduction to the Corpus Poeticum Boreale, Vigfusson and Powell, Oxford, 1883, vol. i. pp. xxii–xxv.

[3] Bishop Brynjólf died in 1675. Arni's visit was made between the years 1702 and 1712. For an account of Arni Magnusson's life and labours, see 'Biographiske Efterretninger om Arne Magnussen'; ved Jon Olafsen fra Grunnavik. Med Indledning, &c., af E. C. Werlauff, contained in, Nordisk Tidskrift for Oldkyndighed, Copenh. 1836, pp. 1–166.

[4] From the farmstead of Bœr (Gaulverjabœr), at which it was obtained.

[Breiþfirser], who went out thither from here, and settled at that place, which has since been called Ericsfirth [Eiríksfiǫrþr]. He gave a name to the country, and called it Greenland, and said, that it must persuade men to go thither, if the land had a good name. They found there, both east and west in the country, the dwellings of men, and fragments of boats, and stone implements [1], such that it may be perceived from these, that that manner of people had been there who have inhabited Wineland, and whom the Greenlanders call Skrellings [Scrælinga, nom. Skrælingjar]. And this, when he set about the colonization of the country, was XIV or XV winters [2] before the introduction of Christianity here in Iceland [3], according to that which a certain man [lit. he], who himself accompanied Eric the Red thither, informed Thorkel [Þorkell] Gellisson.'

This mention of Wineland, which in itself may appear to be of little importance, acquires its greatest value from that which it leaves unsaid; for had Ari not known that his reference to Wineland and its inhabitants would be entirely intelligible to his readers, he would hardly have employed it, as he does, to inform his Greenland chronicle. This passing notice, therefore, indicates a general diffusion of the knowledge of the Wineland discoveries among Ari's contemporaries at the time when the paragraph was composed. The 'libellus' [Íslendingabók] was probably written about the year 1134 [4], and we are accordingly apprised that at that time the facts concerning the Wineland discovery, upon an acquaintance with which Ari seems to rely, were notorious. It is impossible, however, to determine whether Ari presumed upon a knowledge derived from particulars, which he had himself previously published, or upon a prevalent acquaintance with the accounts of the explorers themselves. It is, at least, questionable whether Ari would have been content to presuppose such local historical knowledge if he had not already sealed it with his own authority elsewhere. Nor is the importance which he may have assigned to the Wineland discovery material to this view. He had set about writing a chronicle of his fatherland, and his passing allusion to Wineland, without a word of explanation, appears incompatible with the duty which he had assumed, unless, indeed, he had already dealt with the subject of the Wineland discovery in a previous work. Be this as it may, however, certain it is, that Wineland has found further mention in two Icelandic works, which in their primitive form have been very generally accredited to Ari, namely the Landnámabók [Book of Settlement] and the Kristni-Saga [the Narrative of the Introduction of

[1] Cf. Nordisk Tidskrift for Oldkyndighed, Copenh. 1832, pp. 223–4, where certain of these implements are described.

[2] The customary expression for years, corresponding with our use of the word, 'summers,' as in the expression, he was a lad of twelve summers

[3] Christianity became the legalized religion of Iceland in the year 1000; the settlement of Greenland, therefore, according to Ari's chronology, must have taken place in 985 or 986.

[4] Cf. Möbius, Are's Isländerbuch, pp. xv, xvi; Maurer, loc. cit. p. 315; Íslendingabóc, ed. Jónsson, p. vi.

Christianity into Iceland][1]. The first of these, in a passage already cited[2], expressly acknowledges Ari's share in the authorship[3]. One manuscript of this work, from which the passage is taken, [No. 371, 4to, in the Arna-Magnæan Collection], while it is the oldest extant manuscript containing the Landnámabók [now in an incomplete state] presents this in a later recension of the original work, than that which is contained in the much more modern manuscript, AM. 107, fol. This latter manuscript, like the copy of Íslendingabók, was written by the Rev. John Erlendsson for Bishop Bryniolf Sveinsson[4]. Both of the references to Wineland in the Landnámabók occur incidentally in the course of the history, and are of the briefest. The first of these treats of the adventure of Ari Marsson [Mársson]; it is to be found in Chapter 22, of the second part of the book, and is as follows:

'. . . their[5] son was Ari. He was driven out of his course at sea to White-men's-land [Hvítramanna-land], which is called by some persons Ireland the Great [Írland it mikla] (58); it lies westward in the sea near Wineland the Good [Vínland it góða]; it is said to be six "dœgra[6]" sail west of Ireland; Ari could not depart thence, and was baptized there. The first account of this was given by Rafn who sailed to Limerick (3) [Hlimreksfari], and who remained for a long time at Limerick in Ireland. So Thorkel [Þorkell] Geitisson[7] states that Icelanders report, who have heard Thorfinn, Earl of the Orkneys (4) [Þorfinnr jarl í Orkneyjum] say, that Ari had been recognized there, and was not permitted to leave [lit. could not leave], but was treated with great respect there.'

The names of Ari Marsson's wife, and of his three sons are given in the same passage from which the quotation is made, and additional concurrent evidence is not wanting to serve to establish the existence of this man; any particulars, however, which might serve to enlighten this narrative, or aid in determining whence Rafn and Earl Thorfinn derived their intelligence, are lacking. Without free conjectural

[1] Cf. Storm, Snorre Sturlassöns Historieskrivning, Copenh. 1873, pp. 50, 51; Vigfusson, Prolegomena to Sturlunga Saga, Oxford, 1878, vol. i. pp. xxx, xxxi, and xxxiv; Brenner, Über die Kristni-Saga, Munich, 1878, pp. 4, 5.

[2] Note 3, p. 8.

[3] In the Saga of Bishop Paul it is stated that 'The priest Ari the Learned, who has related much old lore, tells how greatly our land was bowed down upon the death of Bishop Gizur, whom the people looked upon as the foremost man in Iceland.' Páls saga, in Biskupa Sögur, Copenh. 1858, vol. i. p. 145. This passage Vigfusson regards as a recognition of Ari's share in the authorship of the Kristni-Saga. Cf. Prolegomena to Sturlunga Saga, p. xxxiv.

[4] The Landnámabók containing, as it does, the ground-work of Icelandic biographical history, was a favourite subject for the copyist. The editor of the first printed edition states in his preface that his text was diligently compiled and collated from five different manuscripts. Cf. Pref. Sagan Landnáma, Skáholt, 1688.

[5] 'their,' i.e. Már of Reykhólar and Þórkatla.

[6] Cf. note 46.

[7] Or Gellisson. Cf. Grönlands historiske Mindesmærker, Copenh. 1838, vol. i. pp. 167, 8.

emendation to aid in its interpretation, this description of Ari Marsson's visit to Ireland the Great is of the same doubtful historical value as a later account of another visit to an unknown land, to be considered hereafter.

The second reference to Wineland in the Landnámabók is contained in a list of the descendants of Snorri Head-Thord's son [Snorri Høfða-Þórðarson]:

> 'Their[1] son was Thord Horse-head [Þórðr Hest-høfði], father of Karlsefni, who found Wineland the Good, Snorri's father,' &c.[2]

A genealogy which entirely coincides with that of the histories of the discovery of Wineland, as well as with that of the episcopal genealogy appended to the Íslendingabók[3]. The Landnámabók contains no other mention of Wineland, but a more extended notice is contained in the work already named, which, in its present form, is supposed to retain evidence of the learned Ari's pen.

The Kristni-Saga, which is supplementary, historically, to the Landnámabók, is given in its entirety in AM. 105, fol. This is a paper copy of an earlier manuscript made by the same industrious cleric, John Erlendsson, for Bishop Bryniolf. A portion of the same history has also been preserved along with the detached leaves of the Landnámabók now deposited in the Arna-Magnæan Collection, No. 371, 4to. These fragments of the two histories originally belonged to one work, the so-called Hauk's Book [Hauksbók], a vellum manuscript of the fourteenth century, hereafter to be more fully described. The history of the Wineland discovery is contained in the eleventh chapter of the printed edition of the Kristni-Saga, in the following words:

> 'That summer (5) King Olaf [Tryggvason] went from the country southward to Vindland [the land of the Wends]; then, moreover, he sent Leif Ericsson [Leifr Eiríksson] to Greenland, to proclaim the faith there. On this voyage [lit. then] Leif found Wineland the Good; he also found men on a wreck at sea, wherefore he was called Leif the Lucky [Leifr hinn heppni][4].'

Of the same tenor as this brief paragraph of the Kristni-Saga, is a chapter in the Codex Frisianus [Frissbók], number 45, fol., of the Arna-Magnæan manuscripts. This Codex Frisianus, or, as it has been more appropriately called, the Book of Kings [Konungabók], is a beautifully written and well-preserved parchment manuscript of 124 leaves; it obtains its name from a former owner, Otto Friis of Salling; it subse-

[1] 'Their,' i.e. Snorri Head-Thordsson and Thorhild Ptarmigan [Þórhildr rjúpa], the daughter of Thord the Yeller [Þórðr gellir].

[2] Landnámabók, Part III. chap. x.

[3] Cf. Íslendingabóc, ed. Jónsson, p. 18.

[4] 'Þat sumar fór Ólafr konúngr or landi suðr til Vindlands; þá sendi hann ok Leif Eiríkssun til Grœnalands, at boða þar trú; þá fann Leifr Vínland hit góða, hann fann ok menn á skipflaki í hafi, því var hann kallaðr Leifr hinn heppni.' Kristni saga, ed. in Biskupa Sögur, Copenh. 1858, vol. i. p. 20.

quently became the property of one Jens Rosenkranz, and next passed into the possession of Arni Magnusson [1]. Friis' Book was, in all probability, written about the beginning of the fourteenth century [2]; and if the conjectures as to its age are correct, it is, perhaps, the oldest extant Icelandic manuscript containing an account of the Wineland discovery. It is believed, from internal evidence, that the greater part of the Codex was written by an Icelander, in Norway, possibly for a Norwegian, and that the manuscript was never in Iceland [3]. The early history of the Codex is not known. Certain marginal notes appear to have been inserted in the manuscript about the year 1550 by Lawman Laurents Hanssön, and it is conjectured that the book was then owned in Bergen [4]; fifty years later we find it in Denmark; for about the year 1600 a Dane, by the name of Slangerup [Slangendorpius], inserted his name upon a fly-leaf in the book, which leaf, Arni Magnusson tells us, was removed when he had the manuscript bound [5]. In this 'Book of Kings,' the Saga of Olaf Tryggvason, in which the history of the discovery of Wineland occurs, follows closely the same saga as it was written in the two lost parchment manuscripts of the 'Heimskringla,' as we are enabled to determine from the copies of these lost vellums made by the Icelander, Asgeir Jonsson [Ásgeirr Jónsson] [6]. It is not known whether the author of the 'Heimskringla' had access to the history of the Wineland discovery in some such extended form as that contained in Hauk's Book; indeed it has been suggested, that he may only have been acquainted with the brief narrative of the Kristni-Saga [7], but certain it is, that his account of the discovery was not influenced by the version presented in the Flatey Book, which narrative appears in the first printed edition of the 'Heimskringla,' where it was interpolated by the editor, Johann Peringskiöld [8].

[1] Thus Arni Magnusson's entry: 'Bókina hefir átt Otto Friis í Salling. Síðan Etats-Raad Jens Rosencrantz, og eptir hann eignadest eg bókina.' Cf. Katalog over den Arna-Magnæanske Håndskrift-samling, Copenh. 1888, vol. i. p. 33.

[2] Cf. Unger, Codex Frisianus, Christiania, 1871: Forord, p. iii [i.e. p. 1]. Dr. Gustav Storm gives the date as about the year 1300; cf. his Sigurd Ranessön's Proces, Christiania, 1877, p. 44; Vigfusson would make the manuscript still older, namely 'c. 1260–80.' Cf. Corpus Poeticum Boreale, Oxford, 1883, vol. i. p. xlix. If this last view is sound, then the MS. is decidedly older than Hauk's Book, the earliest manuscript mentioning Wineland, of whose date we have certain knowledge.

[3] Cf. Unger, Codex Frisianus, Christiania, 1871, Forord.

[4] Cf. Storm, Sigurd Rannessöns Proces, ubi sup. p. 44.

[5] Cf. Katalog o. d. AM. Hdskrsmlg., vol. i. p. 33.

[6] The two parchment manuscripts belonging to the Library of the University of Copenhagen, called Kringla [i.e. Heimskringla], and Jǫfrskinna (King's vellum), were destroyed by the fire of 1728. The copies, which had, fortunately, been made, have been preserved. Cf. Unger, Heimskringla, Christiania, 1868, Forord, p. iii (i.e. p. 1).

[7] Cf. Storm, Snorre Sturlassöns Historieskrivning, Copenh. 1873, p. 60.

[8] Cf. Peringskiöld's edition, Heimskringla, Eller Snorre Sturlusons Nordlandske Sagor, Stockholm, 1697, chs. civ–cxi. vol. i. pp. 326–50.

Similarly, any trace of the Flatey Book version of the discovery is lacking from Friis' Book, although the author of the saga of Olaf Tryggvason, therein contained, appears to have been acquainted with a somewhat more detailed account of Leif Ericsson's life than that afforded by the Kristni-Saga, if we may judge from his own language, as we find it in column 136, page 34*b*, of the manuscript:

'WINELAND THE GOOD FOUND.

'Leif, a son of Eric the Red, passed this same winter, in good repute, with King Olaf, and accepted Christianity. And that summer[1], when Gizur went to Iceland, King Olaf sent Leif to Greenland to proclaim Christianity there. He sailed that summer to Greenland. He found men upon a wreck at sea and succoured them. Then, likewise, he discovered Wineland the Good, and arrived in Greenland in the autumn. He took with him thither a priest and other spiritual teachers, and went to Brattahlid to make his home with his father, Eric. People afterwards called him Leif the Lucky. But his father, Eric, said that one account should balance the other, that Leif had rescued the ship's crew, and this that he had brought the trickster to Greenland. This[2] was the priest[3].'

Almost identical with the history of the discovery contained in Friis' Book is that of the so-called longer saga of Olaf Tryggvason. This saga, in its printed form, has been compiled from several manuscripts of the Arna-Magnæan collection, the most important of which is No. 61, fol., a codex dating from about the year 1400[4]. This account is contained in the 231st chapter of the printed version[5] as follows:

'King Olaf then[6] sent Leif to Greenland to proclaim Christianity there. The king sent a priest and other holy men with him, to baptize the people there, and to instruct them

[1] The summer of the year in which King Olaf Tryggvason fell, i.e. the summer of the year 1000.

[2] i.e. 'the trickster.'

[3] 'Fvndit Vínland góða. Þenna sama vetr var Leifr son Eiríks hins Rauða með Óláfi konungi vel metinn, ok tók við kristni. Enn þetta svmar, er Gizurr fór til Íslandz sendi Óláfr konungr Leif til Grænlandz, at boða þar kristni. Fór hann þat svmar til Grænlandz. Hann fann í hafi menn á skips-flaki ok hialpaði þeim. Þá fann [hann] ok Vín-land hit góða, ok kom of havstit til Grænlandz. Hann hafði þannig prest ok aðra kenni-menn, ok fór til vistar í Bratta-hlíð til Eiríks føður síns. Menn kolluðu hann síðan Leif hinn hepna. Enn Eiríkr, faðir hans, sagði svá at þat var samskvllda, er Leifr hafði borgit skips-høfn manna í hafi, ok þat er hann hafði flutt skæmanninn til Grænlandz. Þat var prestrinn.'

[4] Cf. Katalog o. d. AM. Hdskrsmlg., Copenh. 1888, vol. i. p. 40.

[5] Fornmanna-sögur, Copenh. 1826, vol. ii. pp. 245, 246.

[6] In the summer of the year 1000, according to Vigfusson's reckoning. If the chronology be controlled by the statement in the same paragraph of the saga corresponding to that of Friis' Book, that Leif made this voyage in the same year in which King Olaf despatched Gizur the White [hvíti] and Hjalti Skeggjason to Iceland on a similar mission, then, according to Vigfusson, the date of Leif's voyage, here described, would appear to have been the year 1000. Cf. Vigfusson, 'Um Tímatal í Íslendínga Sögum,' in, Safn til Sögu Íslands, Copenh. 1856, vol. i. pp. 432, 433.

in the true faith. Leif sailed to Greenland that summer, and rescued at sea the men of a ship's crew, who were in great peril and were clinging to [lit. lay upon] the shattered wreckage of a ship; and on this same voyage he found Wineland the Good, and at the end of the summer arrived in Greenland, and betook himself to Brattahlid, to make his home with his father, Eric. People afterwards called him Leif the Lucky, but his father, Eric, said that the one [deed] offset the other, in that Leif had on the one hand rescued and restored the men of the ship's crew to life, while on the other he had brought the trickster[1] to Greenland, for thus he called the priest[2].'

In composition, doubtless, much more recent than the notices already cited, is a passage in the collectanea of Middle-age wisdom known as No. 194, 8vo, of the Arna-Magnæan Library. This manuscript contains fifty-two pages, part of which are in Icelandic and part in Latin, written between the years 1400–1450[3]. From a slip in Arni Magnusson's hand, inserted in the collection, it appears that Arni obtained it from the Rev. Thorvald Stephensson [Þorvaldr Stefánsson] in the year 1707. Whatever its condition may have been at that time, the parchment upon which it is written is now in a sad state of decay. In this respect page 10 of the vellum, upon the back of which the Wineland chorography is written, in Icelandic, is no exception; fortunately, however, the lacunae are so inconsiderable in this page, that they may be readily supplied from that which survives, and the Wineland passage appears as follows:

'Southward from Greenland is Helluland, then comes [lit. is] Markland; thence it is not far to Wineland the Good, which some men believe extends from Africa, and, if this be so, then there is an open sea flowing in between Wineland and Markland. It is said, that Thorfinn[4] Karlsefni hewed a "house-neat-timber" (6) and then went to seek Wineland the Good, and came to where they believed this land to be, but they did not succeed in exploring it, or in obtaining any of its products (7). Leif the Lucky first found Wineland, and he then found

[1] *Skæmanninn.* This word is employed in old Icelandic to translate the 'hypocrite' of the New Testament. Vide Vigfusson, Dict. s. v. *skí.*

[2] '[Á] því sama vári sendi Óláfr konungr Gizur ok Hjalti til Íslandz, sem ádr er rítað, þá sendi konungr ok Leif Eiríksson til Grænlandz, at boða þar kristni. Fekk konungr honum prest ok nockurra aðra vígda menn, at skíra þar fólk ok kenna þeim trú rétta. Fór Leifr þat sumar til Grænlandz. Hann tók í hafi skipshøfn þeira manna, er þá væri vfærir, ok lágu á skips-flaki albrotnu, ok í þeiri sømv ferð fann hann Vindland (sic) hit góða ok kom at á-liðnu því svmri til Grænlandz, ok fór til vistar í Brattahlíð til Eiríks føþur síns. Kølludu menn hann síþan Leif hinn heppna. En Eiríkr faðir hans sagði at þat var samskullda, er Leifr hafði borgit ok gefit líf skips-høfn manna ok þat er hann hafði flutt skemanninn til Grænlandz, svá kallaði hann prestin. En þó af ráðum ok eggian Leifs var Eiríkr skírðr ok alt fólk á Grænlandi.' AM. 61 fol., col. 2, p. 60 *b*, and col. 1, p. 61.

[3] The date is given upon the authority of Dr. Kålund, the Librarian of the Arna-Magnæan Library.

[4] In the Codex; 'Þorfiðr,' equivalent to Þorfinnr, as in the terminations -ðr, -nnr, in maðr, mannr, 'man.' Cf. Tamm, 'Altnordisch NNR, DR,' in Beiträge zur Geschichte der deutschen Sprache und Literatur, Halle, o. S., 1880, pp. 445–54.

merchants in evil plight at sea, and restored them to life by God's mercy; and he introduced Christianity into Greenland, which waxed there so, that an episcopal seat was established there, at the place called Gardar. England and Scotland are one island, although each of them is a kingdom. Ireland is a great island. Iceland is also a great island [to the north of] Ireland. These countries are all in that part of the world which is called Europe[1].'

In a fascicle of detached vellum fragments, brought together in AM. No. 736, 4to, there are two leaves containing, besides certain astronomical material, a concise geographical compilation. In this Wineland is assigned a location identical with that in the codex from which the quotation has just been made, and the notice of Wineland is limited to this brief statement:

'From Greenland to the southward lies Helluland, then Markland; thence it is not far to Wineland, which some men believe extends from Africa. England and Scotland are one island,' &c.[2]

While the reference to Wineland omits the account of Thorfinn's visit and Leif's discovery, the language in which the location of the land is given, as well as the language of the context, has so great a likeness to that of 194, 8vo, that, although it was perhaps written a few years earlier, there seems to be a strong probability that each of the scribes of these manuscripts derived his material from a common source.

Somewhat similar in character to the above notices is the brief reference written in the vellum fragment contained in AM. 764, 4to. This fragment comprises a so-called 'totius orbis brevis descriptio,' written probably about the year 1400[3]. Upon the second page of this 'brief description' is the passage:

[1] 'Suðr *frá* Grœnla*n*di *er* Helluland, þá er M*ar*kla*n*d: þ[á e]*r* (or, *þaðan er*) *eigi* langt *til* Vínla*n*dz ens góða, *er* sum*ir* m*enn* ætla at g*an*gi af Affríka ok ef *svá er*, þá *er* úthaf in*n*fallanda á milli Vínla*n*dz ok M*ar*kla*n*dz. Þ*at er* sagt ath Þorfiðr Karlsefni hjoggi húsasnotrot*ré*, ok færi síð*an* ath leita Vínla*n*dz ens góða ok kæmi þ*ar er* þ*eir* ætluðu þ*at* la*n*d ok náðu *eigi* ath kan*n*a ok eingu*m* la*n*dzkostu*m*. Leifr hin*n* hepni fan*n* fystr Vínla*n*d, ok þá fan*n* h*ann* kaupm*enn* í hafinu illa stadda ok gaf þ*eim* líf m*eð* gu*ðs* miskun*n*: ok h*ann* ko*m* kr*i*stni á [Grœn]la*n*d ok óx þ*ar* s*vá* ath þ*ar* v*ar* b*isk*u*p*sstóll settr, þ*ar er* í Gǫrð*um* heit*ir*. Eingla*n*d ok Skotla*n*d *er* ein ey, ok *er* þó sitt h[vert] k[*onun*]g[s] rí*ki*. Írla*n*d [er] ey mikil. Ísla*n*d *er* ok ey mikil [í norðr frá Írla*n*di]. Þ*essi* lǫ*n*d ero ǫll í þ*eim* hl*u*ta heim*s* *er* Eyrópa heit*ir*.'

The words or portions of words which are enclosed between brackets are either wholly or partially wanting, by reason of defects in the vellum; they have been supplied either from the traces, which are still decipherable, or from the context. It will be noticed that no considerable break occurs in that part of the paragraph which deals particularly with Wineland.

[2] '*Frá* Grœnla*n*di í suðr lig[g]r Hellv-land, þá Mark-la*n*d, þaðan *er* eigi langt *til* Vinlad (sic), *er* sum*ir* men*n* ætla at gangi af Affríca. England oc Scotla*n*d *eru* ein ey.' AM. 736, I, 4to, p. 1, ll. 28, 29.

[3] The opinion of Dr. Finnur Jónsson, the editor of Íslendingabóc, Eddalieder, &c.

'From Biarmaland uninhabited regions extend from the north, until Greenland joins them. South from Greenland lies Helluland, then Markland. Thence it is not far to Wineland. Iceland is a great island,' &c.[1]

Differing in nature from these geographical notices [but of even greater interest and historical value by reason of the corroborative evidence which it affords of certain particulars set forth in the leading narrative of the Wineland discovery] is the mention of Wineland contained in a chapter of the Eyrbyggja Saga [Saga of the People of Eyrr]. No complete vellum manuscript of this saga has been preserved. The eldest manuscript remnant of the saga is deposited in AM. 162 E, fol., and consists of two leaves written about 1300[2]; these leaves do not, however, contain that portion of the saga with which we are concerned. Of another vellum codex containing this saga, which has entirely perished, we have certain knowledge. This was the so-called Vatnshyrna or Vatnshorn's Book [Vatzhornsbók], a manuscript which at one time belonged to the eminent Danish scholar, Peder Hans Resen, from whom it received the name by which it is sometimes cited, Codex Resenianus. It was bequeathed by Resen to the University Library of Copenhagen, where it was deposited after his death in 1688[3]. It perished in the great fire of October, 1728[4], but fortunately paper copies, which had been made from it, survived the conflagration. The Vatnshorn Codex, it has been conjectured, was prepared for the same John Haconsson, to whom we are indebted for the great Flatey Book, and was, apparently, written about the year 1400, or, possibly, toward the close of the fourteenth century[5]. The most complete vellum manuscript of the Eyrbyggja Saga now extant, forms a part of the so-called Codex Wolphenbuttelensis, belonging to the Ducal Library of Wolfenbüttel, for which it was purchased in the seventeenth century, at a public sale in Holstein. This manuscript was probably written about the middle of the fourteenth century[6], and although the first third of the Eyrbyggja Saga has been lost from the codex, that portion of the history which contains the chapter referring to Wineland has been preserved, and is as follows:

[1] 'Af Biarmal*andi* g*au*ga lǫnd óbygd af n*o*rdr ætt, unz Grænl*a*nd tekr *við*. Sudr *frá* Grænl*andi* liggr Hellu l*and*, þá M*ar*kl*and*. Þ*aðan er eigi* langt t*il* Uínl*andz*.' AM. 764, 4to, p. 1 (b), ll. 27, 28.

[2] Cf. Katalog over den Arnamag. Håndskr. Saml., Copenh. 1888, vol. i. p. 123.

[3] Cf. Fornsögur, ed. Vigfusson and Möbius, Leipzig, 1860, p. xiv; Worm, Lexicon, Helsingøer, 1771, 1 Deel, p. 256.

[4] It was among the most valuable of the manuscripts which were lost in this fire, the same which destroyed many of Arni Magnusson's treasured books, and, no doubt, hastened the end of that ardent bibliophile, for he survived the loss little more than a year, dying on the 6th of January, 1730.

[5] Cf. Fornsögur, ubi sup. pp. xv, xvi; Bárðar saga snæfellsáss, &c., ed. Vigfusson, Copenh. 1860, p. xi.

[6] Vigfusson, Eyrbyggja Saga, Leipzig, 1864, pp. xxiii, xxiv.

'After the reconciliation between Steinthor and the people of Alpta-firth, Thorbrand's sons, Snorri and Thorleif Kimbi, went to Greenland. From him[1] Kimbafirth [Kimbafjǫrðr], (in Greenland), gets its name. Thorleif Kimbi lived in Greenland to old age. But Snorri went to Wineland the Good with Karlsefni; and when they were fighting with the Skrellings there in Wineland, Thorbrand Snorrason[2], a most valiant man, was killed[3].'

The foregoing brief notices of Wineland, scattered through so many Icelandic writings, yield no very great amount of information concerning that country. They do afford, however, a clear insight into the wide diffusion of the intelligence of the discovery in the earlier saga period, and in every instance confirm the Wineland history as unfolded in the leading narrative of the discovery, now to be considered.

[1] i. e. from Thorleif, who was called Þorleifr kimbi.

[2] Cod. Wolph. has Snorri Thorbrandsson, apparently a clerical slip, for other manuscripts have, correctly, Thorbrand Snorrason.

[3] 'Eptir sætt þ*ei*ra Steinðórs ok Álptfirþ*in*ga, *fóru* Þ*or*brandz *synir* til Grænal*an*dz, Snorri ok Þ*or*leifr kimbi, uit [hann] er kendr Kimbafjǫrðr [á Grœnlandi]. Bió Þ*or*leifr kimbi á Grænl*an*di *til* elli. En Snorri fór *til* Uínlandz hins góða með Karlsefni; ok *er* þ*ei*r bǫrðuz á Uínl*an*di u*ið* Skrælinga þá fell S*norri* Þ*or*brandz *son* hin*n* hraustazti ma*ðr*.' Codex Wolphenbuttelensis, p. 20, ll. 12–16.

CHAPTER II.

The Saga of Eric the Red.

The clearest and most complete narrative of the discovery of Wineland, preserved in the ancient Icelandic literature, is that presented in the Saga of Eric the Red. Of this narrative two complete vellum texts have survived. The eldest of these texts is contained in the Arna-Magnæan Codex, No. 544, 4to, which is commonly known as Hauk's Book [Hauksbók]. This manuscript has derived its name from its first owner, for whom the work was doubtless written, and who himself participated in the labour of its preparation. This man, to whom the manuscript traces its origin, has, happily, left, not only in the manuscript itself, but in the history of his time, a record which enables us to determine, with exceptional accuracy, many dates in his life, and from these it is possible to assign approximate dates to that portion of the vellum which contains the narrative of the discovery. This fact possesses the greater interest since of no one of those who participated in the conservation of the elder sagas, have we data so precise as those which have been preserved to us of Hauk Erlendsson [Haukr Erlendsson], to whose care, actual and potential, this manuscript owes its existence.

We know that Jorunn, the mother of this man, was the direct descendant of a famous Icelander[1]. His paternal ancestry is not so clearly established. It has been conjectured that his father, Erlend Olafsson, surnamed the Stout [Erlendr sterki Óláfsson], was the son of a man of humble parentage, and by birth a Norwegian[2]. This view has been discredited, however, and the fact pretty clearly established that Erlend's father, Olaf, was no other than a certain Icelander called Olaf Tot [Óláfr tottr][3]. Hauk's father, Erlend, was probably the 'Ellindr bóndi' of a letter addressed by certain Icelanders to the Norwegian king, Magnus Law-Amender, in the year 1275[4]. In the year 1283 we find indubitable mention of him in

[1] Her genealogy is given at length in Landnámabók, pt. ii. ch. xxv.

[2] Cf. Munch, 'Om Rigsraaden Hr. Hauk Erlendssön,' in Annaler for Nordisk Oldkyndighed, Copenh. 1847, pp. 172, 173.

[3] Cf. Jón Þorkelsson, Nokkur blöð úr Hauksbók, Reykjavík, 1865, pp. iii–vi.

[4] Cf. Diplomatarium Islandicum, Copenh. 1888, vol. ii. p. 125, and, Safn til Sögu Íslands, Copenh. 1861, vol. ii. p. 44.

Icelandic annals as 'legifer,' he having in that year 'come out' to Iceland from Norway vested with the dignity of 'lawman[1].' It is as the incumbent of a similar office, to which he appears to have been appointed in 1294, that we first find Hauk Erlendsson mentioned[2]. It is not unlikely that Hauk had visited Norway prior to 1301; there can be no doubt that he was in that country in the latter part of that year, for he was a 'lawman' in Osló [the modern Christiania] upon the 28th of January, 1302, since upon that date he published an autographic letter, which is still in existence[3]. Whether the rank of knighthood, which carried with it the title of 'herra[4],' had already been conferred upon him at this time is not certain. He is first mentioned with this title, in Icelandic annals, in 1306, elsewhere in 1305[5], although it has been claimed that he had probably then enjoyed this distinction for some years[6], but upon what authority is not clear. While Hauk revisited Iceland upon more than one occasion after the year 1302, much of the remainder of his life appears to have been spent in Norway, where he died in the year 1334[7].

On the back of page 21 of Hauk's Book Arni Magnusson has written, probably with a view to preserve a fading entry upon the same page, the words: 'This book belongs to Teit Paulsson [Teitr Pálsson], if he be not robbed[8].' It is not known who this Teit Paulsson was, but it is recorded that a man of this name sailed from Iceland to Norway in the year 1344[9]. He may have been the one-time owner of the book, and, if the manuscript was then in Norway, may have carried it back to Iceland with him. Apart from this conjecture, the fact remains that the early history of Hauk's Book is shrouded in obscurity. It is first mentioned in the beginning of the seventeenth

[1] Islandske Annaler, ed. Storm, Christiania, 1888, pp. 50, 142, &c.

[2] Islandske Annaler, ubi sup. pp. 144, 198, 485; but on the other hand, one entry [Flatey Annals], p. 385. gives this date, 1293.

[3] Cf. Þorkelsson, loc. cit. p. vii.

[4] Cf. Árna biskups saga: 'A þessu ári gaf Magnús konúngr lendum mönnum barúna nöfn ok herra, en skutilsveinum riddara nöfn ok herra.' ('In this year [1277] King Magnus conferred upon the "landed men" the titles of "baron" and "herra," and upon the table-pages the titles of "knight" and "herra."') Biskupa Sögur, Copenh. 1858, vol. i. p. 706.

[5] Islandske Annaler, ubi sup. passim. He is last named in Norwegian documents without the title in 1304, and is called simply 'Haukr Erlendsson lǫgmaðr,' Diplomatarium Norvegicum, Christiania, 1849, vol. i. p. 93, No. 103. The title 'herra' is first assigned him in these documents in 1305, Dip. Norv. vol. i. p. 96, No. 106.

[6] Cf. Þorkelsson, loc. cit. p. viii; Munch, loc. cit. p. 176.

[7] Islandske Annaler, ubi sup. passim, except p. 219, where the year of his death is given as 1332, which date, however, is not reconcilable with Munklífabók, ed. Christiania, 1845, p. 89. Munch, loc. cit. p. 178, gives the date of his death June 3rd, 1334.

[8] Cf. Formáli, Biskupa Sögur, Copenh. 1858, vol. i. p. xviii, and Katalog over den Arnamagnæanske Håndskriftsamling, Copenh. 1889, vol. i. p. 686.

[9] Islandske Annaler, ubi sup. p. 353.

century by John the Learned [Jón lærði][1], possibly about 1600[2], and a few years later by Arngrim Jonsson [Arngrímr Jónsson][3]; it was subsequently loaned to Bishop Bryniolf Sveinsson, who caused the transcripts of the Landnámabók and the Kristni Saga to be made from it, as has already been related. This part of the codex the Bishop may have returned to the owner, himself retaining the remainder, for, with the exception of the two sagas named, Arni Magnusson obtained the codex from Gaulveriabœr in the south of Iceland, and subsequently the remaining leaves of the missing sagas from the Rev. Olaf Jonsson [Síra Óláfr Jónsson], who was the clergyman at Stad in Grunnavik [Staðr í Grunnavík], in north-western Iceland, between the years 1703 and 1707[4].

Hauk's Book originally contained about 200 leaves[5], with widely varied contents. Certain leaves of the original manuscript have been detached from the main body of the book, and are now to be found in the Arna-Magnæan Collection, under Nos. 371 and 675, 4to; a portion has been lost, but 107 leaves of the original codex are preserved in AM. 544, 4to. With the exception of those portions just referred to, that part of the manuscript which treats of the Wineland discovery is to be found in this last mentioned volume, from leaves 93 to 101 [*back*] inclusive. The saga therein contained has no title contemporary with the text, but Arni Magnusson has inserted, in the space left vacant for the title, the words: 'Here begins the Saga of Thorfinn Karlsefni and Snorri Thorbrandsson' [' Hér hefr upp sǫgu þeirra Þorfinnz

[1] Cf. Arni Magnusson's note in, Katalog over den Arnamagnæanske Håndskriftsamling, vol. i. p. 590.

[2] Formáli, Biskupa Sögur, ubi sup. p. xii.

[3] Arngrimus Ionas, Specimen Islandiae Historicum, Amsterdam, 1643, p. 154.

[4] Arni Magnusson's own words are: 'These leaves of Landnáma book, as well as those of Christendom's saga, I have obtained, for the most part, from Sr. Olaf Jonsson, but Sr. Olaf's father [Sr. John Torfason of Stad in Súgandis-firth] obtained these leaves from a neighbouring farmer there in the west, and took them all apart, separating each sheet from the other to use them for binding. . . . But the volume itself . . . I obtained [if I remember aright] from Gaulveriabær in Flói, whither, without doubt, it drifted after the death of Mag. Bryniolf. . . . It is most probable that the book came first from the West firths, and that its owner, from whom Mag. Bryniolf borrowed it, carried back Landnáma to the West, while the rest remained in the South, unless Landnáma had already been separated from the volume, when it came into Mag. Bryniolf's hands, and he accordingly had the book in two parts.' Arni's notes, in the same codex from which the above is quoted, would indicate, that the greater part of the manuscript had come into his possession before 1702; a few leaves he obtained subsequently, and how greatly he prized this manuscript is indicated by his own words in a letter, which he wrote in the hope that it might still be possible to obtain the missing leaves of Landnáma; in this letter he calls the fragment, which he had already secured, 'inter pretiosissima eorum quae mihi sunt.' Cf. Katalog over den Arnamagnæanske Håndskriftsamling, ubi sup. vol. i. p. 590.

[5] Cf. Formáli, Biskupa Sögur, ubi sup. vol. i. p. xviii; Prolegomena, Sturlunga Saga, Oxford, 1878, vol. i. p. clx.

Karlsefnis oc Snorra Þorbrandzsonar'], although it is not apparent whether he himself invented this title, or derived it from some now unknown source.

The Saga of Thorfinn Karlsefni was written by three different persons; the first portion is in a hand commonly ascribed to Hauk's so-called 'first Icelandic secretary.' On p. 99, l. 14, the ink and the hand change, and beginning with the words *Eiríkr svarar vel*, the chirography is Hauk's own, as is readily apparent from a comparison with the autographic letter of 1302, already referred to [1]. Hauk's own work continues throughout this and the following page, ceasing at the end of the second line on p. 100, with the words *kǫlluðu í Hópi*, where he gives place to a new scribe, his so-called 'second Icelandic secretary.' Hauk, however, again resumes the pen on the back of p. 101, and himself concludes the saga. Two of the leaves upon which the saga is written are of an irregular shape, and there are holes in two other leaves; these defects were, however, present in the vellum from the beginning, so that they in no wise affect the integrity of the text; on the other hand the lower right-hand corner of p. 99 has become badly blackened, and is, in consequence, partially illegible, as is also the left-hand corner of p. 101; similarly pp. 100 and 101 [*back*] are somewhat indistinct, but, in the original, still not undecipherable. Initial letters are inserted in red and blue, and the sub-titles in red ink, which has sadly faded. There are three paginations, of which the latest, in red, is the one here adopted.

The genealogy appended to the saga has been brought down to Hauk's own time, and Hauk therein traces his ancestry to Karlsefni's Wineland-born son. By means of this genealogical list we are enabled to determine, approximately, the date of this transcript of the original saga, for we read in this list of Hallbera, 'Abbess of Reyniness,' and since we know that Hallbera was not consecrated abbess until the year 1299 [2], it becomes at once apparent that the saga could not have been completed before that year. This conclusion is corroborated by additional evidence furnished by this ancestral list, for in this list Hauk has given himself his title 'herra.' As has been stated, Hauk is first accorded this title in 1305, he is last mentioned without the title in 1304; which fact not only confirms the conclusion already reached, but enables us to advance the date, prior to which the transcript of the saga could not have been concluded, to 1304. It is not so easy to determine positively when the saga was finished. As Hauk's own hand brings the saga to a conclusion, it is evident that it must have been completed before, or not later than, the year 1334, the year of his death. If we accept the words of the genealogical list literally, it would appear that Hauk wrote this list not many years before his

[1] A facsimile of this letter is contained in Annaler for Nordisk Oldkyndighed, Copenh. 1847.
[2] Islandske Annaler, ubi sup. p. 199.

death, for it is there stated that Fru Ingigerd's daughter '*was*' Fru Hallbera, the Abbess. But Hallbera lived until 1330[1], and the strict construction of Hauk's language might point to the conclusion that the reference to Hallbera was made after her death, and therefore after 1330. Hauk was in Iceland in the years 1330 and 1331[2], doubtless for the last time. One of the scribes who aided him in writing the codex was probably an Icelander, as may be gleaned from his orthography, and as it is highly probable that the contents of the codex were for the most part copied from originals owned in Iceland, it may be that the transcript of this saga, as well as the book itself, was completed during this last visit. It has been claimed that a portion of Hauk's book, preceding the Saga of Thorfinn, was written prior to Hauk's acquirement of his title, a view founded upon the fact that his name is there cited without the addition of his title, and this view is supported by the corresponding usage of the Annals[3]. If this be true, then, upon the above hypothesis, a period of more than twenty-five years must have elapsed between the inception of the work and the completion of the 'Thorfinn's Saga.' Doubtless a considerable time was consumed in the compilation and transcription of the contents of this manuscript; but it seems scarcely probable that so long a time should have intervened between the preparation of the different portions of the work. Wherefore, if the reference to the Abbess Hallbera be accepted literally, the conjecture that the earlier portion of the codex was written prior to 1299 would appear to be doubtful, and it may be necessary either to advance the date of this portion of the manuscript or place the date of the Saga of Thorfinn anterior to that suggested. However this may be, two facts seem to be clearly established, first, that this saga was not written before 1299, and second, that this eldest surviving detailed narrative of the discovery of Wineland was written not later than the year 1334.

In the vellum codex, known as Number 557, 4to, of the Arna-Magnæan Collection, is an account of the Wineland discovery, so strikingly similar to that of Hauk's Book, that there can be no doubt that both histories were derived from the same source. The history of the discovery contained in the above codex is called the 'Saga of Eric the Red' [Saga Eireks rauða]. This may well have been the primitive title of the saga of Hauk's Book, which, as has been noted, obtains its modern name, 'Thorfinns Saga Karlsefnis,' from the entry made by

[1] Islandske Annaler, ubi sup. p. 219.

[2] Islandske Annaler, ubi sup. pp. 206, 219, 347, 397.

[3] Cf. Munch, loc. cit. p. 209; Íslendínga Sögur, Copenh. 1843, vol. i. pp. xxiv, xxv. Both of these authorities agree in the statement that the title of 'herra' was first applied to Hauk in a Norwegian diploma of 1303, but as they do not cite their authority, it is not apparent whence the statement was derived.

Arni Magnusson, early in the eighteenth century. That both sagas were copied from the same vellum is by no means certain; if both transcripts be judged strictly by their contents it becomes at once apparent that this could not have been the fact, and such a conjecture is only tenable upon the theory that the scribes of Hauk's Book edited the saga which they copied. This, while it is very doubtful in the case of the body of the text of the Hauk's Book Saga of Thorfinn, may not even be conjectured of the Saga of Eric the Red. The latter saga was undoubtedly a literal copy from the original, for there are certain minor confusions of the text, which indicate, unmistakably, either the heedlessness of the copyist, or that the scribe was working from a somewhat illegible original whose defects he was not at pains to supply. If both sagas were copied from different early vellums, the simpler language of the Saga of Eric the Red would seem to indicate that it was a transcript of a somewhat earlier form of the saga than that from which the saga of Hauk's Book was derived. This, however, is entirely conjectural, for the codex containing the Saga of Eric the Red was not written for many years after Hauk's Book, and probably not until the following century. So much the orthography and hand of 557, 4to, indicate, and, from the application of this test, the codex has been determined to date from the fifteenth century[1], and has been ascribed by very eminent authority to *ca.* 1400[2].

The Saga of Eric the Red begins with the thirteenth line of page 27 of the codex [the title appears at the top of this page], and concludes in the fifth line on the back of page 35, the hand being the same throughout. Spaces were left for initial letters, but these were not inserted, except in one case by a different and indifferent penman. With the exception of a very few words, or portions of words, upon page 30 [*back*] and page 31, the manuscript of the saga is clearly legible throughout. Certain slight defects in the vellum have existed from the beginning, and there is, therefore, no material hiatus in the entire text, for the sense of the few indistinct words is either clearly apparent from the context, or may be supplied from the sister text of Hauk's Book.

In his catalogue of parchment manuscripts[3], Arni Magnusson states, that he obtained this manuscript from Bishop John Vidalin [Mag. Jón Vidalín][4] and adds the conjecture, that it had either belonged to the Skálholt Church, or came thither from

[1] Katalog over den Arnamagnæanske Håndskriftsamling, ubi sup. vol. i. p. 708; Íslendínga Sögur, Copenh. 1847, vol. ii. p. xxviii.

[2] Vigfusson, Corpus Poeticum Boreale, Oxford, 1883, vol. i. p. xli, note 1.

[3] AM. 435, 4to.

[4] John Vidalin became bishop of Skálholt in December, 1697, and died in 1720. Cf. Worm, Lexicon, Helsingøer, 1771, 1 Deel, p. 580.

among Bishop Bryniolf's books. This conjecture, that the book belonged to the Church of Skálholt, has, however, been disputed, and the place of its compilation, at the same time, assigned to the north of Iceland[1].

These sagas in Hauk's Book and AM. 557, 4to, are so closely allied, belong so naturally together and each so enlightens the other, that the two texts have been collated, and the translation, which follows, is prepared from both. In the body of the text of the translation, the saga as contained in Hauk's Book has been in the main more closely followed, but the language of the saga of AM. 557, 4to, is occasionally substituted or added, where such treatment has seemed to serve in any degree to inform the narrative. In all cases, however, where any considerable differences exist between the two texts, these differences are recorded in the notes, the abbreviations 'EsR', and 'ÞsK' indicating the language of the Saga of Eric the Red [Eiriks saga Rauða] and that of the Saga of Thorfinn Karlsefni [Þorfinns saga Karlsefnis] respectively.

The Saga of Eric the Red [and both texts are included under this title] presents a clear and graphic account of the discovery and exploration of Wineland the Good. In this narrative the discovery is ascribed to Leif, the son of Eric the Red, who hit upon the land, by chance, during a voyage from Norway to Greenland. This voyage, as has already been stated, probably took place in the year 1000.

After his return to Greenland, Leif's account of the land which he had discovered, seems to have persuaded his brother, Thorstein, and possibly his father, to undertake an expedition to the strange country. This voyage, which was not destined to meet with a successful issue, may well have fallen in the year following Leif's return, and therefore, it may be conjectured, in the year 1001. About this time there had arrived in Greenland an Icelander of considerable prominence, an old friend of Eric's, named Thorbiorn Vifilsson, who had brought with him his daughter, Gudrid, or, as she is also called, Thurid. He must have arrived before Thorstein Ericsson's voyage, for we are told, that it was in Thorbiorn's ship that this voyage was undertaken. It seems probable that Thorbiorn arrived at Brattahlid [Eric's home] during Leif's absence from Greenland, and if this be true, it follows, that Thorbiorn and Gudrid must have been converted to Christianity before its acceptance in Iceland as the legalized religion of the land; for very soon after their arrival in Greenland, Gudrid alludes to the fact of her being a Christian, and, from the language of the saga, there can be no question that her father had likewise embraced the new faith. The presence of these companions in the faith may have materially aided Leif in the work of proselytism, in which he engaged, upon his return to Greenland. We are told, that Thorbiorn

[1] Biskupa Sögur, ubi sup. vol. i. p. lxx.

did not arrive at Brattahlid until the second year after his departure from Iceland, wherefore, if the assumption that he arrived during Leif's absence be sound, it becomes apparent that he must have left Iceland in the summer of the year 998 or 999.

Eric's son, Thorstein, wooed and married Gudrid, and the wedding was celebrated at Brattahlid in the autumn. It is recorded in the saga that Gudrid was regarded as a most desirable match. Thorstein may have promptly recognized her worth, and his marriage may have occurred in the autumn of the same year in which he returned from his unlucky voyage. It could not well have been celebrated in the previous year, for Thorstein's allusions on his death-bed to the religion of Greenland, indicate that Christianity must have been for a longer time the accepted faith of the land than it could have been at the close of the year 1000.

In the winter after his marriage, Thorstein died, and in the spring, Gudrid returned to Brattahlid. Thorfinn Karlsefni arrived at Brattahlid about this time, possibly the next autumn after Thorstein's death, and in his company came Snorri Thorbrandsson. Karlsefni was married to Gudrid shortly after the Yule-tide following his arrival. If he arrived in Greenland in the autumn of the year 1002, this wedding may, accordingly, have taken place about the beginning of the year 1003[1]. In the summer following his marriage, Thorfinn appears to have undertaken

[1] Vigfusson, in his essay, 'Um tímatal í Íslendínga sögum í fornöld,' in Safn til sögu Íslands, loc. cit. vol. i. p. 339, and also in his edition of the Eyrbyggja Saga, loc. cit. p. 129, assigns as the date of Snorri's departure to Greenland, and, by the same token, Karlsefni's, the year 998 [or 999]. This conclusion he reaches from the passage in Eyrbyggja, already cited p. 18, wherein it is stated that 'after the reconciliation of the people of Eyrr and the people of Alpta-firth, Thorbrand's sons, Snorri and Thorleif, went to Greenland.' In Vigfusson's edition of the Erybyggja Saga, the chapter containing this statement is numbered 48, and the next succeeding chapter begins: 'Next to this, Gizur the White and Hialti, his son-in-law, came out to proclaim the gospel, and all the people of Iceland were baptized, and Christianity was legally accepted by the Althing.' The words 'next to this' in the position which they thus occupy seem to refer to the words of the preceding chapter: 'After the reconciliation of the people of Eyrr and the people of Alpta-firth,' that is, 'next after this' reconciliation Gizur and his son-in-law came to Iceland. But Gizur and Hialti came to Iceland on this mission in 999, and the obvious inference is that the reconciliation was accomplished prior to this, according to Vigfusson in the previous year, 998. [Cf. Eyrbyggja Saga, ed. Vigfusson, p. 129.] In the eldest vellum fragment of the Eyrbyggja Saga which we now possess, AM. 162 E. fol., chapter 48 of the Vigfusson text does not occupy the place preceding the account of the arrival of Gizur on his mission. The limited contents of this fragment do not, unfortunately, enable us to determine where the chapter did stand in this text, but presumably it occupied the same position as that in which it occurs in the Codex Wolphenbuttelensis, as well as in the vellum fragment of the saga contained in AM. 445 *b*, 4to, namely, after chapter 55 of the Vigfusson edition. [Cf., in that edition, note 11, p. 91.] To the events described in this chapter 55, Vigfusson [Eyrbyggja, p. 129] assigns the date 1001. The chapter immediately following this chapter 55 begins with the words: 'Snorri Godi dwelt at Helgafell eight years after Christianity became the legal religion

his voyage of exploration to Wineland, that is to say in the summer of the year 1003. A longer time may well have elapsed after Gudrid's arrival before her marriage with Thorstein, and similarly it is even more probable that a longer interval elapsed between Thorstein's death and Gudrid's second marriage. The purpose of this conjectural chronology is to determine, if possible, a date prior to which Thorfinn Karlsefni's voyage to Wineland could not have been undertaken. While, therefore, it is altogether probable that this voyage was made after the year 1003, it does not appear to be possible, for the reasons presented, that it could have taken place before that year.

Problems suggested by the text of another version of the history of the discovery and exploration, namely, that contained in the Flatey Book, are considered elsewhere, as are also points of difference between that narrative and the history as set forth in the Saga of Eric the Red. It remains to be said, that the text of this saga does not present such difficulties as those which are suggested by a critical examination of the narrative of the Flatey Book. This version of the history of the discovery does contain, however, one statement, which is not altogether intelligible and which is not susceptible of very satisfactory explanation, namely, that 'there came no snow' in the land which the Wineland explorers had found. This assertion does not consist with our present knowledge of the winter climate of the eastern coast of that portion of North America situated within the latitude which was probably reached by the explorers. The observation may, perhaps, be best explained upon the theory that the original verbal statement of the explorers was, that there was no snow in Wineland, such as that to which they were accustomed in the countries with which they were more familiar[1]. With this single exception there appears to be no statement in the Saga of Eric the

of Iceland.' The fact, therefore, that the record of the voyage of Thorbrand's sons to Greenland does, in certain other late manuscripts, occupy the place which Vigfusson assigns it, would not seem to afford sufficient reason for establishing the date of this voyage, by the words of a subsequent passage, when, as has been stated, this passage does not indeed follow, but precedes the chapter in the oldest manuscripts now existing. If Snorri [and Karlsefni] sailed to Greenland immediately after the reconciliation, as Vigfusson conjectures, a fatal flaw in the chronology at once appears. By a comparison with the language of the Saga of Eric the Red, it will be seen that if Karlsefni and Snorri sailed to Greenland in 998 or 999, Karlsefni's voyage of exploration, which was undertaken in the year after his arrival in Greenland, would fall either in the year prior to that assigned to Leif's discovery of Wineland, or in the year of that discovery, both of which hypotheses are, of course, impossible. The simpler explanation, and one entirely consistent with the language of the Eyrbyggja Saga, would seem to be that the word 'after' in the sentence, 'Thorbrand's sons went to Greenland after the reconciliation,' does not mean the same year or the next year after the reconciliation, but some time thereafter, and necessarily later than the year 1001, the earliest date assignable for Thorstein Ericsson's ill-fated voyage, and which is also the date of the event immediately preceding this sentence in the elder texts of the Eyrbyggja Saga.

[1] Cf. post, Note No. 55, upon this passage in the saga.

Red which is not lucid, and which is not reasonably consistent with our present knowledge of the probable regions visited. The incident of the adventure with the Uniped may be passed without especial mention in this connection; it gives evidence of the prevalent superstition of the time, it is true, but it in no way reflects upon the keenness of observation or relative credibility of the explorers. It follows, therefore, that the accounts of the discovery contained in Hauk's Book and AM. 557, 4to, whether they present the eldest form of the narrative of the Wineland explorers or not, do afford the most graphic and succinct exposition of the discovery, and, supported as they are throughout by contemporaneous history, appear in every respect most worthy of credence.

The Saga of Eric the Red, also called The Saga of Thorfinn Karlsefni and Snorri Thorbrandsson.

Olaf was the name of a warrior-king[1], who was called Olaf the White. He was the son of King Ingiald, Helgi's son, the son of Olaf, Gudraud's[2] son, son of Halfdan Whiteleg[3], king of the Uplands-men (8). Olaf engaged in a Western freebooting expedition and captured Dublin in Ireland and the Shire of Dublin, over which he became king (9). He married Aud the Wealthy[4], daughter of Ketil Flatnose[5], son of Biorn Buna[6], a famous man of Norway. Their son was called Thorstein the Red[7]. Olaf was killed in battle in Ireland, and Aud (10) and Thorstein went then to the Hebrides (11); there Thorstein married Thurid[8], daughter of Eyvind Easterling[9], sister of Helgi the Lean[10]; they had many children. Thorstein became a warrior-king, and entered into fellowship with Earl Sigurd the Mighty[11], son of Eystein the Rattler[12]. They conquered Caithness and Sutherland, Ross and Moray, and more than the half of Scotland. Over these Thorstein became king, ere he was betrayed by the Scots, and was slain there in battle. Aud was at Caithness when she heard of Thorstein's death; she thereupon caused a ship (12) to be secretly built in the forest, and when she was ready, she sailed out to the Orkneys. There she bestowed Groa, Thorstein the Red's daughter, in marriage; she was the mother of Grelad[13], whom Earl Thorfinn, Skull-cleaver[14], married. After this Aud set out to seek Iceland, and had on board her ship twenty freemen (13). Aud arrived in Iceland, and passed the first winter at Biarnarhöfn with her brother, Biorn.

[1] EsR: 'konungr,' king. [2] ÞsK: Gudred's son; EsR: Gudrid's son. [3] hvítbeinn. [4] EsR: djúpauðga; ÞsK: djúpúðga, i. e. deep-minded, wise. [5] flatnefr. [6] the Ungartered? [7] rauðr. [8] ÞsK: Þuríðr. [9] austmaðr. [10] hinn magri. [11] hinn ríki. [12] glumra. [13] EsR: Gunnlad. [14] hausakljúfr.

Aud afterwards took possession of all the Dale country (14) between Dögurdar river and Skraumuhlaups river. She lived at Hvamm, and held her orisons at Krossholar, where she caused crosses to be erected, for she had been baptized and was a devout believer. With her there came out [to Iceland] many distinguished men, who had been captured in the Western freebooting expedition, and were called slaves. Vifil was the name of one of these: he was a highborn man, who had been taken captive in the Western sea, and was called a slave, before Aud freed him; now when Aud gave homesteads to the members of her crew, Vifil asked wherefore she gave him no homestead as to the other men. Aud replied, that this should make no difference to him, saying, that he would be regarded as a distinguished man wherever he was. She gave him Vifilsdal (15), and there he dwelt. He married a woman whose name was . . . . . [1]; their sons were Thorbiorn and Thorgeir. They were men of promise, and grew up with their father.

Eric the Red finds [2] Greenland.

There was a man named Thorvald; he was a son of Asvald, Ulf's son, Eyxna-Thori's son. His son's name was Eric [3]. He and his father went from Jaederen (16) to Iceland, on account of manslaughter, and settled on Hornstrandir, and dwelt at Drangar (17). There Thorvald died, and Eric then married Thorhild, a daughter of Jorund, Atli's son, and Thorbiorg the Ship-chested [4], who had been married before to Thorbiorn of the Haukadal family [5]. Eric then removed from the North, and cleared land in Haukadal, and dwelt at Ericsstadir by Vatnshorn. Then Eric's thralls caused a land-slide on Valthiof's farm, Valthiofsstadir. Eyiolf the Foul [6], Valthiof's kinsman, slew the thralls near Skeidsbrekkur above Vatnshorn. For this Eric killed Eyiolf the Foul, and he also killed Duelling-Hrafn [7], at Leikskalar. Geirstein and Odd of Jorva, Eyiolf's kinsmen, conducted the prosecution for the slaying of their kinsmen, and Eric was, in consequence, banished from Haukadal. He then took possession of Brokey and Eyxney, and dwelt at Tradir on Sudrey, the first winter (18). It was at this time that he loaned Thorgest his outer daïs-boards (19); Eric afterwards went to Eyxney, and dwelt at Ericsstad. He then demanded his outer daïs-boards, but did not obtain them [8]. Eric then carried the outer daïs-boards away from Breidabolstad, and Thorgest gave chase. They came to blows a short distance from the farm of Drangar (20). There two of Thorgest's sons were killed and certain other men besides. After this

[1] EsR: simply, 'he married a wife.' [2] Lit. 'found.' [3] EsR: 'Eric the Red.'
[4] knarrar-bringa. [5] hinn haukdœlski. [6] saurr. [7] Hólmgǫngu-Hrafn.
[8] EsR: 'He then took possession of Brokey, and dwelt at Tradir. The first winter, however, Eric went to Auxney. He then loaned his outer daïs-boards to Thorgest. He dwelt at Ericsstadir.'

each of them retained a considerable body of men with him at his home. Styr gave Eric his support, as did also Eyiolf of Sviney, Thorbiorn, Vifil's son, and the sons of Thorbrand of Alptafirth; while Thorgest was backed by the sons of Thord the Yeller[1], and Thorgeir of Hitardal, Aslak of Langadal and his son, Illugi. Eric and his people were condemned to outlawry at Thorsness-thing (21). He equipped his ship for a voyage, in Ericsvag; while Eyiolf concealed him in Dimunarvag (22), when Thorgest and his people were searching for him among the islands. He said to them, that it was his intention to go in search of that land which Gunnbiorn (23), son of Ulf the Crow[2], saw when he was driven out of his course, westward across the main, and discovered Gunnbiorns-skerries. He told them that he would return again to his friends, if he should succeed in finding that country. Thorbiorn, and Eyiolf, and Styr accompanied Eric out beyond the islands, and they parted with the greatest friendliness; Eric said to them that he would render them similar aid, so far as it might lie within his power, if they should ever stand in need of his help. Eric sailed out to sea from Snaefells-iokul, and arrived at that ice-mountain (24) which is called Blacksark[3]. Thence he sailed to the southward, that he might ascertain whether there was habitable country in that direction. He passed the first winter at Ericsey, near the middle of the Western-settlement. In the following spring he proceeded to Ericsfirth, and selected a site there for his homestead. That summer he explored the western uninhabited region, remaining there for a long time, and assigning many local names there. The second winter he spent at Ericsholms beyond Hvarfsgnipa. But the third summer he sailed northward to Snaefell, and into Hrafnsfirth. He believed then that he had reached the head of Ericsfirth; he turned back then, and remained the third winter[4] at Ericsey at the mouth of Ericsfirth (25). The following summer he sailed to Iceland, and landed in Breidafirth. He remained that winter with Ingolf (26) at Holmlatr. In the spring he and Thorgest fought together, and Eric was defeated; after this a reconciliation was effected between them. That summer Eric set out to colonize the land which he had discovered, and which he called Greenland, because, he said, men would be the more readily persuaded thither if the land had a good name.

CONCERNING THORBIORN.

Thorgeir, Vifil's son, married, and took to wife Arnora, daughter of Einar of Laugarbrekka, Sigmund's son, son of Ketil Thistil, who settled Thistilsfirth. Einar had another daughter named Hallveig; she was married to Thorbiorn, Vifil's son (27),

[1] gellir. [2] kráka. [3] ÞsK: Bláserkr. EsR: Hvítserkr, Whitesark.
[4] EsR: 'the fourth and third winter.'

who got with her Laugarbrekka-land on Hellisvellir. Thorbiorn moved thither, and became a very distinguished man. He was an excellent husbandman[1], and had a great estate. Gudrid was the name of Thorbiorn's daughter. She was the most beautiful of her sex, and in every respect a very superior woman. There dwelt at Arnarstapi a man named Orm, whose wife's name was Halldis. Orm was a good husbandman, and a great friend of Thorbiorn, and Gudrid lived with him for a long time as a foster-daughter. There was a man named Thorgeir, who lived at Thorgeirsfell (**28**); he was very wealthy and had been manumitted; he had a son named Einar, who was a handsome, well-bred man, and very showy in his dress. Einar was engaged in trading-voyages from one country to the other, and had prospered in this. He always spent his winters alternately either in Iceland or in Norway.

Now it is to be told, that one autumn, when Einar was in Iceland, he went with his wares out along Snaefellsness[2], with the intention of selling them. He came to Arnarstapi, and Orm invited him to remain with him, and Einar accepted this invitation, for there was a strong friendship [between Orm and himself]. Einar's wares were carried into a store-house, where he unpacked them, and displayed them to Orm and the men of his household, and asked Orm to take such of them as he liked. Orm accepted this offer, and said that Einar was a good merchant, and was greatly favoured by fortune. Now, while they were busied about the wares, a woman passed before the door of the store-house. Einar enquired of Orm: 'Who was that handsome woman who passed before the door? I have never seen her here before.' Orm replies: 'That is Gudrid, my foster-child, the daughter of Thorbiorn of Laugarbrekka.' 'She must be a good match,' said Einar; 'has she had any suitors?' Orm replies: 'In good sooth she has been courted, friend, nor is she easily to be won, for it is believed that both she and her father will be very particular in their choice of a husband.' 'Be that as it may,' quoth Einar, 'she is the woman to whom I mean to pay my addresses, and I would have thee present this matter to her father in my behalf, and use every exertion to bring it to a favourable issue, and I shall reward thee to the full of my friendship, if I am successful. It may be that Thorbiorn will regard the connection as being to our mutual advantage, for [while] he is a most honourable man and has a goodly home, his personal effects, I am told, are somewhat on the wane[3]; but neither I nor my father are lacking in lands or chattels, and Thorbiorn would be greatly aided thereby, if this match should be brought about.' 'Surely I believe myself to be thy friend,' replies Orm, 'and yet I am by no means disposed to act in this matter, for Thorbiorn hath a very haughty spirit, and is more-

[1] EsR: 'Godord-man,' cf. note **72**. [2] ÞsK: Snowfells-strand. [3] EsR: 'are much on the wane.'

over a most ambitious man.' Einar replied that he wished for nought else than that his suit should be broached; Orm replied, that he should have his will. Einar fared again to the South until he reached his home. Sometime after this, Thorbiorn had an autumn feast, as was his custom, for he was a man of high position. Hither came Orm of Arnarstapi, and many other of Thorbiorn's friends. Orm came to speech with Thorbiorn, and said, that Einar of Thorgeirsfell had visited him [1] not long before, and that he was become a very promising man. Orm now makes known the proposal of marriage in Einar's behalf, and added that for some persons and for some reasons it might be regarded as a very appropriate match: 'thou mayest greatly strengthen thyself thereby, master, by reason of the property.' Thorbiorn answers: 'Little did I expect to hear such words from thee, that I should marry my daughter to the son of a thrall (29); and that, because it seems to thee that my means are diminishing, wherefore she shall not remain longer with thee [2] since thou deemest so mean a match as this suitable for her.' Orm afterward returned to his home, and all of the invited guests to their respective households, while Gudrid remained behind with her father, and tarried at home that winter. But in the spring Thorbiorn gave an entertainment to his friends, to which many came [3], and it was a noble feast, and at the banquet Thorbiorn called for silence, and spoke: 'Here have I passed a goodly lifetime, and have experienced the good-will of men toward me, and their affection; and, methinks, our relations together have been pleasant; but now I begin to find myself in straitened circumstances, although my estate has hitherto been accounted a respectable one. Now will I rather abandon my farming, than lose my honour, and rather leave the country, than bring disgrace upon my family; wherefore I have now concluded to put that promise to the test, which my friend Eric the Red made, when we parted company in Breidafirth. It is my present design to go to Greenland this summer, if matters fare as I wish.' The folk were greatly astonished at this plan of Thorbiorn's [4], for he was blessed with many friends, but they were convinced that he was so firmly fixed in his purpose, that it would not avail to endeavour to dissuade him from it. Thorbiorn bestowed gifts upon his guests, after which the feast came to an end, and the folk returned to their homes. Thorbiorn sells his lands and buys a ship, which was laid up at the mouth of Hraunhöfn (30). Thirty persons joined him in the voyage; among these were Orm of Arnarstapi, and his wife, and other of Thorbiorn's friends, who would not part from him. Then they put to sea. When they sailed the weather was favourable, but after they came out upon the

[1] Lit. 'had been there.' [2] EsR: 'go with thee.' [3] Lit. 'many men came thither.'

[4] EsK: 'People were greatly astonished at this change of condition.' EsR: 'People thought these great tidings, concerning this design of Eric's.' This may refer to Eric's promise, mentioned above, or, as seems more probable, the 'Eric' has been erroneously inserted for Thorbiorn.

high-seas the fair wind failed, and there came great gales[1], and they lost their way, and had a very tedious voyage that summer. Then illness appeared among their people, and Orm and his wife Halldis died, and the half of their company. The sea began to run high, and they had a very wearisome and wretched voyage in many ways, but arrived, nevertheless, at Heriolfsness in Greenland, on the very eve of winter[2]. At Heriolfsness lived a man named Thorkel. He was a man of ability and an excellent husbandman. He received Thorbiorn and all of his ship's company, and entertained them well during the winter[3]. At that time there was a season of great dearth in Greenland; those who had been at the fisheries had had poor hauls, and some had not returned. There was a certain woman there in the settlement, whose name was Thorbiorg. She was a prophetess, and was called Little Sibyl (31). She had had nine sisters, all of whom were prophetesses, but she was the only one left alive. It was Thorbiorg's custom in the winters, to go to entertainments, and she was especially sought after at the homes of those who were curious to know their fate, or what manner of season might be in store for them; and inasmuch as Thorkel was the chief yeoman in the neighbourhood, it was thought to devolve upon him to find out when the evil time, which was upon them, would cease. Thorkel invited the prophetess to his home, and careful preparations were made for her reception, according to the custom which prevailed, when women of her kind were to be entertained. A high seat was prepared for her, in which a cushion filled with poultry feathers[4], was placed. When she came in the evening, with the man who had been sent to meet her, she was clad in a dark-blue cloak, fastened with a strap, and set with stones quite down to the hem. She wore glass beads around her neck, and upon her head a black lamb-skin hood, lined with white cat-skin. In her hands she carried a staff, upon which there was a knob, which was ornamented with brass, and set with stones up about the knob. Circling her waist she wore a girdle of touch-wood, and attached to it a great skin pouch, in which she kept the charms which she used when she was practising her sorcery. She wore upon her feet shaggy calf-skin shoes, with long, tough latchets, upon the ends of which there were large brass buttons[5]. She had cat-skin gloves upon her hands, which were white inside and lined with fur. When she entered, all of the folk felt it to be their duty to offer her becoming greetings. She received the salutations of each individual according as he pleased her. Yeoman Thorkel took the sibyl by the hand, and led her to the seat which had been made ready for her. Thorkel bade her run her eyes over man and

[1] Thus EsR.

[2] EsR: 'at the winter-night-tide.' The three days which begin the winter season are so called.

[3] EsR adds: 'Thorbiorn and all his shipmates were well pleased.'

[4] Lit. 'in which there should be poultry feathers.'

[5] þsK: 'tin-buttons.'

beast and home. She had little to say concerning all these. The tables were brought forth in the evening, and it remains to be told what manner of food was prepared for the prophetess. A porridge of goat's beestings was made for her, and for meat there were dressed the hearts of every kind of beast, which could be obtained there. She had a brass spoon, and a knife with a handle of walrus tusk, with a double hasp of brass around the haft, and from this the point was broken. And when the tables were removed, Yeoman Thorkel approaches Thorbiorg, and asks how she is pleased with the home, and the character of the folk, and how speedily she would be likely to become aware of that concerning which he had questioned her, and which the people were anxious to know. She replied that she could not give an opinion in this matter before the morrow, after that she had slept there through the night. And on the morrow, when the day was far spent, such preparations were made as were necessary to enable her to accomplish her soothsaying. She bade them bring her those women, who knew the incantation, which she required to work her spells, and which she called Warlocks; but such women were not to be found. Thereupon a search was made throughout the house, to see whether any one knew this [incantation]. Then says Gudrid: 'Although I am neither skilled in the black art nor a sibyl, yet my foster-mother, Halldis, taught me in Iceland that spell-song, which she called Warlocks.' Thorbiorg answered: 'Then art thou wise in season[1]!' Gudrid replies: 'This is an incantation and ceremony of such a kind, that I do not mean to lend it any aid, for that I am a Christian woman.' Thorbiorg answers: 'It might so be that thou couldst give thy help to the company here, and still be no worse woman than before; however I leave it with Thorkel to provide for my needs.' Thorkel now so urged Gudrid, that she said she must needs comply with his wishes. The women then made a ring round about, while Thorbiorg sat up on the spell-daïs. Gudrid then sang the song, so sweet and well, that no one remembered ever before to have heard the melody sung with so fair a voice as this. The sorceress thanked her for the song, and said: 'She has indeed lured many spirits hither, who think it pleasant to hear this song, those who were wont to forsake us hitherto and refuse to submit themselves to us. Many things are now revealed to me, which hitherto have been hidden, both from me and from others. And I am able to announce that this period of famine will not endure longer, but the season will mend as spring approaches. The visitation of disease, which has been so long upon you, will disappear sooner than expected. And thee, Gudrid, I shall reward out of hand, for the assistance, which thou hast vouchsafed us, since the fate in store for thee is now all made manifest to me. Thou shalt make a most worthy match here in Greenland, but it shall not be of long duration for thee, for thy future[2]

[1] EsR: 'wiser than I supposed.'

[2] ÞsK: vegar þínir, thy ways; EsR: vegir þínir.

path leads out to Iceland, and a lineage both great and goodly shall spring from thee, and above thy line brighter rays of light shall shine, than I have power clearly to unfold[1]. And now fare well and health to thee, my daughter!' After this the folk advanced to the sibyl, and each besought information concerning that about which he was most curious. She was very ready in her responses, and little of that which she foretold failed of fulfilment. After this they came for her from a neighbouring farmstead, and she thereupon set out thither. Thorbiorn was then sent for, since he had not been willing to remain at home while such heathen rites[2] were practising. The weather improved speedily, when the spring opened[3], even as Thorbiorg had prophesied. Thorbiorn equipped his ship and sailed away, until he arrived at Brattahlid. Eric received him with open arms[4], and said that it was well that he had come thither. Thorbiorn and his household remained with him during the winter, while quarters were provided for the crew among the farmers. And the following spring Eric gave Thorbiorn land on Stokkaness, where a goodly farmstead was founded, and there he lived thenceforward.

Concerning Leif the Lucky and the Introduction of Christianity into Greenland.

Eric was married to a woman named Thorhild[5], and had two sons; one of these was named Thorstein, and the other Leif. They were both promising men. Thorstein lived at home with his father, and there was not at that time a man in Greenland who was accounted of so great promise as he. Leif had sailed (32) to Norway, where he was at the court of King Olaf Tryggvason. When Leif sailed from Greenland, in the summer, they were driven out of their course to the Hebrides. It was late before they got fair winds thence, and they remained there far into the summer. Leif became enamoured of a certain woman, whose name was Thorgunna. She was a woman of fine family, and Leif observed that she was possessed of rare intelligence[6] (33). When Leif was preparing for his departure Thorgunna (34) asked to be permitted to accompany him. Leif enquired whether she had in this the approval of her kinsmen. She replied that she did not care for it. Leif responded that he did not deem it the part of wisdom to abduct so high-born a woman in a strange country, 'and we so few in number.' 'It is by no means certain that thou

[1] EsR: 'and above thy race shall shine a bright beam of light.'

[2] ÞsK: 'superstitions.'

[3] Omitted in ÞsK.

[4] Lit. 'with both hands.' ÞsK has 'receives him well with graciousness.'

[5] EsR: Thiodhild.

[6] EsR: lit. 'knew more than a little.'

shalt find this to be the better decision,' said Thorgunna. 'I shall put it to the proof, notwithstanding,' said Leif. 'Then I tell thee,' said Thorgunna, 'that I am no longer a lone woman, for I am pregnant, and upon thee I charge it. I foresee that I shall give birth to a male child. And though thou give this no heed, yet will I rear the boy, and send him to thee in Greenland, when he shall be fit to take his place with other men. And I foresee that thou wilt get as much profit of this son as is thy due from this our parting; moreover, I mean to come to Greenland myself before the end comes.' Leif gave her a gold finger-ring, a Greenland wadmal mantle, and a belt of walrus-tusk. This boy came to Greenland, and was called Thorgils. Leif acknowledged his paternity, and some men will have it that this Thorgils came to Iceland in the summer before the Fródá-wonder (35). However, this Thorgils was afterwards in Greenland, and there seemed to be something not altogether natural about him before the end came. Leif and his companions sailed away from the Hebrides, and arrived in Norway in the autumn. Leif went to the court of King Olaf Tryggvason. He was well received by the king, who felt that he could see that Leif was a man of great accomplishments. Upon one occasion the king came to speech with Leif, and asks him, 'Is it thy purpose to sail to Greenland in the summer?' 'It is my purpose,' said Leif, 'if it be your will.' 'I believe it will be well,' answers the king, 'and thither thou shalt go upon my errand, to proclaim Christianity there.' Leif replied that the king should decide, but gave it as his belief that it would be difficult to carry this mission to a successful issue in Greenland. The king replied that he knew of no man who would be better fitted for this undertaking, 'and in thy hands the cause will surely prosper.' 'This can only be,' said Leif, 'if I enjoy the grace of your protection.' Leif put to sea when his ship was ready for the voyage. For a long time he was tossed about upon the ocean, and came upon lands of which he had previously had no knowledge. There were self-sown wheat fields and vines growing there. There were also those trees there which are called 'mausur' (36), and of all these they took specimens. Some of the timbers were so large that they were used in building. Leif found men upon a wreck, and took them home with him, and procured quarters for them all during the winter. In this wise he showed his nobleness and goodness, since he introduced Christianity into the country, and saved the men from the wreck[1]; and he was called Leif the Lucky[2] ever after. Leif landed in Ericsfirth, and then went home to Brattahlid; he was well received by every one. He soon proclaimed Christianity throughout the land, and the Catholic faith, and announced King Olaf Tryggvason's messages to the people, telling them how much excellence and how great glory accompanied this faith. Eric was slow in

[1] EsR: 'as in many other ways, for he brought Christianity to the country.' [2] hinn heppni.

forming the determination to forsake his old belief, but Thiodhild (37) embraced the faith promptly, and caused a church to be built at some distance from the house. This building was called Thiodhild's Church, and there she and those persons who had accepted Christianity, and they were many, were wont to offer their prayers. Thiodhild would not have intercourse with Eric after that she had received the faith, whereat he was sorely vexed.

At this time there began to be much talk about a voyage of exploration[1] to that country which Leif had discovered. The leader of this expedition was Thorstein Ericsson, who was a good man and an intelligent, and blessed with many friends. Eric was likewise invited to join them, for the men believed that his luck and foresight would be of great furtherance. He was slow in deciding, but did not say nay, when his friends besought him to go. They thereupon equipped that ship in which Thorbiorn had come out, and twenty men were selected for the expedition. They took little cargo with them, nought else save their weapons and provisions[2]. On that morning when Eric set out from his home he took with him a little chest containing gold and silver; he hid this treasure, and then went his way. He had proceeded but a short distance, however, when he fell from his horse and broke his ribs and dislocated his shoulder[3], whereat he cried 'Ai, ai[4]!' By reason of this accident he sent his wife word[5] that she should procure the treasure which he had concealed, for to the hiding of the treasure he attributed his misfortune (38). Thereafter they sailed cheerily out of Ericsfirth in high spirits over their plan. They were long tossed about upon the ocean, and could not lay the course they wished. They came in sight of Iceland, and likewise saw birds from the Irish coast[6]. Their ship was, in sooth, driven hither and thither over the sea. In the autumn they turned back, worn out by toil, and exposure to the elements, and exhausted by their labours, and arrived at Ericsfirth at the very beginning of winter. Then said Eric, 'More cheerful were we[7] in the summer, when we put out of the firth, but we still live[8], and it might have been much worse[9].' Thorstein answers, 'It will be a princely deed to endeavour to look well after the wants of all these men who are now in need, and to make provision for them during the winter.' Eric answers, 'It is ever true, as it is said, that "it is never clear ere the answer comes," and so it

[1] EsR: 'From this there began to be much talk, that he should explore.'

[2] EsR: 'mostly weapons and provisions.'

[3] ÞsK: 'injured his arm at the shoulder-joint.'

[4] Lacking in ÞsK.

[5] ÞsK: lit. 'he told his wife.'

[6] Lit. 'had birds from Ireland;' that is, came near enough to the coast of Ireland to see land birds.

[7] EsR has 'ye' instead of 'we' throughout.

[8] Lit. 'but now we are.'

[9] Lit. 'and there is still much good left;' that is, we have still much to be grateful for.

must be here. We will act now upon thy counsel in this matter[1].' All of the men, who were not otherwise provided for, accompanied the father and son. They landed thereupon, and went home to Brattahlid, where they remained throughout the winter.

Thorstein Ericsson weds Gudrid[2]; Apparitions.

Now it is to be told that Thorstein Ericsson sought Gudrid, Thorbiorn's daughter, in wedlock. His suit was favourably received both by herself and by her father, and it was decided that Thorstein should marry Gudrid, and the wedding was held at Brattahlid in the autumn. The entertainment sped well, and was very numerously attended. Thorstein had a home in the Western-settlement at a certain farmstead, which is called Lysufirth. A half interest in this property belonged to a man named Thorstein, whose wife's name was Sigrid. Thorstein went to Lysufirth, in the autumn, to his namesake, and Gudrid bore him company[3]. They were well received, and remained there during the winter. It came to pass that sickness appeared in their home early in the winter. Gard was the name of the overseer there; he had few friends; he took sick first, and died. It was not long before one after another took sick and died. Then Thorstein, Eric's son, fell sick, and Sigrid, the wife of Thorstein, his namesake; and one evening Sigrid wished to go to the house, which stood over against the outer-door, and Gudrid accompanied her; they were facing the outer-door when Sigrid uttered a loud cry[4]. 'We have acted thoughtlessly,' exclaimed Gudrid, 'yet thou needest not cry, though the cold strikes thee[5]; let us go in again as speedily as possible.' Sigrid answers, 'This may not be in this present plight. All of the dead folk are drawn up here before the door now; among them I see thy husband, Thorstein, and I can see myself there, and it is distressful to look upon.' But directly this had passed she exclaimed, 'Let us go now, Gudrid; I no longer see the band!' The overseer[6] had vanished from her sight, whereas it had seemed to her before that he stood with a whip in his hand and made as if he would scourge the flock. So they went in, and ere the morning came she was dead, and a coffin was made ready for the corpse; and that same day the men planned to row out to fish, and Thorstein accompanied them to the landing-place, and in the twilight[7] he went down to see their

[1] EsR: 'Eric answers, "These words shall control here." All of those, who had not been provided for before, [obtained] accommodation with Eric and his son.' The passage, apparently by reason of a clerical confusion, is not clear without emendation.

[2] Lit. 'wedded Thurid.'

[3] Lit. 'both he and Gudrid.'

[4] EsR: 'then Sigrid cried, O!'

[5] Thus the literal rendering; the more intelligible translation would appear to be: 'Give heed lest the cold strike thee!'

[6] ÞsK: Thorstein.

[7] Lit. 'the second light.'

catch. Thorstein, Eric's son, then sent word to his namesake that he should come to him, saying that all was not as it should be there [1], for the housewife was endeavouring to rise to her feet, and wished to get in under the clothes beside him, and when he entered the room she was come up on the edge of the bed. He thereupon seized her hands and held a pole-axe (39) before her breast. Thorstein, Eric's son, died before night-fall. Thorstein, the master of the house, bade Gudrid lie down and sleep, saying that he would keep watch over the bodies during the night; thus she did, and early in the night, Thorstein, Eric's son, sat up and spoke, saying that he desired Gudrid to be called thither, for that it was his wish to speak with her: 'It is God's will that this hour be given me for my own and for the betterment of my condition.' Thorstein, the master, went in search of Gudrid, and waked her, and bade her cross herself, and pray God to help her; 'Thorstein, Eric's son, has said to me that he wishes to see thee [2]; thou must take counsel with thyself now, what thou wilt do, for I have no advice to give thee.' She replies, 'It may be that this is intended to be one of those incidents which shall afterward be held in remembrance, this strange event, and it is my trust that God will keep watch over me; wherefore, under God's mercy, I shall venture to go to him, and learn what it is that he would say, for I may not escape this if it be designed to bring me harm. I will do this, lest he go further, for it is my belief that the matter is a grave one.' So Gudrid went and drew near to Thorstein, and he seemed to her to be weeping. He spoke a few words in her ear, in a low tone, so that she alone could hear them; but this he said so that all could hear, that those persons would be blessed who kept well the faith, and that it carried with it all help and consolation, and yet many there were, said he, who kept it but ill. 'This is no proper usage, which has obtained here in Greenland since Christianity was introduced here, to inter men in unconsecrated [3] earth, with nought but a brief funeral service. It is my wish that I be conveyed to the church, together with the others who have died here; Gard [4], however, I would have you burn upon a pyre, as speedily as possible, since he has been the cause of all of the apparitions which have been seen here during the winter.' He spoke to her also of her own destiny, and said that she had a notable future in store for her, but he bade her beware of marrying any Greenlander; he directed her also to give their property to the church and to the poor [5], and then sank down again a second time. It had been the custom in Greenland, after Christianity was introduced there, to bury persons on the farmsteads where they died, in unconsecrated [3] earth; a pole was

[1] Lit. 'that it was hardly peaceful there.'

[2] EsR: 'and tells, what Thorstein, Eric's son, had said to him; and he wishes to see thee.'

[3] EsR: 'consecrated,' obviously incorrectly.

[4] ÞsK: Garðarr.

[5] EsR: 'or to the poor;' ÞsK: 'and some to the poor.'

erected in the ground, touching the breast of the dead, and subsequently, when the priests came thither, the pole was withdrawn and holy water poured in [the orifice], and the funeral service held there, although it might be long thereafter. The bodies of the dead [1] were conveyed to the church at Ericsfirth, and the funeral services held there by the clergy. Thorbiorn died soon after this, and all of his property then passed into Gudrid's possession. Eric took her to his home and carefully looked after her affairs [2].

Concerning Thord of Höfdi.

There was a man named Thord, who lived at Höfdi on Höfdi-strands. He married Fridgerd, daughter of Thori the Loiterer [3] and Fridgerd, daughter of Kiarval the King of the Irish. Thord was a son of Biorn Chestbutter [4], son of Thorvald Spine [5], Asleik's son, the son of Biorn Iron-side [6], the son of Ragnar Shaggy-breeks [7]. They had a son named Snorri. He married Thorhild Ptarmigan [8], daughter of Thord the Yeller [9]. Their son was Thord Horse-head [10]. Thorfinn Karlsefni [11] was the name of Thord's son (40). Thorfinn's mother's name was Thorunn [12]. Thorfinn was engaged in trading voyages, and was reputed to be a successful merchant. One summer Karlsefni equipped his ship, with the intention of sailing to Greenland. Snorri, Thorbrand's son [13], of Alptafirth (41) accompanied him, and there were forty men on board the ship with them. There was a man named Biarni, Grimolf's son, a man from Breidafirth, and another named Thorhall, Gamli's son (42), an East-firth man. They equipped their ship, the same summer as Karlsefni, with the intention of making a voyage to Greenland; they had also forty men in their ship. When they were ready to sail, the two ships put to sea together [14]. It has not been recorded how long a voyage they had; but it is to be told, that both of the ships arrived at Ericsfirth in the autumn. Eric and other of the inhabitants of the country rode to the ships, and a goodly trade was soon established between them. Gudrid [15] was requested by the skippers to take such of their wares as she wished, while Eric, on his part, showed

[1] ÞsK: 'of Thorstein and the others.'

[2] ÞsK: 'Eric received Gudrid, and acted as a father toward her. Shortly thereafter Thorbiorn died; then all of the property passed into her possession; Eric then took her to his home, and looked well after her affairs.'

[3] híma.

[4] byrðusmiọr.

[5] hryggr.

[6] járnsíða.

[7] loðbrók.

[8] rjúpa.

[9] gellir.

[10] hesthọfði.

[11] Karlsefni, one who gives promise of becoming a man.

[12] EsR: Instead of this genealogical list has: 'There was a man named Thorfinn Karlsefni, a son of Thord Horse-head, who lived in the north, at Reyniness, in Skagafirth, as it is now called. Karlsefni was a man of fine family and was very well-to-do.'

[13] EsR: Þorbiazrson.

[14] ÞsK: 'Karlsefni and the others put to sea with these two ships, when they were ready.'

[15] ÞsK: Eric.

great munificence in return, in that he extended an invitation to both crews to accompany him home for winter quarters at Brattahlid. The merchants accepted this invitation [1], and went with Eric. Their wares were then conveyed to Brattahlid; nor was there lack there of good and commodious store-houses, in which to keep them; nor was there wanting much of that, which they needed, and the merchants were well pleased with their entertainment at Eric's home during that winter. Now as it drew toward Yule, Eric became very taciturn, and less cheerful than had been his wont. On one occasion Karlsefni entered into conversation with Eric, and said: 'Hast thou aught weighing upon thee, Eric? The folk have remarked, that thou art somewhat more silent [2] than thou hast been hitherto. Thou hast entertained us with great liberality, and it behooves us to make such return as may lie within our power. Do thou now but make known the cause of thy melancholy.' Eric answers: 'Ye accept hospitality gracefully, and in manly wise, and I am not pleased that ye should be the sufferers by reason of our intercourse; rather am I troubled at the thought, that it should be given out elsewhere, that ye have never passed a worse Yule than this, now drawing nigh, when Eric the Red was your host at Brattahlid in Greenland.' 'There shall be no cause for that,' replies Karlsefni, 'we have malt, and meal, and corn in our ships, and you are welcome to take of these whatsoever you wish, and to provide as liberal an entertainment as seems fitting to you.' Eric accepts this offer, and preparations were made for the Yule feast **(43)**, and it was so sumptuous, that it seemed to the people they had scarcely ever seen so grand an entertainment before [3]. And after Yule, Karlsefni broached the subject of a marriage with Gudrid to Eric, for he assumed that with him rested the right to bestow her hand in marriage [4]. Eric answers favourably, and says, that she would accomplish the fate in store for her, adding that he had heard only good reports of him [5]. And, not to prolong this, the result was, that Thorfinn was betrothed to Thurid, and the banquet was augmented, and their wedding was celebrated [6]; and this befell at Brattahlid during the winter [7].

[1] ÞsK: adds, 'and thanked him.'

[2] ÞsK: 'less cheerful.'

[3] ÞsK: adds, 'in a poor country.'

[4] EsR: adds, 'and she seemed to him a handsome and accomplished woman.'

[5] EsR: 'Eric answers, saying, that his offer should be well considered, and adding that she was worthy of a goodly match; "moreover, it is probable, that she will fulfil her appointed destiny," even if she should be married to him, and said that good reports had come concerning him.'

[6] ÞsK: 'ok drukkit brullaup þeira,' and their bridal drunk.

[7] EsR: 'There was great good cheer at Brattahlid during the winter. Whereat much discussion arose, that there was much table-play afoot, and story-telling and much of the like which might contribute to the amusement of the household.' The clause 'whereat much discussion arose' appears to have been inserted by accident from the succeeding paragraph.

Beginning of the Wineland Voyages.

About this time there began to be much talk at Brattahlid, to the effect that Wineland the Good should be explored, for, it was said, that country must be possessed of many goodly qualities. And so it came to pass, that Karlsefni and Snorri fitted out their ship, for the purpose of going in search of that country in the spring [1]. Biarni and Thorhall joined the expedition with their ship, and the men who had borne them company [2]. There was a man named Thorvard; he was wedded to Freydis (44), a natural daughter of Eric the Red. He also accompanied them, together with Thorvald, Eric's son, and Thorhall, who was called the Huntsman. He had been for a long time with Eric as his hunter and fisherman during the summer, and as his steward during the winter [3]. Thorhall was stout and swarthy, and of giant stature; he was a man of few words, though given to abusive language, when he did speak, and he ever incited Eric to evil. He was a poor Christian; he had a wide knowledge of the unsettled regions [4]. He was on the same ship with Thorvard and Thorvald [5]. They had that ship which Thorbiorn had brought out. They had in all one hundred and sixty men, when they sailed to the Western-settlement (45), and thence to Bear Island [6]. Thence they bore away to the southward two 'dœgr' (46). Then they saw land, and launched a boat, and explored the land, and

[1] EsR: 'Karlsefni and Snorri determined to go in search of Wineland, and this gave rise to much talk.' [Cf. preceding note.] 'And the end of the matter was, that Karlsefni and Snorri equipped their ship and determined to go in search of Wineland during the summer.'

[2] FsK: 'With them went also that man, who was named Biarni, and likewise Thorhall, who have before been mentioned, with their ship.'

[3] EsR: 'There was a man named Thorvald; he was a relative by marriage of Eric the Red. Thorhall was called the Huntsman [veiðimaðr]; he had long lived with Eric, engaging in fishing and hunting expeditions during the summer, and was general care-taker' [lit. had many things under his charge].

[4] EsR: 'Thorhall was a man of great stature, swart and giant-like; he was rather stricken with years, overbearing in manner, taciturn, and usually a man of few words, underhanded in his dealings, and yet given to offensive language, and always ready to stir up evil; he had concerned himself little with the true faith after its introduction into Greenland. Thorhall was not very popular, but Eric had long been accustomed to seek his advice.'

[5] EsR: 'with Thorvald and his companions, because he had extensive knowledge of the uninhabited regions.'

[6] EsR: 'and they joined Karlsefni and his companions in their expedition, and they were mostly Greenland men on board. There were on their ships forty men off the second hundred [i.e. one hundred and sixty men]. Then they sailed away to the Western-settlement, and to the Bear Isles.' FsK has, 'xl. men and c;' but as the early duodecimal hundred of twelve tens is doubtless meant by 'c,' the numbers agree in both accounts.

found there large flat stones [*hellur*], and many of these were twelve ells wide; there were many Arctic foxes there. They gave a name to the country, and called it Helluland [the land of flat stones][1]. Then they sailed with northerly winds two 'dœgr,' and land then lay before them, and upon it was a great wood and many wild beasts; an island lay off the land to the south-east, and there they found a bear, and they called this Biarney [Bear Island], while the land where the wood was they called Markland [Forest-land][2]. Thence they sailed southward along the land for a long time, and came to a cape; the land lay upon the starboard; there were long strands and sandy banks there. They rowed to the land and found upon the cape there the keel of a ship (**47**), and they called it there Kialarnes [Keelness]; they also called the strands Furdustrandir [Wonder-strands], because they were so long to sail by[3]. Then the country became indented with bays, and they steered their ships into a bay[4]. It was when Leif was with King Olaf Tryggvason, and he bade him proclaim Christianity to Greenland, that the king gave him two Gaels (**48**); the man's name was Haki, and the woman's Haekia. The king advised Leif to have recourse to these people, if he should stand in need of fleetness, for they were swifter than deer[5]. Eric and Leif had tendered Karlsefni the services of this couple. Now when they had sailed past Wonder-strands, they put the Gaels ashore, and directed them to run to the southward, and investigate the nature of the country, and return again before the end of the third half-day. They were each clad in a garment, which they called 'kiafal[6],' which was so fashioned, that it had a hood at the top, was open at the sides, was sleeveless, and was fastened between the legs with buttons and loops, while elsewhere they were naked. Karlsefni and his companions cast anchor, and lay there during

[1] EsR: 'Thence they sailed away beyond the Bear Isles, with northerly winds. They were out two "dœgr;" then they discovered land, and rowed thither in boats, and explored the country, and found there many flat stones [hellur], so large, that two men could well spurn soles upon them' [i.e. lie at full length upon them, sole to sole]; 'there were many Arctic foxes there.'

[2] ÞsK: 'Thence they sailed two "dœgr," and bore away from the south toward the south-east, and they found a wooded country, and on it many animals; an island lay there off the land toward the south-east; they killed a bear on this [island], and called it afterwards Bear Isle, but the country Forest-land.'

[3] EsR: 'Then when two "dœgr" had elapsed, they descried land, and they sailed off this land; there was a cape to which they came. They beat into the wind along this coast, having the land upon the starboard side. This was a bleak coast, with long and sandy shores. They went ashore in boats, and found the keel of a ship, so they called it Keelness there; they likewise gave a name to the strands, and called them Wonder-strands, because they were long to sail by.'

[4] EsR: 'to the bays.'

[5] ÞsK: 'King Olaf Tryggvason had given Leif two Gaelic people, the man's name was Haki, and she Hekia. They were fleeter than deer. These people were on board Karlsefni's ship.'

[6] EsR: 'biafal.'

their absence[1]; and when they came again, one of them carried[2] a bunch of grapes, and the other an ear of new-sown wheat[3]. They went on board the ship, whereupon Karlsefni and his followers held on their way, until they came to where the coast was indented with bays. They stood into a bay with their ships. There was an island out at the mouth of the bay, about which there were strong currents, wherefore they called it Straumey [Stream Isle]. There were so many birds there, that it was scarcely possible to step between the eggs[4]. They sailed through the firth, and called it Straumfiord [Streamfirth], and carried their cargoes ashore from the ships, and established themselves there. They had brought with them all kinds of live-stock. It was a fine country there. There were mountains thereabouts. They occupied themselves exclusively with the exploration of the country. They remained there during the winter, and they had taken no thought for this during the summer. The fishing began to fail, and they began to fall short of food[5]. Then Thorhall the Huntsman disappeared. They had already prayed to God for food, but it did not come as promptly as their necessities seemed to demand. They searched for Thorhall for three half-days, and found him[6] on a projecting crag. He was lying there, and looking up at the sky, with mouth and nostrils agape, and mumbling something[7]. They asked him why he had gone thither; he replied, that this did not concern anyone[8]. They asked him then to go home with them, and he did so. Soon after this a whale appeared there, and they captured it[9], and flensed it, and no one could tell what manner of whale it was[10]; and when the cooks had prepared

[1] Lit. 'for this period.'

[2] Lit. 'had in the hand.'

[3] EsR: 'and when three days [sic] had passed, they ran down from the land, and one of them carried in the hand a wine-vessel' [vín-ker, doubtless a clerical error for 'vín-ber,' grapes], 'and the other wheat self-sown. Karlsefni said that they seemed to have found goodly indigenous products!'

[4] ÞsK: 'There were so many eider-ducks on the island, that it was scarcely possible to walk for the eggs.'

[5] EsR: 'they explored the nature of the land. There were mountains there, and the country round about was fair to look upon. They did nought but explore the country. There was tall grass there. They remained there during the winter, and they had a hard winter, for which they had not prepared, and they grew short of food, and the fishing fell off. Then they went out to the island, in the hope that something might be forthcoming in the way of fishing or flotsam. There was little food left, however, although their live-stock fared well there. Then they invoked God, that he might send them food, but they did not get response so soon as they needed. Thorhall disappeared,' &c.

[6] EsR: 'on the fourth half-day Karlsefni and Biarni found him.'

[7] EsR: 'and with eyes, mouth and nostrils wide-stretched, and was scratching himself, and muttering something.'

[8] EsR adds, 'he told them not to be surprised at this; adding that he had lived sufficiently long to render it unnecessary for them to take counsel for him.'

[9] Lit. 'they went to it.'

[10] EsR adds, 'Karlsefni had much knowledge of whales, but he did not know this one.'

it, they ate of it, and were all made ill by it. Then Thorhall, approaching them, says: 'Did not the Red-beard (49) prove more helpful than your Christ? This is my reward for the verses which I composed to Thor, the Trustworthy[1]; seldom has he failed me.' When the people heard this, they cast the whale down into the sea, and made their appeals to God[2]. The weather then improved, and they could now row out to fish, and thenceforward they had no lack of provisions, for they could hunt game on the land, gather eggs on the island, and catch fish from the sea[3].

Concerning Karlsefni and Thorhall.

It is said, that Thorhall wished to sail to the northward beyond Wonder-strands, in search of Wineland, while Karlsefni desired to proceed to the southward, off the coast[4]. Thorhall prepared for his voyage out below the island, having only nine men in his party, for all of the remainder of the company went with Karlsefni. And one day when Thorhall was carrying water aboard his ship, and was drinking, he recited this ditty:

When I came, these brave men told me,
  Here the best of drink I'd get,
Now with water-pail behold me,—
  Wine and I are strangers yet.
Stooping at the spring, I've tested
  All the wine this land affords;
Of its vaunted charms divested,
  Poor indeed are its rewards[5].

[1] fulltrúann, lit. a person in whom one reposes all confidence.

[2] EsR: 'and when the people knew this, none of them would eat, and they cast [it] down over the rocks, and invoked God's mercy.'

[3] EsR: 'They were then able to row out to fish, and they had no longer any lack of the necessities of life. In the spring they went into Streamfirth, and obtained provisions from both regions, hunting on the mainland, gathering eggs, and deep-sea fishing.'

[4] EsR: This introductory paragraph reads: 'Now they took counsel together concerning their expedition, and came to an agreement. Thorhall the Huntsman wished to go northward around Wonder-strands, and past Keelness, and so seek Wineland; while Karlsefni wished to proceed southward along the land and to the eastward, believing that country to be greater, which is farther to the southward, and it seemed to him more advisable to explore both.'

[5] The order of the words of the verse is as follows: Meiðar [trees] málm þings [of the metal-meeting, i. e. of battle, trees of battle, warriors, men] kváðu mik hafa [said that I should have] drykk inn bazta [the best of drink], er ek kom hingat [when I came hither], mér samir lasta land fyrir lýðum [it behooves me to blame the land 'fore all]; bílds hattar [bíldr, an instrument for letting blood, i. e. a sword, bílds hattar, the sword's hat, i. e. the helmet] beiðitýr [the god who demands, wherefore, bílds hattar

And when they were ready, they hoisted sail; whereupon Thorhall recited this ditty[1]:

Comrades, let us now be faring
  Homeward to our own again!
Let us try the sea-steed's daring,
  Give the chafing courser rein.
Those who will may bide in quiet,
  Let them praise their chosen land,
Feasting on a whale-steak diet,
  In their home by Wonder-strand[2].

Then they sailed away to the northward past Wonder-strands and Keelness, intending to cruise to the westward around the cape. They encountered westerly gales, and were driven ashore in Ireland, where they were grievously maltreated and thrown into slavery. There Thorhall lost his life, according to that which traders have related.

It is now to be told of Karlsefni, that he cruised southward off the coast, with Snorri and Biarni, and their people. They sailed for a long time, and until they came

beiðitýr, he, or the god, who demands the helmet, the warrior, i. e. man], ek verð at reiða byttu [I must bear the pail]; heldr er svá at ek krýp at keldu [I have rather to stoop to the spring]; komat vín á grǫn mína [wine has not touched my lips].

The prose sense of the verse is: Men promised me, when I came hither, that I should have the best of drink, it behooves me before all to blame the land, [ÞsK] ['little to blame it,' EsR]. See, oh, man! how I must raise the pail; instead of drinking wine, I have to stoop to the spring.

[1] EsR: 'Then they put to sea, and Karlsefni accompanies them out off the island. Before they hoisted sail, Thorhall uttered this ditty.'

[2] The order of the words in the verse is as follows: Fǫrum aptr þar er órir landar eru [Let us go back where our countrymen are], látum kenni sandhimins [sandhiminn, the canopy of the sands, the sea, kenni sandhimins, the knowing one of the sea, the sailor, wherefore, látum kenni sandhimins, let the sailor], val kanna [explore well] en breiðu knarrarskeið [the broad courses of the ships, i. e. the sea]; meðan bilstyggvir [while the rest-hating] laufaveðrs bellendr [laufaveðr, sword-storm, i. e. battle, bellendr, wagers, givers, laufaveðrs bellendr, the givers of battle, rest-hating givers of battle, warriors, men], þeir er leyfa lǫnd [they who praise the land], byggja ok vella hval á Furðustrǫndum [live and cook whale on Wonder-strands].

The prose sense of the verse is: Let us return to our countrymen, leaving those, who like the country here, to cook their whale on Wonder-strands.

EsR has ærir for órir, and kæti for kenni, which words are not readily intelligible. The paper manuscripts have still other variants, certain of them clearly unintelligible. The verse, as given in ÞsK, appears to be the least corrupted. The form órir, nom. plur. from várr, disappeared at the beginning of the thirteenth century, being supplanted by the form várir. [Cf. Konr. Gislason, Ældre og nyere Böining af Første Persons Plural-possessiv i Oldnordisk-Islandsk., in Aarb. for nord. Oldk. og Hist. 1889, pp. 343 et seq.] From this it is apparent that the verse is much older than either text of the saga which we have, and must have been composed at least a hundred years before Hauk's Book was written; although it may well be much older than the beginning of the thirteenth century.

at last to a river, which flowed down from the land into a lake, and so into the sea. There were great bars at the mouth of the river, so that it could only be entered at the height of the flood-tide. Karlsefni and his men sailed into the mouth of the river, and called it there Hóp [a small land-locked bay]. They found self-sown wheat-fields on the land there, wherever there were hollows, and wherever there was hilly ground, there were vines (**50**). Every brook there was full of fish. They dug pits, on the shore where the tide rose highest, and when the tide fell, there were halibut (**51**) in the pits. There were great numbers of wild animals of all kinds in the woods. They remained there half a month, and enjoyed themselves, and kept no watch. They had their live-stock with them. Now one morning early, when they looked about them, they saw a great number of skin-canoes[1], and staves (**52**) were brandished from the boats, with a noise like flails, and they were revolved in the same direction in which the sun moves. Then said Karlsefni: 'What may this betoken?' Snorri, Thorbrand's son, answers him: 'It may be, that this is a signal of peace, wherefore let us take a white shield (**53**) and display it.' And thus they did. Thereupon the strangers rowed toward them, and went upon the land, marvelling at those whom they saw before them. They were swarthy men[2], and ill-looking, and the hair of their heads was ugly. They had great eyes, and were broad of cheek (**54**). They tarried there for a time looking curiously at the people they saw before them, and then rowed away, and to the southward around the point.

Karlsefni and his followers had built their huts above the lake, some of their dwellings being near the lake, and others farther away[3]. Now they remained there that winter. No snow came there[4], and all of their live-stock lived by grazing (**55**). And when spring opened, they discovered, early one morning, a great number of skin-canoes, rowing from the south past the cape, so numerous, that it looked as if coals had been scattered broadcast out before the bay; and on every boat staves were waved. Thereupon Karlsefni and his people displayed their shields, and when they came together, they began to barter with each other. Especially did the strangers wish to buy red cloth[5], for which they offered in exchange peltries and quite grey skins. They also desired to buy swords and spears, but Karlsefni and Snorri forbade this. In exchange for perfect unsullied skins, the Skrellings would take red stuff a span in length, which they would bind around their heads. So their trade went on for a time, until Karlsefni and his people began to grow short of cloth, when they divided it into such narrow pieces, that it was not more than a

[1] EsR: 'nine skin-canoes.'
[2] EsR: 'small men,' instead of 'swarthy men.'
[3] EsR: 'some dwellings were near the mainland, and some near the lake.'
[4] EsR: 'no snow whatever.'
[5] ÞsK: skrúð, a kind of stuff; EsR: klæði, cloth.

finger's breadth wide, but the Skrellings still continued to give just as much for this as before, or more.

It so happened, that a bull, which belonged to Karlsefni and his people, ran out from the woods, bellowing loudly. This so terrified the Skrellings, that they sped out to their canoes, and then rowed away to the southward along the coast. For three entire weeks nothing more was seen of them. At the end of this time, however, a great multitude of Skrelling boats was discovered approaching from the south, as if a stream were pouring down, and all of their staves were waved in a direction contrary to the course of the sun, and the Skrellings were all uttering loud cries. Thereupon Karlsefni and his men took red shields (53) and displayed them. The Skrellings sprang from their boats, and they met then, and fought together. There was a fierce shower of missiles, for the Skrellings had war-slings. Karlsefni and Snorri observed, that the Skrellings raised up on a pole[1] a great ball-shaped body, almost the size of a sheep's belly, and nearly black in colour, and this they hurled from the pole up on the land above Karlsefni's followers, and it made a frightful noise, where it fell. Whereat a great fear seized upon Karlsefni, and all his men, so that they could think of nought but flight, and of making their escape up along the river bank, for it seemed to them, that the troop of the Skrellings was rushing towards them from every side, and they did not pause, until they came to certain jutting crags, where they offered a stout resistance. Freydis came out, and seeing that Karlsefni and his men were fleeing, she cried: 'Why do ye flee from these wretches, such worthy men as ye, when, meseems, ye might slaughter them like cattle. Had I but a weapon, methinks, I would fight better than any one of you!' They gave no heed to her words. Freydis sought to join them, but lagged behind, for she was not hale[2]; she followed them, however, into the forest, while the Skrellings pursued her; she found a dead man in front of her; this was Thorbrand, Snorri's son, his skull cleft by a flat stone; his naked sword lay beside him; she took it up, and prepared to defend herself with it. The Skrellings then approached her, whereupon she stripped down her shift, and slapped her breast with the naked sword. At this the Skrellings were terrified and ran down to their boats, and rowed away. Karlsefni and his companions, however, joined her and praised her valour. Two of Karlsefni's men had fallen, and a great number of the Skrellings[3]. Karlsefni's party had been overpowered by dint of superior numbers. They now returned to their dwellings, and bound up their wounds, and weighed carefully what throng of men that could have been, which had seemed to descend upon them from the land[4]; it now seemed to them, that there

[1] EsR: 'on poles.'

[2] 'eigi heil,' a euphemism for pregnant.

[3] EsR: 'four of the Skrellings.'

[4] EsR: simply 'from the land.'

could have been but the one party, that which came from the boats, and that the other troop must have been an ocular delusion[1]. The Skrellings, moreover, found a dead man, and an axe lay beside him. One of their number picked up the axe, and struck at a tree with it, and one after another [they tested it], and it seemed to them to be a treasure, and to cut well; then one of their number seized it, and hewed at a stone with it, so that the axe broke, whereat they concluded that it could be of no use, since it would not withstand stone, and they cast it away[2].

It now seemed clear to Karlsefni and his people, that although the country thereabouts was attractive, their life would be one of constant dread and turmoil by reason of the [hostility of the] inhabitants[3] of the country, so they forthwith prepared to leave, and determined to return to their own country. They sailed to the northward off the coast, and found five Skrellings, clad in skin-doublets, lying asleep near the sea. There were vessels beside them, containing animal marrow, mixed with blood. Karlsefni and his company concluded that they must have been banished from their own land. They put them to death. They afterwards found a cape, upon which there was a great number of animals, and this cape looked as if it were one cake of dung, by reason of the animals which lay there at night[4]. They now arrived again at Streamfirth, where they found great abundance of all those things of which they stood in need. Some men say, that Biarni and Freydis[5] remained behind here with a hundred men, and went no further; while Karlsefni and Snorri proceeded to the southward with forty men, tarrying at Hóp barely two months, and returning again the same summer. Karlsefni then set out with one ship, in search of Thorhall the Huntsman, but the greater part of the company remained behind. They sailed to the northward around Keelness, and then bore to the westward, having land to the larboard. The country there was a wooded wilderness, as far as they could see, with scarcely an open space[6]; and when they had journeyed a considerable distance, a river flowed down from the east toward the west. They sailed into the mouth of the river, and lay to by the southern bank.

The Slaying of Thorvald, Eric's Son.

It happened one morning, that Karlsefni and his companions discovered in an open space in the woods above them, a speck, which seemed to shine toward them, and they shouted at it: it stirred, and it was a Uniped (56), who skipped down to the

[1] EsR: 'þversýningar,' lit. cross-sight.

[2] EsR has instead of the above: 'one of their people hewed at a stone, and broke the axe; it seemed to him of no use, since it would not withstand stone, and he cast it down.'

[3] EsR: 'for those who dwelt there before.'

[4] EsR: 'during the winter.'

[5] ÞsK: Gudrid.

[6] EsR has simply, 'there were wooded wildernesses there.'

bank of the river by which they were lying. Thorvald, a son of Eric the Red, was sitting at the helm, and the Uniped shot an arrow into his inwards. Thorvald drew out the arrow, and exclaimed: 'There is fat around my paunch; we have hit upon a fruitful country, and yet we are not like to get much profit of it[1].' Thorvald died soon after from this wound. Then the Uniped ran away back toward the north. Karlsefni and his men pursued him, and saw him from time to time[2]. The last they saw of him, he ran down into a creek. Then they turned back; whereupon one of the men recited this ditty:

Eager, our men, up hill down dell,
  Hunted a Uniped;
Hearken, Karlsefni, while they tell
  How swift the quarry fled![3]

Then they sailed away back toward the north, and believed they had got sight of the land of the Unipeds; nor were they disposed to risk the lives of their men any longer. They concluded that the mountains of Hóp, and those which they had now found, formed one chain, and this appeared to be so because they were about an equal distance removed from Streamfirth, in either direction[4]. They sailed back, and passed the third winter at Streamfirth. Then the men began to divide into factions[5], of which the women were the cause; and those who were without wives, endeavoured to seize upon the wives of those who were married, whence the greatest trouble arose. Snorri, Karlsefni's son, was born the first autumn, and he was three winters' old[6] when they took their departure. When they sailed away from Wineland, they had a southerly wind, and so came upon Markland, where they found five Skrellings, of whom one was bearded, two were women, and two were children. Karlsefni and his people took the boys, but the others escaped, and these Skrellings sank down into the earth. They bore the lads away with them, and taught them to speak, and they were baptized. They said, that their mother's name was Vætilldi, and their

[1] In EsR the text of this passage seems to be somewhat confused, apparently through a clerical error. It reads: 'and runs down thither to where, they [the companions of] Thorvald, the son of Eric the Red, lay; then said Thorvald: "We have found a good land." Then the Uniped runs away, back toward the north, having first shot an arrow into Thorvald's intestines; he drew out the arrow, then Thorvald said: "There is fat about the paunch." They pursued the Uniped,' &c.

[2] EsR adds, 'and it seemed as if he were trying to escape.'

[3] Lit. 'The men pursued, most true it is, a Uniped down to the shore, but the strange man took to running swift over the banks. Hear thou, Karlsefni!'

[4] EsR: 'They intended to explore all the mountains, those which were at Hóp, and [those] which they discovered.'

[5] EsR: 'gengu menn þá mjǫk sleitum,' the men then began to grow quarrelsome [?].

[6] EsR: 'ok var þar þann er þeir fóru á brott,' and was there 'that' when they went away. It is not clear to what the 'þann' refers.

father's Uvægi[1]. They said, that kings governed the Skrellings[2], one of whom was called Avalldamon[3], and the other Valldidida (57). They stated, that there were no houses there, and that the people lived in caves or holes. They said, that there was a land on the other side over against their country, which was inhabited by people who wore white garments, and yelled loudly, and carried poles before them, to which rags were attached[4]; and people believe that this must have been Hvítramanna-land [White-men's-land[5]], or Ireland the Great (58). Now they arrived in Greenland, and remained during the winter with Eric the Red[6].

Biarni, Grimolf's son, and his companions were driven out into the Atlantic[7], and came into a sea, which was filled with worms, and their ship began to sink beneath them[8]. They had a boat[9], which had been coated with seal-tar; this the sea-worm does not penetrate. They took their places in this boat, and then discovered that it would not hold them all[10]. Then said Biarni: 'Since the boat will not hold more than half of our men, it is my advice, that the men who are to go in the boat, be chosen by lot, for this selection must not be made according to rank.' This seemed to them all such a manly offer, that no one opposed it[11]. So they adopted this plan, the men casting lots; and it fell to Biarni to go in the boat, and half[12] of the men with him, for it would not hold more[13]. But when the men were come into the boat, an Icelander[14], who was in the ship, and who had accompanied Biarni from Iceland, said: 'Dost thou intend, Biarni, to forsake me here?' 'It must be even so,' answers Biarni. 'Not such was the promise thou

[1] EsR: 'they called their mother Vætilldi and Uvægi,' apparently a clerical error.

[2] EsR: 'the land of the Skrellings.'

[3] ÞsK: 'Avalldama' [?]

[4] EsR: 'and they yelled loudly, and carried poles, and went with rags.'

[5] EsR simply, 'men believe that White-men's-land.'

[6] In ÞsK this sentence is lacking.

[7] ÞsK: Írlands haf, lit. Ireland's sea. EsR: Grœnlands haf, lit. Greenland's sea, the term used of the sea between Iceland and Greenland.

[8] EsR: 'they did not discover this, before the ship was all worm-eaten beneath them. Thereupon they debated what they should do.'

[9] EsR: 'an after-boat,' a jolly-boat usually towed 'after' the ship, whence the name.

[10] EsR: 'people say, that the shell-worm does not bore in wood, which has been coated with seal-tar. It was the advice and decision of most of the men, to transfer to the boat as many as it would contain. But when this was tried, the boat would not hold more than half the men.'

[11] EsR: 'Biarni said then, that men should go in the boat, and that this should be determined by casting lots, and not by rank. For all of the men who were there wished to go in the boat; it would not carry all, wherefore they adopted this plan, to choose men by lot for the boat, and from the ship.'

[12] EsR: 'nearly half.'

[13] EsR: 'Then they, who had been chosen, left the ship and entered the boat.'

[14] EsR: 'a young Icelander.'

gavest my father,' he answers, 'when I left Iceland with thee, that thou wouldst thus part with me, when thou saidst, that we should both share the same fate.' 'So be it, it shall not rest thus,' answers Biarni; 'do thou come hither, and I will go to the ship, for I see that thou art eager for life [1].' Biarni thereupon boarded the ship, and this man entered the boat, and they went their way, until they came to Dublin in Ireland, and there they told this tale; now it is the belief of most people, that Biarni and his companions perished in the maggot-sea, for they were never heard of afterward [2].

Karlsefni and his Wife Thurid's Issue.

The following summer Karlsefni sailed to Iceland and Gudrid [3] with him, and he went home [4] to Reyniness (59). His mother believed that he had made a poor match, and she [5] was not at home the first winter. However, when she became convinced that Gudrid was a very superior woman, she returned to her home, and they lived happily together. Hallfrid was a daughter of Snorri, Karlsefni's son, she was the mother of Bishop Thorlak, Runolf's son (60). They had a son named Thorbiorn, whose daughter's name was Thorunn, [she was] Bishop Biorn's mother. Thorgeir was the name of a son of Snorri, Karlsefni's son, [he was] the father of Ingveld, mother of Bishop Brand the Elder [6]. Steinunn was a daughter of Snorri, Karlsefni's son, who married Einar, a son of Grundar-Ketil, a son of Thorvald Crook [7], a son of Thori of Espihol. Their son was Thorstein the Unjust [8], he was the father of Gudrun, who married Jorund of Keldur. Their daughter was Halla, the mother of Flosi, the father of Valgerd, the mother of Herra Erlend the Stout [9], the father of Herra Hauk the Lawman. Another daughter of Flosi was Thordis, the mother of Fru Ingigerd the Mighty [10]. Her daughter was Fru Hallbera, Abbess of Reyniness at Stad (59). Many other great people in Iceland are descended from Karlsefni and Thurid, who are not mentioned here. God be with us, Amen!

[1] EsR: '"Such was not thy promise to me," says he, "when I set out from Iceland with thee, from my father's home." Biarni says: "I see no other course left here, however; but" [answers] "what suggestion hast thou to offer?" He says: "I have to suggest, that we change places, do thou come hither, and I will go thither." Biarni answers: "So be it. I see, indeed, that thou clingest eagerly to life, and holdest it hard to die." So they changed places.'

[2] EsR: 'And men say, that Biarni perished there in the maggot-sea, together with those men, who were there with him in the ship. But the boat, and they who were in it, went their way, until they reached land, and afterwards told this tale.'

[3] EsR: 'Snorri.' [4] EsR: 'to his home.' [5] ÞsK: 'Gudrid.'

[6] 'hinn fyrri.' EsR: 'and there this saga ends.' [7] krókr.

[8] ranglátr. [9] sterki. [10] ríka.

CHAPTER III.

The Wineland History of the Flatey Book.

The Flatey Book [Flateyjarbók] is the most extensive and most perfect of Icelandic manuscripts. It is in itself a comprehensive historical library of the era with which it deals, and so considerable are its contents, that they fill upwards of 1700 large octavo pages of printed text[1]. On the title-page of the manuscript[2] we are informed, that it belonged originally to John Haconsson [Jón Hákonarson], for whom it was written by the priests John Thordsson [Jón Þórðarson] and Magnus Thorhallsson [Magnús Þórhallsson]. We have no information concerning the date when the book was commenced by John Thordsson; but the most important portion of the work appears to have been completed in the year 1387[3], although additions were made to the body of the work by one of the original scribes[4], and the annals, appended to the book, brought down to the year 1394. Toward the close of the fifteenth century, the then owner of the book, whose name is unknown, inserted three quaternions of additional historical matter in the manuscript[5], to fill a hiatus in the historical sequence of the work, not, however, in that part of the manuscript which treats of Wineland.

It has been conjectured that the manuscript was written in the north of Iceland[6],

[1] 'Five pages or ten columns of it fill twenty-eight printed pages.' Vigfusson, Preface to the Rolls Ed. 'Icelandic Sagas,' London, 1887, vol. i. p. xxvii.

[2] 'The only title-page found in any Icelandic MS.' Ibid. p. xxv.

[3] Cf. Storm, Islandske Annaler, Christiania, 1888, pp. xxxiv–xxxvi. This view, however, conflicts with the opinion held by others that this date should be 1380. Cf. Flateyjarbók, ed. Vigfusson and Unger, Christiania, 1860–68, vol. iii, Fortale, i–iii; Finnur Jónsson, Eddalieder, Halle, o. S., 1888, i. p. viii.

[4] Magnus Thorhallsson.

[5] Cf. Preface, Icelandic Sagas, ubi sup. vol. i. p. xxx.

[6] 'Annales non in occidentali Islandia, sed potius aut Vididalstungae aut in monasterio Thingeyrensi [qui uterque locus in septentrionali Islandia situs est] scripti esse videntur.' Islenzkir Annálar, Copenh. 1847, p. xv. This opinion is partially sanctioned by Storm, who suggests that Magnus' predecessor probably had his home in the north of Iceland. Cf. Storm, Islandske Annaler, Christiania, 1888, p. xxxiv.

but, according to the editors of the printed text, the facts are that the manuscript was owned in the west of Iceland as far back as we possess any knowledge of it, and there is no positive evidence where it was written [1]. We have, indeed, no further particulars concerning the manuscript before the seventeenth century, when we find that it was in the possession of John Finsson [Jón Finsson], who dwelt in Flatey in Breidafirth [Breiðafjörðr], as had his father, and his father's father before him. That the book had been a family heirloom is evident from an entry made in the manuscript by this same John Finsson:

'This book I, John Finsson, own; the gift of my deceased father's father, John Biarnsson [2],' &c.

From John Finsson the book descended to his nephew, John Torfason [3], from whom that worthy bibliophile, Bishop Bryniolf of Skálholt, sought, in vain, to purchase it, as is related in an anecdote in the bishop's biography:

'Farmer John of Flatey, son of the Rev. Torfi Finsson, owned a large and massive parchment-book in ancient monachal writing, containing sagas of the Kings of Norway, and many others; and it is, therefore, commonly called Flatey Book [4]. This, Bishop Bryniolf endeavoured to purchase, first for money, and then for five hundreds of land. But he, nevertheless, failed to obtain it; however, when John bore him company, as he was leaving the island, he presented him the book; and it is said, that the Bishop rewarded him liberally for it [5].'

The Flatey Book was among a collection of vellum manuscripts intrusted to the care of Thormod Torfæus, in 1662, as a present from Bishop Bryniolf to King Frederick the Third of Denmark, and thus luckily escaped the fate of others of the bishop's literary treasures. In the Royal Library of Copenhagen it has ever since remained, where it is known as No. 1005, fol. of the Old Royal Collection.

Interpolated in the Saga of Olaf Tryggvason in the Flatey Book are two minor historical narratives. The first of these, in the order in which they appear in the manuscript, is called, a Short Story of Eric the Red [Þáttr Eireks Rauða], the second, a Short Story of the Greenlanders [Grœnlendinga Þáttr]. Although these short histories are not connected in any way in the manuscript, being indeed separated by over fifty columns of extraneous historical matter, they form, if brought together,

[1] Cf. Flateyjarbók, Fortale, ubi sup. p. vi. John Haconsson appears to have lived at one time in the north of Iceland at Víðidalstunga (cf. Safn til sögu Íslands, Copenh. 1861, vol. ii. p. 77), which in some measure may tend to confirm the view that the book originated in the north of Iceland.

[2] Ibid. p. iii.

[3] Cf. Vigfusson, Icelandic Sagas, ubi sup. vol. i. p. xxx.

[4] That is from Flatey [Flat Island], the home of the owners of the book.

[5] Cf. Vigfusson, 'Prolegomena' in Sturlunga Saga, Oxford, 1878, vol. i. p. cxliii, note 1.

what may be called, the Flatey Book version of the history of the Wineland discovery, —a version which varies materially from the accounts of the discovery, as they have been preserved elsewhere. Before considering these points of difference, it may be stated that, as we have no certain knowledge where the Flatey Book was written, neither have we any definite information concerning the original material from which the transcripts of these two narratives were made. The original manuscripts of these narratives would appear to have shared a common fate with the other originals from which the scribes of the Flatey Book compiled their work ;—all of this vast congeries of early manuscripts has entirely disappeared. This is the conclusion reached by that eminent authority, the late Dr. Vigfusson [1], whose profound knowledge of the written literature of the North was supplemented in the present instance by that close acquaintance which he had gained with the Flatey Book, by reason of his having transcribed the entire manuscript for publication [2].

This total disappearance of all trace of the archetypes of the Flatey Book, although it is by no means the only case of the kind in the history of Icelandic paleography [3], is especially to be deplored in connection with the Wineland narrative, since it leaves us without a clue, which might aid us in arriving at a solution of certain enigmas which this narrative presents.

In the Flatey Book version of the discovery it is stated that Biarni Heriulfsson, during a voyage from Iceland to Greenland, having been driven to the southward out of his course, came upon unknown lands; that, following upon this, and as the direct result of Biarni's reports of his discoveries, Leif Ericsson was moved to go in search of the strange lands which Biarni had seen but not explored ; that he found these in due course, 'first that land which Biarni had seen last,' and finally the southernmost land, to which, 'after its products,' he gave the name of Wineland. This account differs entirely from the history contained in the other manuscripts which deal with

[1] He says: 'Though I believe I have had in my hands every scrap of the Old Norse or Icelandic vellum writing existing in Scandinavia, I have never been able to identify a scrap of the material they used, nay more, I never remember having found a line in the well-known hand of either John or Magnus, though it is not probable that the Flatey Book was their first or only work, so great has been the destruction of MSS. Again, there would have seemed great likelihood of the Flatey Book being much copied; it was easy to read, and very complete in its contents. Yet, with one exception, there is no vellum transcript of it, and the great book for some 250 years apparently lay unseen. The one exception is AM. 309 fol., which contains parts of Tryggwasson's Saga, and gives its date thus: "He was then king when the book was written, when there had passed from the Incarnation of our Lord Jesus Christ 1387 years, but there be now gone at the time when this book is written 1498 years."' Vigfusson, Pref. Icelandic Sagas, ubi sup. vol. i. p. xxix.

[2] Cf. Corpus Poeticum Boreale, Oxford, 1883, vol. i. p. xlix.

[3] Cf. e.g. Corp. Poet. Boreale, ubi sup. vol. i. p. xlii.

this subject, all of which agree in ascribing the discovery to Leif Ericsson, and unite in the statement that he found Wineland *accidentally*, during a voyage from Norway to Greenland, which he had undertaken at the instance of King Olaf Tryggvason, for the purpose of introducing Christianity to his fellow-countrymen in Greenland. Not only is Biarni's discovery unknown to any other Icelandic writing now existing, but the man himself, as well as his daring voyage, have failed to find a chronicler elsewhere, although his father was 'a most distinguished man,' the grandson of a 'settler,' and a kinsman of the first Icelandic colonist.

The first portion of the Flatey Book version, the 'Short Story of Eric the Red,' concludes with the words, 'Biarni now went to his father, gave up his voyaging, and remained with his father during Heriulf's lifetime, and continued to dwell there after his father.' The second portion of this version of the Wineland history, the 'Short Story of the Greenlanders,' begins with the words, 'It is now next to this, that Biarni Heriulfsson came out from Greenland on a visit to Earl Eric,' &c. As has already been stated, the two portions of the history of the Wineland discovery, as they appear in the Flatey Book, are not in any way connected with each other. The first narrative occupies its appropriate place in the account of the life of King Olaf Tryggvason, as do the other narratives, similar in character, which are introduced into this as into the other sagas in the manuscript, and there appears to be no reason why the second narrative, 'A Short Story of the Greenlanders,' should be regarded as having received treatment different, in this respect, from other interpolated narratives of the same class. If, therefore, we interpret the opening words of this story of the Greenlanders, 'It is now next to this,' to mean that the incident which follows is related next in chronological order after that part of the saga which has immediately preceded it, it becomes apparent that Biarni's visit must have taken place after the battle of Svoldr, in which King Olaf Tryggvason fell, and Earl Eric was victorious [1]. This battle took place on the 9th of September, in the year 1000. As it is not probable that Biarni would have undertaken his voyage to Norway before the summer following, the earliest date which could reasonably be assigned for Biarni's sojourn at the Earl's court would appear to be the winter of the years 1001-1002 [2]. We are told in the same place that Biarni returned to Greenland the following summer, and that subsequent to

[1] Schöning, who adopted the narrative of the Flatey Book in his edition of Heimskringla, assigns the date of Biarni's visit to the Earl to the year 988 or 989. With him, in this view, the editors of Grönlands historiske Mindesmærker seem inclined to agree, but the Flatey Book itself does not appear to furnish any support for this conjecture. Cf. Grönlands historiske Mindesmærker, Copenh. 1838, vol. i. pp. 266-7.

[2] Arngrímr Jónsson, in his Gronlandia, the earliest account of the Wineland discovery printed in Iceland, gives as the date of Biarni's voyage the year 1002. Cf. Gronlandia, Skálholt, 1688, ch. ix.

his return Leif purchased his ship, and went in search of the land which Biarni had seen, but had failed to explore, in the year 985, according to the chronology of the 'Short Story.'

Leif's voyage of exploration, as described in the Flatey Book, could, therefore, scarcely have taken place before the year 1002[1]. But, according to the other historical data already cited, Leif discovered Wineland during a voyage to Greenland, undertaken at the request, and during the lifetime, of King Olaf Tryggvason, hence obviously not later than the year 1000. The Flatey Book refers to this voyage in the following words: 'That same summer he [King Olaf Tryggvason] sent Gizur and Hialti to Iceland, as has already been written. At that time King Olaf sent Leif to Greenland to preach Christianity there. The King sent with him a priest and certain other holy men to baptize the folk, and teach them the true faith. Leif went to Greenland that summer and took [on board his vessel] a ship's-crew of men, who were at the time in great peril upon a wreck. He arrived in Greenland late in the summer, and went home to his father, Eric, at Brattahlid. The people afterwards called him Leif the Lucky, but his father, Eric, said that Leif's having rescued the crew and restored the men to life, might be balanced against the fact that he had brought the impostor to Greenland, so he called the priest. Nevertheless, through Leif's advice and persuasion, Eric was baptized, and all of the people of Greenland[2].'

It will be observed, that, in this record of Leif's missionary voyage, no allusion is made to the discovery of Wineland, as in the other accounts of the same voyage, with which, in other respects, this passage agrees. By this variation a conflict with Biarni's claim to the priority of discovery, previously promulgated in the 'Short Story of Eric the Red,' is avoided. A portion of this passage may not, however, be so happily reconciled. It is said that, through Leif's advice and persuasion, Eric the Red was baptized, while we find in the 'Short Story of the Greenlanders,' the statement, that 'Eric the Red died before Christianity.' Moreover we have, in the 'Short Story of the Greenlanders,' in addition to this direct conflict of statement, an apparent repetition of the incident of the rescue of the shipwrecked mariners, when we are told that Leif effected a rescue of castaways on his return from a voyage of exploration to Wineland, and was therefore called Leif the Lucky. If this be not a repetition of the same incident, then we must conclude that Leif upon two different voyages saved

[1] Munch, the eminent Norwegian historian, says 1001. Concerning this date there may well be a difference of opinion, but Munch, while accepting the Flatey Book's account of Biarni's discovery, fixes the date of it in the year 1000, a date which does not at all agree with the chronology afforded by the narrative itself. Cf. Munch, Det norske Folks Historie, Christiania, 1853, Part i. vol. ii. p. 461.

[2] Flateyjarbók, Christiania, 1860, vol. i. p. 448.

the lives of a crew of ship-wrecked mariners, for which he twice received the same title from the same people! In the description of the rescue, contained in the 'Short Story of the Greenlanders,' we read that the leader of the castaways was one Thori Easterling [Þórir austmaðr], whose wife, Gudrid, Thorbiorn's daughter [Guðríðr Þorbjarnardóttir], seems to have been among the rescued. This Thori is mentioned nowhere save in the Flatey Book. His wife was so famous a personage in Icelandic annals that it seems passing strange this spouse should have been so completely ignored by other Icelandic chronicles, which have not failed to record Gudrid's marriage to Thorstein Ericsson, and subsequently to Thorfinn Karlsefni. Indeed, according to the biography of this 'most noble lady,' as written in the Saga of Eric the Red, there is no place for Thori, for Gudrid is said to have come to Greenland in much less romantic fashion, namely, as an unmarried woman, in the same ship with, and under the protection of her father, Thorbiorn.

Another chronological error occurs in that paragraph of the 'Short Story of Eric the Red,' wherein it is stated that, 'after sixteen winters had lapsed from the time when Eric the Red went to colonize Greenland, Leif, Eric's son, sailed out from Greenland to Norway. He arrived in Drontheim in the autumn when King Olaf Tryggvason was come down from the North out of Halogaland.' It has previously been stated in this same chronicle that Eric set out to colonize Greenland fifteen years before Christianity was legally adopted in Iceland, that is to say in the year 985. Whence it follows, from this chronology, that Leif's voyage must have been undertaken in the year 1001, but since Olaf Tryggvason was killed in the autumn of the year 1000, this is, from the context, manifestly impossible. If we may suppose that the scribe of the Flatey Book, by a careless verbal substitution, wrote 'fór at byggja' [went to colonize], instead of 'fór at leita' [went in search of], the chronology of the narrative becomes reconcilable.

In the 'Short Story of the Greenlanders' inaccuracies of lesser import occur, one of which, at least, appears to owe its origin to a clerical blunder. In the narrative of Freydis' voyage, we are told, that she waited upon the brothers Helgi and Finnbogi, and persuaded them to join her in an expedition to Wineland; according to the text, however, she enters into an agreement governing the manning of their ships, not with them, but with Karlsefni. Yet it is obvious, from the context, that Karlsefni did not participate in the enterprise, nor does it appear that he had any interest whatsoever in the undertaking. The substitution of Karlsefni's name for that of Helgi or Finnbogi, by a careless scribe, may have given rise to this lack of sequence. A blunder, which has crept into the genealogical list, at the conclusion of the history, may, perhaps, owe its origin to a somewhat similar cause. In this list, it will be noted, Bishop Thorlak [Þorlákr] is called the grandson of Hallfrid [Hallfriðr], Snorri's daughter; in the words of the manuscript, 'Hallfrid was the name of the daughter of Snorri, Karlsefni's son; she was the mother of Runolf [Runólfr], the father of Bishop Thorlak.' Now Runolf was, indeed, the father of Bishop Thorlak, but he was the husband and not the son of Hallfrid. If we may suppose the heedless insertion of the word 'mother' in the place of 'wife,' the palpable error, as the text now stands, would be removed.

It has been conjectured that the Wineland History of the Flatey Book has been drawn from a more primitive source than the narrative of the discovery which has been preserved in the two manuscripts, Hauk's Book and AM. 557, 4to[1]. Two passages in the Flatey Book narrative lend a certain measure of plausibility to this conjecture. In the 'Short Story of Eric the Red' it is stated, that Eric called his land-fall in Greenland, Midiokul [Miðjǫkull], in the words of the history; 'this is now called Blacksark [Bláserkr].' In Hauk's Book this mountain is also called Blacksark; in AM. 557, 4to, it is called Whitesark [Hvítserkr]; neither of these manuscripts, however, recalls the earlier name. Again, in the list of the descendants of Snorri, Karlsefni's Wineland-born son, appended to the 'Short Story of the Greenlanders,' Bishop Brand is so called without qualification, while in both texts of the Saga of Eric the Red he is referred to as Bishop Brand the Elder [hin fyrri]. The second Bishop Brand was ordained in 1263[2]. This fact, while it would, without the other evidence which we possess, establish a date prior to which neither Hauk's Book nor AM. 557, 4to, could have been written, seems, at the same time, to afford negative evidence in support of the claim for the riper antiquity of the source from which the Flatey Book narrative was drawn. However this may be, the lapses already noted, together with the introduction of such incidents as that of the apparition of the big-eyed Gudrid to her namesake, Karlsefni's spouse; the narrative of Freydis' unpalliated treachery; the account of Wineland grapes which produced intoxication, and which apparently ripened at all seasons of the year, of honey-dew grass, and the like, all seem to point either to a deliberate or careless corruption of the primitive history. Nevertheless, despite the discrepancies existing between the account of the Wineland discovery, as it has been preserved in the Flatey Book and as it is given elsewhere, so striking a parallelism is apparent in these different versions of this history, in the chief points of historical interest, as to point conclusively to their common origin.

The two disjoined 'accounts' of the Flatey Book, which relate to the Wineland discovery, are brought together in the translation which follows.

[1] Cf. Maurer, 'Grönland im Mittelalter,' contained in Die zweite deutsche Nordpolarfahrt, Leipsic, 1873, vol. i. n. 2, p. 206.

[2] Cf. Biskupa tal á Íslandi, in Safn til Sögu Íslands, Copenh. 1856, vol. i. p. 4.

A Brief History of Eric the Red[1].

There was a man named Thorvald, a son of Osvald, Ulf's son, Eyxna-Thori's son. Thorvald and Eric the Red, his son, left Jaederen [in Norway], on account of manslaughter, and went to Iceland. At that time Iceland was extensively colonized. They first lived at Drangar on Horn-strands, and there Thorvald died. Eric then married Thorhild, the daughter of Jorund and Thorbiorg the Ship-chested[2], who was then married to Thorbiorn of the Haukadal family. Eric then removed from the north, and made his home at Ericsstadir by Vatnshorn. Eric and Thorhild's son was called Leif.

After the killing of Eyiulf the Foul[3], and Duelling-Hrafn, Eric was banished from Haukadal, and betook himself westward to Breidafirth, settling in Eyxney at Ericsstadir. He loaned his outer daïs-boards to Thorgest, and could not get these again when he demanded them. This gave rise to broils and battles between himself and Thorgest, as Eric's Saga relates[4]. Eric was backed in the dispute by Styr Thorgrimsson, Eyiulf of Sviney, the sons of Brand of Alptafirth and Thorbiorn Vifilsson, while the Thorgesters were upheld by the sons of Thord the Yeller[5] and Thorgeir of Hitardal. Eric was declared an outlaw at Thorsness-thing. He thereupon equipped his ship for a voyage, in Ericsvag, and when he was ready to sail, Styr and the others[6] accompanied him out beyond the islands. Eric told them, that it was his purpose to go in search of that country which Gunnbiorn, son of Ulf the Crow[7], had seen, when he was driven westward across the main, at the time when he discovered Gunnbiorns-skerries; he added, that he would return to his friends, if he should succeed in finding this country. Eric sailed out from Snaefellsiokul, and found the land. He gave the name of Midiokul to his landfall[8]; this is now called Blacksark. From thence he proceeded southward along the coast, in search of habitable land. He passed the first winter at Ericsey, near the middle of the Eastern-settlement, and the following spring he went to Ericsfirth, where he selected a dwelling-place. In the summer he visited the western uninhabited country, and assigned names to many of the localities. The second winter he remained at Holmar by Hrafnsgnipa[9], and the third summer he sailed northward to Snæfell, and all the way into Hrafnsfirth; then he said

[1] [Flatey Book, column 221.] [2] knarrarbringa. [3] saurr.
[4] 'sem segir í sǫgu Eireks:' lit. as it says in Eric's Saga. [5] gellir.
[6] 'þeir Styrr:' lit. they Styrr. [7] kráka.
[8] 'kom utan at því, þar sem hann kallaði Miðjǫkul:' lit. came out to that, which he called M.
[9] The Saga of Eric the Red and Landnáma have: 'Hvarfsgnipa.'

he had reached the head of Ericsfirth. He then returned and passed the third winter in Ericsey at the mouth of Ericsfirth. The next summer he sailed to Iceland, landing in Breidafirth. He called the country, which he had discovered, Greenland, because, he said, people would be attracted thither, if the country had a good name. Eric spent the winter in Iceland, and the following summer set out to colonize the country. He settled at Brattahlid in Ericsfirth, and learned men say, that in this same summer, in which Eric set out to settle Greenland, thirty-five[1] ships sailed out of Breidafirth and Borgarfirth; fourteen of these arrived there safely, some were driven back and some were lost. This was fifteen years before Christianity was legally adopted in Iceland[2]. During the same summer Bishop Frederick and Thorvald Kodransson (61) went abroad [from Iceland]. Of those men, who accompanied Eric to Greenland, the following took possession of land there: Heriulf, Heriulfsfirth, he dwelt at Heriulfsness; Ketil, Ketilsfirth; Hrafn, Hrafnsfirth; Solvi, Solvadal; Helgi Thorbrandsson, Alptafirth; Thorbiorn Gleamer[3], Siglufirth; Einar, Einarsfirth; Hafgrim, Hafgrimsfirth and Vatnahverfi; Arnlaug, Arnlaugsfirth; while some went to the Western-settlement.

Leif the Lucky baptized[4].

After that sixteen winters had lapsed, from the time when Eric the Red went to colonize Greenland, Leif, Eric's son, sailed out from Greenland to Norway. He arrived in Drontheim[5] in the autumn, when King Olaf Tryggvason was come down from the north, out of Halagoland. Leif put in to Nidaros with his ship, and set out at once to visit the king. King Olaf expounded the faith to him, as he did to other heathen men who came to visit him. It proved easy for the king to persuade Leif, and he was accordingly baptized, together with all of his shipmates. Leif remained throughout the winter with the king, by whom he was well entertained.

Biarni goes in quest of[6] Greenland.

Heriulf (62) was a son of Bard Heriulfsson. He was a kinsman of Ingolf, the first colonist. Ingolf allotted land to Heriulf[7] between Vág and Reykianess,

[1] 'hálfr fjórði tøgr:' lit. half of the fourth ten, i. e. three decades and a half: the ancient Icelandic method of numeration. [2] Hence, A. D. 985. [3] glóra.
[4] 'var skírðr:' lit. was baptized. [5] Þrándheimr, Throndhjem. [6] Lit. sought.
[7] 'þeim Herjúlfi:' lit. to them Heriulf, i. e. to Heriulf and his people.

and he dwelt at first at Drepstokk. Heriulf's wife's name was Thorgerd, and their son, whose name was Biarni, was a most promising man. He formed an inclination for voyaging[1] while he was still young, and he prospered both in property and public esteem. It was his custom to pass his winters alternately abroad and with his father. Biarni soon became the owner of a trading-ship, and during the last winter that he spent in Norway, [his father], Heriulf determined to accompany Eric on his voyage to Greenland, and made his preparations to give up his farm[2]. Upon the ship with Heriulf was a Christian man from the Hebrides[3], he it was who composed the Sea-Rollers' Song (63), which contains this stave:

Mine adventure to the Meek One,
  Monk-heart-searcher[4], I commit now[5];
He, who heaven's halls doth govern[6],
  Hold the hawk's-seat[7] ever o'er me!

Heriulf settled at Heriulfsness, and was a most distinguished man. Eric the Red dwelt at Brattahlid, where he was held in the highest esteem, and all men paid him homage[8]. These were Eric's children: Leif, Thorvald, and Thorstein, and a daughter whose name was Freydis; she was wedded to a man named Thorvard, and they dwelt at Gardar, where the episcopal seat now is. She was a very haughty woman, while Thorvard was a man of little force of character, and Freydis had been wedded to him chiefly because of his wealth[9]. At that time the people of Greenland were heathen.

Biarni arrived with his ship at Eyrar [in Iceland] in the summer of the same year,

[1] 'fýstisk utan:' lit. hankered to go abroad.

[2] 'brá búi sínu,' broke up his home.

[3] 'Suðreyskr maðr,' a Sodor man, a man from the Suðreyjar, or Southern Islands, as the Hebrides were called.

[4] 'meinalausan múnka reyni:' lit. the faultless monk prover; meina-lauss, faultless; múnka reynir, lit. prover of monks, or searcher of monks; the faultless or innocent searcher of monks, a poetical epithet for Christ.

[5] Arranged in prose order, the passage would read: I bid the faultless monk-prover forward my travels.

[6] 'dróttinn foldar hattar hallar:' lit. the lord of the halls of the earth's hood; foldar hǫttr, earth's hat, or hood, i.e. the sky; hallar foldar hattar, the halls of the sky, i.e. the heavens; dróttinn foldar hattar hallar, the lord of the heavens, i.e. Christ.

[7] 'heiðis stallr,' the seat of the hawk, i.e. the hand. Haldi heiðis stalli yfir mér, hold the hand above me, i.e. protect me.

[8] 'lutu allir til hans,' all bowed down [louted] to him.

[9] 'var hon mjǫk gefin til fjár:' lit. she was chiefly given for money.

in the spring of which his father had sailed away. Biarni was much surprised when he heard this news [1], and would not discharge his cargo. His shipmates enquired of him what he intended to do, and he replied that it was his purpose to keep to his custom, and make his home for the winter with his father [2]; 'and I will take the ship to Greenland, if you will bear me company.' They all replied that they would abide by his decision. Then said Biarni, 'Our voyage must be regarded as foolhardy, seeing that no one of us has ever been in the Greenland Sea [3].' Nevertheless they put out to sea when they were equipped for the voyage, and sailed for three days, until the land was hidden by the water, and then the fair wind died out, and north winds arose, and fogs, and they knew not whither they were drifting, and thus it lasted for many 'dœgr.' Then they saw the sun again, and were able to determine the quarters of the heavens [4]; they hoisted sail, and sailed that 'dœgr' through before they saw land. They discussed among themselves what land it could be, and Biarni said that he did not believe that it could be Greenland. They asked whether he wished to sail to this land or not. 'It is my counsel' [said he], 'to sail close to the land.' They did so, and soon saw that the land was level, and covered with woods [5], and that there were small hillocks upon it. They left the land on their larboard, and let the sheet turn toward the land. They sailed for two 'dœgr' before they saw another land. They asked whether Biarni thought this was Greenland yet. He replied that he did not think this any more like Greenland than the former, 'because in Greenland there are said to be many great ice-mountains.' They soon approached this land, and saw that it was a flat and wooded country. The fair wind failed them then, and the crew took counsel together, and concluded that it would be wise to land there, but Biarni would not consent to this. They alleged that they were in need of both wood and water. 'Ye have no lack of either of these,' says Biarni—a course, forsooth, which won him blame among his shipmates. He bade them hoist sail, which they did, and turning the prow from the land they sailed out upon the high seas, with south-westerly gales, for three 'dœgr,' when they saw the third land; this land was high and mountainous, with ice-mountains upon it (64). They asked Biarni then whether he would land there, and he replied that he was not disposed to do so, 'because this land does not appear to me to offer any attractions [6].' Nor did they lower their sail, but held their course off the land, and saw that it was an island. They left this land

[1] 'þau tíðindi þóttu Bjarna mikil:' lit. these tidings seemed great to Biarni.

[2] 'þiggja at fǫður sínum vetr-vist:' lit. receive from his father winter-quarters.

[3] That part of the ocean between Iceland and Greenland was so called.

[4] 'deila ættir,' to distinguish the airts, i.e. as we should say, to tell the points of the compass.

[5] 'ófjǫllótt ok skógi vaxit:' lit. not mountainous and grown with woods.

[6] 'ógagnvænligt:' lit. unprofitable, i.e. sterile.

astern [1], and held out to sea with the same fair wind. The wind waxed amain, and Biarni directed them to reef, and not to sail at a speed unbefitting their ship and rigging. They sailed now for four 'dœgr,' when they saw the fourth land. Again they asked Biarni whether he thought this could be Greenland or not. Biarni answers, 'This is likest Greenland, according to that which has been reported to me concerning it, and here we will steer to the land.' They directed their course thither, and landed in the evening, below a cape upon which there was a boat, and there, upon this cape, dwelt Heriulf (65), Biarni's father, whence the cape took its name, and was afterwards called Heriulfsness. Biarni now went to his father, gave up his voyaging, and remained with his father while Heriulf lived, and continued to live there after his father.

Here begins the Brief History of the Greenlanders [2].

Next to this is now to be told how Biarni Heriulfsson came out from Greenland on a visit to Earl Eric, by whom he was well received. Biarni gave an account of his travels [upon the occasion] when he saw the lands, and the people thought that he had been lacking in enterprise [3], since he had no report to give concerning these countries, and the fact brought him reproach. Biarni was appointed one of the Earl's men, and went out to Greenland the following summer. There was now much talk about voyages of discovery. Leif, the son of Eric the Red, of Brattahlid, visited Biarni Heriulfsson and bought a ship of him, and collected a crew, until they formed altogether a company of thirty-five men [4]. Leif invited his father, Eric, to become the leader of the expedition, but Eric declined, saying that he was then stricken in years, and adding that he was less able to endure the exposure of sea-life than he had been. Leif replied that he would nevertheless be the one who would be most apt to bring good luck [5], and Eric yielded to Leif's solicitation, and rode from home when they were ready to sail. When he was but a short distance from the ship, the horse which Eric was riding stumbled, and he was thrown from his back and wounded his foot, whereupon he exclaimed, 'It is not designed for me to discover more lands than the one in which we are now living, nor can we now continue longer together.' Eric returned home to Brattahlid, and Leif pursued his way to the ship with his

[1] 'settu enn stafn við því landit:' lit. moreover they set the 'stafn' against that land. 'Stafn,' stem, is used of both the bow and stern of a vessel.

[2] [Flatey Book, column 281.]

[3] 'úforvitinn:' lit. incurious.

[4] See note 1, p. 61.

[5] 'hann enn mundi mestri heill stýra af þeim frændum:' lit. he would, nevertheless, win the greatest luck of them, the kinsmen.

companions, thirty-five men; one of the company was a German[1] named Tyrker. They put the ship in order, and when they were ready, they sailed out to sea, and found first that land which Biarni and his ship-mates[2] found last. They sailed up to the land and cast anchor, and launched a boat and went ashore, and saw no grass there; great ice mountains lay inland back from the sea[3], and it was as a [table-land of] flat rock all the way from the sea to the ice mountains, and the country seemed to them to be entirely devoid of good qualities. Then said Leif, 'It has not come to pass with us in regard to this land as with Biarni, that we have not gone upon it. To this country I will now give a name, and call it Helluland[4]'. They returned to the ship, put out to sea, and found a second land. They sailed again to the land, and came to anchor, and launched the boat, and went ashore. This was a level wooded land, and there were broad stretches of white sand, where they went, and the land was level by the sea[5]. Then said Leif, 'This land shall have a name after its nature, and we will call it Markland[6].' They returned to the ship forthwith, and sailed away upon the main with north-east winds, and were out two 'dœgr' before they sighted land. They sailed toward this land, and came to an island which lay to the northward off the land. There they went ashore and looked about them, the weather being fine, and they observed that there was dew upon the grass, and it so happened that they touched the dew with their hands, and touched their hands to their mouths, and it seemed to them that they had never before tasted anything so sweet as this. They went aboard their ship again and sailed into a certain sound, which lay between the island and a cape, which jutted out from the land on the north, and they stood in westering past the cape. At ebb-tide there were broad reaches of shallow water there, and they ran their ship aground there, and it was a long distance from the ship to the ocean[7]; yet were they so anxious to go ashore that they could not wait until the tide should rise under their ship, but hastened to the land, where a certain river flows out from a lake. As soon as the tide rose beneath their ship, however, they took the boat and rowed to the ship, which they conveyed up the river, and so into the lake, where they cast anchor and carried their hammocks ashore from the ship, and built themselves booths there. They afterwards determined to establish themselves there for the winter, and they accordingly built a large house. There was no lack of salmon there either in the

[1] 'Suðrmaðr:' lit. a Southern man; a German was so called as contradistinguished from Norðmaðr, a Northman.

[2] 'þeir Bjarni:' lit. they Biarni.

[3] 'allt hit efra:' lit. all the upper part, i. e. away from the shore.

[4] Helluland, the land of flat stone; from hella, a flat stone.

[5] ósæbrattr: lit. un-sea-steep, i. e. not steep toward the sea.

[6] Markland, Forest-land; from mǫrk, a forest.

[7] 'var þá langt til sjóvar at sjá frá skipinu:' lit. it was far to see from the ship to the sea.

river or in the lake, and larger salmon than they had ever seen before. The country thereabouts seemed to be possessed of such good qualities that cattle would need no fodder there during the winters. There was no frost there in the winters [1], and the grass withered but little. The days and nights there were of more nearly equal length than in Greenland or Iceland. On the shortest day of winter the sun was up between 'eyktarstad' and 'dagmalastad (66) [2].' When they had completed their house Leif said to his companions, 'I propose now to divide our company into two groups, and to set about an exploration of the country; one half of our party shall remain at home at the house, while the other half shall investigate the land, and they must not go beyond a point from which they can return home the same evening, and are not to separate [from each other].' Thus they did for a time; Leif himself, by turns, joined the exploring party or remained behind at the house. Leif was a large and powerful man, and of a most imposing bearing, a man of sagacity, and a very just man in all things.

LEIF THE LUCKY FINDS [3] MEN UPON A SKERRY AT SEA.

It was discovered [4] one evening that one of their company was missing, and this proved to be Tyrker, the German. Leif was sorely troubled by this, for Tyrker had lived with Leif and his father [5] for a long time, and had been very devoted to Leif, when he was a child. Leif severely reprimanded his companions, and prepared to go in search of him, taking twelve men with him. They had proceeded but a short distance from the house, when they were met by Tyrker, whom they received most cordially. Leif observed at once that his foster-father was in lively spirits. Tyrker had a prominent forehead, restless eyes, small features [6], was diminutive in stature, and rather a sorry-looking individual withal, but was, nevertheless, a most capable handicraftsman. Leif addressed him, and asked: 'Wherefore art thou so belated, foster-father mine, and astray from the others?' In the beginning Tyrker spoke for some time in German, rolling his eyes, and grinning, and they could not understand him; but after a time he addressed them in the Northern tongue: 'I

[1] 'þar kvámu engi frost á vetrum,' no frost came there in the winters.

[2] 'sól hafði þar eyktarstað ok dagmálastað um skamdegi:' lit. the sun had there 'eyktarstad' and 'dagmalastad' on the short-day.

[3] Lit. found.

[4] 'bar þat til tíðinda:' lit. it came to tidings.

[5] 'með þeim feðgum:' lit. with them, the father and son.

[6] 'smáskitligr í andliti:' lit. very small in face.

did not go much further [*than you*], and yet[1] I have something of novelty to relate. I have found vines and grapes.' 'Is this indeed true, foster-father?' said Leif. 'Of a certainty it is true,' quoth he, 'for I was born where there is no lack of either grapes or vines.' They slept the night through, and on the morrow Leif said to his shipmates: 'We will now divide our labours[2], and each day will either gather grapes or cut vines and fell trees, so as to obtain a cargo of these for my ship.' They acted upon this advice, and it is said, that their after-boat was filled with grapes. A cargo sufficient for the ship was cut, and when the spring came, they made their ship ready, and sailed away; and from its products Leif gave the land a name, and called it Wineland. They sailed out to sea, and had fair winds until they sighted Greenland, and the fells below the glaciers; then one of the men spoke up, and said, 'Why do you steer the ship so much into the wind?' Leif answers: 'I have my mind upon my steering, but on other matters as well. Do ye not see anything out of the common[3]?' They replied, that they saw nothing strange[4]. 'I do not know,' says Leif, 'whether it is a ship or a skerry that I see.' Now they saw it, and said, that it must be a skerry; but he was so much keener of sight than they, that he was able to discern men upon the skerry. 'I think it best to tack,' says Leif, 'so that we may draw near to them, that we may be able to render them assistance, if they should stand in need of it; and if they should not be peaceably disposed, we shall still have better command of the situation than they[5].' They approached the skerry, and lowering their sail, cast anchor, and launched a second small boat, which they had brought with them. Tyrker inquired who was the leader of the party. He replied that his name was Thori, and that he was a Norseman; 'but what is thy name?' Leif gave his name. 'Art thou a son of Eric the Red of Brattahlid?' says he. Leif responded that he was. 'It is now my wish,' says Leif, 'to take you all into my ship, and likewise so much of your possessions as the ship will hold.' This offer was accepted, and [with their ship] thus laden, they held away to Ericsfirth, and sailed until they arrived at Brattahlid. Having discharged the cargo, Leif invited Thori, with his wife, Gudrid, and three others, to make their home with him, and procured quarters for the other members of the crew, both for his own and Thori's men. Leif rescued fifteen persons from

[1] If the word in the MS. be 'þit' and not 'þó' [cf. Icelandic text, page 147, line 59], the words 'and yet' should be italicised as supplied, and the words now italicised in the translation should then stand unbracketed.

[2] 'hafa tvennar sýslur fram:' lit. carry on two occupations.

[3] 'eðr hvat sjái þér til tíðinda:' lit. but what do you see of tidings.

[4] 'er tíðindum sætti,' which amounted to tidings.

[5] 'þá eigum vér allan kost undir oss, en þeir ekki undir sér:' lit. we shall have all the choice under us [in our control], but they not under themselves.

the skerry. He was afterward called Leif the Lucky. Leif had now goodly store both of property and honour. There was serious illness that winter in Thori's party, and Thori and a great number of his people died. Eric the Red also died that winter. There was now much talk about Leif's Wineland journey, and his brother, Thorvald, held that the country had not been sufficiently explored. Thereupon Leif said to Thorvald: 'If it be thy will, brother, thou mayest go to Wineland with my ship, but I wish the ship first to fetch the wood, which Thori had upon the skerry.' And so it was done.

Thorvald goes to Wineland[1].

Now Thorvald, with the advice of his brother, Leif, prepared to make this voyage with thirty men. They put their ship in order, and sailed out to sea; and there is no account of their voyage before their arrival at Leif's-booths in Wineland. They laid up their ship there, and remained there quietly during the winter, supplying themselves with food by fishing. In the spring, however, Thorvald said that they should put their ship in order, and that a few men should take the after-boat, and proceed along the western coast, and explore [the region] thereabouts during the summer. They found it a fair, well-wooded country; it was but a short distance from the woods to the sea, and [there were] white sands, as well as great numbers of islands and shallows. They found neither dwelling of man nor lair of beast; but in one of the westerly islands, they found a wooden building for the shelter of grain (67). They found no other trace of human handiwork, and they turned back, and arrived at Leifs-booths in the autumn. The following summer Thorvald set out toward the east with the ship[2], and along the northern coast. They were met by a high wind off a certain promontory, and were driven ashore there, and damaged the keel of their ship, and were compelled to remain there for a long time and repair the injury to their vessel. Then said Thorvald to his companions: 'I propose that we raise the keel upon this cape, and call it Keelness[3],' and so they did. Then they sailed away, to the eastward off the land, and into the mouth of the adjoining firth, and to a headland, which projected into the sea there, and which was entirely covered with woods. They found an anchorage for their ship, and put out the gangway to the land, and Thorvald and all of his companions went ashore. 'It is a fair region here,' said he, 'and here I should like to make my home.' They then returned to the ship, and discovered on the sands, in beyond the headland, three mounds; they went up to these, and saw that they were three skin-canoes, with three men under each. They, thereupon

[1] Lit. Thorvald went to Wineland.

[2] 'kaupskipit:' lit. merchant-ship.

[3] Kjalarnes.

divided their party, and succeeded in seizing all of the men but one, who escaped with his canoe. They killed the eight men, and then ascended the headland again, and looked about them, and discovered within the firth certain hillocks, which they concluded must be habitations. They were then so overpowered with sleep[1] that they could not keep awake, and all fell into a [heavy] slumber, from which they were awakened by the sound of a cry uttered above them[2]; and the words of the cry were these: 'Awake, Thorvald, thou and all thy company, if thou wouldst save thy life; and board thy ship with all thy men, and sail with all speed from the land!' A countless number of skin-canoes then advanced toward them from the inner part of the firth, whereupon Thorvald exclaimed: 'We must put out the war-boards (68), on both sides of the ship, and defend ourselves to the best of our ability, but offer little attack.' This they did, and the Skrellings, after they had shot at them for a time, fled precipitately, each as best he could. Thorvald then inquired of his men, whether any of them had been wounded, and they informed him that no one of them had received a wound. 'I have been wounded in my arm-pit[3],' says he; 'an arrow flew in between the gunwale and the shield, below my arm. Here is the shaft, and it will bring me to my end[4]!' I counsel you now to retrace your way with the utmost speed. But me ye shall convey to that headland which seemed to me to offer so pleasant a dwelling-place; thus it may be fulfilled, that the truth sprang to my lips, when I expressed the wish to abide there for a time[5]. Ye shall bury me there, and place a cross at my head, and another at my feet, and call it Crossness[6] for ever after.' At that time Christianity had obtained in Greenland; Eric the Red died, however, before [the introduction of] Christianity.

Thorvald died, and when they had carried out his injunctions, they took their departure, and rejoined their companions, and they told each other of the experiences which had befallen them[7]. They remained there during the winter, and gathered grapes and wood with which to freight the ship. In the following spring they returned to Greenland, and arrived with their ship in Ericsfirth, where they were able to recount great tidings to Leif.

[1] 'sló á þá hǫfga svá miklum, at,' they were stricken with so heavy a sleep, that—

[2] 'Þá kom kall yfir þá:' lit. then there came a call over them.

[3] 'undir hendi:' lit. under the arm.

[4] 'mun mik þetta til bana leiða:' lit. this must lead me to my bane [death]; i.e. this will be the death of me.

[5] 'at ek muni þar búa á um stund:' lit. that I should dwell up there for a time.

[6] Krossanes.

[7] 'sǫgðu hvárir ǫðrum slík tíðindi sem vissu:' lit. they told each other such tidings as they knew.

THORSTEIN ERICSSON DIES[1] IN THE WESTERN SETTLEMENT.

In the meantime it had come to pass in Greenland, that Thorstein of Ericsfirth had married, and taken to wife Gudrid, Thorbiorn's daughter, [she] who had been the spouse of Thori Eastman (69), as has been already related. Now Thorstein Ericsson, being minded to make the voyage[2] to Wineland after the body of his brother, Thorvald, equipped the same ship, and selected a crew of twenty-five men[3] of good size and strength[4], and taking with him his wife, Gudrid, when all was in readiness, they sailed out into the open ocean, and out of sight of land. They were driven hither and thither over the sea all that summer, and lost all reckoning[5], and at the end of the first week of winter they made the land at Lysufirth in Greenland, in the Western-settlement. Thorstein set out in search of quarters for his crew, and succeeded in procuring homes for all of his shipmates; but he and his wife were unprovided for, and remained together upon the ship for two or more days[6]. At this time Christianity was still in its infancy in Greenland. It befell, early one morning, that men came to their tent, and the leader inquired who the people were within the tent. Thorstein replies: 'We are twain,' says he; 'but who is it who asks?' 'My name is Thorstein, and I am known as Thorstein the Swarthy[7], and my errand hither is to offer you two, husband and wife, a home with me.' Thorstein replied, that he would consult with his wife, and she bidding him decide, he accepted the invitation. 'I will come after you on the morrow with a sumpter-horse, for I am not lacking in means wherewith to provide for you both, although it will be lonely living with me, since there are but two of us, my wife and myself, for I, forsooth, am a very hard man to get on with[8]; moreover, my faith is not the same as yours[9], albeit methinks that is the better to which you hold.' He returned for them on the morrow, with the beast, and they took up their home with Thorstein the Swarthy, and were well treated by him. Gudrid was a woman of fine presence, and a clever woman, and very happy in adapting herself to strangers.

Early in the winter Thorstein Ericsson's party was visited by sickness, and many of his companions died. He caused coffins to be made for the bodies of the dead, and had them conveyed to the ship, and bestowed there; 'for it is my purpose to have all the bodies taken to Ericsfirth in the summer.' It was not long before

[1] 'andaðisk:' lit. died.
[2] 'fýstisk . . . at fara:' lit. hankered to go.
[3] 'hálfan þriðja tǫg,' half of the third ten; cf. note 1, p. 61.
[4] 'valdi hann lið at afli ok vexti:' lit. selected a company for their strength and size.
[5] 'vissu eigi hvar þau fóru:' lit. they did not know where they went.
[6] 'tvau nǫkkurar nætr:' lit. some two nights.
[7] svartr.
[8] 'er einþykkr mjǫk:' am very obstinate.
[9] i.e. he was not a Christian.

illness appeared in Thorstein's home, and his wife, whose name was Grimhild, was first taken sick. She was a very vigorous woman, and as strong as a man, but the sickness mastered her; and soon thereafter Thorstein Ericsson was seized with the illness, and they both lay ill at the same time; and Grimhild, Thorstein the Swarthy's wife, died, and when she was dead Thorstein went out of the room to procure a deal, upon which to lay the corpse. Thereupon Gudrid spoke. 'Do not be absent long, Thorstein mine!' says she. He replied, that so it should be. Thorstein Ericsson then exclaimed: 'Our house-wife is acting now in a marvellous fashion, for she is raising herself up on her elbow, and stretching out her feet from the side of the bed, and groping after her shoes.' At that moment Thorstein, the master of the house[1], entered, and Grimhild laid herself down, wherewithal every timber in the room creaked. Thorstein now fashioned a coffin for Grimhild's body, and bore it away, and cared for it. He was a big man, and strong, but it called for all [his strength], to enable him to remove the corpse from the house. The illness grew upon Thorstein Ericsson, and he died, whereat his wife, Gudrid, was sorely grieved. They were all in the room at the time, and Gudrid was seated upon a chair before the bench, upon which her husband, Thorstein, was lying. Thorstein, the master of the house[1], then taking Gudrid in his arms, [carried her] from the chair, and seated himself, with her, upon another bench, over against her husband's body, and exerted himself in divers ways to console her, and endeavoured to reassure her, and promised her that he would accompany her to Ericsfirth with the body of her husband, Thorstein, and those of his companions: 'I will likewise summon other persons hither,' says he, 'to attend upon thee, and entertain thee.' She thanked him. Then Thorstein Ericsson sat up, and exclaimed: 'Where is Gudrid?' Thrice he repeated the question, but Gudrid made no response. She then asked Thorstein, the master, 'Shall I give answer to his question, or not?' Thorstein, the master, bade her make no reply, and he then crossed the floor, and seated himself upon the chair, with Gudrid in his lap, and spoke, saying: 'What dost thou wish, namesake?' After a little while, Thorstein replies: 'I desire to tell Gudrid of the fate which is in store for her[2], to the end that she may be better reconciled to my death, for I am indeed come to a goodly resting-place[3]. This I have to tell thee, Gudrid, that thou art to marry an Icelander, and that ye are to have a long wedded life together, and a numerous and noble progeny, illustrious, and famous, of good odour and sweet virtues. Ye shall go from Greenland to Norway, and thence to Iceland, where ye shall build your home. There ye shall dwell together

[1] 'Þorsteinn bóndi:' the word bóndi signifies a man who is the owner and manager of a home.

[2] 'segja Guðríði forlǫg sín:' tell Gudrid her fate.

[3] 'hvíldar-staðr:' lit. place of rest, i.e. paradise; cf. Fritzner, Ordbog, s. v.

for a long time, but thou shalt outlive him, and shalt then go abroad and to the South [1], and shalt return to Iceland again, to thy home, and there a church shall then be raised, and thou shalt abide there and take the veil, and there thou shalt die.' When he had thus spoken, Thorstein sank back again, and his body was laid out for burial, and borne to the ship. Thorstein, the master, faithfully performed all his promises to Gudrid. He sold his lands and live-stock in the spring, and accompanied Gudrid to the ship, with all his possessions. He put the ship in order, procured a crew, and then sailed to Ericsfirth. The bodies of the dead were now buried at the church, and Gudrid then went home to Leif at Brattahlid, while Thorstein the Swarthy made a home for himself on Ericsfirth, and remained there as long as he lived, and was looked upon as a very superior man.

Of the Wineland Voyages of Thorfinn and his Companions.

That same summer a ship came from Norway to Greenland. The skipper's name was Thorfinn Karlsefni [2]; he was a son of Thord Horsehead [3], and a grandson of Snorri, the son of Thord of Höfdi. Thorfinn Karlsefni, who was a very wealthy man, passed the winter at Brattahlid with Leif Ericsson. He very soon set his heart upon Gudrid, and sought her hand in marriage; she referred him to Leif for her answer, and was subsequently betrothed to him, and their marriage was celebrated that same winter. A renewed discussion arose concerning a Wineland voyage, and the folk urged Karlsefni to make the venture, Gudrid joining with the others [4]. He determined to undertake the voyage, and assembled a company of sixty men and five women, and entered into an agreement with his shipmates that they should each share equally in all the spoils of the enterprise [5]. They took with them all kinds of cattle, as it was their intention to settle the country, if they could. Karlsefni asked Leif for the house in Wineland, and he replied, that he would lend it but not give it. They sailed out to sea with the ship, and arrived safe and sound at Leifs-booths, and carried their hammocks ashore there. They were soon provided with an abundant and goodly supply of food, for a whale of good size and quality was driven ashore there, and they secured it, and flensed it, and had then no lack of provisions. The cattle were turned out

[1] 'ganga suðr,' go to the South; an expression employed here, doubtless, as in many other places in Icelandic sagas, to signify a pilgrimage to Rome.

[2] Karls-efni: a person who has about him the promise of becoming a capable man.

[3] hesthọfði.

[4] 'bæði Guðríðr ok aðrir menn:' lit. both Gudrid and others.

[5] 'er þeir fengi til gœða:' lit. which they might get of good things.

upon the land[1], and the males soon became very restless and vicious; they had brought a bull with them. Karlsefni caused trees to be felled, and to be hewed into timbers, wherewith to load his ship, and the wood was placed upon a cliff to dry. They gathered somewhat of all of the valuable products of the land, grapes, and all kinds of game and fish, and other good things. In the summer succeeding the first winter, Skrellings were discovered[2]. A great troop of men came forth from out the woods. The cattle were hard by, and the bull began to bellow and roar with a great noise, whereat the Skrellings were frightened, and ran away, with their packs wherein were grey furs, sables, and all kinds of peltries. They fled towards Karlsefni's dwelling, and sought to effect an entrance into the house, but Karlsefni caused the doors to be defended [against them]. Neither [people] could understand the other's language. The Skrellings put down their bundles then, and loosed them, and offered their wares [for barter], and were especially anxious to exchange these for weapons, but Karlsefni forbade his men to sell their weapons, and taking counsel with himself, he bade the women carry out milk[3] to the Skrellings, which they no sooner saw, than they wanted to buy it, and nothing else. Now the outcome of the Skrellings' trading was, that they carried their wares away in their stomachs, while they left their packs and peltries behind with Karlsefni and his companions, and having accomplished this [exchange] they went away. Now it is to be told, that Karlsefni caused a strong wooden palisade to be constructed and set up around the house. It was at this time that Gudrid, Karlsefni's wife, gave birth to a male child, and the boy was called Snorri. In the early part of the second winter the Skrellings came to them again, and these were now much more numerous than before, and brought with them the same wares as at first. Then said Karlsefni to the women: 'Do ye carry out now the same food, which proved so profitable before, and nought else.' When they saw this they cast their packs in over the palisade. Gudrid was sitting within, in the doorway, beside the cradle of her infant son, Snorri, when a shadow fell upon the door, and a woman in a black namkirtle (70) entered. She was short in stature, and wore a fillet about her head; her hair was of a light chestnut colour, and she was pale of hue, and so big-eyed, that never before had eyes so large been seen in a human skull. She went up to where Gudrid was seated, and said: 'What is thy name?' 'My name is Gudrid; but what is thy name?' 'My name is Gudrid,' says she. The housewife, Gudrid, motioned her with her hand to a seat beside her; but it so happened, that,

[1] 'gekk þar á land upp:' lit. went up on the land there.

[2] 'þá urðu þeir varir við Skrælingja:' lit. they became aware of Skrellings.

[3] 'búnyt:' milk, or an article of food prepared from milk; cf. Fritzner, Ordbog, s. v.

at that very instant Gudrid heard a great crash, whereupon the woman vanished, and at that same moment one of the Skrellings, who had tried to seize their weapons [1], was killed by one of Karlsefni's followers. At this the Skrellings fled precipitately, leaving their garments and wares behind them; and not a soul, save Gudrid alone, beheld this woman. 'Now we must needs take counsel together,' says Karlsefni, 'for that I believe they will visit us a third time, in great numbers [2], and attack us. Let us now adopt this plan: ten of our number shall go out upon the cape, and show themselves there, while the remainder of our company shall go into the woods and hew a clearing for our cattle, when the troop approaches from the forest. We will also take our bull, and let him go in advance of us.' The lie of the land was such that the proposed meeting-place had the lake upon the one side, and the forest upon the other. Karlsefni's advice was now carried into execution. The Skrellings advanced to the spot which Karlsefni had selected for the encounter, and a battle was fought there, in which great numbers of the band of the Skrellings were slain. There was one man among the Skrellings, of large size and fine bearing, whom Karlsefni concluded must be their chief. One of the Skrellings picked up an axe, and having looked at it for a time, he brandished it about one of his companions, and hewed at him, and on the instant the man fell dead. Thereupon the big man seized the axe, and after examining it for a moment, he hurled it as far as he could, out into the sea; then they fled helter-skelter into the woods, and thus their intercourse came to an end. Karlsefni and his party [3] remained there throughout the winter, but in the spring Karlsefni announces, that he is not minded to remain there longer, but will return to Greenland. They now made ready for the voyage, and carried away with them much booty in vines and grapes [4], and peltries. They sailed out upon the high seas, and brought their ship safely to Ericsfirth, where they remained during the winter.

FREYDIS CAUSES [5] THE BROTHERS TO BE PUT TO DEATH.

There was now much talk anew, about a Wineland-voyage, for this was reckoned both a profitable and an honourable enterprise. The same summer that Karlsefni arrived from Wineland, a ship from Norway arrived in Greenland. This ship was

[1] 'þvíat hann hafði viljat taka vápn þeira:' lit. because he had wished to take their weapons.

[2] 'með úfriði ok fjǫlmenni:' lit. with un-peace [war] and a multitude of men.

[3] 'Þeir Karlsefni,' they Karlsefni.

[4] 'vínviði ok berjum:' lit. 'wine-wood' and berries. Vines are called in Icelandic 'wine-wood,' and grapes 'wine-berries.' The relation between the words of the sentence would indicate that the 'berries' here named are 'wine-berries' or grapes.

[5] 'lét drepa:' lit. caused to be put to death.

commanded by two brothers, Helgi and Finnbogi, who passed the winter in Greenland. They were descended from an Icelandic family of the East-firths [1]. It is now to be added, that Freydis, Eric's daughter, set out from her home at Gardar, and waited upon the brothers, Helgi and Finnbogi, and invited them to sail with their vessel to Wineland, and to share with her equally all of the good things which they might succeed in obtaining there. To this they agreed, and she departed thence to visit her brother, Leif, and ask him to give her the house which he had caused to be erected in Wineland, but he made her the same answer [as that which he had given Karlsefni], saying, that he would lend the house, but not give it. It was stipulated between Karlsefni and Freydis, that each should have on ship-board thirty able-bodied men [2], besides the women; but Freydis immediately violated this compact, by concealing five men more [than this number], and this the brothers did not discover before they arrived in Wineland. They now put out to sea, having agreed beforehand, that they would sail in company, if possible, and although they were not far apart from each other, the brothers arrived somewhat in advance, and carried their belongings up to Leif's house. Now when Freydis arrived, her ship was discharged, and the baggage carried up to the house, whereupon Freydis exclaimed: 'Why did you carry your baggage in here?' 'Since we believed,' said they, 'that all promises [3] made to us would be kept.' 'It was to me that Leif loaned the house,' says she, 'and not to you.' Whereupon Helgi exclaimed: 'We brothers cannot hope to rival thee in wrong-dealing.' They thereupon carried their baggage forth, and built a hut, above the sea, on the bank of the lake, and put all in order about it; while Freydis caused wood to be felled, with which to load her ship. The winter now set in, and the brothers suggested, that they should amuse themselves by playing games. This they did for a time, until the folk began to disagree [4], when dissensions arose between them, and the games came to an end, and the visits between the houses ceased; and thus it continued far into the winter. One morning early, Freydis arose from her bed, and dressed herself, but did not put on her shoes and stockings. A heavy dew had fallen [5], and she took her husband's cloak, and wrapped it about her, and then walked to the brothers' house, and up to the door, which had been only partly closed [6] by one of the men, who had gone out a short time before. She pushed

[1] 'Íslenzkir at kyni, ok ór Austfjǫrðum:' lit. of Icelandic descent and from the East-firths.

[2] 'vígir menn:' lit. men capable of bearing arms.

[3] 'ákveðin orð:' lit. fixed words, i. e. explicit agreements.

[4] 'menn bárusk verra í milli:' lit. men introduced a worse condition among them.

[5] 'veðri var svá farit, at dǫgg var fallin mikil:' the weather was of such a character that a heavy dew had fallen.

[6] 'lokit hurð aptr á miðjan klofa:' lit. closed the door behind to the middle of the groove.

the door open, and stood, silently, in the doorway for a time. Finnbogi, who was lying on the innermost side of the room, was awake, and said: 'What dost thou wish here, Freydis?' She answers: 'I wish thee to rise, and go out with me, for I would speak with thee.' He did so, and they walked to a tree, which lay close by the wall of the house, and seated themselves upon it. 'How art thou pleased here?' says she. He answers: 'I am well pleased with the fruitfulness of the land, but I am ill-content with the breach which has come between us, for, methinks, there has been no cause for it.' 'It is even as thou sayest,' says she, 'and so it seems to me; but my errand to thee is, that I wish to exchange ships with you brothers, for that ye have a larger ship than I, and I wish to depart from here.' 'To this I must accede,' says he, 'if it is thy pleasure.' Therewith they parted, and she returned home, and Finnbogi to his bed. She climbed up into bed, and awakened Thorvard with her cold feet, and he asked her why she was so cold and wet. She answered, with great passion: 'I have been to the brothers,' says she, 'to try to buy their ship, for I wished to have a larger vessel, but they received my overtures so ill, that they struck me, and handled me very roughly; what time thou, poor wretch, wilt neither avenge my shame nor thy own, and I find, perforce, that I am no longer in Greenland, moreover I shall part from thee unless thou wreakest vengeance for this.' And now he could stand her taunts no longer, and ordered the men to rise at once, and take their weapons, and this they did, and they then proceeded directly to the house of the brothers, and entered it, while the folk were asleep [1], and seized and bound them, and led each one out, when he was bound; and as they came out, Freydis caused each one to be slain. In this wise all of the men were put to death, and only the women were left, and these no one would kill. At this Freydis exclaimed: 'Hand me an axe!' This was done, and she fell upon the five women, and left them dead. They returned home, after this dreadful deed, and it was very evident that Freydis was well content with her work. She addressed her companions, saying: 'If it be ordained for us, to come again to Greenland, I shall contrive the death of any man who shall speak of these events. We must give it out, that we left them living here, when we came away.' Early in the spring, they equipped the ship, which had belonged to the brothers, and freighted it with all of the products of the land, which they could obtain, and which the ship would carry. Then they put out to sea, and, after a prosperous voyage, arrived with their ship in Ericsfirth early in the summer. Karlsefni was there, with his ship all ready to sail, and was awaiting a fair wind; and people say, that a ship richer laden, than that which he commanded, never left Greenland.

[1] 'at þeim sofǫndum:' lit. to them sleeping.

Concerning Freydis.

Freydis now went to her home, since it had remained unharmed during her absence. She bestowed liberal gifts upon all of her companions, for she was anxious to screen her guilt. She now established herself at her home; but her companions were not all so close-mouthed, concerning their misdeeds and wickedness, that rumours did not get abroad at last. These finally reached her brother, Leif, and he thought it a most shameful story. He thereupon took three of the men, who had been of Freydis' party, and forced them all at the same time to a confession of the affair, and their stories entirely agreed. 'I have no heart,' says Leif, 'to punish my sister, Freydis, as she deserves, but this I predict of them, that there is little prosperity in store for their offspring.' Hence it came to pass, that no one from that time forward thought them worthy of aught but evil. It now remains to take up the story from the time when Karlsefni made his ship ready, and sailed out to sea. He had a successful voyage[1], and arrived in Norway safe and sound. He remained there during the winter, and sold his wares, and both he and his wife were received with great favour by the most distinguished men of Norway. The following spring he put his ship in order for the voyage to Iceland; and when all his preparations had been made, and his ship was lying at the wharf, awaiting favourable winds, there came to him a Southerner[2], a native of Bremen in the Saxonland, who wished to buy his 'house-neat[3].' 'I do not wish to sell it,' said he. 'I will give thee half a "mörk" in gold for it' (71), says the Southerner. This Karlsefni thought a good offer, and accordingly closed the bargain. The Southerner went his way, with the 'house-neat,' and Karlsefni knew not what wood it was, but it was 'mösur[4],' come from Wineland.

Karlsefni sailed away, and arrived with his ship in the north of Iceland, in Skagafirth. His vessel was beached there during the winter, and in the spring he bought Glaumbœiar-land (59), and made his home there, and dwelt there as long as he lived, and was a man of the greatest prominence. From him and his wife, Gudrid, a numerous and goodly lineage is descended. After Karlsefni's death, Gudrid, together with her son, Snorri, who was born in Wineland, took charge of the farmstead; and when Snorri was married, Gudrid went abroad, and made a pilgrimage to the South[5], after which she returned again to the home of her son, Snorri, who had caused a church to be built at Glaumbœr. Gudrid then took the veil and became an anchorite, and lived there the rest of her days. Snorri had a son, named Thorgeir, who was the

[1] 'Honum fórsk vel:' lit. it went well with him.

[2] Suðrmaðr: a Southerner, i.e. a German; cf. note 1, p. 65.

[3] húsa-snotra. Cf. note 6.

[4] Or 'mausur,' as in the MS.; cf. note 36.

[5] Cf. note 1, p. 72.

father of Ingveld, the mother of Bishop Brand. Hallfrid was the name of the daughter of Snorri, Karlsefni's son; she was the mother of Runolf, Bishop Thorlak's father. Biorn was the name of [another] son of Karlsefni and Gudrid; he was the father of Thorunn, the mother of Bishop Biorn. Many men are descended from Karlsefni, and he has been blessed with a numerous and famous posterity; and of all men Karlsefni has given the most exact accounts of all these voyages, of which something has now been recounted.

CHAPTER IV.

Wineland in the Icelandic Annals.

In addition to the longer sagas of the discovery and exploration of Wineland, and the scattered references in other Icelandic historical literature, already adduced, the country finds mention in still another class of Icelandic records. These records are the chronological lists of notable events, in and out of Iceland, which are known as the Icelandic Annals. It has been conjectured that the archetype of these Annals was compiled either by the learned Ari, the father of Icelandic historiography, or in the century in which he lived[1]. Although there is the best of reasons for the belief, that the first writer of Icelandic Annals was greatly indebted to Ari the Learned for the knowledge of many of the events which he records, such written evidence as we have from the century in which Ari lived, would seem to indicate that this kind of literature had not then sprung into being[2].

A recent writer in an able disquisition upon this subject arrives at the conclusion, that the first book of Annals was written in the south of Iceland about the year 1280[3]. While this theory is apparently well grounded, it is, nevertheless, true that the first writer of Icelandic Annals of whom we have definite knowledge, was an Icelandic priest named Einar Haflidason [Einarr Hafliðason], who was born in 1307, and died in 1393[4]. The fact that Einar was the compiler of such a book is gleaned from his

[1] Cf. Langebek, Scriptores rerum Danicarum, Copenh. 1773, vol. ii. p. 177; Björn Jónsson á Skarðsá. Annálar, Hrappsey, 1774, vol. i. p. 4; Grönlands historiske Mindesmærker, Copenh. 1838, vol. ii. pp. 577–8; Antiquarisk Tidskrift, Copenh. 1846–8, p. 122.

[2] Cf. Snorra Edda, Copenh. 1852, vol. ii. p. 12: 'Á þessu landi bæði lög og áttvísi eða þýðingar helgar, eða svá hin spakligu fræði, er Ari Þorgilsson hefir á bækr sett af skynsamligu viti.' ['In this land both laws and genealogical lore, or translations of sacred writings, or also of those learned records, which through a gifted wisdom, Ari Thorgilsson has committed to books.'] 'Learned records' ['spakligu fræði'] does not explicitly exclude the Annals, but the language of Hungrvaka, a work contemporary with that from which the above quotation is made, does, in the following passage: 'þat er á norrænu er ritað; lög, eðr sögur, eðr mannfræði' ['that which is written in the Northern tongue [Icelandic] laws, or sagas, or genealogies']. Biskupa Sögur, Copenh. 1858, vol. i. p. 59.

[3] Storm, Islandske Annaler, Christiania, 1888, pp. lxviii–lxxxiii, &c.

[4] Cf. Finnr Jónsson, Historia Ecclesiastica Islandiæ, Copenh. 1772, vol. i. pp. 592, 593.

own work, through an entry under the year 1304, in which his birth is recorded in such wise as to point unmistakably to his authorship[1]. This collection of Annals is contained in the parchment manuscript AM. 420 *b*, 4to, which has received the name, Lawman's Annals [Lögmanns-Annáll], probably from the office held by some one of its former owners[2]. Under the year 1121, we find in these Annals the entry: 'Bishop Eric Uppsi[3] sought Wineland[4].'

The next considerable collection of Annals, the date of which we are enabled to determine with tolerable accuracy, is that appended to the Flatey Book, the manuscript of which has already been described. These Annals were written by the priest Magnus Thorhallsson[5], and doubtless completed before the year 1395, for all entries cease in the previous year. Among the recorded events of the year 1121 it is stated that 'Eric, Bishop of Greenland, went in search of Wineland[6].'

Of a riper antiquity than either of the foregoing works, are, in all likelihood, the so-called Annales Reseniani, the original vellum manuscript of which was destroyed by the fire of 1728. A paper copy from this original, written by Arni Magnusson, is preserved in AM. 424, 4to. The dates included in these Annals extend from the year 228 to 1295 inclusive, and it has been conjectured that these records were compiled before the year 1319[7]. Here, under the year 1121, occurs the statement: 'Bishop Eric sought Wineland[8].'

[1] The entry is as follows: 'Rev. Einar Haflidason born, "in octava nativitatis gloriosæ virginis Mariæ." I, a sinful man, bid you who may read or hear these letters pray to God for me, that at the day of judgment I may be numbered among his chosen men,' &c. ['Fœddr Síra Einar Hafliðason, in Octava nativitatis gloriosæ virginis Marie. Bið ek syndugr maðr þetta letr lesandi eðr heyrandi, at þér biðit fyrir mér til Guðs, svá at ek mætti reiknast á dómsdegi í meðal hans valdra manna.'] Prof. Storm agrees with Arni Magnusson in the opinion that Einar himself wrote these Annals, from the beginning down to the year 1362. Cf. Storm, Isl. Ann. ubi sup. pp. xxi and 264.

[2] Cf. Hálfdan Einarsson, Sciagraphia Historiæ Literariæ Islandicæ, Copenh. 1777, p. 133; Storm, Isl. Ann. p. xxiv.

[3] Vigfusson [Dict. s. v.] translates uppsi, the fish '*gadus virens*;' Ivar Aasen [Dict. s.v. Ufs], on the other hand, renders the Norwegian word 'store Sei [large coal-fish], Isl. [i. e. Icelandic] Upsi.' This is confirmed by Benedikt Gröndal [Dýrafræði, Reykjavík, 1878, p. 89], who calls the Upsi, *Merlangus carbonarius*, deriving the descriptive *carbonarius*, from the black colour of the mouth of the full-grown fish.

[4] 'Eiríkr bis*ku*p vppse leitade Vínlandz.'

[5] Cf. Introductory notice of authorship in Flatey Book. Flateyjarbók, loc. cit. vol. i.

[6] 'Eir*ikr* bisk*u*p af Grônlandi *fór* at leita Vín l*an*dz.' The verb 'leita' has the double significance, 'to go to for aid,' and 'to go in search of.' The entry here seems to point clearly to the latter interpretation, literally, '*went to seek*.'

[7] Cf. Storm, Isl. Ann. p. vii; Íslenzkir Annálar, Copenh. 1847, pp. xxxi, xxxii.

[8] 'Eiríkr byscop leitaði Vín landz.' In another copy of these Annals, contained in the de la Gardie Collection in the Upsala University Library, Nos. 25–29, the original entry under the year 1121 appears

A parchment manuscript is preserved in the Royal Library of Copenhagen, No. 2087, 4to, old collection, which contains the annals known as Annales regii. These are written in various hands, and are brought down to the year 1341. From the first entry down to the year 1306, the hand is the same, and from this fact the conclusion has been drawn, that this portion of the manuscript was completed not later than 1307[1]. Against the year 1121 we find the entry: 'Bishop Eric of Greenland went in search of Wineland[2].'

Similar entries to these occur in two other collections of Icelandic Annals, which may be mentioned here, for, while these are, in their present form, of much more recent creation than those already noticed, they still seem to have drawn their material from elder lost vellums. One of these, Henrik Höyer's Annals, derives its name from its first owner, who died in Bergen in the year 1615. It is a paper manuscript contained in AM. 22, fol., and bears strong internal evidence of having been copied from an Icelandic original, which has since disappeared[3]. The entry in this manuscript under the year 1121 is: 'Bishop Eric sought Wineland[4].'

The other modern collection, known as Gottskalk's Annals, is contained in a parchment manuscript in the Royal Library of Stockholm, No. 5, 8vo, which it is believed was chiefly written by one Gottskalk Jonsson [Gottskálk Jónsson], a priest, who lived in the north of Iceland in the sixteenth century, and it has been conjectured, from internal evidence, that the portion of the compilation prior to the year 1394 was copied from a lost manuscript[5]. The entry under the year 1121 corresponds with those already quoted: 'Eric, the Greenlanders' bishop, sought Wineland[6].'

From these different records, varying slightly in phraseology, but all of the same purport, we may safely conclude that, in the year 1121, a certain Bishop of Greenland, called Eric Uppsi, went upon a voyage in search of Wineland. It is the sum of information which the Annals have to give concerning that country, and is meagre enough, for we are not only left unenlightened as to why the voyage was undertaken,

to have been confused or misunderstood by the copyist. It reads: 'Thorgils Erche biskup leitati Vínlands.' ['Arch-bishop Thorgils sought Wineland.'] The name Eiríkr appears to have been misread, and that of Thorgils carried over from the preceding sentence, as may be better seen by comparison with Arni Magnusson's entry of the same year: 'Sætt Hafliða oc Þorgils, Eiríkr byscop leitaði Vínlandz.'

[1] Cf. Langebek, Scr. rer. Dan. vol. iii. p. 2; Storm, Isl. Ann. p. xi.

[2] 'Eiríkr b*i*sk*u*p af Grônlan*n*di fór at leita Vínlan*n*dz.'

[3] Cf. Katalog over den Arnamagn. Handskr. Saml. Copenh. vol. i. pp. 19, 20; Storm, Isl. Ann. p. x.

[4] 'Eirikr b*i*sk*u*p leitad*i* Uínl*an*ds.'

[5] Cf. Storm, Isl. Ann. pp. xxv–xxviii.

[6] 'Eirekr Grœnlendinga byskup leitadi Vindlands.' A variant of this collection of Annals, AM. 412, 4to, the so-called Hóla-Annáll, has, correctly, 'Vínlands.'

but we are not even informed whether the bishop succeeded in finding the country of which he went in search. It is not possible to obtain much additional knowledge concerning this Bishop Eric elsewhere. It seems altogether probable that he was the 'Greenlanders' bishop Eric Gnup's son,' mentioned in a genealogical list in Landnáma [1], and it is clear that if this be the same Eric, he was by birth an Icelander. This view is in a slight measure confirmed by an entry in the Lawman's Annals under the year 1112 [in the Annals of the Flatey Book under the year 1113] wherein the journey of Bishop Eric is recorded [2], a 'journey' presumably undertaken away from Iceland, and probably to Greenland. In the ancient Icelandic scientific work called Rímbegla, in a list of those men who had been bishops at Gardar, the episcopal seat in Greenland, Eric heads the list [3], while in a similar list of Greenland bishops in the Flatey Book, Eric's name is mentioned third [4]. No record of Bishop Eric's ordination has been preserved, and none of his fate, unless indeed, it be written in the brief memorial of his Wineland voyage. It has been conjectured that this voyage to Wineland was undertaken as a missionary enterprise, a speculation which seems to have been suggested solely by the ecclesiastical office of the chief participant. It has been further conjectured, since we read in the Annals of the ordination of a new bishop for Greenland in 1124 [5], that Eric must have perished in the undertaking. The date of his death is nowhere given, and it is possible that the entry in the Annals, under the year 1121, is a species of necrological record. It is, in any event, the last surviving mention of Wineland the Good in the elder Icelandic literature.

Although no subsequent visit to Wineland is recorded, a portion of the American coastland, seen by the original explorers, does appear to have been visited by certain of the Greenland colonists, more than a hundred years after Bishop Eric's Wineland voyage.

A parchment manuscript, AM. 420 *a*, 4to, contains a collection of Annals, known as the Elder Skálholt Annals [Skálholts-Annáll hinn forni], not heretofore cited because of a lacuna covering the year 1121. This manuscript, which Arni Magnusson obtained from Skálholt, in the south of Iceland, and which he conjectures may have belonged to Skálholt church, or to Bishop Bryniolf's private library [6], is believed to

[1] Landnáma, Part i. ch. xiii.

[2] 'Ferd Eireks *biskups*.'

[3] Similarly the MS. AM. 415, 4to. Cf. Langebek, Scr. rer. Dan. vol. vi. p. 620.

[4] Rymbegla, Copenh. 1780, p. 320; Flateyjarbók, loc. cit. vol. iii. p. 454.

[5] Bishop Arnold [Arnaldr]; he was duly ordained Bishop of Greenland, at Lund, and was clearly the first bishop of Greenland so ordained. Cf. Grœnlendinga þáttr [Einars þáttr Sokkasonar], Flateyjarbók, Christiania, 1868, vol. iii. pp. 445, 446. Annales Reseniani, Annales regii, Flatey Book Annals, Gottskalk's Annals, and Höyer's Annals all give this date 1124, the Lawman's Annals alone assigns the event to 1125.

[6] Katalog o. d. AM. Håndskr. Saml. vol. i. p. 625.

have been written about the year 1362[1]. We find in this, against the year 1347, the following record: 'There came also a ship from Greenland, less in size than small Icelandic trading vessels. It came into the outer Stream-firth. It was without an anchor. There were seventeen men on board, and they had sailed to Markland, but had afterwards been driven hither by storms at sea[2].' The Annals of Gottskalk record the simple fact in the same year: 'a ship from Greenland came into the mouth of Stream-firth[3].' On the other hand the Annals of the Flatey Book, under the year 1347, have the following more particular record: 'A ship came then from Greenland, which had sailed to Markland, and there were eighteen men on board[4].'

This scanty record is the last historical mention of a voyage undertaken by Leif's fellow-countrymen to a part of the land which he had discovered three hundred years before. The nature of the information indicates that the knowledge of the discovery had not altogether faded from the memories of the Icelanders settled in Greenland. It seems further to lend a measure of plausibility to a theory that people from the Greenland colony may, from time to time, have visited the coast to the south-west of their home for supplies of wood, or for some kindred purpose. The visitors in this case had evidently intended to return directly from Markland to Greenland, and had they not been driven out of their course to Iceland, the probability is that this voyage would never have found mention in Icelandic chronicles, and all knowledge of it must have vanished as completely as did the colony to which the Markland visitors belonged.

[1] Storm, Isl. Ann. pp. xv, xvi.

[2] 'Þá ko*m* ok skip af Grænl*an*di min*n*a at vexti en*n* smá Íslan*dz* fór. Þ*at* ko*m* í Strau*m* fiörð in*n* *ytra*. Þ*at var* akk*er*is laust. Þ*ar váru* á xvij *menn* ok höfðu farit *til* M*ark*l*an*dz en*n* síðan vorðit hingat hafreka.'

[3] 'Kom skip j Straumfiardar ós af Grænlandi.'

[4] 'Þá ko*m* skip af Grænl*an*di, þ*at* *er* sótt hafdi *til* M*ark*l*an*dz, ok áttián m*enn* á.'

CHAPTER V.

NOTICES OF DOUBTFUL VALUE; FICTIONS.

IT will be remembered that a passage in the Book of Settlement [Landnámabók] recites the discovery, by one Ari Marsson, of a country lying westward from Ireland, called White-men's-land, or Ireland the Great. This White-men's-land is also mentioned in the Saga of Eric the Red, and in both places is assigned a location in the vicinity of Wineland the Good. Many writers have regarded this White-men's-land as identical with a strange country, the discovery of which is recounted in the Eyrbyggja Saga, having been led to this conclusion, apparently, from the fact that both unknown lands lay to the 'westward,' and that there is a certain remote resemblance between the brief particulars of the Eric's Saga and the more detailed narrative of Eyrbyggja.

It is related in the Eyrbyggja Saga[1] that a certain Biorn Asbrandsson [Bjǫrn Ásbrandsson] became involved in an intrigue with a married woman named Thurid, which resulted in his wounding the affronted husband and slaying two of the husband's friends, for which he was banished from Iceland for the term of three years. Biorn went abroad, led an adventurous life, and received the name of 'kappi' [champion, hero] on account of his valorous deeds. He subsequently returned to Iceland, where he was afterwards known as the Broadwickers'-champion [Breiðvíkingakappi]. He brought with him on his return not only increase of fame, but the added graces of bearing due to his long fellowship with foreign chieftains, and he soon renewed his attentions to his former mistress. The husband, fearing to cope alone with so powerful a rival, invoked the aid of one skilled in the black art to raise a storm, which should overwhelm the object of his enmity. The hero, however, after three days of exposure to the preternaturally-agitated elements, returned exhausted, but in safety, to his home. The husband then prevailed upon his powerful brother-in-law, the godi (72) Snorri, to come to his assistance, and as a result of Snorri's intervention, Biorn agreed to leave the country. He accordingly rode 'south, to a ship in Lava-haven[2], in which he took

[1] Eyrbyggja Saga, ed. Gudbrand Vigfusson, Leipsic, 1864, chaps. 29, 40, 47.

[2] Hraunhöfn, situated on the southern side of the promontory of Snæfellsness in western Iceland.

passage that same summer, but they were rather late in putting to sea. They sailed away with a north-east wind, which prevailed far into the summer, but nothing was heard of this ship for a long time afterwards[1].'

Further on in the same saga we read of the fortuitous discovery of this same Biorn by certain of his fellow-countrymen, and as the account of their strange meeting contains the sole description of this unknown land, it may best be given in the words of the saga. 'It was in the latter days of Olaf the Saint[2] that Gudleif [Guðleifr Guðlaugsson] engaged in a trading-voyage westward to Dublin, and when he sailed from the west it was his intention to proceed to Iceland. He sailed to the westward of Ireland, and had easterly gales and winds from the north-east, and was driven far to the westward over the sea and toward the south-west, so that they had lost all track of land. The summer was then far spent, and they uttered many prayers that they might be permitted to escape from the sea, and it befell thereupon that they became aware of land. It was a great country, but they did not know what country it was. Gudleif and his companions determined to sail to the land, for they were weary with battling with the tempestuous sea. They found a good harbour there, and they had been alongside the land but a short time when men came toward them. They did not recognize a single man, but it rather seemed to them that they were speaking Irish; soon so great a throng of men had drawn about them that they amounted to several hundreds. These people thereupon seized them all and bound them, and then drove them up upon the land. They were then taken to a meeting, at which their case was considered. It was their understanding that some [of their captors] wished them to be slain, while others would have them distributed among the people[3] and thrown into bondage. While this was being argued they descried a body of men riding, and a banner was carried in their midst[4], from which they concluded that some manner of chieftain must be in the company; and when this band drew near they saw a tall and warlike man riding beneath the banner; he was far advanced in years, however, and his hair was white. All of the people assembled bowed before this man, and received him as he had been their lord; they soon observed that all questions and matters for decision were submitted to him. This man then summoned Gudleif and his fellows, and when they came before him he addressed them in the Northern tongue [i.e. Icelandic], and asked them to what country they belonged. They responded that they were, for the most part, Icelanders. This man asked which of them were the Icelanders.

[1] 'Annan dag eptir reið Björn suðr í Hraunhöfn til skips ok tók sér þar þegar fari um sumarit, ok urðu heldr síðbúnir. Þeir tóku út landnyrðing, ok viðraði þat löngum um sumarit, en til skips þess spurðist eigi síðan langan tíma.' Eyrbyggja Saga, loc. cit. p. 91.

[2] That is to say, toward the end of Olaf's reign. Olaf died in 1030.

[3] Lit. 'divided for their sustenance.'

[4] Lit. 'in the company.'

Gudleif then advanced before this man, and greeted him worthily, and he received his salutations graciously, and asks from what part of Iceland they came, and Gudleif replies that he comes from Borgarfirth. He then enquired from what part of Borgarfirth he came, and Gudleif informs him. After this he asked particularly after every one of the leading men of Borgarfirth and Breidafirth, and in the course of the conversation he asks after Snorri Godi and Thurid, of Fróda [Fróðá], his sister, and he enquired especially after all details concerning Fróda, and particularly regarding the boy Kiartan[1], who was then the master at Fróda. The people of the country, on the other hand, demanded that some judgment should be reached concerning the ship's crew. After this the tall man left them, and called about him twelve of his men, and they sat together for a long time in consultation, after which they betook themselves to the [general] meeting. Thereupon the tall man said to Gudleif and his companions: "We, the people of this country, have somewhat considered your case, and the inhabitants have given your affair into my care, and I will now give you permission to go whither ye list; and even though it may seem to you that the summer is far spent, still I would counsel you to leave here, for the people here are untrustworthy and hard to deal with, and have already formed the belief that their laws have been broken." Gudleif replied: "If it be vouchsafed us to reach our native land, what shall we say concerning him who has granted us our freedom." He answers: "That I may not tell you, for I cannot bear that my relatives and foster-brothers should have such a voyage hither, as ye would have had if ye had not had my aid; but now I am so advanced in years," said he, "that the hour may come at any time when age shall rise above my head; and even though I should live yet a little longer, still there are those here in the land who are more powerful than I who would offer little mercy to strangers, albeit these are not in this neighbourhood where ye have landed." Afterward this man aided them in equipping their ship, and remained with them until there came a fair wind, which enabled them to put to sea. But before he and Gudleif parted, this man took a gold ring from his hand and handed it to Gudleif, and with it a goodly sword; and he then said to Gudleif: "If it be granted thee to come again to thy father-land, then do thou give this sword to Kiartan, the master at Fróda, and the ring to his mother." Gudleif said: "What shall I reply as to who sends these precious things?" He answers: "Say that he sends them who was more of a friend of the mistress at Fróda, than of the Godi at Helgafell, her brother. But if any persons shall think they have discovered from this to whom these treasures belonged, give them my message, that I forbid any man to go in search of me, for it would be a most desperate undertaking, unless he should fare as successfully as ye have in finding

[1] This Kiartan was Thurid's son.

a landing-place; for here is an extensive country with few harbours, and over all a disposition to deal harshly with strangers, unless it befall as it has in this case." After this they parted. Gudleif and his men put to sea, and arrived in Ireland late in the autumn, and passed the winter in Dublin; but in the summer they sailed to Iceland, and Gudleif delivered the treasures, and all men held of a verity that this man was Biorn Broadwickers'-champion; but people have no other proof of this, save these particulars, which have now been related (73).'

It will be observed that the narrator of the saga does not in this incident once connect this unknown land with White-men's-land, nor does he offer any suggestion as to its situation. The work of identifying this strange country with White-men's-land, and so with Wineland the Good, has been entirely wrought by the modern commentator[1]. If we accept as credible a meeting so miraculous as the one here described, if we disregard the statements of the narrative showing the existence of horses in this unknown land, which the theorist has not hesitated to do[2], and, finally, if we assume that there was at this time an Irish colony or one speaking a kindred tongue in North America, we may conclude that Biorn's adopted home was somewhere on the eastern North-American coast. If, however, we read the statements of the saga as we find them, they seem all to tend to deny this postulate, rather than to confirm it. The entire story has a decidedly fabulous appearance, and, as has been suggested by a learned editor of the saga, a romantic cast, which is not consonant with the character of the history in which it appears[3]. A narrative, the truth of which the narrator, himself, tells us had not been ratified by collateral evidence, and whose details are so vague and indefinite, seems to afford historical evidence of a character so equivocal, that it may well be dismissed without further consideration.

Of an altogether different nature from the narrative of discovery above recited, is the brief notice of the finding of a new land, set down in the Icelandic Annals toward the end of the thirteenth century. In the Annales regii, in the year 1285, the record

[1] Cf. Torfæus, Historia Vinlandiæ Antiquæ, Copenh. 1715, p. 72: 'Nescio an ad hanc Vinlandiam aut incertam aliam Americæ partem referenda sit terra illa, ad quam historia Eyrbyggensium memorat Gudleifum Gunnlaugi filium,' &c. Other later writers have spoken with less hesitancy.

[2] 'Dass Biörn zu Pferde an den Strand gekommen, könnte einer von den gewöhnlichen Zusätzen der Sagaschreiber seyn, die keinen Anstand nehmen, die einzelnen Umstände nach Wahrscheinlichkeit auszumählen, damit die Sache anschaulicher werde.' Müller, Sagaenbibliothek, aus der Dänischen Handschrift übers. v. Lachmann, Berlin, 1816, p. 144.

[3] 'Die Geschichte von Björn Breiðvíkingakappi ursprünglich vielleicht eine selbstständige kleine Erzählung, hier aber vom Verf. ohne weiteres der Eb. eingefügt, [sie] hat etwas romanhaftes, das nichts weniger als mit dem sonstigen Ernste der Saga übereinstimmt.' Vigfusson, ed. Eyrbyggja, p. xvii.

reads: 'Adalbrand and Thorvald, Helgi's sons, found New-land[1];' in the Annals of the Flatey Book, under the same year, 'Land was found to the westward off Iceland[2];' and again in Gottskalk's Annals an entry exactly similar to that of the Flatey Book. In Höyer's Annals the entry is of a different character: 'Helgi's sons sailed into Greenland's uninhabited regions[3].'

In the parchment manuscript AM. 415, 4to, written, probably, about the beginning of the fourteenth century[4], is a collection of annals, called 'Annales vetustissimi,' and here, under the year 1285, is an entry similar to that of the Flatey Book: 'Land found to the westward off Iceland[5].' In the Skálholt Annals, on the other hand, the only corresponding entry against the year 1285, is: 'Down-islands discovered[6].'

It required but the similarity between the names New-land and Newfoundland to arouse the effort to identify the two countries; and the theory thus created was supposed to find confirmation in a passage in a copy of a certain document known as Bishop Gizur Einarsson's Register [bréfa-bók], for the years 1540–47, which is contained in a paper manuscript of the seventeenth century[7], AM. 266, fol. This passage is as follows: 'Wise men have said, that you must sail to the south-west from Krisuvik mountain to Newland[8].' Krísuvík mountain is situated on the promontory of Reykianess, the south-western extremity of Iceland, and, as has been recently pointed out[9], to sail the course suggested by Bishop Gizur would in all probability land the adventurous mariner in south-eastern Greenland. The record of the Annals, however, is so explicit, that, in determining the site of 'Newland,' we do not need to orient ourselves by extraneous evidence. We are informed, that, in 1285, Helgi's sons sailed into Greenland's 'óbygðir,' the name by which the Greenland colonists were wont to designate the uninhabited east coast of Greenland; and as it is elsewhere distinctly stated that the 'Newland,' which these men discovered in the same year, lay to the 'westward off Iceland[10],' there can be little room for hesitancy in reaching the conclusion that 'Newland,' the 'óbygðir' and the 'Down-islands,' all lie together, and

[1] 'Fu*n*du Helga syn*ir* n*ý*ia l*an*d Adalbrandr ok Þorvalldr.' These men were priests of some prominence in their time. Cf. Árna saga biskups, Biskupa Sögur, Copenh. 1858, vol. i. The above entry is in a later hand than that of the other entries under the same year.

[2] 'Fanz l*an*d vestr undan Ísl*an*di.' [3] 'Helga sy*nir* sigldu í Grœnl*an*dz óbijoðir (óbygðir).'

[4] Cf. Katalog over den AM. Handskriftsamling, vol. i. p. 619.

[5] 'Fandz l*an*d vestr vndan Ísl*an*de.' [6] 'Funduz Dúneyiar.'

[7] Cf. Katalog AM. Handskrifter, vol. i. p. 240. It is, perhaps, worthy of note that Adalbrand was a priest in the south of Iceland, not far from Skálholt, where Bishop Gizur's book was, doubtless, written, and whither any record which Adalbrand or his brother may have left, might easily have found its way.

[8] 'Hafa vitrir menn sagt at suðvestr skal sigla til Nýalands undir Krísuvíkr bergi.'

[9] Storm, Historisk Tidskrift, Christiania, 1888, p. 264. [10] 'vestr undan Íslandi.'

are probably only different names for the same discovery. However this may be, it is at least manifest, from the record, that if Newland was not a part of the eastern coast of Greenland[1], there is nothing to indicate that it was anywhere in the region of Newfoundland.

A few years after this discovery is recorded, namely in 1289, we find the following statement in the Flatey Annals: 'King Eric sends Rolf to Iceland to seek New-land[2];' and again in the next year: 'Rolf travelled about Iceland soliciting men for a New-land voyage[3].' No additional information has been preserved touching this enterprise, and it therefore seems probable that if the voyage was actually undertaken, it was barren of results. The Flatey Annals note the death of Rolf, Land-Rolf [Landa-Rólf] as he was called, in 1295[4], and as no subsequent seeker of Newland is named in Icelandic history, it may be assumed that the spirit of exploration died with him.

This brief record of the Annals is unquestionably historically accurate, moreover there may be somewhat of an historical foundation for the adventures of the Broad-wickers'-champion recounted in the Eyrbyggja Saga; neither of these notices of discovery, however, appears to have any connection with the discovery of Wineland; they have been considered here chiefly because of the fact that they have been treated in the past as if they had a direct bearing upon the Wineland history.

The historical and quasi-historical material relating to the discovery of Wineland, has now been presented. A few brief notices of Helluland, contained in the later Icelandic literature, remain for consideration. These notices necessarily partake of the character of the sagas in which they appear, and as these sagas are in a greater or less degree pure fictions, the notices cannot be regarded as possessing any historical value.

First among these unhistorical sagas is the old mythical tale [fornsaga] of Arrow-Odd [Ǫrvar-Odds Saga], of which two recensions exist; the more recent[5] and inferior version[6] is that which contains the passages wherein Helluland is mentioned, as follows: '"But I will tell thee where Ogmund [Ǫgmundr] is; he is come into that firth which is called Skuggi[7], it is in Helluland's deserts . . .; he has gone thither because

[1] It has even been suggested that the supposed land may have been an ice-floe. Cf. Zahrtmann, 'Om Zeniernes Reiser i Norden,' in Nordisk Tidskrift for Oldkyndighed, Copenh. 1833, p. 24.

[2] 'Eir*ík*r *konung*r sendi Rólf t*il* Ísl*an*dz at leita nýia l*an*dz.' The 'Eiríkr konungr' was King Eric Magnusson of Norway, who died 1299.

[3] 'F*ór* Rólfr *vm* Ísl*an*d ok kr*a*fdi m*enn* t*il* nýia l*an*dz f*er*dar.'

[4] 'And*aðiz* L*an*da-Rólfr.'

[5] Cf. Boer, Ǫrvar-Odds Saga, Leiden, 1888, p. xxiv.

[6] Maurer, Ueber die Ausdrücke: altnord., altnorw., u. isländ., Sprache, Munich, 1867, p. 210.

[7] This firth is also referred to in the fictitious Gunnars saga keldugnúpsfífls, Copenh. 1866, p. 51. Although Helluland is not mentioned by name, the context appears to indicate that the firth was intended to have a location similar to that assigned it in Arrow-Odd's Saga.

he does not wish to meet thee; now thou mayest track him home, if thou wishest, and see how it fares." Odd said thus it should be. Thereupon they sail until they come into Greenland's sea, when they turn south and west around the land. . . . They sail now until they come to Helluland, and lay their course into the Skuggi-firth. And when they had reached the land the father and son went ashore, and walked until they saw where there was a fortification, and it seemed to them to be very strongly built[1].'

In the same category with Arrow-Odd's Saga may be placed two other mythical sagas, the Saga of Halfdan Eysteinsson [Hálfdanar saga Eysteinssonar], and the Saga of Halfdan Brana's-fosterling [Hálfdanar saga Brǫnufóstra]; in the first of these the passage containing the mention of Helluland is as follows: 'Raknar brought Helluland's deserts under his sway, and destroyed all the giants there[2].' In the second of these last-mentioned sagas the hero is driven out of his course at sea, until he finally succeeds in beaching his ship upon 'smooth sands' beside 'high cliffs;' 'there was much drift-wood on the sands, and they set about building a hut, which was soon finished. Halfdan frequently ascended the glaciers, and some of the men bore him company . . . . The men asked Halfdan what country this could be. Halfdan replied that they must be come to Helluland's deserts[3].'

Belonging to a class of fictitious sagas known as 'landvættasögur' [stories of a country's guardian spirits], is the folk-tale of Bard the Snow-fell-god [Bárðar saga Snæfellsáss]. The first chapter of this tale begins: 'There was a king named Dumb, who ruled over those gulfs, which extend northward around Helluland and are now called Dumb's sea[4].' Subsequently we find brief mention of a king of Helluland, of

[1] '"En segja mun ek þér til, hvar Ǫgmundr er; hann er kominn í fjǫrð þann, er Skuggi heitir, hann er í Hellulands úbygðum, . . .; er hann því þar kominn, at hann hirðir ekki þik at finna; nú máttu sækja hann heim, ef þú vilt, ok vita hversu er gengr." Oddr sagði svá skyldu vera. Síðan sigla þeir þar til er þeir kómu í Grœnlands haf, snúa þá suðr ok vestr fyrir landit. . . . Sigla þar til, at þeir koma til Hellulands, ok leggja inn á fjǫrðinn Skugga. En er þeir eru landfastir orðnir, ganga þeir feðgar á land, ok þar til sem þeir sjá, hvar virki stendr, ok sýniz þeim þat harðla rammgǫrt.' Ǫrvar-Odds Saga, ed. Boer, Leyden, 1888, pp. 131, 132; cf. also the verse in the Ævidrápa, same edition, p. 206.

[2] 'Raknar lagði undir sik Hellulands óbygðir, ok eyddi þar öllum jötnum.' Hálfdánar saga Eystein-sonar, ed. Rafn, Fornald. sögur Nordrl. Copenh. 1830, vol. iii. p. 556.

[3] 'Viðr var þar rekinn mikill á sandinn, ok taka þeir þar til skálasmíðar, ok var skjótt algjör. Hálfdán gengr á jökla jafnan, ok nökkrir men með honum, . . . Menn Hálfdánar spurðu, hvat land þetta væri. Hálfdán kvað þá mundu vera komna at Hellulands óbygðum.' Hálfdánar saga Brönufóstra, ed. Rafn, Fornald. sög. Nordrl. vol. iii. p. 568.

[4] 'Dumbr hefir konúngr heitið, hann réð fyrir hafsbotnum þeim, er ganga norðr um Helluland ok nú er kallat Dumbshaf.' Bárðar saga Snæfellsás, ed. Vigfusson, Copenh. 1860. The edition of this saga, contained in Biörn Marcusson's Nockrer Marg-Frooder Sogu-Þætter Íslendinga, Hólar, 1756, however, gives Dumb dominion over the gulfs, which extend from Risaland to the south-east: 'Hann

whom Gest, the son of the hero of the saga, says: 'I have never seen him before, but I have been told by my relatives that the king was called Rakin[1], and from their account I believe I recognize him; he at one time ruled over Helluland and many other countries, and after he had long ruled these lands he caused himself to be buried alive, together with five hundred men, at Raknslodi; he murdered his father and mother, and many other people; it seems to me probable, from the reports of other people, that his burial-mound is northward in Helluland's deserts[2].' Gest goes in quest of this mound, sails to Greenland's deserts, where, having traversed the lava-fields [!] for three days on foot, he at length discovers the burial-mound upon an island near the sea-coast; 'some men say that this mound was situated to the northward off Helluland, but wherever it was, there were no settlements in the neighbourhood[3].'

The brief extracts here quoted will suffice to indicate not only the fabulous character of the sagas in which they appear, but they serve further to show how completely the discoveries of Leif, and the explorations of Karlsefni had become distorted in the popular memory of the Icelanders at the time these tales were composed, which was probably in the thirteenth or fourteenth century[4]. The Helluland of these stories is an unknown region, relegated, in the popular superstition, to the trackless wastes of northern Greenland.

ried fyri hafs Botnum þeim er gánga af Risalande, i Lands-sudur,' l. c. p. 163. This text was probably drawn from Vatnshyrna; cf. Bárðar saga Snæfellsáss, ed. Vigfusson, p. 1, n. 1.

[1] The edition of the saga of 1756 has Ragnar; cf. the quotation from Hálfd. saga Eysteinssonar.

[2] 'Ekki hef ek sèt hann fyrr, en sagt hefir mèr verit af frændum mínum, at konúngr hefir heitið Rakin, ok af þeirri sögn þikkjumst ek kenna hann; hefir hann ráðit fyrir Hellulandi ok mörgum öðrum löndum, ok er hann hafði lengi ráðit lèt hann kviksetja sik með ccccc manna á Rakns1óða; hann myrði föður sinn ok móður, ok mart annat fólk; þikki mèr ván, at haugr hans muni vera norðarliga í Hellulands óbygðum at annarra manna frásögn.' Bárðar saga, ed. Vigfusson, pp. 38, 39.

[3] 'Segja sumir menn, at sjá haugr hafi staðit norðarliga fyrir Hellulandi, en hvar sem þat hefir verit, þá hafa þar engar bygðir í nánd verit.' Bárðar saga, loc. cit. p. 41.

[4] Cf. Maurer, Ueber die Ausdrücke, &c., p. 25; Vigfusson, Prolegomena, Sturlunga Saga, p. lxii.

CHAPTER VI.

THE PUBLICATION OF THE DISCOVERY.

THE earliest foreign mention of Wineland appears in the work of the prebendary, Adam of Bremen, called *Descriptio insularum aquilonis*[1]. The material for this work was obtained by its author during a sojourn at the court of the Danish king, Svend Estridsson, after the year 1069, and probably, very soon thereafter, for his history appears to have been completed before the year 1076, the date of king Svend's death[2]. The most important manuscript of Adam's longer work, the *Gesta Hammaburgensis ecclesiæ pontificum*, is the Codex Vindobonensis, deposited in the Imperial Library of Vienna under the number 413. This manuscript, written in the thirteenth century[3], contains also the complete 'description of the Northern islands,' which is partially lacking in the fine manuscript of the same century, contained in the Royal Library of Copenhagen. This 'description' was first printed[4] in Lindenbruch's edition of Adam's work, published in 1595[5], and is the first printed reference to Wineland, being as follows: 'Moreover he[6] spoke of an island in that ocean discovered by many, which is called Wineland, for the reason that vines grow wild there, which yield the best of wine. Moreover that grain unsown grows there abundantly, is not a fabulous fancy, but, from the accounts of the Danes, we know to be a fact. Beyond this island, it is said, that there is no habitable land in that ocean, but all those regions which are beyond are filled with insupportable ice and boundless gloom, to which Martian thus refers: "One day's sail beyond Thile the sea is frozen." This was essayed not long since by that very enterprising Northmen's prince, Harold[7], who explored the extent of the northern ocean with his ship, but was scarcely able by retreating to escape in

[1] Also called by editors 'De situ Daniæ;' cf. ed. Lindenbruch, 1595, Stephanius, 1629.

[2] Cf. Adami gesta Hammaburgensis ecclesiæ pontificum, ex recensione Lappenbergii, 2nd ed. Hanover, 1876, p. ii.

[3] Adami gesta Hammab. ed. 1876, p. vii.

[4] Idem, p. xiv.

[5] 'M. Adami Historia Ecclesiastica, . . . eivsdem avctoris libellvs de Sitv Daniæ,' . . . Cura ac labore Erpoldi Lindenbrvch, Lugd. Bat. 1595.

[6] Cf. preceding lines: 'Itaque rex Danorum cum multis aliis contestatus est,' &c.

[7] Probably King Harold Hardrede, who was slain in 1066.

safety from the gulf's enormous abyss [1], where before his eyes the vanishing bounds of earth were hidden in gloom [2].'

The learned cleric, it will be observed, is very careful to give his authority for a narrative, which evidently impressed him as bordering sharply upon the fabulous. The situation, which he would ascribe to the strange country is inaccurate enough, but the land where vines grow wild and grain self-sown, stripped of the historian's adornments, would accord sufficiently well with the accounts of the discoverers of Wineland to enable us to identify the country, if Adam had not himself given us the name of this land, and thus arrested all uncertainty [3]. It is not strange, however, that with the lapse of time the knowledge of such a land should have been erased from the recollection of the outer world. The author of the so-called 'Breve Chronicon Norvegiæ [4]' is, therefore, constrained to omit all reference to this wonderful land, although his reference to Greenland indicates an acquaintance with that tradition, which in Icelandic geographical notices, already cited, would ascribe Wineland to a more southerly clime, bordering indeed, upon Africa. The manuscript of this history, which has been preserved, belongs to the Earl of Dalhousie [5], and was probably written between the years 1443 and 1460 [6]. The passage mentioned, while it is not strictly pertinent, in a

[1] As to the possible significance of these words and the passage in AM. 194, 8vo, 'then there is an open sea flowing in between Wineland and Markland,' quoted page 15, ante, cf. Storm, 'Ginnungagap i Mythologien og i Geografien,' in Arkiv for nordisk Filologi, Lund, 1890, pp. 340–50.

[2] 'Praeterea unam adhuc insulam recitavit a multis in eo repertam occeano, quae dicitur Winland, eo quod ibi vites sponte nascantur, vinum optimum ferentes. Nam et fruges ibi non seminatas habundare, non fabulosa opinione, sed certa comperimus relatione Danorum. Post quam insulam, ait, terra non invenitur habitabilis in illo occeano, sed omnia quae ultra sunt glacie intolerabili ac caligine inmensa plena sunt. Cuius rei Marcianus ita meminit: "Ultra Thilen," inquiens, "navigatione unius diei mare concretum est." Temptavit hoc nuper experientissimus Nordmannorum princeps Haraldus. Qui latitudinem septentrionalis occeani perscrutatus navibus, tandem caligantibus ante ora deficientis mundi finibus, inmane abyssi baratrum retroactis vestigiis pene vix salvus evasit.' Ed. 1876, p. 187.

[3] As late as 1673 [1689?] Olof Rudbeck would seek to identify this 'Winland,' which Adam mentions, with Finland. 'Ne tamen poetis solis hoc loquendi genus in suis regionum laudationibus familiare fuisse quis existimet, sacras adeat literas quæ Palæstinæ fæcunditatem appellatione *fluentorum lactis & mellis* designant. Tale aliquid, sine omni dubio, Adamo Bremensi quondam persuaserat insulam esse in ultimo septentrione sitam, mari glaciali vicinam, vini feracem, & ea propter fide tamen Danorum, *Vinlandiam* dictam prout ipse in de situ Daniæ p. m. 37. fateri non dubitat. Sed deceptum eum hac sive Danorum fide, sive credulitate sua planum facit affine isti vocabulum *Finlandiæ* provinciæ ad Regnum nostrum pertinentis, pro quo apud Snorronem & in Hist. Regum non semel occurrit *Vinlandiæ* nomen, cujus promontorium ad ultimum septentrionem & usque ad mare glaciale sese extendit.' Ole Rudbeks, Atland eller Manheim, Upsala. n. d. [1689?], pp. 291, 292.

[4] First printed by Munch in Symbolæ ad Historiam Antiquiorem Rerum Norvegicarum, Christiania, 1850.

[5] Cf. Storm, Monumenta Historica Norvegiæ, Christiania, 1880, p. xvi.

[6] Idem, p. xvii; Munch, Symbolæ, p. ii.

measure indicates, perhaps, the information accessible at this period, to an author who must have been more or less acquainted with the current lore of the land in which the Wineland history was still preserved. Greenland, this author writes, 'which country was discovered and settled by the inhabitants of Thule [Telensibus], and strengthened by the Catholic faith, lies at the western boundary of Europe, almost bordering upon the African isles, where the overflowing sea spreads out[1].' No quickening evidence came from Iceland until long afterward, and those who saw Adam's Wineland recital, probably regarded it as the artless testimony of a too-credulous historian.

After the publication of Adam of Bremen's work, in 1595, the name of Wineland next recurs in print, in a poem written by the Danish clergyman, Claus Christoffersson Lyschander, called 'Den Grønlandske Chronica' [the Chronicle of Greenland], which was published in Copenhagen in 1608. Founded, apparently, upon the scantiest of historical material, which material was treated with the broadest of poetic licence, the Chronicle is devoid of historical value[2]. Lyschander seems to have derived from Icelandic Annals[3] the knowledge of Bishop Eric's Wineland voyage, and to have elaborated this entry, with the aid of his vivid imagination, into three lines of doggerel in somewhat the following manner:

And Eric of Greenland did the deed,
Planted in Wineland both folk and creed,
Which are there e'en now surviving[4].

A few years prior to this rhapsody of Lyschander's, the geographer Ortelius had ascribed to the Northmen the credit of the discovery of America. According to Alexander von Humboldt, Ortelius announced this opinion in 1570, and he cites Ortelius' work, 'Theatrum orbis terrarum,' in the edition of 1601[5]. The edition of 1584 of Ortelius' work does not so credit the discovery, but the English edition of

[1] 'Que patria a Telensibus reperta et inhabitata ac fide catholica roborata terminus est ad occasum Europe fere contingens affricanas insulas ubi inundant oceani refluenta.' Munch, Symbolæ, p. 2.

[2] Cf. Storm, Om Kilderne till Lyschanders Grønlandske Chronica,' in Aarb. f. Nord. Oldk. og Hist., 1888, pp. 197–218.

[3] Idem, pp. 210, 211.

[4] 'Oc Erich paa Grønland lagde haand oppaa
Plandtet paa Vjnland baade Folck oc Tro
Som er der endnu ved ljge.'

[5] 'Le mérite d'avoir reconnu la première découverte de l'Amérique continentale par les Normands, appartient indubitablement au géographe Ortelius, qui annonca cette opinion dès l'année 1570, presque encore du vivant de Barthélemi de Las Casas, le célèbre contemporaine de Colomb et de Cortez.' Alex. v. Humboldt, Examen critique de l'histoire de la géographie du Nouveau Continent, Paris, 1837, vol. ii, p. 120.

1606 does explicitly, and clearly sets forth upon what foundation the author rests his statement[1]. Ortelius does not seem to have had, and could not well have had at the time he wrote, any acquaintance with Icelandic records; his opinion, as he himself tells us, was based upon the marvellous relation of the voyages of the brothers Zeni, first published in 1558. It is not pertinent to dwell here upon the authenticity of the Zeni discoveries, and while it is true that Ortelius stated the fact, when he announced that the 'New World was entered upon many ages past by certain "islanders" of Greenland and Iceland,' he travelled to it by a circuitous route, and hit upon it, after all, by a happy chance.

The debased taste in Iceland, which followed the age when the greater sagas were committed to writing, found its gratification in the creation of fictitious tales, in recounting the exploits of foreign heroes, and for a time, the garnered wealth of their historical literature was disregarded or forgotten by the people of Iceland. With the revival of learning, which came in post-Reformation times, after a long period of comparative literary inactivity, came a reawakening of interest in the elder literature, and the Icelandic scholars of this era heralded abroad the great wealth of the discarded treasures which their ancestors had amassed.

The first writer in modern times to glean from Icelandic records, and to publish, as thus established, the discovery made by his countrymen, was Arngrim Jonsson [Arngrímr Jónsson], who was born in Iceland in 1568. His various historical works, published during his life-time, were written in Latin, and all, with the exception of the first edition of a single work, issued from presses on the Continent. His writings were, for the most part, devoted to the history of his fatherland and to its defence, but incidentally two of these, at least, refer to the Wineland discovery. The first of these works, 'Crymogœa, sive Rerum Islandicarum,' was published in Hamburg in 1610, 1614, 1630. The notice in this book refers to the discovery of 'New Land' in 1285, and Land-Rolf's expedition to Iceland [undertaken with a view to the exploration of this land], diverges into a consideration of the Frislanda of the Zeni narrative, which

[1] 'Iosephus Acosta in his booke *De Natura noui orbis* indeuors by many reasons to proue, that this part of *America* was originally inhabited by certaine Indians, forced thither by tempestuous weather ouer the South sea which now they call Mare del Zur. But to me it seemes more probable, out of the historie of the two *Zeni*, gentlemen of *Venice* [which I haue put down before the Fable of the South sea, and before that of Scandia] that this New World many ages past was entred vpon by some islanders of *Europe*, as namely of *Groenland*, *Island*, and *Frisland*; being much neerer thereunto than the Indians, nor disioyned thence [as appeares out of the Map] by an Ocean so huge, and to the Indians so vnnauigable. Also, what else may we coniecture to be signified by this *Norumbega* [the name of a North region of *America*] but that from *Norway*, signifying a North land, some Colonie in times past hath hither beene transplanted?' The Theatre of the Whole World: Set forth by that Excellent Geographer Abraham Ortelius, London, 1606, p. 5.

the author regards as Iceland, and concludes: 'In truth we believe the country which Land-Rolf sought to be Wineland, formerly so-called by the Icelanders, concerning which island of America, in the region of Greenland, perhaps the modern Estotelandia, elsewhere[1];' a statement chiefly interesting from the fact that it is the first printed theory as to the location of Wineland.

In a second book, written *ca.* 1635[2], but not published until 1643, Arngrim refers at some length to Karlsefni and his Wineland voyage[3], which information he states he draws from Hauk's history, and also makes mention of Bishop Eric's Wineland voyage, noting incidentally Adam of Bremen's reference to that country[4].

Arngrim died in 1648, leaving behind him an unprinted Latin manuscript, which was subsequently translated into Icelandic and published in Iceland under the title 'Gronlandia[5].' In this treatise he deals more minutely with the Wineland discovery, but it is probable that this book failed to obtain as wide a circulation among the scholars of Europe as his earlier works, and even though it had become well known, it was destined to be followed, a few years later, by a much more exhaustive work, which must have supplanted it.

Although the Icelandic discovery had now been published, the chief documents from which the knowledge of the discovery was drawn, remained for many years in Iceland, where they were practically inaccessible to the foreign student. Arngrim Jonsson was himself, probably, the first to set the example, which, actively followed after his death, soon placed the Icelandic manuscripts within comparatively easy reach of the students of the Continent[6]. We have already seen, incidentally, how certain of these codices were exported; it remained for the tireless bibliophile, Arni Magnusson, to complete the deportation of manuscripts from his fatherland, so that early in the eighteenth century all of the more important early vellums containing the Wineland narrations were lodged in the libraries of Copenhagen. The hugest of all these

[1] 'Terram veró Landa Rolfoni quæsitam existamarem esse Vinlandiam olim Islandis sic dictam; de qua alibi insulam nempe Americæ e regione Gronlandiæ, quæ fortè hodie Estotelandia,' &c. Crymogœa, p. 120.

[2] Vigfusson and Powell, Corp. Poet. Bor. vol. i. p. xx.

[3] Specimen de Islandiæ historicvm, et Magna ex parte Chorographicvm, Amsterdam, 1643, pp. 153, 154.

[4] Idem, p. 148.

[5] Gronlandia edur Grænlands Saga Vr Islendskum Sagna Bookum og Añalum samañtekin og á Latinski mál Skrifud af þeim heidurliga & hálærda Manni, Syra Arngrime Jonssine . . . Eñ a Norrænu utløgd af Einare Ejolfssjne. Þryckt i Skalhollte Af Hendrick Kruse, Anno, 1688.

[6] Arngrim presented a manuscript of Edda to the Danish scholar, Ole Worm, about 1628. It was, perhaps, the first Icelandic manuscript thus sent from Iceland. Cf. Vigfusson, Sturlunga Saga, Prolegomena, p. cxlv.

manuscripts, the Flatey Book, had been brought by the talented Icelander, Thormod Torfæus[1], from Iceland to Denmark, as a gift to King Frederick the Third.

In the year 1715 Torfæus published the first book devoted exclusively to the discovery of Wineland. In this little work the place of priority is assigned to the account of the discovery as unfolded in the Flatey Book[2]; this is followed by a compendium of the Saga of Eric the Red [Thorfinns Saga], with which the author seems to have become acquainted through a transcript of the Hauk's Book Saga, made by Biorn of Skardsá [Björn á Skarðsá][3]. The interest which Torfæus' little book elicited was of such a character that the general dissemination of the knowledge of the discovery may almost be said to date from its appearance; the publication of the texts of the sagas upon which Torfæus' book was based was not accomplished, however, until the present century.

In 1837 the sumptuous work entitled 'Antiquitates Americanæ[4]' was published by the Royal Society of Northern Antiquaries of Copenhagen. The book was edited by Carl Christian Rafn, with whom were associated Finn Magnusen and Sveinbiörn Egilsson; the associate editors, however, especially the last-named, seem to have shared to a very limited extent in the preparation of the work; all were scholarly men, well versed in the literature of Iceland. This book was by far the most elaborate which had been published up to that time upon the subject of the Icelandic discovery of America, and in it the texts of the sagas relating to the discovery were first printed, and with these the lesser references bearing upon the discovery, which were scattered through other Icelandic writings. Side by side with the Icelandic texts, Latin and Danish versions of these texts were presented, and along with these the interpretations and theories of the gifted editor, Rafn. The book obtained a wide circulation, and upon it have been based almost all of the numerous treatises upon the same subject, which have since appeared. Rafn's theories touching the Old Stone Tower at Newport, R. I., and the Dighton Picture Rock near Taunton, Mass., have latterly fallen into disfavour, but others of his errors, less palpable than these, if we may judge by

[1] Þormóðr Torfason was born in Iceland in 1636, and died at his home in Norway in 1719. Cf. Worm, Lexicon.

[2] Justin Winsor states, in his Narrative and Critical History of America [vol. i. note 1, pp. 91, 92], that, 'the Codex Flatoyensis . . . seems to have been unknown to Torfæus.' A mistake rendered the more inexplicable by the fact that the learned editor reproduces a page of Torfæus' 'Vinlandia,' the contents of which work so clearly confute this statement.

[3] Cf. Torfæus, Historia Vinlandiæ Antiquæ, p. 29.

[4] Antiquitates Americanæ, sive Scriptores rerum Ante-Columbianarum in America. Samling af de Nordens Oldskrifter indeholdte Efterretninger om de gamle Nordboers Opdagelsesreiser til America fra det 10de til det 14de Aarhundrede. Edidit Societas Regia Antiquarior. Septentrionalium, Copenh. 1837.

recent publications, still exercise potent sway. While the editor of the 'Antiquitates Americanæ' deserves great praise for having been the first to publish to the world the original records, he has seriously qualified the credit to which he is entitled by the extravagant theories and hazardous statements to which he gave currency, and which have prejudiced many readers against the credibility of the records themselves.

Since the publication of the 'Antiquitates Americanæ' the most important and original treatise upon the Wineland discovery which has appeared, is that recently published by Dr. Gustav Storm, Professor of History in the University of Christiania, entitled, 'Studies relating to the Wineland voyages, Wineland's Geography and Ethnography[1].' These 'Studies' appear to have been the natural sequence of an article upon the vexed question, affecting the site of Wineland, to which reference has already been made[2]. Professor Storm's method of treatment is altogether different from that of Rafn; it is philosophical, logical, and apparently entirely uninfluenced by preconceived theories, being based strictly upon the records. These records of the Icelandic discovery have now been presented here. They clearly establish the fact that some portion of the eastern coast of North America was visited by people of Iceland and the Icelandic colony in Greenland early in the eleventh century. In matters of detail, however, the history of the discovery leaves wide the door to conjecture as to the actual site of Wineland. It was apparently not north of the latitude of northern Newfoundland; present climatic conditions indicate that it was situated somewhat south of this latitude, but how far south the records do not show.

[1] 'Studier over Vinlandsreiserne, Vinlands Geografi og Ethnografi,' in Aarb. f. Nord. Oldk. og Hist., Copenh. 1887, pp. 293-372.

[2] Cf. ante, p. 6.

CHAPTER VII.

The Icelandic Texts.

The following texts of the leading sagas, relating to the discovery of Wineland, have been edited to conform, line by line, with the manuscripts, but with normalized orthography, since the reproduction of the manuscripts in type would have no especial significance where the facsimiles of the vellums are themselves given. The chief difficulty which the reading of these manuscripts offers to the unpractised reader is that of supplying the numerous contractions. This is a difficulty which they share with all other Icelandic manuscripts, but, except in a very slight measure, it is not complicated by the real crux, which many Icelandic vellums offer, in their faded writing or blackened parchment; and the phototypic reproductions are therefore, except in portions of two of the pages of Hauk's Book, substantially as legible as the originals.

Although there are many paper copies of the so-called Þorfinns saga karlsefnis of Hauk's Book, and of Eiríks saga rauða of AM. 557, 4to (74), they are based upon the vellum manuscripts of these sagas here given in facsimile, and it has not, therefore, been deemed necessary to record the variants which they contain, or to make especial note of their readings, except in cases where the vellum manuscripts are now indistinct. Certain paper manuscripts, notably AM. 281, 4to, 770 *b*, 4to, and 118, 8vo, appear to have derived their texts of Þorfinns saga karlsefnis from Hauk's Book, when the two pages 100 *b* and 101 were in better state than they now are, and these have been of great assistance in the preparation of the printed text[1]; in the few minor instances in which the vellum originals are not clearly to be read, the words of the paper manuscripts are given.

If it be remembered that *i* and *j*, *i* and *y*, *u* and *v*, are used in these manuscripts more or less interchangeably, the unskilled reader should have little difficulty in following the facsimiles of these sagas and comparing these with the normalized texts.

[1] In editing the text of these two pages of Hauk's Book I have been very materially aided by Dr. Valtýr Guðmundsson. Portions of these pages would be well-nigh undecipherable in the original manuscript, without the help afforded by the paper manuscripts, but these indistinct portions are very inconsiderable.

THE HAUK'S BOOK TEXT.

The first scribe of Þorfinns saga karlsefnis, as the Hauk's Book text of the Saga of Eric the Red has been called, has been known as Hauk's 'first Icelandic secretary.' He is, perhaps, chiefly distinguished from his collaborators, particularly from Hauk himself, by the variety of forms which he employs, many of which are, doubtless, due to carelessness. He generally writes both *æ* and *æ*, *ę*, but frequently simply *e*. He uses *v* for the most part for both *u* and *v*, but in a few instances reverses this usage and employs *u* in the dual capacity. He distinguishes between *ð* and *þ*, and occasionally between *ð* and *d*, although he generally writes *d* for both *ð* and *d*, in one instance, however, writing the same word upon the same page with both *ð* and *d*, as on p. 93, *Auð*, *Aud*. He writes both *fyrsta* and *fysta*, *fyri* and *firi*, *cristni* [p. 97, l. 3] and *kristni* [p. 97, l. 11], *Vivils* and *Vifvils*, and once, apparently a slip, *emeirr* [*emeiR*] for *meirr*. Many words are written with a single instead of a double consonant, as *þoka* for *þokka*, *knor* for *knǫrr*, *Snori* for *Snorri*, *skapstor* for *skapstórr*, many verbs, on the other hand, are written with double in place of single *l*, as *giallda* [*gjalda*], *villdi* [*vildi*]. He writes the genitive [in *s*] for the most part with *s*, frequently with double *s*, as *Kelliss*, *Einarss*, the leading exception being in the case of proper names, as *Íslandz*, *Grœnlandz*, *Asvalldz*, *Þorbrandz*, although he also writes [p. 98, l. 12] *til moz* [*til móts*], and [p. 93 *b*, l. 32] *landz* [*lands*.] He writes *fodr* for *fǫður*, *broðr* for *bróður*, *besti* for *bezti*, *semiligaz* for *sæmiligast*. The prepositions *í* and *á* he usually connects with the succeeding noun, writing both preposition and noun as one word, as *iskogi* [*í skógi*], *avaldiofs st*[*ǫðum*] [*á Valþjófs stǫðum*]. He uses for his negative prefix *o* [*ó*] almost exclusively, although he writes [p. 99, l. 3] *vgledi* [*úgleði*], and for the feminine pronoun he employs the form *hvn*, *hun* [*hon*], and writes *gera* [*gera*, *gøra*], *voro* [*váru*]. He writes his reflexive forms only with a *z*, as *bordnz* [*bǫrðusk*], *gerdiz* [*gerðisk*], *kvez* [*kvezk*]. The forms which he uses seem to indicate clearly, however, that the scribe was, indeed, an Icelander, for they belong to Icelandic, not to Norse, paleography. A single expression, however, which he employs, acquires a certain noteworthiness when contrasted with the language of the scribe of Eiríks saga rauða. This 'first Icelandic secretary' writes [p. 94, ll. 30–1] *Einarr var á Íslandi*, while the scribe of AM. 557, 4to, has [p. 28, l. 28] *Einarr var út hér*. The first expression would ordinarily have no significance whatever in determining where the 'Icelandic secretary' was writing, and in all likelihood has none here. If, however, the secretary had written *út hér* ['out here'] as the scribe of EsR has, instead of *á Íslandi* ['in Iceland'], we should be better warranted in concluding that his work was done in Iceland.

Hauk, who follows the 'first Icelandic secretary,' if he wrote in Iceland, wrote with one of the peculiarities to be found in Norse vellums, the uniform omission of *h* before the sibilant *l* in such words as *lioðlyndr* [*hljóðlyndr*], *lutaðir* [*hlutaðir*], *laupa* [*hlaupa*]. He, unlike any of the other scribes of these manuscripts [except the second secretary, as noted below], distinguishes between *æ* and *œ*, and usually discriminates these correctly, although he writes [p. 99 *b*, l. 16] *bœði* for *bæði*. Hauk distinguishes between *d* and *ð*, and between *ð* and *þ*, but writes *siþan* [*síðan*], and *hefþi* [*hefði*]. He uses *v* for both *u* and *v* throughout his work, and again, in contrast with the first scribe, writes *en* in place of *enn*. He writes *ck* instead of *kk*, as *ecki* for *ekki*, *ockr* for *okkr*, *nockot* (*nǫkkut*), and also *qvað* for *kvað*. He writes *iamnan* for *jafnan*, and substitutes *f* for *p* in such words as *aptr*, *lopt*, *knept*; he writes *sun* for *son*, and not only many verbs with double *ll*, but such words as *helldr*, *sialldan*. He uses the same reflexive terminations as the first writer.

The third scribe of Þorfinns saga karlsefnis is Hauk's so-called 'second Icelandic secretary.' If this secretary was, indeed, an Icelander, he must have been brought under strong Norwegian influence, for he employs throughout such Norse forms as *vurdu* [*urðu*], *rid* [*hrið*], *liop* [*hljóp*] and *huggj* [*hjó*]. He writes, for the most part, both *æ* and *œ* with *e*, although he also writes *nðr* [*nœr*], and *einfðtingr* [*Einfœtingr*]; while discriminating between *þ* and *ð*, as in the normalized orthography, he writes both *ð* and *d* with *d*. He differs from Hauk in using both *u* and *v*, and from both Hauk and the first secretary in writing *haar* [*hár*], *saad* [*sáð*, *sáit*], and also in writing *sealf* [*sjálf*], *sea* [*sjá*]. For *eigi* he writes both *eige* and *eighe*; *medr* for *með*, *vidr* for *við*, *iammykit* for *jafnmikit*, *iamlangt* for *jafnlangt*. He has *hafdu* for *hǫfðu*, *bamadu* for *bǫnnuðu*, and writes his reflexive verbal forms as Hauk and the first secretary, as *komaz* [*komask*], *byz* [*býsk*], but also *fundust* [*fundusk*], *biuggust* [*bjoggusk*], and parallel with Hauk's *lutaðu* [*hlutuðu*], he writes *skemtadu* [*skemtuðu*]. No one of the three scribes uses accents, and the *ǫ* of the printed texts, except in the verbal forms above noted, is generally written *o*, although occasionally *au*.

The AM. 557, 4to Text.

The peculiarities of the text of the Saga Eireks rauda, as it is called in the Codex, AM. 557, 4to; many of them point to a later date for this text than that of either Hauk's Book or the Flatey Book, for we find here such forms as *giora* [*gøra*], *sied* [*séð*], *þier* [*þér*], *hier* [*hér*], *hiellt* [*helt*], and also other forms indicating the modern pronunciation, as *eirn* [*einn*], *iall* [*jarl*], Þ*osteirn* [Þ*orsteinn*]. The scribe does not discriminate between *u* and *v*, nor between *ð* and *d*, writing *d* throughout, although he employs *þ* as in the normalized orthography. He writes both *æ* and *œ* with *æ*; and *ǫ*, while frequently written simply *o*, is occasionally also written *au*, as *maurg* [*mǫrg*], *baurn* [*bǫrn*], *laund* [*lǫnd*], &c. He writes *á* both 'ꜳ' and *a*, *q* is writtenin *qvat* [*kvað*], *ck* for *kk*, as *þickia* [*þykkja*], *ecki* [*ekki*], *ockr* [*okkr*]. *Fysta* is written for *fyrsta*; *dreing* for *dreng*, and similarly *leingi* for *lengi*, *geingr* for *gengr*, *þveingi* for *þvengi*; *hafva* is written for *hafa*, *kvonnu* for *kvánnu* [*könnu*], and while *i* is usually employed as in the normalized texts, the scribe also writes *Eireckr*, *saker*, *epter*. He writes many proper names as *Styrr*, *Einarr*, *Þorgeirr* in the nominative with a single final *r*, and occasionally omits the second *r* in other words; *fǫður* is written both *fedr* and *faudr*, *bróður* is written *brodr*, and the omission of the *u* in such inflected forms, and in the nominative plural of certain nouns is very common. He generally writes the genitive form [in *s*] with *s*, although occasionally with *z*, as *Ingiallz* [*Ingjalds*], *agætz manz* [*ágæts manns*], *lambskinz* [*lambskinns*]; he also writes *leingzt* [*lengst*], *sæmiligazt* [*sæmiligast*], *likazt* [*likast*]. He generally writes *hun* [*hon*] while his contraction indicates *hon*, but he also writes *haun* [*hon*], and *haunum* [*honum*]. He uses throughout the same reflexive forms [except in one instance *skyzz* for *skýzk*], writing *giordizt* [*gørðisk*], *lituduzt* [*lituðusk*], *kvezt* [*kvezk*], &c. Finally, as has already been suggested, the errors, verbal and textual, of which there are many scattered through the saga, seem to point pretty clearly to the faults of a copyist, working, perhaps, from a somewhat illegible original.

THE FLATEY BOOK TEXT.

In the reproduction of the original manuscript of this version of the history it has been found necessary, in order to preserve the text in its actual size, and at the same time have this conform in size to the page of the quarto manuscripts, to divide each column of the Flatey Book text into two parts, and as there are two columns to each page of this folio manuscript, each page of this phototypic reproduction represents one-fourth of the page of the original. The first portion of the narrative, Eiriks þáttr rauða, begins with the second line from the bottom of col. 221 of the Flatey Book, and ends in col. 223, twenty lines from the bottom, with the words '*meðan Herjólfr lifði, ok siðan bjó haun þar eptir fǫður sinn.*' The second part of the narrative, Grœnlendinga þáttr, begins in col. 281, fifteen lines from the bottom of the page, and is brought to a conclusion in col. 288, in the twenty-sixth line from the top of the page. The hand, which is the same throughout, is that of John Thordsson. In the photographic reproduction of the manuscript it has, of course, been impossible to preserve the colours of the illuminated initials, which are inserted in the original in red and green and blue; the sub-titles, which, like those of Hauk's Book, are written in red, have, like the Hauk's Book titles, been printed in bolder type.

Contrasted with the other texts, the most marked peculiarity of this scribe is, perhaps, the use of *æ* for *e*, for which, with very few exceptions, it is uniformly written at the beginning of words, as *ægi* [*eigi*], *æinn* [*einn*], *Æireckr* [*Eirikr*], and very frequently, though not so constantly, in the body of such words as *mæira* [*meira*], *ræida* [*reiða*], *læitan* [*leitan*], *Læifr* [*Leifr*]. This *æ* of the scribe, which has more the appearance of *æ* than that of his co-worker Magnus, is used generally for both *æ* and *ę*, although *ę* is occasionally similarly used, there being no discrimination between *æ* and *æ*; *ǫ* is generally written *ó*, but occasionally also *au*, and yet again simply *o*; *á* is in a few instances written 'æ'; *j* is uniformly used for the preposition *í*, as is generally the case in the other manuscripts, and accented *í* is occasionally written *ij*, as *vijda* [*víða*], *Vijnland* [*Vínland*]; *e* is almost constantly used in the place of *i* at the end of words, and sometimes elsewhere, as *aller* [*allir*]; *e* is occasionally written for *j*, as in *fear* [*fjár*], *sea* [*sjá*]; *u* and *v* are used interchangeably; *d* is written throughout for both *ð* and *d*; *þ* is written normally, although in the initial at the beginning of Eiríks þáttr we find *Ðorualldr* [*Þorvaldr*]; *n* and *l* are frequently reduplicated in such words as *nafnn* [*nafn*], *Biarnne* [*Bjarni*]. The double forms *mig* and *mik*, *eftir* and *eptir* occur, although the usual forms are *mig*, *sig* [*mik*, *sik*] and *eftir*, *aftr* [*eptir*, *aptr*]. *Fyrst* is written *fyst*, the forms *id* [*it*], *ad* [*at*] occur, as also *ath* [*at*], *audith* [*auðit*], *voth* [*vát*], *vær* [*vér*], *kallar* [*karlar*], &c. *Síðast* is written *sidazst*, as are other similar forms, and reflexive forms are written with the same termination, as *fystizst* [*fýstisk*], *kuetzst* [*kvezk*]. The genitive [in *s*] is usually written with *s*, although the forms *Íslandz*, as also *lanz*, *Branz* occur; *q* is, for the most part, substituted for *k* in *kveða* and its inflected forms. In this manuscript, as in Hauk's Book, and AM. 557, 4to, *með* is almost always written with the contracted equivalent, and so also is *ok* (and) with a sign corresponding to our symbol (&).

The facsimiles are throughout exact reproductions of the manuscripts, so far as it is possible to reproduce these by photographic process.

[HAUKSBÓK, p. 93.] ÞORFINNS SAGA KARLSEFNIS—I.

Hér hefr upp sǫgu þeira Þor-
finns karlsefnis ok Snorra Þorbrandssonar.
17. Óláfr hét herkonungr, er kallaðr, var Óláfr[1] hvíti,
18. hann var son Ingjakls konungs Helgasonar, Óláfssonar, Guðrǿðarsonar[2], Hálfdanar-
19. sonar hvítbeins Upplendinga konungs. Óláfr herjaði í vestrvíking, ok vann
20. Dyflinni á Írlandi, ok Dyflinnarsker[3]. Þar gerðisk hann konungr yfir. Hann fekk
21. Auðar djúpúðgu, dóttur Ketils flatnefs, Bjarnarsonar bunu, ágæts manns ór Noregi;
22. Þorsteinn rauðr hét son þeira. Óláfr fell á Írlandi í orrostu, en Auðr ok Þorsteinn fóru þá í Suðr-
23. eyjar; þar fekk Þorsteinn Þuríðar[4], dóttur Eyvindar austmanns, systur Helga hins ma-
24. gra; þau áttu mǫrg bǫrn. Þorsteinn gerðisk herkonungr. Hann rézk til lags með
25. Sigurði jarli hinum ríka, syni Eysteins glumru; þeir unnu Katanes ok Suðr-
26. land, Ros ok Merævi, ok meirr en hálft Skotland. Gerðisk Þorsteinn þar konungr yfir,
27. áðr Skotar sviku hann, ok fell hann þar í orrostu. Auðr var þá á Katanesi, er hon
28. spurði fall Þorsteins; hon lét þá gǿra knǫrr í skógi á laun, ok er hon var búin, helt
29. hon út í Orkneyjar; þar gipti hon Gró, dóttur Þorsteins rauðs; hon var móðir Grela-
30. ðar[5], er Þorfinnr jarl hausakljúfr átti. Eptir þat fór Auðr at leita Íslands;
31. hon hafði á skipi xx karla frjálsa. Auðr kom til Íslands, ok var hinn fyrsta

[1] MS. oloafr. [2] MS. gudredarsonar. [3] i.e. Dyflinnarskíri. [4] MS. þoridar.
[5] Laxdæla Saga has Greiladar; cf. Laxdæla Saga, ed. Kålund, Copenh. 1889, p. 8.

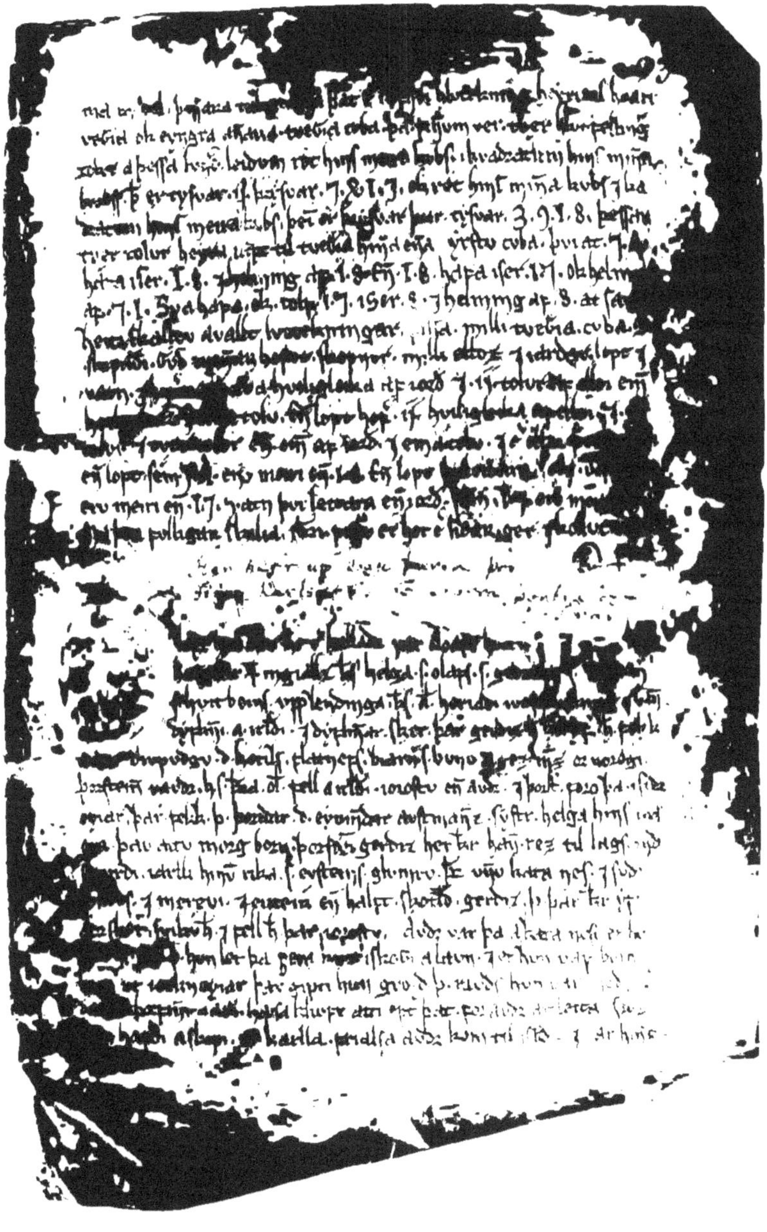

verþ i bratrí hof[illegible] [illegible] [illegible] hon vá [illegible] nefn [illegible]
[illegible] milli dogurdar ár. ok lækiar [illegible] hlaupr ok hoggvo [illegible]
bena [illegible] i kross holu þar let hon reisa kross [illegible]
skird. ok vel trvud med [illegible] hon ut margt goþra manna [illegible] [illegible]
verit i vestr viking. ok vero kallad ansaudir. einar [illegible]
var ærstor madr. ok hafdi [illegible] fyrir vestan haf [illegible]
suiudigr [illegible] aude [illegible] ok er audr gaf bustadi [illegible] [illegible]
þa spurdi vifill hui audr gefi hanum aungan bustad. sem [illegible] [illegible]
[illegible] lunda [illegible] eingu [illegible] skaptar [illegible] þar [illegible] [illegible]
sem [illegible] hon gaf hanum vifils [illegible] þar [illegible] þa [illegible]
Þa [illegible] voro [illegible] ok þorgeir [illegible] [illegible] ok [illegible]
[illegible] het madr [illegible] [illegible] [illegible]
[illegible] asvaldr [illegible] [illegible] [illegible] [illegible]
[illegible] til islandz fyrir vigsakir. ok nam [illegible] [illegible]
[illegible] þar andadiz þorvalldr. en eirikr [illegible] þorhallo
[illegible] [illegible] ok þorbiargar [illegible] [illegible] þa atti [illegible] [illegible]
ok bio a eiriksstodum [illegible] [illegible] [illegible] þar [illegible]
þa [illegible] eiriks [illegible] [illegible] [illegible] [illegible]
[illegible] [illegible] [illegible] [illegible] [illegible]
[illegible] [illegible] [illegible] ok holmgongo [illegible] [illegible] [illegible] [illegible]
[illegible] [illegible] eiriks [illegible] [illegible] [illegible] þa var eirikr [illegible]
[illegible] nam þa [illegible] ok [illegible] ok bio at [illegible] [illegible] en [illegible]
þa [illegible] þorgesti setstokka sina [illegible] ok bio a eiriks
[illegible] heimti þa setstokkana [illegible] eiriks [illegible] þa setstok
[illegible] a bolstad en þorgestr [illegible] [illegible]
[illegible] [illegible] [illegible] [illegible] synir þorgests ok nokkur
[illegible] [illegible] [illegible] [illegible] [illegible]
ok eyiolfr [illegible] [illegible] [illegible] [illegible] [illegible]
[illegible] synir þorbrandz [illegible] [illegible]
[illegible] synir þordar gellis ok þorgeirr [illegible] [illegible]
[illegible] [illegible] eirikr [illegible] [illegible] [illegible] [illegible] [illegible]
[illegible] en eyiolfr [illegible] [illegible] [illegible] menn þorgestz
[illegible] [illegible] [illegible] [illegible] [illegible]
[illegible] [illegible] [illegible] vestr um haf [illegible]
[illegible] [illegible] hann [illegible] [illegible] leita til vina sinna ef [illegible]

[HAUKSBÓK, p. 93 *b*.] ÞORFINNS SAGA KARLSEFNIS—2.

vetr í Bjarnarhǫfn með Birni, bróður sínum. Síðan nam Auðr ǫll Dalalǫnd milli Dǫgurðarár ok Skrámuhlaupsár[1]. Hon bjó í Hvammi. Hon hafði bœnahald[2] í Krosshólum; þar lét hon reisa krossa, því at hon var skírð ok vel trúuð. Með henni kómu út margir gǫfgir menn, þeir er herteknir hǫfðu verit í vestrvíking, ok váru kallaðir ánauðgir. Einn af þeim hét Vífill; hann var ættstórr maðr, ok hafði verit hertekinn fyri vestan haf, ok var kallaðr ánauðigr áðr Auðr[3] leysti hann; ok er Auðr gaf bústaði skipverjum sínum, þá spurði Vífill hví Auðr gæfi honum øngan bústað, sem ǫðrum mǫnnum. Auðr kvað þat engu[4] mundu skipta, kallaði hann þar gǫfgan mundu þikkja, sem hann var. Hon gaf honum Vífilsdal, ok bjó hann þar. Hann átti konu, er hét þeira synir váru þeir Þorbjǫrn ok Þorgeirr. Þeir váru efniligir menn, ok óxu upp Þorvaldr hét maðr; hann var son **Eiríkr rauði fann Grœnland.** með fǫður sínum. Ásvalds Úlfssonar, Øxna-Þórissonar[5]. Eiríkr hét son hans. Þeir feðgar fóru af Jaðri til Íslands, fyri vígа sakir, ok námu land á Hornstrǫndum, ok bjoggu at Drǫngum. Þar andaðisk Þorvaldr; en Eiríkr fekk þá Þórhildar, dóttur Jǫrundar Atlasonar ok Þorbjargar knarrarbringu, er þá átti Þorbjǫrn hinn haukdœlski, ok bjó á Eiríksstǫðum síðan, er Eiríkr rézk norðan; þat er hjá Vatnshorni. Þá feldu þrælar Eiríks skriðu á bœ Valþjófs á Valþjófsstǫðum[6]. Eyjólfr saurr, frændi hans, drap þrælana hjá Skeiðsbrekkum, upp frá Vatnshorni. Fyri þat vá Eiríkr Eyjólf saur; hann vá ok Hólmgǫngu-Hrafn at Leikskálum[7]. Geirsteinn ok Oddr á Jǫrva, frændr Eyjólfs, vildu eptir hann mæla; þá var Eiríkr gerr brott ór[8] Haukadal. Hann nam þá Brokey ok Øxney, ok[9] bjó at Trǫðum í Suðrey enn fyrsta vetr. Þá léði hann Þorgesti setstokka. Síðan fór Eiríkr í Øxney, ok bjó á Eiríksstǫðum. Hann heimti þá setstokkana, ok náði eigi. Eiríkr sótti þá setstokkana á Breiðabólstað, en Þorgestr fór eptir honum. Þeir bǫrðusk skamt frá[10] garði at Drǫngum. Þar fellu II synir Þorgests ok nǫkkurir menn aðrir. Eptir þat hǫfðu hvárirtveggju setu fjǫlmenna. Styrr veitti Eiríki, ok Eyjólfr ór Svíney, Þorbjǫrn Vífilsson[11] ok synir Þorbrands í Álptafirði. En Þorgesti veittu synir Þórðar gellis, ok Þorgeirr ór Hítardal, Áslákr ór Langadal ok Illugi, son hans. Þeir Eiríkr urðu sekir á Þórsnessþingi. Hann bjó skip í Eiríksvági, en Eyjólfr leyndi honum í Dímunarvági, meðan þeir Þorgestr leituðu hans um eyjarnar. Hann sagði þeim, at hann ætlaði at leita lands þess, er Gunnbjǫrn, son Úlfs kráku, sá, er hann rak vestr um haf, ok hann fann Gunnbjarnarsker. Hann kvezk aptr mundu leita til vina sinna, ef hann

1 MS. skravmv hlavps ar.
2 MS. bena halld.
3 Auðr repeated in MS.
4 MS. eyngv.
5 MS. yxna þoriss *sonar*.
6 MS. valdiofs avaldiofs stǫð*um*.
7 MS. leikslalum.
8 MS. o.
9 MS. i.
10 skamt fra repeated in MS.
11 MS. vivils *son*.

[HAUKSBÓK, p. 94.] ÞORFINNS SAGA KARLSEFNIS—3.

fyndi landit. Þeir Þorbjǫrn ok Eyjólfr ok Styrr fylgðu Eiríki út um eyjarnar. Skilðusk þeir með hinni mestu vináttu. Kvezk Eiríkr þeim skyldu verða at þvílíku trausti, ef hann mætti sér við koma, ok kynni þeir hans at þurfa. Sigldi Eiríkr á haf undan Snjófellsjǫkli; hann kom utan at jǫkli þeim, er heitir Bláserkr. Fór hann þaðan suðr, at leita ef þar væri byggjanda. Hann var hinn fyrsta vetr í Eiríksey, nær miðri hinni vestri bygð. Um várit eptir fór hann til Eiríksfjarðar, ok tók sér þar bústað. Hann fór þat sumar í vestri óbygð, ok var þar lengi. Hann gaf þar víða ørnefni. Hann var annan vetr í Eiríkshólmum fyri Hvarfsgnúpi. En hit þriðja sumar fór hann allt norðr til Snjófells, ok inn í Hrafnsfjǫrð. Þá kvezk hann kominn fyri botn Eiríksfjarðar; hverfr hann þá aptr, ok var hinn þriðja vetr í Eiríksey fyri mynni Eiríksfjarðar. En eptir, um sumarit, fór hann til Íslands, ok kom í Breiðafjǫrð. Hann var þann vetr með Ingólfi á Hólmlátri. Um várit bǫrðusk þeir Þorgestr, ok fekk Eiríkr úsigr. Eptir þat váru þeir sættir. Þat sumar fór Eiríkr at byggja land þat, sem hann hafði fundit, ok kallaði Grœnland, því at hann kvað menn þat mjǫk mundu fýsa þangat, ef landit héti vel. **Af Þorbirni.** Þorgeirr Vífilsson[1] kvángaðisk, ok fekk Arnóru, dóttur Einars frá Laugarbrekku, Sigmundarsonar, Ketilssonar þistils, er numit hafði Þistilsfjǫrð. Ǫnnur dóttir Eiríks[2] hét Hallveig; hennar fekk Þorbjǫrn, ok tók með Laugarbrekkuland á Hellisvǫllum. Rézk Þorbjǫrn þangat bygðum, ok gerðisk gǫfugmenni mikit. Hann var góðr bóndi, ok hafði rausnar ráð. Guðríðr hét dóttir Þorbjarnar; hon var kvenna vænst ok hinn mesti skǫrungr í ǫllu athæfi sínu. Maðr hét Ormr, er bjó at Arnastapa; hann átti konu, er Halldís hét. Ormr var góðr bóndi, ok vinr Þorbjarnar mikill, ok var Guðríðr þar lǫngum at fóstri með honum. Þorgeirr hét maðr; hann bjó at Þorgeirsfelli. Hann var auðigr at fé, ok hafði verit leysingi; hann átti son, er Einarr hét; hann var vænn maðr, ok vel mannaðr, hann var ok skartsmaðr mikill. Einarr var í siglingum meðal landa, ok tóksk honum þat vel; var hann jafnan sinn vetr hvárt á Íslandi eða í Noregi. Nú er frá því at segja eitt haust, þá er Einarr var á Íslandi, fór hann með varning sinn út eptir Snjófellsstrǫnd, ok vildi selja. Hann kemr til Arnastapa; Ormr býðr honum þar at vera, ok þat þiggr Einarr, því at þar var vinátta. Var borinn inn varningr hans í eitt útibúr. Einarr braut upp varning sinn, ok sýndi Ormi

[1] MS. vífvils *son*.

[2] Obviously erroneously for, Einars.

fyrdi landit. fr þorbr. eyrbygr. ok styrr. fylgdu eiriki vt um eyiar
... thildr ... med honum mestu vinattu huers. eirikr þeir skylldu
... at þau ... eirikr. en h. mettr sem uid konu ...
... at þurfa. sigldi eirikr ehaf undan snęfellz iokli han ko
... at iokli þeir er h. blaserkr fór h þadan sudr at leita ef
... vęri byggiandi. h var hinn fyrsta vetr ... ey ... ui
... hinni vestri bygd um uarit eptir fór h til eiriks f. ok tok sér
... h for þat sumar vestr i obygd. ok uar þar longum ok gaf
þar uida ornefni. h var annan vetr i eiriks holmum fyri hvarfs
gnupi. en hit þridia sumar fór h allt nordr til snęfellz ok inn i
hrafns f. þa ... h komin fyri botn eiriks f. hvarf h þa aptr
ok uar hinn þridia vetr i eiriks ey fyri mynni eiriks f. en eptir
um sumarit fór h til islandz ok kom i breida. f. h. v þann vetr med
ingolfi a holmlatri. um varit borduzt þr þorgestr ok fekk
eirikr v sigr. eptir þ voro þr sętt. þat sumar fór eirikr at byggia
land. þ sem h hapdi fundit ok kalladi grœnland. þui at h kuad men þ
miok mundu fysa þangat ef landit hefdi nafn gott.

Þorgeirr vifils. s. kuangadiz ok fekk arnoru d. einars fra
laugar brekku. sigmundar. s. ketils. s. þistils. er þistil hapdi þist
ils. f. ... d. eir. h. hallveig hon fekk þorb. ok tok med land
brekku ... a hellis vollu. rez þorb. þangat byggdu ok gerdiz
gofugmenni mikit. h v godr bondi ok hapdi rausnar rad. Gudr
idr. h. d. þorb. hon v kuenna uęnst ok hinn mesti skorungr i ollu
at hepa sinu. Madr. h. ormr e bio at arnarstapa h atti konu
er halldors. h. ormr v godr bondi ok vinr þorb. mikill. ok v gudridr
þar longum at fostri med hinn. þorgeirr. h m. h bio at þorgeirs fell.
hann v audigr at fe ok hapdi vit leysingi. h atti. s. e ein. h. hvar
venn madr ok vel mannadr h v ok skart m mikill. einar var i sig
lingum medal landa ok tokz hm þat vel v h iafnan sinn vetr hvart
a islandi eda a i noreg. nu er fra þui at segia eitt haust ... e.
var a islandi fór h med var ning sinn vt eptir snęfell ... ...
di selia. h kemr til arnarstapa ormr budr hm þar ...
þar bitr. en. ... þar var vinatta var ...
... einar ... bar upp vdi ... ...

ok heita vin ok bad hann at at hefia slikt e h vildi eigi þat þa
ok tala en var godan fardin ok audru mann mikinn en er þa
hellu a varningiunu gekk kona fyri utburi dyrin ein s. eini
hver er su hin fagra kona er þar gekk fyri dyrnar ok hefi ek
hana h fyrr set. O. s. þ er gudridr fostr min d. þorb' [illegible]
E in mun hon mun vera kostr godr. eda hefir nokkurr m til
bedit at biðia hennar. O. s. bedit hefr hen vist ver ok liggr þ ei laust
fyrir. finnr þ a at hun mun vera mannvond ok sva f. hen. sva
med þvi. sagdi ein at her er su kona er ek etla m biðia ok vill
da ek at þessa mala leitadir þu vid þorb' fodr hennar ok legdir
allan hug a at flytia metti fram gengit vida sk ek þ fullkomna
vinattu fyri giallda. ef ek get radit. ma þorb' bondi þ [illegible]
at ekki er vel hendar tengdir þui at h er sæmda madr mikill
ok a stadfestu goda en lausa fe h er mer sagt hellzt a þrot
en mik skortir huarki til ne lausa fe ok ekki fedga ok mundi þat
vel at þessu hinn mesti styrkr. ef þetta tekz. O. s. vist þikiumz
vinr þin vera en þo em ek ei vid mitt rad þess at vid berim
þetta upp þui at þorb' er skapstor ok þo metnadarmadr mikill
ein kvez ekki vilia annat en upp se borit bonordit. O. kvad h ra
da skyldu. ferr ein sudr aptr unz h kom heim. nokkuru sidarr ha
fdi þorb' haustbod sem h atti vanda til þui at h var stormenni mik
it kom þar ormr fra arnastapa ok marg annarr vin þorb'. O. kom at mali
h vid þorb' ok sagdi at einar var þar skomu fra þorbergi [illegible] gerdiz
hinn efniligsti madr hefr O. nu upp bonordit fyrir hond einars
ok s. þ vel hent. fyrir sumra hluta sakir ma þer bondi vida at
styrkr mikill fyri fiar hlutar sakir. þorb' s. ei vendi mik slikra
orda af þer at ek mundi gipta þrælssyni d. mina ok þ finn þer nu at
[illegible] þverr er slik rad gefr mer ok eigi skal hun med þer vera lengr er
þer þotti hun sva litils giafordz verd. sidan for ormr heim ok hver
annarra bodsmanna til sins heimilis. Gudridr var eptir med f. sinu
ok var heima þann vetr en at vari hafdi þorb' vinabod ok kom þar
mart manna ok var hin bezta veizla ok at veizlunni krafdi þorb' ser
hlioðs ok m. her hefi ek buit langa efi ok hefi ek reynt godvilia
manna vid mik ok astud kalla ek vel farit hafa var skipti. en nu

[HAUKSBÓK, p. 94 *b*.] ÞORFINNS SAGA KARLSEFNIS—4.

1. ok heimamǫnnum, ok bauð honum af at hafa slíkt er hann vildi. Ormr þá þetta,
2. ok taldi Einar vera góðan fardreng ok auðnumann mikinn. En er þeir
3. heldu á varninginum gekk kona fyri útibúrs dyrrin. Einarr spyrr Orm:
4. 'Hver væri sú hin fagra kona, er þar gekk fyri dyrrin. Ek hefi eigi
5. hana hér fyrri sét.' Ormr svarar: 'Þat er Guðríðr, fóstra mín, dóttir Þorbjarnar at Laugarbrekku.'
6. Einarr mælti: 'Hon mun vera kostr góðr, eða hafa nǫkkurir menn til
7. komit at biðja hennar?' Ormr segir: 'Beðit hefir hennar víst verit, ok liggr þat eigi laust
8. fyri; finnsk þat á, at hon mun vera mannvǫnd, ok svá faðir hennar.' 'Svá
9. með því,' sagði Einarr, 'at hér er sú kona, er ek ætla mér [at] biðja, ok vil-
10. da ek at þessa mála leitaðir þú við Þorbjǫrn, fǫður hennar, ok legðir
11. allan hug á, at þetta mætti framgengt verða. Skal ek þér fullkomna
12. vináttu fyri gjalda, ef ek get ráðit. Má Þorbjǫrn bóndi þat sjá,
13. at okkr væri vel hendar tengðir, því at hann er sómamaðr mikill
14. ok á staðfestu góða, en lausafé hans er mér sagt heldr á fǫrum;
15. en mik skortir hvárki land né lausafé, ok okkr feðga, ok mundi Þorbirni
16. verða at þessu hinn mesti styrkr, ef þetta tœkisk.' Ormr segir: 'Víst þykkjumk [ek]
17. vinr þinn vera, en þó em ek eigi við mitt ráð fúss, at vit berim
18. þetta upp, því at Þorbjǫrn er skapstórr, ok þó metnaðarmaðr mikill.
19. Einarr kvezk ekki vilja annat en [at] upp væri borit bónorðit. Ormr kvað hann rá-
20. ða skyldu. Ferr Einarr suðr aptr unz hann kemr heim. Nǫkkuru síðar ha-
21. fði Þorbjǫrn haustboð, sem hann átti vanda til, því at hann var stórmenni mik-
22. it. Kom þar Ormr frá Arnastapa, ok margir aðrir vinir Þorbjarnar. Ormr kom at má-
23. li við Þorbjǫrn, ok sagði, at Einarr var þar skǫmmu frá Þorgeirsfelli, ok gerðisk
24. hinn efniligsti maðr. Hefr Ormr nú upp bónorðit fyri hǫnd Einars,
25. ok segir þat vel hent fyri sumra hluta sakir, 'má þér, bóndi, verða at því
26. styrkr mikill fyri fjárkosta sakir.' Þorbjǫrn svarar: 'Eigi varði mik slíkra
27. orða af þér, at ek munda[1] gipta þræls syni dóttur mína; ok þat finni þér nú, at
28. fé mitt þverr, er slík ráð gefið mér; ok eigi skal hon með þér vera lengr, er
29. þér þótti hon svá lítils gjaforðs verð.' Síðan fór Ormr heim, ok hverr
30. annarr bóndmanna[2] til síns heimilis. Guðríðr var eptir með fǫður sínum,
31. ok var heima þann vetr. En at vári hafði Þorbjǫrn vinaboð, ok kom þar
32. mart manna, ok var hin bezta veizla. Ok at veizlunni krafði Þorbjǫrn sér
33. hljóðs, ok mælti: 'Hér hefi ek búit langa æfi, ok hefi ek reynt[3] góðvilja
34. manna við mik ok ástúð; kalla ek vel farit hafa vár skipti; en nú

[1] MS. mundi. [2] *sic*. [3] MS. reyn.

[HAUKSBÓK, p. 95.] ÞORFINNS SAGA KARLSEFNIS—5.

tekr[1] hagr minn at úhœgjask fyri lausafjár sakir, en hér til hefir kallat verit heldr virðingar ráð. Nú vil ek fyrr búinu bregða, en sœmðinni týna. Ætla ek ok fyrr af landi fara, en ætt mína svívirða, ok vitja heita Eiríks hins rauða, vinar míns, er hann hafði, þá er vit skilðum á Breiðafirði. Ætla ek nú at fara til Grœnlands í sumar, ef svá ferr sem ek vildi. Mǫnnum þótti mikil þessi ráðabreytni, því at Þorbjǫrn var vinsæll maðr, en þóttusk vita at Þorbjǫrn mundi svá fremi þetta upp hafa kveðit, at ekki mundi tjóa at letja hann. Gaf Þorbjǫrn mǫnnum gjafir, ok var brugðit veizlunni; síðan fór hverr til síns heima. Þorbjǫrn selr lǫnd sín, ok kaupir sér skip, er uppi stóð í Hraunhafnarósi. Réðusk til ferðar með honum XXX manna; var þar í ferð Ormr frá Arnastapa, ok kona hans, ok aðrir vinir Þorbjarnar, þeir er eigi vildu við hann skilja. Síðan létu þeir í haf, ok er þeir váru í hafi tók af byri; fengu þeir hafvillur, ok fórsk þeim ógreitt um sumarit. Því næst kom sótt í lið þeira, ok andaðisk Ormr ok Halldís, kona hans, ok helmingr liðs þeira. Sjó tók at stœra, ok þolðu menn hit mesta vás ok vesǫld á marga vega; en tóku þó Herjólfsnes á Grœnlandi við vetr sjálfan. Sá maðr hét Þorkell, er bjó á Herjólfsnesi; hann var hinn bezti bóndi. Hann tók við Þorbirni ok ǫllum skipverjum hans um vetrinn. Þorkell veitti þeim skǫruliga. Í þenna tíma var hallæri mikit á Grœnlandi; hǫfðu menn fengit lítit fang, þeir er í veiðiferðir hǫfðu farit, en sumir ekki aptr komnir. Sú kona var þar í bygð[2], er Þorbjǫrg hét; hon var spákona, ok var kǫlluð lítil vǫlva. Hon hafði átt sér IX systur, ok váru allar spákonur, en hon ein var þá á lífi. Þat var háttr Þorbjargar um vetrum, at hon fór at veizlum, ok [buðu[3]] þeir menn henni mest heim, er forvitni var á at vita forlǫg sín eða árferð; ok með því at Þorkell var þar mestr bóndi, þá þótti til hans koma at vita, nær létta mundi óárani þessu, sem yfir stóð. Býðr Þorkell spákonunni heim, ok er henni þar vel fagnat, sem siðr var til, þá er við þess háttar konum skyldi taka. Var henni búit hásæti, ok lagt undir hana hœgindi, þar skyldi í vera hœnsafiðri[4]; en er hon kom um kveldit, ok sá maðr, er móti henni var sendr, þá var hon svá búin, at hon hafði yfir sér tuglamǫttul blán, ok var settr steinum allt í skaut ofan;

[1] MS. tek. [2] MS. byð. [3] MS. ok *þeir menn* hen*ni* *þeir* mest hei*m*. [4] MS. hesna fidri, i.e. hœsnafiðri.

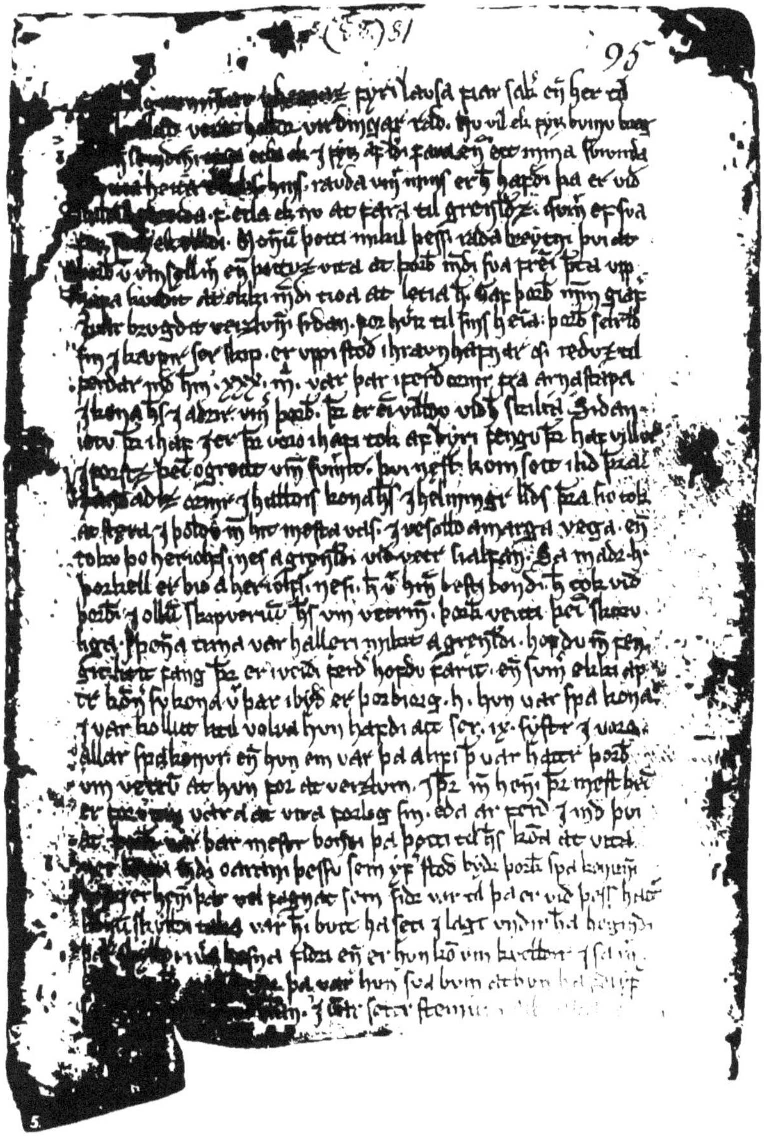

hon hafði a halsi ser glertolur ok lambskinns [illegible]
a hofði ok við innan kattskinn hvit. ok hon hafði staf [illegible]
ok var a knappr. hann var buinn með messingu ok settr steinum
um knappinn. hon hafði um sik hnioskulinda ok var þar
a skioðu pungr mikill. ok varðveitti hon þar i taufr sin
þau er hon þurfti til froðleiks at hafa. hon hafði a fotum
kalfskinns skva loðna. ok i þvengi langa ok a tinknappar mikla
a endunum. hon hafði a hondum ser kattskinns glofa ok voro hv-
itir innan ok loðnir. en er hon kom inn þotti ollum monnum skylt at velia
henni sęmiligar kveðiur. hon tok þvi sem henni voru menn geðiaðir til. tok þork.
bondi hond henni ok leiddi hana til þess sętis sem henni var buit. þork. bað
hana þa renna þar augum yfir hiu ok hiorð ok sva hibyli. hon var fa-
malug um allt. borð voro upp tekin um kveldit ok er fra þvi
at segia hvat spakonunni var matbuit. henni var gerr graut-
r a kiðia miolk ok mat buin hiortu or ollum kykvendum þeim
er þar voru til. hon hafði messingar spon ok knif tannskeptan tvihol-
kaðan af eiri ok var brotinn af oddrinn. en er borð voro upp tekin þa
gengr þork. b. fyrir þorb. ok spyrr hversu henni þikki þar um at litast
eða hversu skapfellt henni eru þar hibyli eða hęttir manna. eða hversu
fliotliga hon mun vis verða þess er hann hefir spurt hana ok monnum er
mest forvitni at vita. hon kallaz ekki munu segia fyrr
en um morguninn eptir er hon hefði aðr sofit um nottina.
En um morgininn at aliðnum d. var henni veittr sa umbunin-
gr sem hon þurfti at hafa til at fremia seiðinn. hon bað ok
fa sor konur þer er kunnu frędi þat sem til seiðsins þarf ok varðlokkur hetu. en þer konur funduz eigi. þa var leitat at
um bęinn ef nokkur kynni. þa s. Guðriðr hvarki em ek fiolkunn-
ig ne visinda kona. en þo kendi halldis fostra min mer a islandi kvęði er hon kallaði varðlokkur. þork. s. þa ertu happfroð.
hon s. þetta er þat eitt atferli er ek ętla i engum atbeina at
vera þvi at ek em kristin kona. þorb. s. sva metti verða at þu
yrðir monnum at liði her um en þu vęrir þa kona ekki verri en
[illegible]. en við þork. mun ek meta at fa þa hluti til er hafa

[HAUKSBÓK, p. 95 *b*.] ÞORFINNS SAGA KARLSEFNIS—6.

hon hafði á hálsi sér glertǫlur, ok lambskinns kofra svartan á hǫfði, ok við innan kattskinn hvít, ok hon hafði staf í hendi, ok var á knappr; hann var búinn með mersingu, ok settr steinum ofan um knappinn; hon hafði um sik hnjóskulinda, ok var þar á skjóðupungr mikill, ok varðveitti hon þar í taufr sín, þau er hon þurfti til fróðleiks at hafa. Hon hafði á fótum kálfskinns-skúa loðna, ok í þvengi langa ok á tinknappar miklir á endunum; hon hafði á hǫndum sér kattskinns-glófa, ok váru hvítir innan ok loðnir. En er hon kom inn, þótti ǫllum mǫnnum skylt at velja henni sœmiligar kveðjur. Hon tók því sem henni váru menn geðjaðir til. Tók Þorkell bóndi [í] hǫnd henni, ok leiddi hana til þess sætis, sem henni var búit. Þorkell bað hana þá renna þar augum yfir hjú ok hjǫrð[1] ok svá híbýli. Hon var fámálug um allt. Borð váru upp tekin um kveldit, ok er frá því at segja, hvat spákonunni var matbúit. Henni var gerr grautr á kiðjamjólk, ok matbúin hjǫrtu ór ǫllum kykvendum þeim, er þar váru til. Hon hafði mersingarspón ok kníf tannskeptan[2], tvíholkaðan af eiri, ok var brotinn af oddrinn[3]. En er borð váru upp tekin, þá gengr Þorkell bóndi fyri Þorbjǫrgu, ok spyrr hversu henni þikki þar um at lítask, eða hversu skapfeld henni eru þar híbýli eða hættir manna, eða hversu fljótliga hon mun vís verða þess, er hann hefir spurt hana ok mǫnnum er mest forvitni at vita. Hon kallask ekki munu segja fyrr en um morgininn eptir, er hon hafði áðr sofit um nóttina. En um morgininn at áliðnum degi, var henni veittr sá umbúningr, sem hon þurfti at hafa til at fremja seiðinn. Hon bað ok fá sér konur þær, er kunnu frœði þat, sem til seiðsins þarf, ok varðlokkur hétu; en þær konur fundusk eigi. Þá var leitat at um bœinn, ef nǫkkur kynni. Þá segir Guðríðr: 'Hvárki em ek fjǫlkunnig né vísinda kona, en þó kendi Halldís, fóstra mín, mér á Íslandi þat kvæði, er hon kallaði varðlokkur.' Þorkell segir: 'Þá ertu happfróð.' Hon segir: 'Þetta er þat eitt atferli, er ek ætla í øngum atbeina at vera, því at ek em kristin kona.' Þorbjǫrg segir: 'Svá mætti verða, at þú yrðir mǫnnum at liði hér um, en þú værir þá kona ekki verri en áðr; en við Þorkel mun ek meta, at fá þá hluti, er hafa

[1] MS. evidently by a slip, hrord.

[2] MS. tan*n* skepan.

[3] MS. oddin*n*.

[HAUKSBÓK, p. 96.] ÞORFINNS SAGA KARLSEFNIS—7.

þarf.' Þorkell herðir nú á Guðríði, en hon kvezk gøra mundu sem hann vildi. Slógu þá konur hring um hjallinn, en Þorbjǫrg sat á uppi. Kvað Guðríðr þá kvæðit svá fagrt ok vel, at engi þóttisk heyrt hafa með fegri rǫdd kvæði kveðit, sá er þar var hjá. Spákonan þakkar henni kvæðit, ok kvað: 'Margar þær náttúrur nú til hafa sótt, ok þikkja fagrt at heyra, er kvæðit var svá vel flutt, er áðr vildu við oss skiljask, ok enga hlýðni oss veita. En mér eru nú margir þeir hlutir auðsýnir, er áðr var ek dulið, ok margir aðrir. En ek kann þér þat at segja, Þorkell, at hallæri þetta mun ekki haldask lengr en í vetr, ok mun batna árangr sem várar. Sóttarfar þat, sem á hefir legit, man ok batna vánu bráðara. En þér, Guðríðr, skal ek launa í hǫnd liðsinni þat, er oss hefir af þér staðit, því at þín forlǫg eru mér nú allglǫggsæ. Þú munt gjaforð fá hér á Grœnlandi, þat er sœmiligast er, þó at þér verði þat eigi til langæðar, því at vegar þínir liggja út til Íslands, ok man þar koma frá þér bæði mikil ætt ok góð, ok yfir þínum kynkvíslum skína bjartari geislar, en ek hafa megin til at geta slíkt vandliga sét; enda far þú nú heil ok vel, dóttir!' Síðan gengu menn at vísindakonunni, ok frétti þá hverr þess, er mest forvitni var á at vita. Hon var ok góð af frásǫgnum; gekk þat ok lítt í taum, er hon sagði. Þessu næst var komit eptir henni af ǫðrum bœ. Fór hon þá þangat. Þá var sent eptir Þorbirni, því at hann vildi eigi heima vera meðan slík hindrvitni var framið. Veðrátta batnaði skjótt, sem Þorbjǫrg hafði sagt. Býr Þorbjǫrn skip sitt, ok ferr þar til er hann kemr í Brattahlíð. Eiríkr tekr vel við honum með blíðu, ok kvað þat vel er hann var þar kominn. Var Þorbjǫrn með honum um vetrinn, ok skuldalið hans, en þeir vistuðu háseta með bóndum. Eptir um várit gaf Eiríkr Þorbirni land á Stokkanesi, ok var þar gerr sœmiligr bœr, ok bjó hann þar síðan.

Af Leif onum heppna ok kristni kom á Grœnland.

Eiríkr átti þá konu, er Þórhildr hét, ok við henni II sonu; hét annarr Þorsteinn, en annarr Leifr. Þeir váru báðir efniligir menn, ok var Þorsteinn heima með fǫður sínum, ok var eigi sá maðr á Grœnlandi, er jafnmannvænn þótti sem hann. Leifr hafði siglt til Noregs, ok var með Óláfi konungi Tryggvasyni. En er Leifr sigldi af Grœnlandi um sumarit,

þarf. þeir hlyta nu a gudridi en hun kuez ga undir sem h[ann] villdi
slogu þa konur hring um hiallin en þorbiorg sat a uppi. kuad þa
gudr[idr] þa kuædit. sua fagurt ok vel at engi þottiz heyrt hafa med
fegri rodd kuedi kuedit sa er þar var hia. spakonan þakkar
h[enni] kuædit. ok kuad margar þær natturur nu til hafa sott
ok þikkia fagurt at heyra er kuædit var sua vel flutt er adr
villdu vid oss skiliaz ok enga hlydni oss veita. en m[er] eru nu marg
ir þeir hlutir audsynir er adr var ek dulit ok margir adrir. en ek
kann þer. þat at segia þork[ell] at hallæri þetta mun ekki halldaz
lengr en i uetr ok mun batna arangr sem uarar. sottar far
þat sem a hef[ir] legit man ok batna uanu bradara. en þer gud
ridr. sk[al] ek launa i hond lidsinni þat er oss hef[ir] af þ[er] stadit. þui
at þin forlog eru m[er] nu allglogg se. þu m[un]t giaford fa h[er]
a grænlandi þat er sæmiligaz er þo at þer uerdi þat ei til langædar
þuiat uegir þin[ir] liggia ut til isl[an]dz ok man þar koma fra þ[er]
bædi mikil ætt ok god ok yfir þinu[m] kynkuislum skina biar
tari geislar en ek hafa megin til at geta slikt uandliga
set en far þu nu heil ok uel dott[ir]. Sidan gengu m[enn] at uisinda
konunni ok frettu þa hverr þess er mest forvitni var a at uita hun
var ok god af frasognu[m] gekk þat ok litt i tauma er hun sagdi þessu
nest var komit epter henni af odru[m] bæ. for hun þa þangat
þa var sent ept[ir] þorbirni þui at h[ann] villdi ei heima uera medan
slik heidni var framit. uedratta batnadi skiott sem þorb[iorg]
hafdi sagt. byr þorbiorn skip sitt ok ferr þar til er h[ann] kemr i bratta
hlid. eirikr tekr uel vid h[onu]m med blidu ok kuad þat uel er h[ann] var þar
komi[n]. var þorbiorn med h[onu]m um uetrin ok skulldalid h[an]s en hus[karlar]
uistudu sik med bondu[m]. ept[ir] um uarit gaf eirikr þorb[irni]
[land] a stokkanesi ok uar þar gert sæmiligr bær ok bio h[ann] þar sidan
Eirikr atti þa konu er þiodhilldr h[et]
[o]k atto þau .ij. s[onu] het annar þorsteinn en annar leif[r] [illegible]
[illegible] efniligir m[enn] ok u[ar] þorst[einn] heima med f[odur] sinu[m] ok uar ei [illegible]
[illegible] er [illegible] man uænn þotti sem h[ann]. leifr hafdi s[illegible]
[illegible] en er leifr sigldi af [illegible]

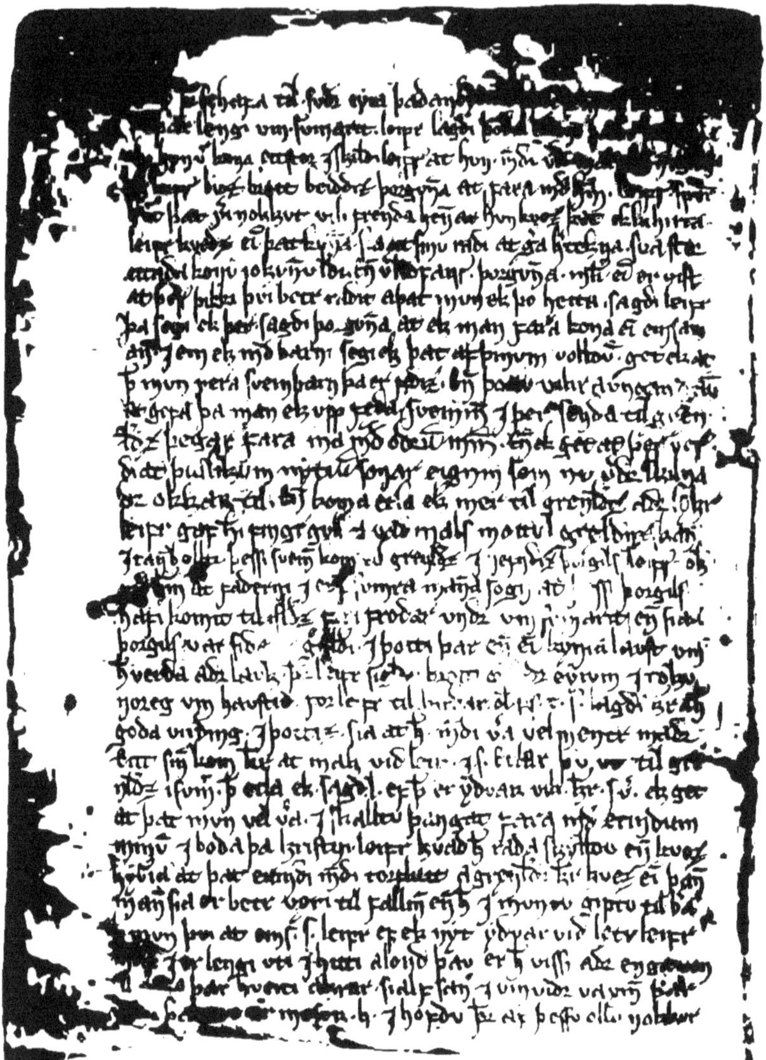

[illegible] skiheita til. fóðr eina þaðan [illegible]
[illegible] þar lengi um sumarit. leifr lagði þokka [illegible]
[illegible] kona [illegible] ok skildi leifr at hon mundi [illegible]
[illegible] leifr bióz brott beiddiz þorgunna at fara með honum. leifr spurði
hvat þat [illegible] nokkut vili frænda hennar. hon kvez ekki hirða.
leifr kvez ei þat kunna sjá at sínu ráði at gera hertekna svá stórættaða konu í ókunnu landi en vér fáir. þorgunna mælti eigi er víst
at þér þykki því betr ráðit. á þat mun ek þó hætta sagði leifr.
þá segi ek þér sagði þorgunna at ek man fara kona eigi einsaman ok em ek með barni segi ek þat af þínum völdum. get ek at
þat mun vera sveinbarn þá er fæðiz. en þóttu vilir engan gaum
at gefa þá man ek upp fæða sveininn ok þér senda til grænlands
þegar fara má með öðrum mönnum. en ek get at þér verði
at því líkum nytjar at sonar eign sem nú verðr skilnaðr
okkarr til. en koma ætla ek mér til grænlands áðr lýkr.
leifr gaf henni fingrgull ok vaðmálsmöttul grænlenzkan
ok tannbelti. þessi sveinn kom til grænlands ok nefndiz þorgils. leifr tók
við honum at faðerni ok er þat sumra manna sögn at sjá þorgils
hafi komit til íslands fyrir fróðárundr um sumarit. en síðan
var þorgils á grænlandi ok þótti þar eigi einkamálalaust um
verða áðr lyki. þeir leifr sigldu brott ór suðreyjum ok tóku
noreg um haustit. fór leifr til hirðar óláfs konungs tryggvasonar. lagði konungr á hann
góða virðing ok þóttiz sjá at hann mundi vera vel menntr maðr.
eitt sinn kom konungr at máli við leif ok segir ætlar þú út til grænlands
í sumar. þat ætla ek sagði leifr ef þat er yðvarr vili. konungr svarar ek get
at þat mun vel vera ok skaltu þangat fara með erindum
mínum ok boða þar kristni. leifr kvað hann ráða skyldu en kvez
hyggja at þat erindi mundi torsótt á grænlandi. konungr kvez eigi þann
mann sjá er betr væri til fallinn en hann ok muntu giptu til bera.
því at eins sagði leifr ef ek nýt yðvar við. lét leifr
[illegible] ok var lengi úti ok hitti á lönd þau er hann vissi áðr engar ván
[illegible] þar hveitiakrar sjálfsánir ok vínviðr vaxinn. þar
[illegible] er mösurr heita ok höfðu þeir af þessu öllu nokkur

[HAUKSBÓK, p. 96 *b*.] ÞORFINNS SAGA KARLSEFNIS.—8.

1. urðu þeir sæhafa til Suðreyja. Þaðan byrjaði þeim seint, ok dvǫlðusk
2. þeir þar lengi um sumarit. Leifr lagði þokka á konu þá, er Þórgunna
3. hét. Hon var kona ættstór, ok skilði Leifr, at hon mundi vera margkunnig. En
4. er Leifr bjósk brott, beiddisk Þórgunna at fara með honum. Leifr spurði
5. hvárt þat væri nǫkkut vili frænda hennar. Hon kvezk þat ekki hirða[1].
6. Leifr kvezk eigi þat kunna sjá at sínu ráði, at gøra hertekna svá stór-
7. ættaða konu í ókunnu landi; 'en vér liðfáir.' Þórgunna mælti: 'Eigi er víst,
8. at þér þikki því betr ráðit.' 'Á þat mun ek þó hætta,' sagði Leifr,
9. 'Þá segi ek þér,' sagði Þórgunna, 'at ek man fara kona eigi einsam-
10. an, ok em ek með barni; segi ek þat af þínum vǫldum. Get ek at
11. þat mun vera sveinbarn, þá er fœðisk. En þóttú vilir ǿngvan gaum
12. at gefa, þá man ek upp fœða sveininn, ok þér senda til Grœn-
13. lands, þegar fara má með ǫðrum mǫnnum. En ek get, at þér ver-
14. ði at þvílíkum nytjum sonareignin, sem nú verðr skilna-
15. ðr okkar til. En koma ætla ek mér til Grœnlands, áðr lýkr.'
16. Leifr gaf henni fingrgull, ok vaðmáls mǫttul grœnlenzkan
17. ok tannbelti. Þessi sveinn kom til Grœnlands, ok nefndisk Þorgils. Leifr tók
18. við honum at faðerni, ok er þat sumra manna sǫgn, at þessi Þorgils
19. hafi komit til Íslands fyri Fróðárundr um sumarit. En sjá
20. Þorgils var síðan á Grœnlandi, ok þótti þar enn eigi kynjalaust um
21. hann verða, áðr lauk. Þeir Leifr sigldu brott ór Suðreyjum, ok tóku
22. Noreg um haustit. Fór Leifr til hirðar Óláfs konungs Tryggvasonar. Lagði konungr á hann
23. góða virðing, ok þóttisk sjá, at hann mundi vera vel mentr maðr.
24. Eitt sinn kom konungr at máli við Leif, ok segir: 'Ætlar þú út til Grœ-
25. nlands í sumar?' 'Þat ætla ek,' sagði Leifr, 'ef þat er yðvarr vili.' Konungr svarar:
'Ek get,
26. at þat mun vel vera, ok skaltu þangat fara með ǿrindum
27. mínum, ok boða þar kristni.' Leifr kvað hann ráða skyldu, en kvezk
28. hyggja, at þat ǿrindi mundi torflutt á Grœnlandi. Konungr kvezk eigi þann
29. mann sjá, er betr væri til fallinn en hann, 'ok muntu giptu til bera.'
30. 'Þat mun því at eins,' segir Leifr, 'ef ek nýt yðvar við.' Lætr Leifr
31. í haf, ok er lengi úti, ok hitti á lǫnd þau, er hann vissi áðr enga ván
32. til. Váru þar hveitiakrar sjálfsánir, ok vínviðr vaxinn. Þar
33. váru þau tré, er mǫsurr heita, ok hǫfðu þeir af þessu ǫllu nǫkkur

[1] MS. hirta.

[HAUKSBÓK, p. 97.] ÞORFINNS SAGA KARLSEFNIS—9.

merki, sum tré svá mikil, at í hús váru lǫgð. Leifr fann menn á skipflaki, ok flutti heim með sér. Sýndi hann í því hina mestu stórmensku ok drengskap, sem mǫrgu ǫðru, er hann kom kristni á landit, ok var jafnan síðan kallaðr Leifr hinn heppni. Leifr tók land í Eiríksfirði, ok fór heim síðan í Brattahlíð; tóku þar allir menn vel við honum. Hann boðaði brátt kristni um landit ok almenniliga trú, ok sýndi mǫnnum orðsending Óláfs konungs Tryggvasonar, ok sagði hversu mǫrg ágæti ok mikil dýrð fylgði þessum sið. Eiríkr tók því máli seint, at láta sið sinn, en Þjóðhildr gekk skjótt undir, ok lét gøra kirkju eigi allnær húsunum. Þat hús var kallat Þjóðhildar kirkja. Hafði hon þar fram bœnir sínar, ok þeir menn sem við kristni tóku. Þjóðhildr vildi ekki samræði við Eirík, síðan hon tók trú, en honum var þetta mjǫk móti skapi. Á þessu gørðisk orð mikit, at menn mundu leita lands þess, er Leifr hafði fundit. Var þar formaðr at Þorsteinn Eiríksson, fróðr maðr ok vinsæll. Eiríkr var ok til beðinn, ok trúðu menn hans gæfu framast ok forsjá. Hann var lengi fyri, en kvað eigi nei við, er vinir hans báðu hann til, bjoggu síðan skip þat, er Þorbjǫrn hafði út haft, ok váru til ráðnir XX menn, ok hǫfðu lítit fé, eigi meira en vápn ok vistir. Þann morgin reið Eiríkr heiman, tók hann einn kistil, ok var þar í gull ok silfr; fal hann þat, ok fór síðan leiðar sinnar, ok bar svá til at hann fell af baki, ok brotna rifin í síðunni, en lesti hǫndina í axlarliðnum. Af þeim atburð sagði hann Þórhildi, konu sinni, at hon tœki féit á brott, lézk þess hafa at goldit, er hann hafði féit fólgit. Síðan sigldu þeir út ór Eiríksfirði með gleði mikilli; þótti þeim allvænt sitt efni. Þá velkti úti lengi í hafi, ok kómu þeir ekki á þær slóðir, sem þeir vildu. Þeir kómu í sýn við Ísland, ok svá hǫfðu þeir fugl af Írlandi. Rak þá skip þeira um haf innan. Fóru aptr um haustit, ok váru allmjǫk væstir ok þrekaðir; koma við vetr sjálfan á Eiríksfjǫrð. Þá mælti Eiríkr: 'Kátari sigldu vér í sumar út ór firðinum, en nú eru vér, ok eru þó enn mǫrg góð at.' Þorsteinn svarar: 'Þat er nú hǫfðingligt bragð, at sjá nǫkkut gott ráð fyri þeim mǫnnum ǫllum, sem hér eru nú ráðstafalausir, ok fá þeim vist í vetr.' Eiríkr svarar: 'Þat er

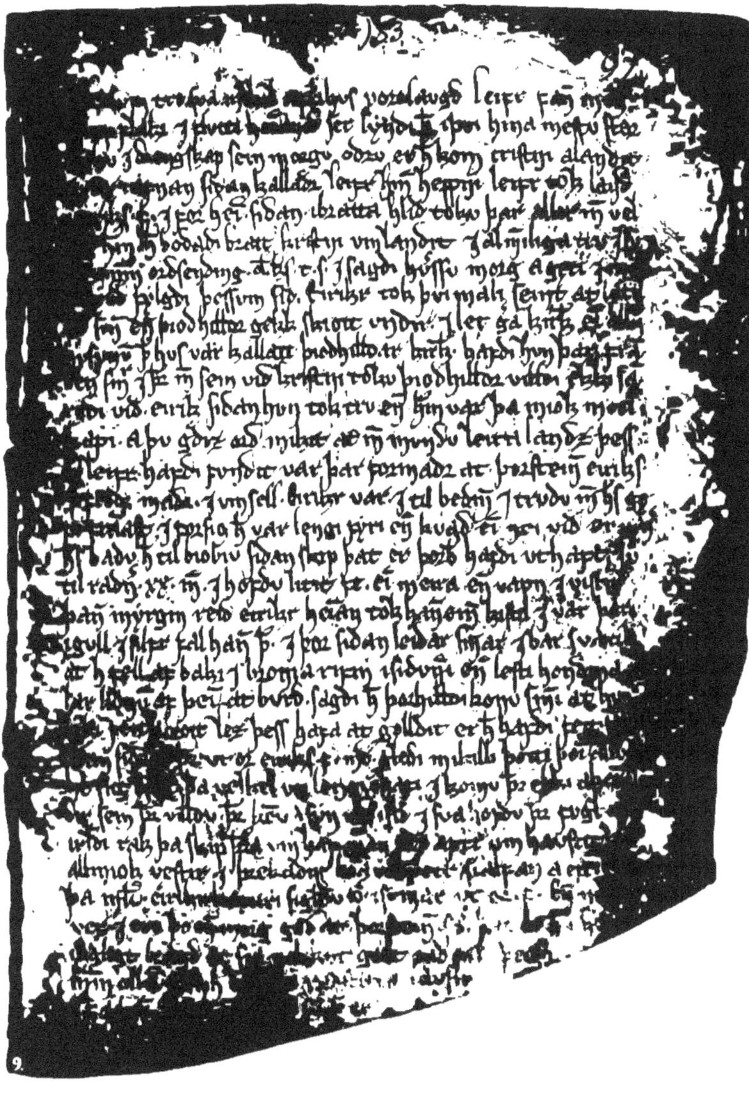

9.

iafnan latt leng[illegible] at ei veri [illegible] en svarar [illegible]
her þara sk. nu hafa rad þin um þetta þars nu all[illegible] [illegible]
hofdu [illegible] vistir [illegible] þeir fodgu sidan þaus þa heim [illegible]
ok vas þar um vetrinn [illegible]

Nu er fra þui at segia at þorsteinn eiriks. s. vakti bonord
vid. gudridi ok var þui mali vel svarat. bædi af h. ok af
f. h. ok er þat at radi gert. þorst. gengr at eiga gudridi ok
þeira brudkaup i brattahlid um haustit. for sv veizla vel fram ok
allfiolmenn. þorst. atti bu i vestri bygd a bæ þeim er h. i lysu f. en
sa madr atti þar helming i bui er þorsteinn h. sigridr h. kona hs.
for þorst. i lysu. f. um haustit til nafna sins ok þau gudridr bædi.
var þar vid þeim vel tekit. voro þau þar um vetrinn. þ. gerdiz þ[illegible]
tidindi at sott kom i bæ þeira er lit[illegible] var [illegible] h. het
verkstiori. h. v. eigi vinsell m[illegible] [illegible] sott [illegible]
en v. skamt at bida at huerr [illegible] þa tok [illegible]
s. ok sigridr kona þorsteins nafna [illegible] utt at vella [illegible]
ganga til. nadahuss. er stod i gegnt vid durum. gudridr [illegible]
ok horfdu þær moti vid durunum. þa kvad hon vid hatt. sigr. gud
r. mitt vid hofum ovarliga farit ok attu eigi [illegible] stand vid [illegible]
kalld hun a þig ok foru vid heim sem skiotaz. sigridr. sv. ei er
at sva buit her ei nu vildir þat allt hit dauda i fyrir durunum ok
[illegible] bondi þinn ok þar kenni ek mik ok er illt hoyrning at sia ok
[illegible] leid ef nisti hun for vid nu gudridr. nu se ek ekki lidit
þa þorsteinn baesinn hi þottiz hafa hafa svipu i hendi
ok vilia beria lidit. sidan gengu þær inn. ok adr morgun kemi þa
var hon latin ok var gert kista at likinu. ok þenna sama dag ætlu
[illegible] at roa ok leiddi þorst. þa til vara ok i rökkrinu fors h. at
[illegible] skap fari. þa sendi þorst. eiriks. s. nafna sinum ord at han
[illegible] ok sagdi sva at þar veri varla kyrt. ok husfreyia vill
[illegible] a fot. ok villdi undir kledin hia h. ok er h. kom
[illegible] upp a rekkiu stokkinn þa tok h.
[illegible] hondum ok lagdi boleyxi fyrir briost
[illegible] stein eiriks. s. andadiz

[HAUKSBÓK, p. 97 *b*.] ÞORFINNS SAGA KARLSEFNIS—10.

jafnan satt, sem mælt er, at eigi veit fyrr en svarat er, ok svá man hér fara. Skal nú hafa ráð þín um þetta.' Fóru nú allir, þeir er eigi hǫfðu aðrar vistir, með þeim feðgum. Síðan fóru þeir heim í Brattahlíð, ok váru þar um vetrinn.

Þorsteinn Eiríksson fekk Guðríðar. Aptrgǫngur.

Nú er frá því at segja, at Þorsteinn Eiríksson vakði bónorð við Guðríði, ok var því máli vel svarat, bæði af henni ok af fǫður hennar. Er þetta at ráði gert. Þorsteinn gengr at eiga Guðríði, ok var þetta brúðkaup í Brattahlíð um haustit. Fór sjá veizla vel fram, ok var allfjǫlmennt. Þorsteinn átti bú í Vestrbygð, á bœ þeim, er hét í Lýsufirði. En sá maðr átti þar helming í búi, er Þorsteinn hét; Sigríðr hét kona hans. Fór Þorsteinn í Lýsufjǫrð, um haustit, til nafna síns, ok þau Guðríðr bæði. Var þar við þeim vel tekit. Váru þau þar um vetrinn. Þat gerðisk til tíðinda, at sótt kom í bœ þeira, er lítit var af vetri. Garðr hét þar verkstjóri; hann var ekki vinsæll maðr; hann tók fyrst sótt, ok andaðisk. Síðan var skamt at bíða, at hverr lézk at ǫðrum. Þá tók sótt Þorsteinn Eiríksson, ok Sigríðr, kona Þorsteins, nafna hans; ok eitt kveld fýstisk Sigríðr at ganga til náðahúss, er stóð í gegn útidyrum. Guðríðr fylgði henni, ok horfðu þær móti útidurunum. Þá kvað hon við hátt, Sigríðr. Guðríðr mælti: 'Vit hǫfum óvarliga farit, ok áttu øngan[1] stað við at kalt komi á þik, ok fǫru vit heim sem skjótast.' Sigríðr svarar: 'Eigi er fœrt at svá búnu. Hér er nú liðit þat allt hit dauða fyri durunum, ok Þorsteinn, bóndi þinn, ok þar kenni ek mik, ok er slíkt hǫrmung at sjá.' Ok er þetta leið af, mælti hon: 'Fǫru vit nú, Guðríðr. Nú sé ek ekki liðit.' Var þá Þorsteinn horfinn henni; þótti hann áðr haft hafa svipu í hendi, ok vilja berja liðit. Síðan gengu þær inn, ok áðr morginn kœmi, þá var hon látin; ok var ger kista at líkinu. Ok þenna sama dag ætluðu menn at róa, ok leiddi Þorsteinn þá til vara, ok í annan lit fór hann at sjá veiðiskap þeira. Þá sendi Þorsteinn Eiríksson nafna sínum orð, at hann kœmi til hans, ok sagði svá, at þar væri varla kyrt, ok húsfreyja vildi fœrask á fœtr, ok vildi undir klæðin hjá honum, ok er hann kom inn, var hon komin upp á rekkjustokkinn. Þá tók hann hana hǫndum, ok lagði bolǫxi fyri brjóst henni. Þorsteinn Eiríksson andaðisk

[1] MS. eyngan.

[HAUKSBÓK, p. 98.] ÞORFINNS SAGA KARLSEFNIS—11.

nær dagsetri[1]. Þorsteinn bóndi bað Guðríði leggjask niðr ok sofa; en hann kvezk vaka mundu um nóttina yfir líkinu. Hon gǫrir svá, ok er skamt leið á nóttina, settisk Þorsteinn Eiríksson upp, ok mælti; kvezk vilja at Guðríðr væri þangat kǫlluð, ok kvezk vilja tala við hana: 'Guð vill at þessi stund sé mér gefin til leyfis ok umbótar míns ráðs.' Þorsteinn bóndi gengr á fund Guðríðar, ok vakði hana, biðr hana signa sik ok biðja sér guð hjálpar, ok segir hvat Þorsteinn Eiríksson hafði talat við hann; 'ok hann vill finna þik. Verðr þú ráð fyri at sjá hvat þú vill upp taka, því at ek kann hér um hvárskis at fýsa.' Hon svarar: 'Vera kann, at þetta sé ætlat til nǫkkurra þeira hluta, er síðan sé í minni hafðir, þessi hinn undarligi hlutr, en ek vænti at guðs gæzla[2] mun yfir mér standa; mun ek á hætta með guðs miskunn, at fara til móts við hann, ok vita hvat hann vill tala, því at ek mun eigi forðask mega, ef mér skal mein at verða. Vil ek síðr at hann gangi víðara; en mik grunar, at þat man á liggja.' Nú fór Guðríðr, ok hitti Þorstein; sýndisk henni sem hann feldi tár. Hann mælti í eyra henni nǫkkur orð hljótt, svá at hon ein vissi. En þat mælti hann svá at allir heyrðu, at þeir menn væri sælir, er trúna heldu, ok henni fylgði ǫll hjálp ok miskunn, ok sagði þó, at margir heldi hana illa; 'er þat engi háttr, sem hér hefir verit á Grœnlandi, síðan kristni kom hér, at setja menn niðr í úvígða mold við lítla yfirsǫngva. Vil ek mik láta flytja til kirkju ok aðra þá menn, sem hér hafa andazk, en Garðar vil ek brenna láta á báli sem skjótast, því at hann veldr ǫllum aptrgǫngum þeim, sem hér hafa verit í vetr.' Hann sagði henni ok um sína hagi, ok kvað hennar forlǫg mikil mundu verða, en bað hana varask at giptask grœnlenzkum mǫnnum; bað at hon legði fé þeira til kirkju, ok sumt fátœkum mǫnnum, ok þá hné hann aptr ǫðru sinni. Sá hafði háttr verit á Grœnlandi, síðan kristni kom þangat, at menn váru grafnir á bœjum, þar sem ǫnduðusk, í úvígðri moldu; skyldi setja staur upp af brjósti hinum dauða. En

[1] MS. dag satri.

[2] MS. gętla.

[illegible] dag setan þa [illegible] guðriðr hvart vaki ok sofa en þ ku-
[illegible] heyrandi [illegible] hyn [illegible] sva ok [illegible] skat leida a
nottina settizk þorst. eirik. s. upp ok mælti hvers vilia at guðriði se
þingat kollud ok vers vilia tala við hana. guð vill at þessi stund se
mer gefin til leyfis ok umbotar mins raðs. þorst. bondi gengr a fund. guðriðar vakti hana biðr hana signa sik ok biðia ser guð hialpar
ok segir hvat þorst. eirik. s. hafði talat við hann ok hann vill finna þig
verðr þu rad fyrir at sia hvat þu vill upp taka þui at ek kann her
um hvartveggi [illegible] at fysa. hon svarar. vera kann at þetta se ætlat til nok-
kurra þeira hluta er siðan se i minni hafðir. þessi inn undarligi hlutr en ek vænti at guðs gæzla mun yfir mer standa. mun ek
ok a hættu hætta með guðs miskunn at fara til mots við hann ok vita hvat
hann vill tala þui at ek mun eigi forðaz mega ef mer skal mein
at verða vil ek siðr at hann gangi viðara en mik grunar at þat
muni a liggia. nu for guðriðr ok hitti þorst. syndiz henni sem
hann felldi tar ok mælti i eyra henni nokkur orð hliott sva at hon
ein vissi. en þat mælti hann sva at allir heyrði at þeir menn væri
sælir er truna heldu ok þeim fylgði oll hialp ok miskunn ok sagði
þo at margir heldi hana illa. er þat engi hattr sem her hefir
verit a grænlandi siðan kristni kom her at setia menn niðr i o vi-
gða moldu við litla yfirsongva vil ek mik lata flytia
til kirkiu ok aðra þa menn sem her hafa andaz. en garðar
vil ek brenna lata a bali sem skiotaz þui at hann velldr
ollum aptrgongum þeim sem her hafa verit i vetr. hann sagði
henni ok um sina hagi ok kvað hennar forlog mikil mundu v-
erða. en bað hana varaz at giptaz grænlenzkum monnum
bað at hon legði fe þeira til kirkiu ok sumt fatæ-
kum monnum. ok þa hneig hann aptr aðru sinni. sa hafði
hattr verit a grænlandi siðan kristni kom
þangat at menn væru grafnir a bæium
þar sem onduðuz i ovigðri moldu
skyldi setia staur upp af
briosti hinum dauða en

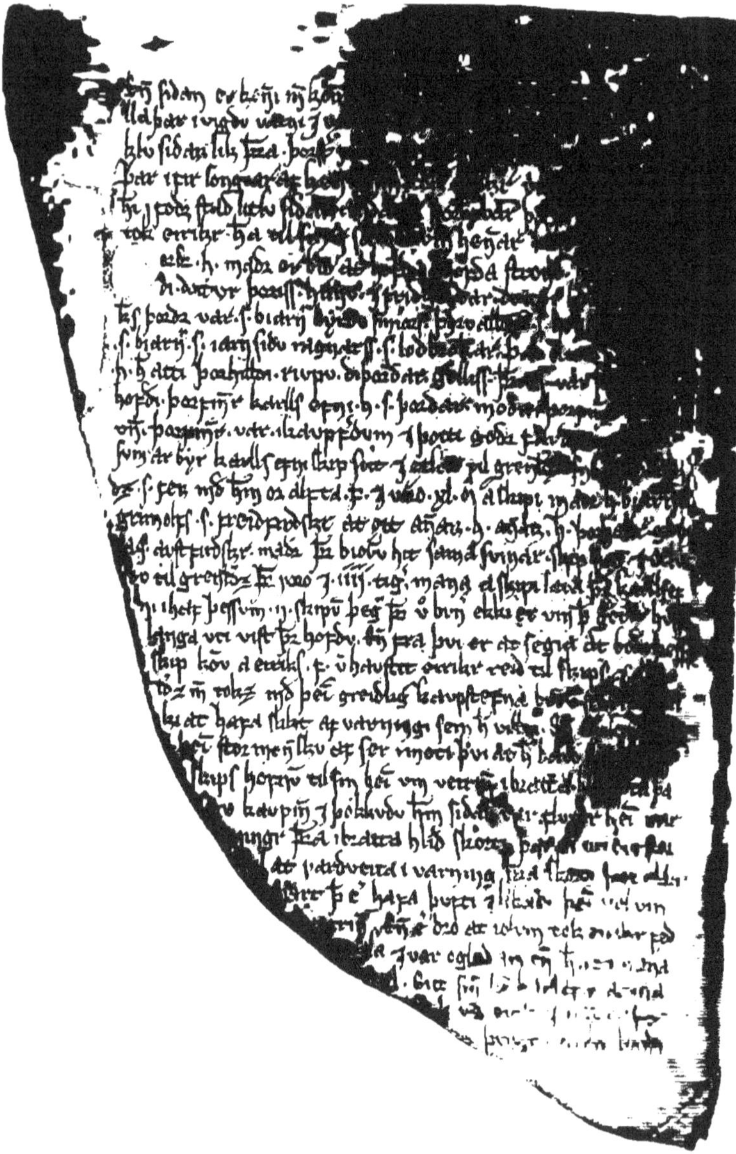

[HAUKSBÓK, p. 98 *b*.] ÞORFINNS SAGA KARLSEFNIS—12.

En[1] síðan, er kennimenn kómu til, þá skyldi upp kippa staurinum, ok hella þar í vígðu vatni, ok veita þar yfirsǫngva, þótt þat væri miklu síðar. Lík þeira Þorsteins váru fœrð til kirkju í Eiríksfjǫrð, ok veittir þar yfirsǫngvar af kennimǫnnum. Tók Eiríkr við Guðríði, ok var henni í fǫður stað. Litlu síðar andaðisk Þorbjǫrn; bar þá fé allt undir Guðríði. Tók Eiríkr hana til sín, ok sá vel um hennar kost. **Af Hǫfða-Þórði.** Þórðr hét maðr, er bjó at Hǫfða á Hǫfðaströnd. Hann átti Friðgerði, dóttur Þóris hímu ok Friðgerðar, dóttur Kjarvals Írakonungs. Þórðr var son Bjarnar byrðusmjǫrs, Þorvaldssonar hryggs, Ásleikssonar, Bjarnarsonar járnsíðu, Ragnarssonar loðbrókar. Þau áttu son, er Snorri hét; hann átti Þórhildi rjúpu, dóttur Þórðar gellis. Þeira son var Þórðr hesthǫfði. Þorfinnr karlsefni hét son Þórðar. Móðir Þorfinns hét Þórunn. Þorfinnr var í kaupferðum, ok þótti góðr fardrengr. Eitt sumar býr Karlsefni skip sitt, ok ætlar til Grœnlands. Snorri Þorbrandsson ferr með honum ór Álptafirði, ok váru XL manna á skipi. Maðr hét Bjarni Grímólfsson, breiðfirzkr[2] at ætt. Annarr hét[3] Þórhallr Gamlason, austfirzkr maðr. Þeir bjoggu hit sama sumar skip sitt, ok ætluðu til Grœnlands; þeir váru ok IIII tigir manna á skipi. Láta þeir Karlsefni í haf þessum II skipum, þegar þeir váru búnir. Ekki er um þat getit, hversu langa útivist þeir hǫfðu. En frá því er at segja, at bæði þessi skip kómu á Eiríksfjǫrð um haustit. Eiríkr reið til skips, ok aðrir landsmenn. Tóksk með þeim greiðlig kaupstefna. Buðu stýrimenn Eiríki at hafa slíkt af varningi, sem hann vildi. En Eiríkr sýnir þeim stórmensku af sér í móti, því at hann bauð þessum II skipshǫfnum til sín heim um vetrinn í Brattahlíð. Þetta þágu kaupmenn, ok þǫkkuðu honum. Síðan var fluttr heim varningr þeira í Brattahlíð. Skorti þar eigi útibúr stór til at varðveita í varning þeira; skorti þar ekki mart þat, er hafa þurfti, ok líkaði þeim vel um vetrinn. En er dró at jólum, tók Eiríkr fæð mikla, ok var óglaðari en hann átti vana til. Eitt sinn kom Karlsefni at máli við Eirík, ok mælti: 'Er þér þungt, Eiríkr bóndi?

[1] En*n* repeated in MS.

[2] MS. freidfirdskr, obviously a clerical slip.

[3] an*narr* h*ét* repeated in MS.

[HAUKSBÓK, p. 99.] ÞORFINNS SAGA KARLSEFNIS—13.

1. Menn þikkjask finna, at þú ert óglaðari en þú átt vana til. Þú hefir
2. veitt oss með hinni mestu rausn, ok eru vér skyldir til at launa þér
3. slíku góðu, sem vér hǫfum fǫng á. Nú segðu hvat úgleði [þinni veldr].' Eiríkr svarar:
4. 'Ér þiggit vel ok góðmannliga. Nú leikr mér þat eigi í hug, at á yðr verði
5. hallt um vár skipti, hitt er heldr, at mér þikki uggligt, þá er þér
6. komit annarsstaðar, at þat flytisk, at þér hafit engi jól verri haft
7. en þessi, er nú koma, ok Eiríkr hinn rauði veitti yðr í Brattahlíð á Grœn-
8. landi.' 'Þat mun eigi svá fara, bóndi,' segir Karlsefni, 'vér hǫfum [á] skipi vá-
9. ru bæði malt ok korn, ok hafið þar af slíkt, er þér vilið, ok gørið
10. veizlu svá stórmannliga, sem yðr líkar fyri því.' Þetta þiggr Eiríkr, ok
11. var þá búit til jólaveizlu, ok var hon hin sœmiligsta, svá at menn
12. þóttusk trautt þvílíka rausn sét hafa í fátœku landi. Ok eptir jól-
13. in vekr Karlsefni bónorð fyri Eirík um Guðríði, því at honum
14. leizk sem hann mundi forræði á hafa. Eiríkr svarar vel, ok segir, at hon man sínum for-
15. lǫgum verða at fylgja, ok kvezk góða eina frétt af honum hafa; ok lauk svá, at Þorfinnr festi
16. Þuríði, ok var þá aukin veizlan, ok drukkit brullaup þeira, ok var þetta í Brattahlíð um vetrinn.
17. Í Brattahlíð hófusk miklar umrœður, at menn skyldu leita Vínlands **Hófsk Vínlandsferð.**
18. ens góða, ok var sagt, at þangat mundi vera at vitja góðra landskosta. Ok þar kom, at Karlse-
19. fni ok Snorri bjoggu skip sitt, at leita landsins um várit. Með þeim fór ok sá maðr, er Bjarni
20. hét, ok annarr Þórhallr, er fyrr eru nefndir, með sínu skipi. Maðr hét Þorvarðr; hann átti Frey-
21. dísi, dóttur Eiríks rauða, laungetna. Hann fór ok með þeim, ok Þorvaldr, son Eiríks, ok Þórhallr,
22. er kallaðr var veiðimaðr. Hann hafði lengi verit með Eiríki, veiðimaðr hans um sumrum, en
23. bryti um vetrum. Hann var mikill maðr, ok sterkr ok svartr ok þursligr, hljóðlyndr ok illorðr, þat er hann
24. mælti, ok eggjaði jafnan Eirík ens verra. Hann var illa kristinn. Honum var víða kunnigt í úbygðum.
25. Hann var á skipi með Þorvarði ok Þorvaldi. Þeir hǫfðu þat skip, er Þorbjǫrn hafði út haft.
26. Þeir hǫfðu alls XL manna ok C, er þeir sigldu til Vestribygðar, ok þaðan til Bjarneyjar.
27. Þaðan sigldu þeir II dœgr í suðr. Þá sá þeir land, ok skutu báti ok kǫnnuðu landit, funnu
28. þar hellur stórar, ok margar XII álna víðar; fjǫlði var þar melrakka. Þeir gáfu
29. þar nafn, ok kǫlluðu Helluland. Þaðan sigldu þeir II dœgr, ok brá til landsuðrs ór suðri,
30. ok fundu land skógvaxit, ok mǫrg dýr á. Ey lá þar undan í landsuðr, þar í drápu þeir
31. einn bjǫrn, ok kǫlluðu þar síðan Bjarney, en landit Markland. Þaðan sigldu þeir suðr með
32. landinu langa stund, ok kómu at nesi einu, lá landit á stjórn; váru þar strandir langar
33. ok sandar. Þeir reru til lands, ok fundu þar á nesinu kjǫl af skipi, ok kǫlluðu þar
34. Kjalarnes. Þeir kǫlluðu ok strandirnar Furðustrandir, því at langt þótti fyr[1] at sigla.

[1] þótti fyr, supplied from paper MSS., AM. 281, 4to, 597 b, 4to; the words are not decipherable in the vellum.

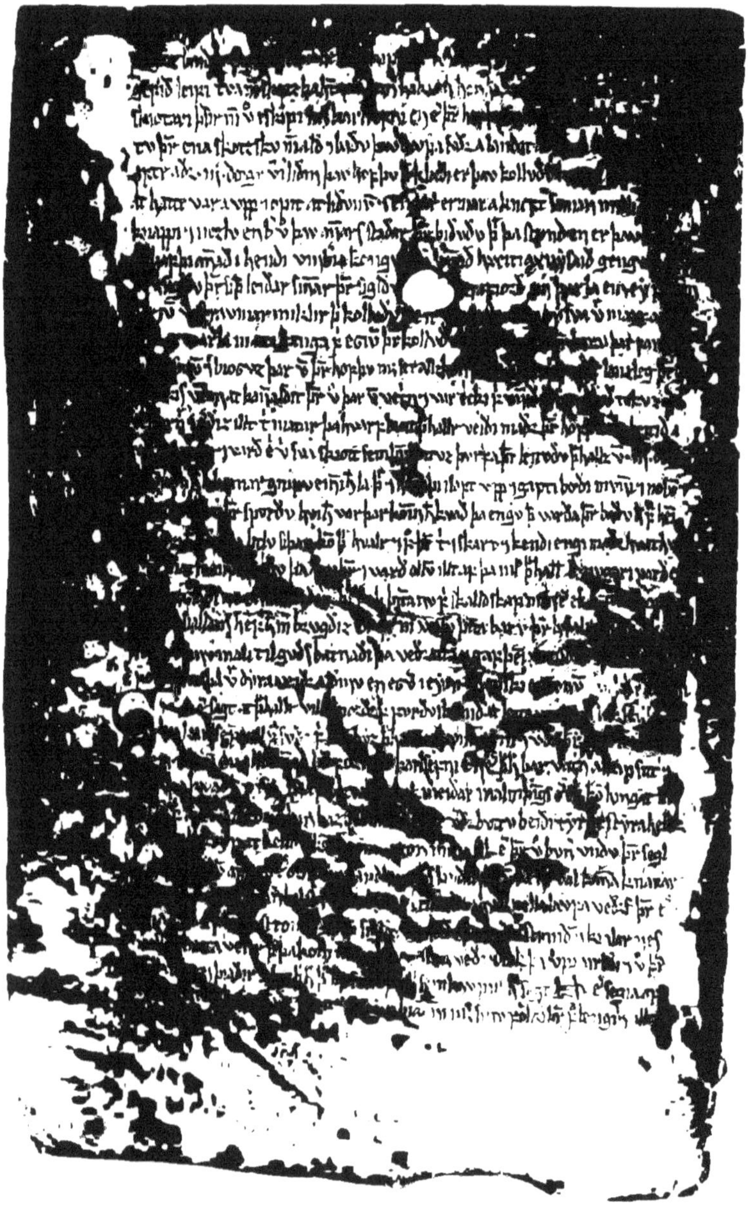

1. Þá gørðisk landit vágskorit. Þeir heldu skipunum í einn vág. Óláfr konungr Tryggvason hafði
2. gefit Leifi tvá menn skozka, hét maðrinn Haki, en hon Hekja [1]. Þau váru dýrum
3. skjótari. Þessir menn váru í skipi með Karlsefni; en er þeir hǫfðu siglt fyrir Furðustrandir, þá lé-
4. tu þeir ena skozku menn á land, ok báðu þau hlaupa suðr á landit, at leita landskosta ok koma
5. aptr áðr III dœgr væri liðin. Þau hǫfðu þat klæði, er þau kǫlluðu kjafal, þat var svá gǫrt,
6. at hattr var á upp, ok opit at hliðunum, ok engar ermar á, knept saman milli fóta með
7. knappi ok nezlu, en ber váru þau annarsstaðar. Þeir biðuðu þar þá stund, en er þau kómu ap-
8. tr, hafði annat í hendi vínberja kǫngul, en annat hveitiax nýsáit. Gengu þau á skip
9. út, ok sigldu þeir síðan leiðar sinnar. Þeir sigldu inn á fjǫrð einn; þar lá ein ey fyrir utan;
10. þar um váru straumar miklir; því kǫlluðu þeir hana Straumey. Svá var mǫrg æðr í
11. eynni, at varla mátti ganga fyrir eggjum. Þeir kǫlluðu þar Straumfjǫrð. Þeir báru þar farm af
12. skipum sínum, ok bjoggusk þar um. Þeir hǫfðu með sér allskonar fénað. Þar var fagrt landsleg. Þeir gá-
13. ðu enkis utan at kanna landit. Þeir váru þar um vetrinn, ok var ekki fyrir unnit um sumarit. Tókusk af
14. veiðarnar, ok gørðisk illt til matar. Þá hvarf brott Þórhallr veiðimaðr. Þeir hǫfðu áðr heitit á
15. guð til matar, ok varð eigi við svá skjótt, sem þeir þóttusk þurfa. Þeir leituðu Þórhalls um III dœgr,
16. ok fundu hann á hamargnípu einni. Hann lá þar, ok horfði í lopt upp, ok gapti bæði munni ok nǫsum, ok
17. þulði nǫkkut. Þeir spurðu hví hann var þar kominn. Hann kvað þá engu þat varða. Þeir báðu hann fara heim
18. með sér, ok hann gørði svá. Lítlu síðar kom þar hvalr, ok fóru þeir til, ok skáru, ok kendi engi maðr hvat hvala
19. var, ok er matsveinar suðu, þá átu þeir, ok varð ǫllum illt af. Þá mælti Þórhallr: 'Drjúgari varð enn
20. rauðskeggjaði nú en Kristr yðarr. Hefir ek þetta nú fyrir skáldskap minn, er ek orta um Þór fu-
21. lltrúann; sjaldan hefir hann mér brugðizk.' Ok er menn vissu þetta, báru þeir hvalinn allan á kaf,
22. ok skutu sínu máli til guðs. Batnaði þá veðrátta, ok gaf þeim útróðra, ok skorti þá síðan
23. eigi fǫng, því at þá var dýraveiðr á landinu. en eggver í eynni, en fiski ór sjónum. **Af Karlsefni**
24. Svá er sagt, at Þórhallr vill fara norðr fyrir Furðustrandir, at leita Vínlands, **ok Þórhalli.**
25. en Karlsefni vill fara suðr fyrir landit. Býsk Þórhallr út undir eynni, ok verða þeir eigi fleiri saman
26. en IX menn; en allt annat lið fór með Karlsefni. En er Þórhallr bar vatn á skip sitt, ok
27. drakk. þá kvað hann vísu: 'Hafa kváðu mik meiðar málmþings, er ek kom hingat, mér
28. samir land fyrir lýðum lasta, drykkinn bazta. Bilds hattar verðr buttu beiðitýr at stýra, heldr
29. er svá at ek krýp at keldu; komat vín á grǫn mína.' Ok er þeir váru búnir, undu þeir segl.
30. Þá kvað Þórhallr: 'Fǫrum aptr þar er órir eru, sandhimins, landar, látum kenni val kanna knarrar
31. skeið en breiðu; meðan bilstyggvir byggja bellendr, ok hval vella, laufa veðrs, þeir er
32. leyfa lǫnd á Furðustrǫndum.' Síðan sigldu þeir norðr fyrir Furðustrandir ok Kjalarnes,
33. ok vildu beita vestr fyrir. Þá kom móti þeim vestanveðr, ok rak þá upp á Írlandi, ok váru þeir
34. þar barðir ok þjáðir, ok lét Þórhallr þar líf sitt, eptir því sem kaupmenn hafa sagt. Nú er [at] segja af
35. Karlsefni, at hann fór suðr fyrir landit, ok Snorri ok Bjarni með sínu fólki. Þeir fóru lengi, ok allt þar

[1] MS., apparently through a clerical slip, en hon haki en hon hekia.

1. til er þeir kómu at á einni, er ſell aſ landi oſan ok í vatn eitt til sjóvar. Eyrar váru þar miklar,
2. ok mátti eigi komask í ána utan at háflœðum. Þeir Karlsefni sigldu í ósinn, ok kǫlluðu í Hópi.
3. Þeir fundu þar á landi sjálfsána hveitiakra, þar sem lægðir
4. váru, en vínvið allt þar sem holta vissi. Hverr lœkr var þar fullr aſ
5. fiskum. Þeir gǫrðu graſir þar sem mœttisk landit, ok flóðit gekk oſast,
6. ok þá er út ſell sjórinn, váru helgir fiskar í grǫſunum. Þar var mikill ſjǫl-
7. ði dýra á skóginum með ǫllu móti. Þeir váru þar hálfan má-
8. nað, ok skemtuðu[1] sér, ok urðu[2] við ekki varir. Fé sitt hǫſ-
9. ðu þeir með sér. Ok einn morgin snemma, er þeir litu-
10. ðusk[3] um, sá þeir mikinn ſjǫlða húðkeipa, ok var veiſt
11. trjám[4] á skipunum, ok lét því líkast sem í hálmþust, [ok]
12. var veiſt sólarsinnis. Þá mælti Karlsefni: 'Hvat man þetta hafa [at]
13. teikna?' Snorri Þorbrandsson svarar honum: 'Vera kann at þetta sé ſriðar-
14. mark, ok tǫkum skjǫld hvítan, ok berum at móti;' ok svá gǫrðu þeir. Þá
15. reru þeir í mót, ok undruðusk[5] þá, sem ſyrir váru, ok gengu á land upp. Þeir váru svar-
16. tir menn ok illiligir, ok hǫſðu illt hár á hǫſði. Þeir váru mjǫk eygðir ok breiðir
17. í kinnum. Dvǫlðusk þeir oſ stund, ok undruðusk[5] þá, sem ſyrir váru, ok reru sí-
18. ðan í brott, ok suðr ſyrir nesit. Þeir Karlsefni hǫſðu gǫrt búðir sínar upp frá
19. vatninu, ok váru sumir skálarnir nær vatninu, en sumir firr. Nú váru þeir þar þann
20. vetr. Þar kom enginn snjór, ok allt gekk fé þeira sjálfala fram. En er vá-
21. ra tók, sá þeir einn morgin snemma, at ſjǫlði húðkeipa reri sunnan
22. ſyrir nesit, svá mart sem kolum væri sáit ſyrir hópit; var þá ok veiſt [á] hverju
23. skipi trjánum[6]. Þeir Karlsefni brugðu þá skjǫldum upp, ok er þeir fundusk, tó-
24. ku þeir kaupstefnu sín[7] á milli, ok vildi þat fólk helzt hafa rautt
25. skrúð. Þeir hǫſðu móti [at] gefa skinnavǫru ok algrá skinn. Þeir vildu ok kaupa sverð
26. ok spjót, en þat bǫnnuðu þeir Karlsefni ok Snorri. Þeir Skrælingar tóku sp-
27. annarlangt rautt skrúð ſyrir úſǫlvan belg, ok bundu um hǫfuð sér. Gekk
28. svá kaupstefna þeira um hríð. Þá tók at fættask skrúðit með þeim
29. Karlsefni, ok skáru þeir þá svá smátt í sundr, at eigi var breiðara en þvers
30. fingrs, ok gáfu Skrælingar þó jafnmikit ſyrir sem áðr eða meira. Þat bar
31. til, at graðungr hljóp ór skógi, er þeir Karlsefni áttu, ok gellr hátt. Þetta fæ-
32. lask Skrælingar, ok hlaupa út á keipana ok reru síðan suðr ſyrir landit.
33. Verðr þá ekki vart við þá þrjár vikur í samt. En er sjá stund var liðin,
34. sjá þeir fara sunnan mikinn ſjǫlða Skrælinga skipa, svá sem straumr stœði, var
35. þá trjánum[6] ǫllum veiſt andsœlis, ok ýla upp allir mjǫk hátt. Þá tóku

[1] MS. skemtadu. [2] MS. uordu, i.e. vurðu. [3] MS. litadust. [4] MS. triom.
[5] MS. undradust. [6] MS. trionum. [7] sin repeated in MS.

[HAUKSBÓK, p. 100 *b*.] ÞORFINNS SAGA KARLSEFNIS—16.

þeir Karlsefni rauðan skjǫld, ok báru at móti. Skrælingar hljópu[1] af skipum, ok síðan gengu þeir saman, ok bǫrðusk. Varð þar skothríð hǫrð, því at Skrælingar hǫfðu valslǫngur. Þat sá þeir Karlsefni, at Skrælingar fœrðu upp á stǫng knǫtt stundar mikinn, því nær til at jafna sem sauðarvǫmb, ok helzt blán at lit, ok fleygðu af stǫnginni upp á landit yfir lið þeira Karlsefnis, ok lét illiliga við, þar sem niðr kom. Við þetta sló ótta miklum á Karlsefni ok allt lið hans, svá at þá fýsti engis annars en flýja, ok halda undan upp með ánni, því at þeim þótti lið Skrælinga drífa at sér ǫllum megin, ok létta eigi fyrr en þeir koma til hamra nǫkkurra, ok veittu þar viðrtǫku harða. Freydís kom út, ok sá at þeir Karlsefni heldu undan, ok kallaði: 'Hví renni þér undan þessum auvirðismǫnnum, svá gildir menn sem þér eruð, er mér þótti sem þér mættið drepa niðr svá sem búfé; ok ef ek hefða vápn, þótti mér sem ek skylda betr berjask, en einnhverr yðar!' Þeir gáfu engan gaum hennar[2] orðum. Freydís vildi fylgja þeim, ok varð seinni, því at hon var eigi heil; gekk hon þó eptir þeim í skóginn. En Skrælingar sœkja at henni. Hon fann fyrir sér mann dauðan, þar var Þorbrandr Snorrason, ok stóð hellusteinn í hǫfði honum; sverðit lá bert í hjá honum; tók hon þat upp, ok býsk at verja sik. Þá kómu Skrælingar at henni, en hon dró þá út brjóstit undan klæðunum, ok slettir á beru sverðinu. Við þetta óttask Skrælingar, ok hljópu[1] undan á skip sín, ok reru í brott. Þeir Karlsefni finna [nú] hana[3], ok lofa kapp hennar. Tveir menn fellu af þeim Karlsefni, en fjǫldi af þeim Skrælingum. Urðu þeir Karlsefni ofrliði bornir, ok fóru nú heim eptir þetta til búða sinna, ok bundu sár sín, ok hugsa hvat fjǫlmenni þat myndi verit hafa, er at þeim sótti af landinu ofan. Sýnisk þeim nú sem þat eina mun liðit verit hafa, er af skipunum kom, en hitt fólkit man verit hafa sjónhverfingar. Þeir Skrælingar fundu einn mann dauðan, ok lá øx í hjá. Einn þeira tók upp øxina, ok hjó[4] með tré, ok þá hverr at ǫðrum, ok þótti þeim vera gǫrsimi, ok bíta vel[5]; síðan tók einn ok hjó[4] í stein, svá at brotnaði øxin, ok þá þótti þeim engu nýt, er eigi stóðsk grjótit, ok kǫstuðu[6] niðr. Þeir Karlsefni þóttusk nú sjá, þótt þar væri landskostir góðir, at þar myndi jafnan ótti ok úfriðr á liggja af þeim, er þar bjoggu. Síðan bjoggusk þeir á brott, ok ætluðu til síns lands, ok sigldu norðr fyrir landit, ok funnu V Skrælinga í skinnhjúpum

[1] MS. lupu.
[2] MS. adds syllable 'or,' repeated in next line.
[3] Björn á Skarðsá [AM. 118, 8vo] writes in place of 'finna nú hana,' which is not clear in the vellum, 'finna nú Freydís.'
[4] MS. huggj.
[5] MS. val.
[6] MS. kastadu.

[HAUKSBÓK, p. 101.] ÞORFINNS SAGA KARLSEFNIS—17.

sofnaða nær sjó; þeir hǫfðu með sér stokka, ok í dýramerg dreyra blandinn. Þóttusk þeir Karlsefni þat skilja, at þessir menn myndu hafa verit gørvir brott af landinu; þeir drápu þá. Síðan fundu þeir Karlsefni nes eitt, ok á fjǫlða dýra; var nesit at sjá, sem mykiskán væri, af því at dýrin lágu þar um nætrnar. Nú koma þeir Karlsefni aptr í Straumfjǫrð, ok váru þar fyrir alls gnóttir, þess er þeir þurftu at hafa. Þat er sumra manna sǫgn, at þau Bjarni ok Guðríð[1] hafi þar eptir verit, ok X tigir manna með þeim, ok hafi eigi farit lengra. En þeir Karlsefni ok Snorri hafi suðr farit, ok XL manna með þeim, on hafi eigi lengr verit í Hópi en vart tvá mánaði, ok hafi sama sumar aptr komit. Karlsefni fór þá einu skipi at leita Þórhalls veiðimanns, en annat liðit var eptir; ok fóru þeir norðr fyrir Kjalarnes, ok berr þá fyrir vestan fram, ok var landit á bakborða þeim. Þar váru þá eyðimerkr einar allt at sjá fyrir þeim, ok nær hvergi rjóðr í. Ok er þeir hǫfðu lengi farit, fellr á af landi ofan ór austri ok í vestr; þeir lǫgðu inn í árósinn, ok lágu við hinn syðra bakkann. Þat var einn morgin, er þeir Karlsefni sá fyrir ofan **Víg Þorvalds Eiríkssonar.** rjóðrit flekk nǫkkurn, sem glitraði við þeim, ok æptu þeir á þat; þat hrœrðisk, ok var þat Einfœtingr, ok skauzk ofan á þann árbakkann, sem þeir lágu við. Þorvaldr, Eiríks son rauða, sat við stýri, ok skaut Einfœtingr ǫr í smáþarma honum. Þorvaldr dró út ǫrina, ok mælti: 'Feitt er um ístruna, gott land hǫfum vér fengit kostum, en þó megum vér varla njóta!' Þorvaldr dó af sári þessu lítlu síðar. Þá hleypr Einfœtingr á braut, ok norðr aptr. Þeir Karlsefni fóru eptir honum, ok sá hann stundum. Þat sá þeir síðast til hans, at hann hljóp á vág nǫkkurn. Þá hurfu þeir Karlsefni aptr. Þá kvað einn maðr kviðling þenna: 'Eltu seggir, allsatt var þat, einn Einfœting ofan til strandar; en kynligr maðr kostaði rásar hart um stopir. Heyrðu Karlsefni!' Þeir fóru þá í brott, ok norðr aptr, ok þóttusk sjá Einfœtingaland. Vildu þeir þá eigi hætta liði sínu lengr. Þeir ætluðu ǫll ein fjǫll, þau er í Hópi váru, ok þessi, er nú fundu þeir, ok þat stœðisk mjǫk svá á, ok væri jafnlangt ór Straumfirði beggja vegna. Hinn þriðja vetr váru þeir í Straumfirði. Gengu menn þá mjǫk í sveitir, ok varð þeim til um konur, ok vildu þeir, er úkvændir váru, sœkja til í hendr þeim, sem kvændir váru, ok stóð af því hin mesta úró. Þar kom til hit fyrsta haust Snorri, son Karlsefnis, ok var hann þá þrévetr, er þeir fóru brott. Þá er þeir sigldu af Vínlandi tóku þeir suðrœn veðr, ok hittu þá Markland, ok fundu þar Skrælinga V, ok var einn skeggjaðr, konur váru II, ok bǫrn tvau. Tóku þeir Karlsefni sveinana, en hinir kómusk undan, ok sukku þeir Skrælingar í jǫrð niðr. Sveina þessa II hǫfðu þeir með sér Þeir kendu þeim mál, ok váru skírðir. Þeir nefndu móður sína Vethilldi, ok fǫður Uvege. Þeir sǫgðu at konungar stjórnuðu Skrælingum, ok hét annarr þeira Avalldama, en annarr Avilldudida[2]. Þeir kváðu þar engin hús, lágu menn þar í hellum eða holum. Þeir sǫgðu þar liggja land ǫðrum megin gagnvart sínu landi, er þeir menn bygði, er váru í hvítum klæðum, ok báru stangir fyrir sér, ok váru festar við flíkar, ok æpðu hátt, ok ætla menn, at þat hafi verit Hvítramannaland eða Írland et mikla. Þá Bjarna Grímólfsson bar í Írlands haf, ok kómu í maðksjó, ok

[1] MS. *sic.*   [2] Björn á Skardsá [AM. 118, 8vo] has 'Avalldainna' and 'Valldidida.

[HAUKSBÓK, p. 101 *b*.] ÞORFINNS SAGA KARLSEFNIS—18.

1. søkk drjúgum skipit undir þeim; þeir høfðu bát þann, er bræddr var með seltjøru, því at þar fær eigi sjómaðkr
2. á. Þeir gengu í bátinn, ok sá þeir þá, at þeim mátti hann eigi øllum vinnask. Þá mælti Bjarni: 'Af því at bátrinn tekr
3. eigi meira en helming manna várra, þá er þat mitt ráð, at menn sé hlutaðir í bátinn, því at þetta skal ekki fara at
4. mannvirðingu.' Þetta þótti øllum svá drengiliga boðit, at engi vildi móti mæla. Gørðu þeir svá, at [þeir]
5. hlutuðu mennina, ok hlaut Bjarni at fara í bátinn, ok helmingr manna með honum, því at bátrinn tók ekki meira.
6. En er þeir váru komnir í bátinn, þá mælti einn íslenzkr maðr, er þá var í skipinu, ok Bjarna hafði fylgt af
7. Íslandi: 'Ætlar þú, Bjarni, hér at skiljask við mik?' Bjarni svarar: 'Svá verðr nú at vera.' Hann svarar: 'Qðru hézk
8. þú føður mínum, þá er ek fór af Íslandi með þér, en skiljask svá við mik, þá er þú sagðir, at eitt sk-
9. yldi ganga yfir okkr báða.' Bjarni svarar: 'Eigi skal ok svá vera, gakk þú hingat í bátinn, en ek man upp
10. fara í skipit, því at ek sé, at þú ert svá fúss til fjørsins.' Gekk Bjarni þá upp í skipit, en þessi maðr í
11. bátinn, ok fóru þeir síðan leiðar sinnar, til þess er þeir kómu til Dyflinnar á Írlandi, ok søgðu þar þessa søgu; en
12. þat er flestra manna ætlan, at Bjarni ok hans kumpánar hafi látizk í maðksjónum, því at ekki spurðisk til þeira
13. Annat sumar eptir fór Karlsefni til Íslands, ok Guðríðr **Ættartala frá Karlsefni ok Þuríði, konu hans.** síðan[1].
14. með honum, ok fór heim í Reynisnes. Móður hans þótti sem hann hefði lítt til kostar tekit, ok var Guðr-
15. íðr eigi heima enn fyrsta vetr. En er hon prófaði, at Guðríðr var kvennskørungr mikill, fór
16. hon heim, ok váru samfarar þeira góðar. Dóttir Snorra Karlsefnissonar var Hallfríðr, móðir Þorláks biskups
17. Runólfssonar. Þau áttu son, er Þorbjørn hét; hans dóttir hét Þórunn, móðir Bjarnar biskups. Þorgeirr hét
18. son Snorra Karlsefnissonar, faðir Yngvildar, móður Brands biskups hins fyrra. Dóttir Snorra, Karlsefnis-
19. sonar var ok Steinunn, er átti Einarr, son Grundar-Ketils, Þorvaldssonar króks, Þórissonar
20. á Espihóli. Þeira son var Þorsteinn ranglátr, hann var faðir Guðrúnar, er átti Jørundr at Keldum;
21. þeira dóttir var Halla, móðir Flosa, føður Valgerðar, móður herra Erlends sterka, føður herra Hauks
22. løgmanns. Qnnur dóttir Flosa var Þórdís, móðir frú Ingigerðar ríku. Hennar dóttir var frú Hallbera, ab-
23. badís í Reynisnesi at Stað. Mart stórmenni er komit annat á Íslandi frá Karlsefni ok Þuríði, þat er ekki
24. er hér skráð. Veri guð með oss, amen.

[1] 'síðan' to be read at the end of line 12.

[AM. 557, 4to, p. 27.] EIRÍKS SAGA RAUÐA[1]—1.

[Ó]láfr[2] hét konungr, er kallaðr var Óláfr hvíti. Hann var son Ingjalds konungs Helgasonar, Óláfssonar, Guðrøðarsonar[3], Hálfdanarsonar hvítbeins Upplendinga konungs. Óláfr herjaði í vestrvíking, ok vann Dyflinni[4] á Írlandi ok Dyflinnarskíri, ok gørðisk konungr yfir. Hann fekk[5] Auðar djúpauðgu, dóttur Ketils flatnefs, Bjarnarsonar bunu, ágæts manns ór Noregi; Þorsteinn rauðr hét son þeira. Óláfr fell á Írlandi í orrostu, en Auðr ok Þorsteinn fóru þá í Suðreyjar; þar fekk Þorsteinn Þuríðar, dóttur Eyvindar austmanns[6], systur Helga hins magra; þau áttu mǫrg bǫrn. Þorsteinn gørðisk herkonungr. Hann rézk til lags með Sigurði enum ríka, syni Eysteins glumru. Þeir unnu Katanes ok Suðrland, Ros ok Mœri, ok meirr en hálft Skotland. Gørðisk Þorsteinn þar konungr yfir, áðr Skotar sviku hann, ok fell hann þar í orrostu. Auðr var þá á Katanesi, er hon spurði fall Þorsteins. Hon lætr þá gøra knǫrr í skógi á laun, en er hon var búin, helt hon út í Orkneyjar. Þar gipti hon Gró, dóttur Þorsteins, ok hon var móðir Gunnlaðar, er Þorfinnr jarl hausakljúfr átti. Eptir þat fór Auðr at leita Íslands; hon hafði á skipi tuttugu karla frjálsa. Auðr kom til Íslands, ok var hinn fyrsta vetr í Bjarnarhǫfn með Birni bróður sínum. Síðan nam Auðr ǫll Dalalǫnd, milli Dǫgurðarár ok Skrámuhlaupsár, ok bjó í Hvammi. Hon hafði bœnahald í Krosshólum. Þar lét hon reisa krossa, því at hon var skírð ok vel

[1] MS. saga eircks rauda. [2] MS. [O]leifr. [3] MS. gudridar sonar. [4] MS. diflina.
[5] *hann* feck repeated in MS. [6] MS. austz *manns*.

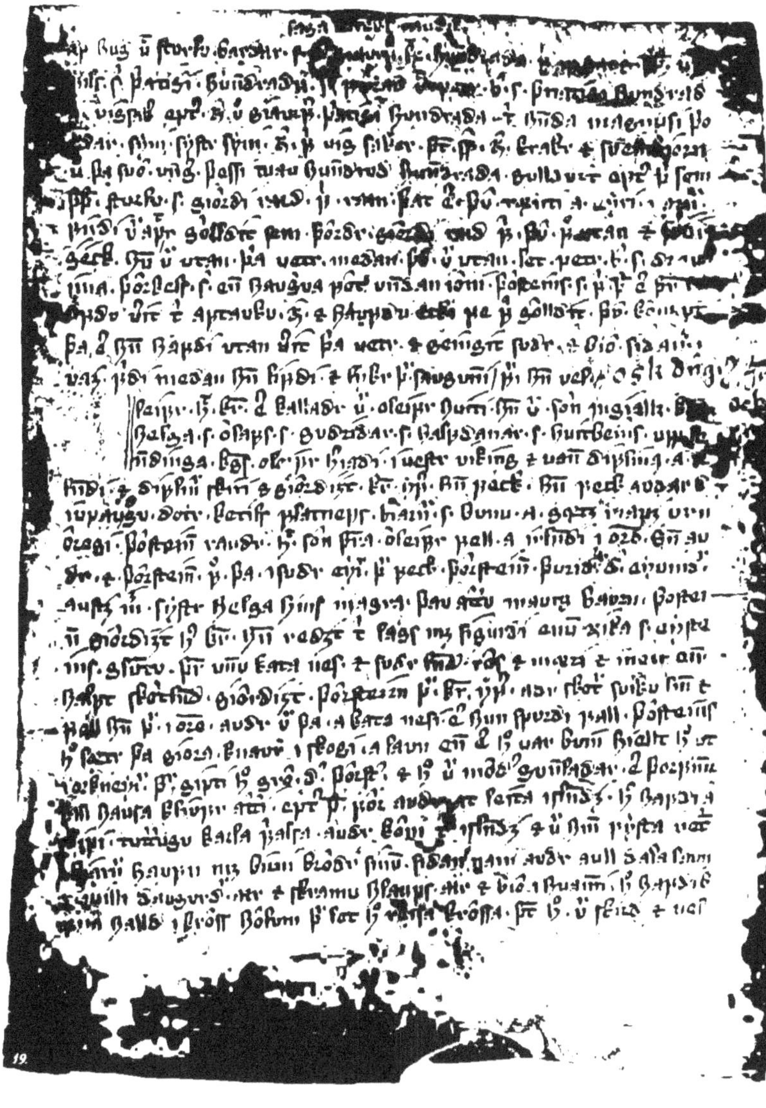

19

mma . af h̄m . bianny ar ingor [illegible]
[illegible] i vestr viking . ok v̄ kallaðr . a nauðg[illegible] [illegible]
[illegible] fyrir . iii . ok hafði ǿrt [illegible] þ. vestan [illegible] kallaðir
augr . aðr auðr . keypti h̄m . ok a . auðr gaf bu stað [illegible]
[illegible] . vífill þ. auðr gaf h̄m bustað . sem auðr [illegible]
[illegible] skiptu . q̄ð h̄m þ. [illegible] [illegible] sam h̄u [illegible]
[illegible] vífils . dal . ok bió . [illegible] h̄m . [illegible] kona . [illegible] þorg[illegible]
[illegible] . [illegible] . [illegible] ey . [illegible] rauði [illegible]
Þorvalldr . [illegible] h̄m v . son . asvalds . ulfs son . [illegible] þo[illegible]
[illegible] rauði . [illegible] . [illegible] fóru af iaðri [illegible]
[illegible] . námu lond . a hornstrondu . ok bjuggu at drǫngum . þ. [illegible]
[illegible] . Þorvalldr . eirekr [illegible] . þa . þorhilldar [illegible]
þorbiargar knarrar bringu . en þa [illegible] . þorbiorn [illegible] haukdælsk[illegible]
[illegible] . eirekr þa norðan . ok ruddi . lond i hauka . dal . ok bio a eireks stǫðum . [illegible] . þa [illegible] þrælar . eir . skriðu . a [illegible] valþiofs . a valþiofs stǫðum . eyiolfr saurr . [illegible] . [illegible] . þrælana . [illegible]
[illegible] skeiðs brekku . upp fra vatz horni . [illegible] nó eirekr . eyiolf saur
[illegible] ok holmgǫngu . hrafn . at leikskalum . [illegible] . ok oddr . a [illegible]
þa . [illegible] eyiolfs . mæltu eptir h̄m . þa v̄ . eirekr gǫrr a brott [illegible]
hauka dal . h̄n nam þa brokey . ok bio . at [illegible] i suðr ey . [illegible]
[illegible] [illegible] . [illegible] . i [illegible] ey . þa ledi h̄n þorgesti set stokka
h̄n bio a . eireks stǫðum . þa heimti h̄n set . stokkana ok [illegible]
[illegible] . [illegible] set stokkana . a . breiða bolstað . en þorgestr [illegible]
[illegible] [illegible] [illegible] a drǫngum . þ. fellu tveir synir . þorg[illegible]
ok nǫkkurir [illegible] . [illegible] hauguðu [illegible] [illegible] . [illegible]
[illegible] . eireki ok eyiolfr [illegible] . þorbiorn vífils . s. þorvalds [illegible]
a . þ. en . þorgesti [illegible] . [illegible] . [illegible] ok þorgeirr [illegible] dal [illegible]
[illegible] langa . dal ok illugi . son . [illegible] [illegible] [illegible] . [illegible] . a þor[illegible]
[illegible] . h̄n bio . skip sitt . i eireks vogi . en eyiolfr [illegible] . h̄m . i [illegible]
[illegible] vogi . [illegible] þorgestr [illegible] . h̄m [illegible] . h̄n sagði [illegible]
at h̄n ætlaði at leita . lands [illegible] . gunnbiorn . son ulfs . kraku . [illegible]
[illegible] vestr um haf . þa [illegible] gunnbiarnar sker . h̄n [illegible]
[illegible] . [illegible] una [illegible] af h̄m [illegible] . [illegible] þorbiorn ok [illegible]

[illegible]

[AM. 557, 4to, p. 27 *b*.] EIRÍKS SAGA RAUÐA—2.

trúuð. Með[1] henni kvámu út margir gǫfgir menn, þeir er herteknir hǫfðu verit í vestrvíking, ok váru kallaðir ánauðgir. Einn af þeim hét Vífill; hann varr ættstórr maðr, ok hafði verit hertekinn fyrir vestan haf, ok var kallaðr ánauðigr, áðr Auðr leysti hann; ok er Auðr gaf bústaði[2] skipverjum sínum, þá spurði Vífill því Auðr gæfi honum eigi bústað, sem ǫðrum mǫnnum. Auðr kvað eigi mundu skipta, kvað hann þar gǫfgan þikkja mundu, sem hann væri. Honum gaf Auðr Vífilsdal, ok bjó hann þar. Hann átti konu; þeira synir váru þeir Þorgeirr ok Þorbjǫrn. Þeir váru efniligir menn, ok óxu upp með fǫður sínum.

Þorvaldr hét maðr; hann var son Ásvalds, Úlfssonar, Øxna-Þórissonar[3]. Eiríkr rauði hét son hans. Þeir feðgar fóru af Jaðri til Íslands, fyrir víga sakir, ok námu land á Hornstrǫndum, ok bjoggu at Drǫngum. Þar andaðisk Þorvaldr; Eiríkr fekk þá Þórhildar, dóttur Jǫrundar Atlasonar ok Þorbjargar knarrarbringu, en þá átti áðr Þorbjǫrn hinn haukdœlski.

Rézk Eiríkr þá norðan, ok ruddi land í Haukadal, ok bjó á Eiríksstǫðum, hjá Vatnshorni. Þá feldu þrælar Eiríks skriðu[4] á bœ Valþjófs á Valþjófsstǫðum. Eyjólfr saurr, frændi hans, drap þrælana hjá Skeiðsbrekkum, upp frá Vatnshorni. Fyrir þat vá Eiríkr Eyjólf saur; hann vá ok Hólmgǫngu-Hrafn at Leikskálum. Geirsteinn ok Oddr á Jǫrva[5], frændr Eyjólfs, mæltu eptir hann; þá var Eiríkr gǫrr á brott ór Haukadal. Hann nam þá Brokey, ok bjó at Trǫðum í Suðrey. En hinn fyrsta vetr fór Eiríkr í Øxney. Þá léði hann Þorgesti setstokka.

Hann bjó á Eiríksstǫðum; þá heimti hann setstokkana, ok náði eigi. Eiríkr sótti setstokkana á Breiðabólstað, en Þorgestr fór eptir honum.

Þeir bǫrðusk skamt frá garði á Drǫngum. Þar fellu tveir synir Þorgests, ok nǫkkurir menn aðrir. Eptir þat hǫfðu hvárirtveggju setu fjǫlmenna. Styrr veitti Eiríki, ok Eyjólfr ór Svíney, Þorbjǫrn Vífilsson[6], (ok) synir Þorvalds ór Álptafirði[7]. En Þorgesti veittu[8] synir Þórðar gellis, ok Þorgeirr ór Hítardal, ok Áslákr ór Langadal ok Illugi son hans. Þeir Eiríkr urðu sekir á Þórnesþingi. Hann bjó skip sitt í Eiríksvági, en Eyjólfr leyndi honum í Dímunarvági, meðan þeir Þorgestr leituðu hans um eyjarnar. Hann sagði þeim, at hann ætlaði at leita lands þess, er Gunnbjǫrn, son Úlfs kráku, sá, er hann rak vestr um haf, þá [er] hann fann Gunnbjarnarnessker. Hann kvezk aptr mundu leita til vina sinna, ef hann fyndi landit. Þeir Þorbjǫrn ok Styrr ok Ey-

[1] MS. af. [2] MS. bvstad. [3] MS. eyxna þoris *sonar*. [4] MS. skylldv.
[5] MS. iorfa. [6] MS. uifils, the son has been omitted. [7] MS. alt-a *firði*. [8] MS. veitti.

[AM. 557, 4to, p. 28.] EIRÍKS SAGA RAUÐA.—3.

jólfr fylgðu Eiríki út um eyjar, ok skilðu með hinni mestu vináttu. Kvezk Eiríkr þeim skyldu verða at þvílíku trausti, sem hann mætti sér við koma, ef þeir kynni hans at þurfa. Sigldi Eiríkr á haf undan Snæfellsjǫkli, ok kom utan at jǫkli þeim, er Hvítserkr heitir. Hann fór þaðan suðr, at leita ef þangat er byggjanda. Hann var hinn fyrsta vetr í Eiríkseyju, nær miðri enni vestri bygðinni. Um várit eptir fór hann til Eiríksfjarðar, ok tók sér þar bústað. Hann fór þat sumar í hina vestri óbygð, ok gaf víða ǫrnefni. Hann var annan vetr í Eiríkshólmum við Hvarfsgnípu[1]. En hit þriðja sumar fór hann allt norðr til Snæfells, ok inn í Hrafnsfjǫrð. Þá þóttisk hann kominn fyrir botn Eiríksfjarðar; hverfr hann þá aptr, ok var hinn fjórða ok þriðja vetr í Eiríkseyju fyrir munni Eiríksfjarðar. Eptir um sumarit fór hann til Íslands, ok kom í Breiðafjǫrð. Hann var þann vetr með Ingólfi á Hólmlátri[2]. Um várit bǫrðusk þeir Þorgestr, ok fekk Eiríkr úsigr; eptir þat váru þeir sáttir gǫrðir. Þat sumar fór Eiríkr at byggja landit, þat er hann hafði fundit, ok hann kallaði Grœnland. Hann kvað þess menn mundu mjǫk fýsa þangat, ef landit héti vel. Þorgeirr Vífilsson kvángaðisk, ok fekk Arnóru, dóttur Einars frá Laugarbrekku, Sigmundarsonar, Ketilssonar Þistils, er numit hafði Þistilsfjǫrð. Ǫnnur dóttir Einars hét Hallveig; hennar fekk Þorbjǫrn Vífilsson, ok tók með land á[3] Laugarbrekku á Hellisvǫllum. Rézk Þorbjǫrn þangat bygðum, ok gǫrðisk gǫfugmenni mikit. Hann var goðorðsmaðr, ok hafði rausnar bú. Guðriðr hét dóttir Þorbjarnar; hon var kvenna vænst ok hinn mesti skǫrungr í ǫllu athæfi sínu. Maðr hét Ormr, er bjó at Arnarstapa; hann átti konu þá, er Halldís hét. Ormr var góðr bóndi, ok vinr Þorbjarnar mikill; var Guðríðr þar lǫngum at fóstri með honum. Maðr hét Þorgeirr, er bjó at Þorgeirsfelli; hann var vellauðigr at fé, ok hafði verit leysingi[4]; hann átti son, er Einarr hét, hann var vænn maðr ok vel mannaðr, ok skartsmaðr[5] mikill. Einarr var í siglingum landa í milli, ok teksk þat vel; var jafnan sinn hvárt vetr á Íslandi eða í Noregi. Nú er frá því at segja eitt haust, er Einarr var út hér, at hann fór með varning sinn út eptir Snæfellsnesi, ok skyldi selja. Hann kemr til Arnarstapa; Ormr býðr honum þar at vera, ok þat þiggr Einarr, því at þar var vinátta við kǫrin. Varningrinn Einars var borinn í eitthvert útibúr. Einarr brýtr upp varninginn, ok sýndi Ormi ok heimamǫnnum, ok bauð Ormi sí-

[1] MS. hv*ar*fsnipv.

[2] MS. holatri.

[3] MS. apparently by a clerical slip, l*and* a lan*n*di a.

[4] MS. lavsin*n*g.

[5] MS. skazz ma*ðr*.

[illegible]

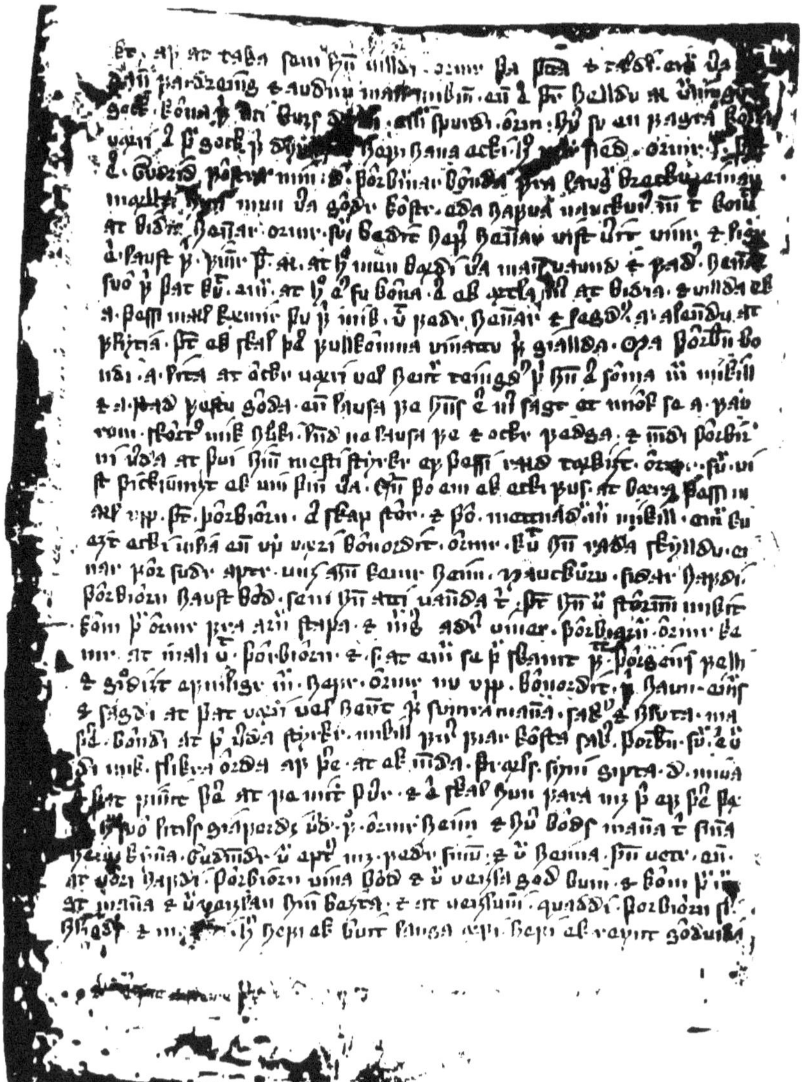

[AM. 557, 4to, p. 28 *b*.] EIRÍKS SAGA RAUÐA.—4.

kt aſ at taka sem hann vildi. Ormr þá þetta, ok talði Einar vera góðan ſardreng ok auðnumann mikinn. En er þeir heldu á varninginum, gekk kona ſyrir útibúrs dyrnar. Einarr spurði Orm hver sú en ſagra kona væri, er þar gekk ſyrir dyrnar; 'ek heſi hana ekki hér ſyrr sét.' Ormr segir: 'Þat er Guðríð[1], ſóstra mín, dóttir Þorbjarnar bónda ſrá Laugarbrekku.' Einarr mælti: 'Hon mun vera góðr kostr, eða haſa nǫkkurir menn til komit at biðja hennar?' Ormr svarar: 'Beðit heſir hennar víst verit, vinr, ok liggr eigi laust ſyrir; finnr þat á, at hon mun vera mannvǫnd, ok ſaðir hennar.' 'Svá ſyrir þat,' kvað Einarr, 'at hon er sú kona, er ek ætla mér at biðja, ok vilda ek á þessi mál kœmir þú ſyrir mik við ſǫður hennar, ok legðir á alendu[2] at flytja, því at ek skal þér ſullkomna vináttu ſyrir gjalda. Má Þorbjǫrn bóndi á líta, at okkr væri vel hentar tengðir, því at hann er sómamaðr mikill ok á staðſestu góða, en lausaſé hans er mér sagt at[3] mjǫk sé á ſǫrum. Skortir mik hvárki land né lausaſé, ok okkr ſeðga, ok mundi Þorbirni verða at því hinn mesti styrkr, eſ þessi ráð tœkisk.' Ormr svarar: 'Víst þikkjumk ek vin þinn vera. En þó em ek ekki ſúss at bera þessi mál upp, því at Þorbjǫrn er skapstórr ok þó metnaðarmaðr mikill.' Einarr kvezk ekki vilja [annat] en [at] upp væri [borit] bónorðit. Ormr kvað hann ráða skyldu. Einarr ſór suðr aptr unz hann kemr heim. Nǫkkuru síðar haſði Þorbjǫrn haustboð, sem hann átti vanda til, því at hann var stórmenni mikit. Kom þar Ormr ſrá Arnarstapa ok margir aðrir vinir Þorbjarnar. Ormr kemr at máli við Þorbjǫrn, ok segir, at Einarr sé þar skamt[4] ſrá Þorgeirsſelli, ok gǫrðisk eſniligr maðr; heſr Ormr nú upp bónorðit ſyrir hǫnd[5] Einars, ok sagði at þat væri vel hent ſyrir sumra manna sakir ok hluta. 'Má þér, bóndi, at því verða styrkr mikill ſyrir ſjárkosta sakir.' Þorbjǫrn svarar: 'Eigi varði mik slíkra orða aſ þér, at ek munda þræls syni gipta dóttur mína; ok þat finnið þér at ſé mitt þverr, ok eigi skal hon ſara með þér, eſ þér þœtti hon svá lítils gjaſorðs verð.' Fór Ormr heim, ok hverr boðsmanna til sinna heimkynna. Guðríðr[6] var eptir með ſǫður sínum, ok var heima þann vetr. En at vári haſði Þorbjǫrn vinaboð, ok var veizla góð búin, ok kom þar margt manna, ok var veizlan hin bezta. Ok at veizlunni kvaddi Þorbjǫrn sér hljóðs, ok mælti: 'Hér heſi ek búit langa æſi; heſi ek reynt góðvilja

[1] MS. *sic*. [2] MS. ale*nn*da. [3] MS. apparently et.
[4] Properly, skǫmmu. [5] MS. haun. [6] MS. Guðm*un*dr.

[AM. 557, 4to, p. 29.] EIRÍKS SAGA RAUDA—5.

manna við mik ok ástúð; kalla ek vel vár skipti farit hafa. En nú tekr fjárhagr[1] minn at úhœgjask, en kallat hefir verit hingat til ekki úvirðuli-gt[2] ráð. Nú vil ek fyrr búi mínu bregða, en sœmð minni týna; fyrr af landi fara, en ætt mína svívirða. Ætla ek nú at vitja um mál Eiríks[3] rauða, vinar míns, er hann hafði, þá er vér skilðumsk á Breiðafirði. Ætla ek nú at fara til Grœnlands í sumar, ef svá ferr sem ek vilda.' Mǫnnum þ-ótti mikil tíðindi um þessa ráðagørð Þorbjarnar[3]. Þorbjǫrn hafði len-gi vinsæll verit, en[4] þóttusk vita, at Þorbjǫrn mundi þetta hafa sv-á framt upp kveðit, at[5] hann mundi ekki stoða at letja. Gaf Þorbjǫrn mǫnnum gja-fir, ok var veizlu brugðit eptir þetta, ok fóru menn heim til heimkynna sinna. Þorbjǫrn selr lendur sínar, ok kaupir skip, er stóð uppi í Hraunhafnarósi. Ré-ðusk til ferðar með honum þrír tigir manna. Var þar Ormr frá Arnarstapa ok kona hans, ok þeir vinir Þorbjarnar, er eigi vildu við hann skilja. Síðan létu þeir í haf. Þá er þeir hǫfðu út látit, var veðr hagstœtt. En er þeir kvámu í haf, tók af byri, ok fengu þeir mikil veðr, ok fórsk þeim úgreitt um sumarit. Því næ-st kom sótt í lið þeira, ok andaðisk Ormr ok Halldís, kona hans, ok helmingr þeira. Sjó tók at stœrka[6], ok fengu þeir vás mikit ok vesǫld á marga vega, ok tóku þó Herjólfsnes á Grœnlandi við vetrnætr sjálfar. Sá maðr bjó á Herjólfsnesi, er Þorkell hét. Hann var nytjamaðr[7] ok hinn bezti bóndi. Hann t-ók við Þorbirni ok ǫllum skipverjum hans um vetrinn. Þorkell veitti þeim skǫr-uliga. Líkaði Þorbirni vel ok ǫllum skipverjum hans. [lítit, þeir sem í v-[8], [Í] þenna tíma var hallæri mikit á Grœnlandi; hǫfðu menn fengit eiðiferð[9] hǫfðu verit, en sumir eigi aptr komnir. Sú kona var í by-gð, er Þorbjǫrg hét; hon var spákona; hon var kǫlluð lítil vǫlva[10]. Hon hafði átt sér níu systr, ok var hon ein eptir á lífi. Þat var háttr Þorbjargar á vetr-um, at hon fór á veizlur, ok buðu menn henni heim, mest þeir, er forvitni var á um forlǫg sín eða atferðir; ok með því at Þorkell var þar mestr bóndi, þ-á þótti til hans koma at vita hvenær[11] létta mundi úárani þessu, sem yf-ir stóð. Þorkell býðr spákonu þangat, ok er henni búin góð viðtaka, sem siðr var til, þá er við þess háttar konum skyldi taka. Búit var henni hásæti, ok lagt undir hœgindi; þar skyldi í vera hœnsafiðri. En er hon kom um kveldit, ok sá maðr, er í móti henni var sendr, þá var hon svá búin, at hon hafði yfir sér tuglamǫttul[12] blán, ok var settr steinum allt í sk-aut ofan. Hon hafði á hálsi sér glertǫlur; hon hafði á hǫfði lamb-skinns kofra svartan, ok við innan kattarskinn hvítt. Staf hafði hon í hendi, ok

[1] MS. fiarhugr. [2] MS. *virdvligt*. [3] MS. Eircks.
[4] ek is added in MS. after en, obviously by a slip: menn should be supplied in its stead. [5] MS. *er*.
[6] MS. sta*rka*. [7] nytiv *maðr*. [8] The bracketed words belong at the end of line 22.
[9] MS. vedr *ferd*. [10] MS. litill volve. [11] MS. hven*ær* at vita. [12] MS. tygla mauttvl.

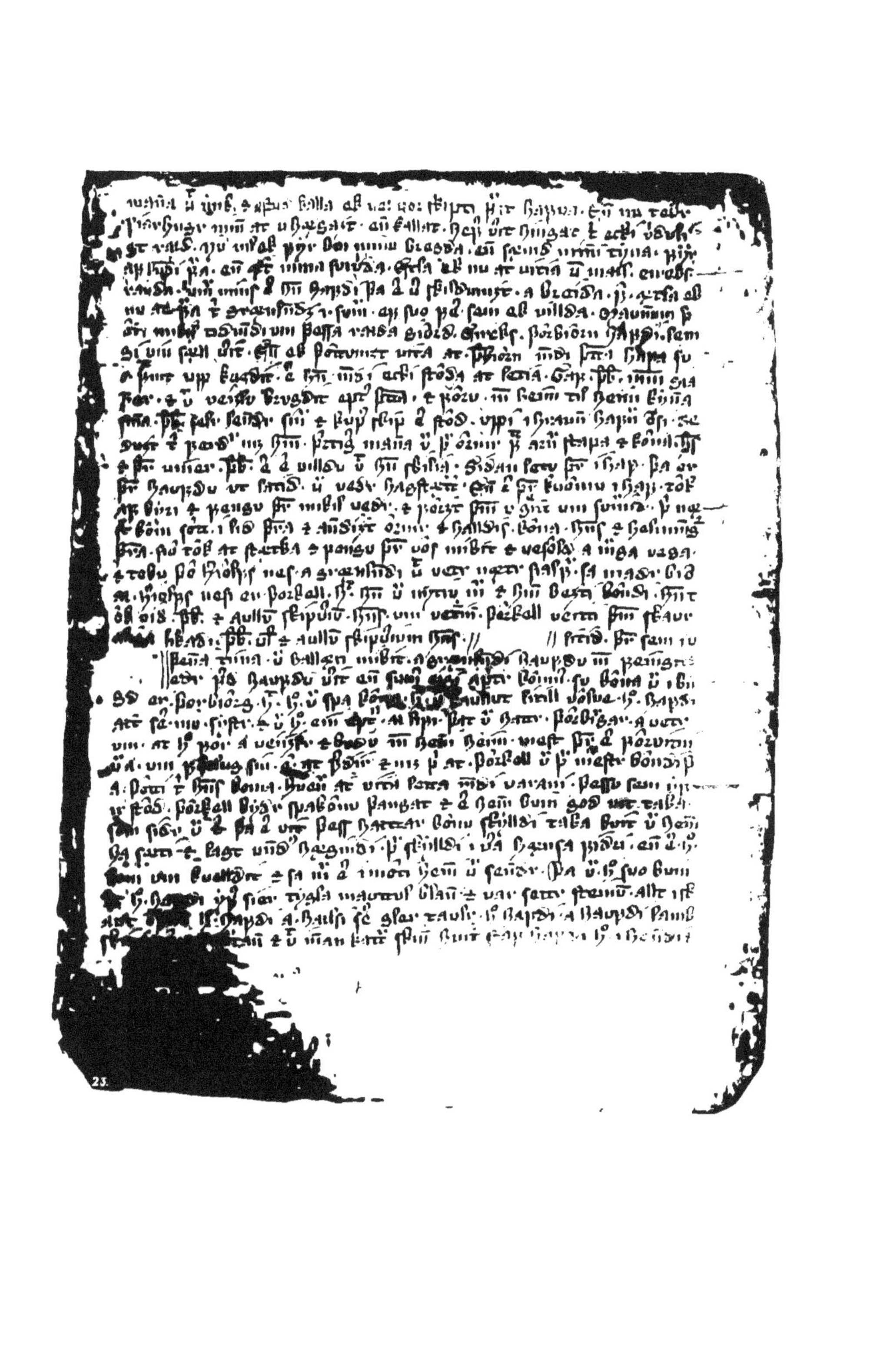

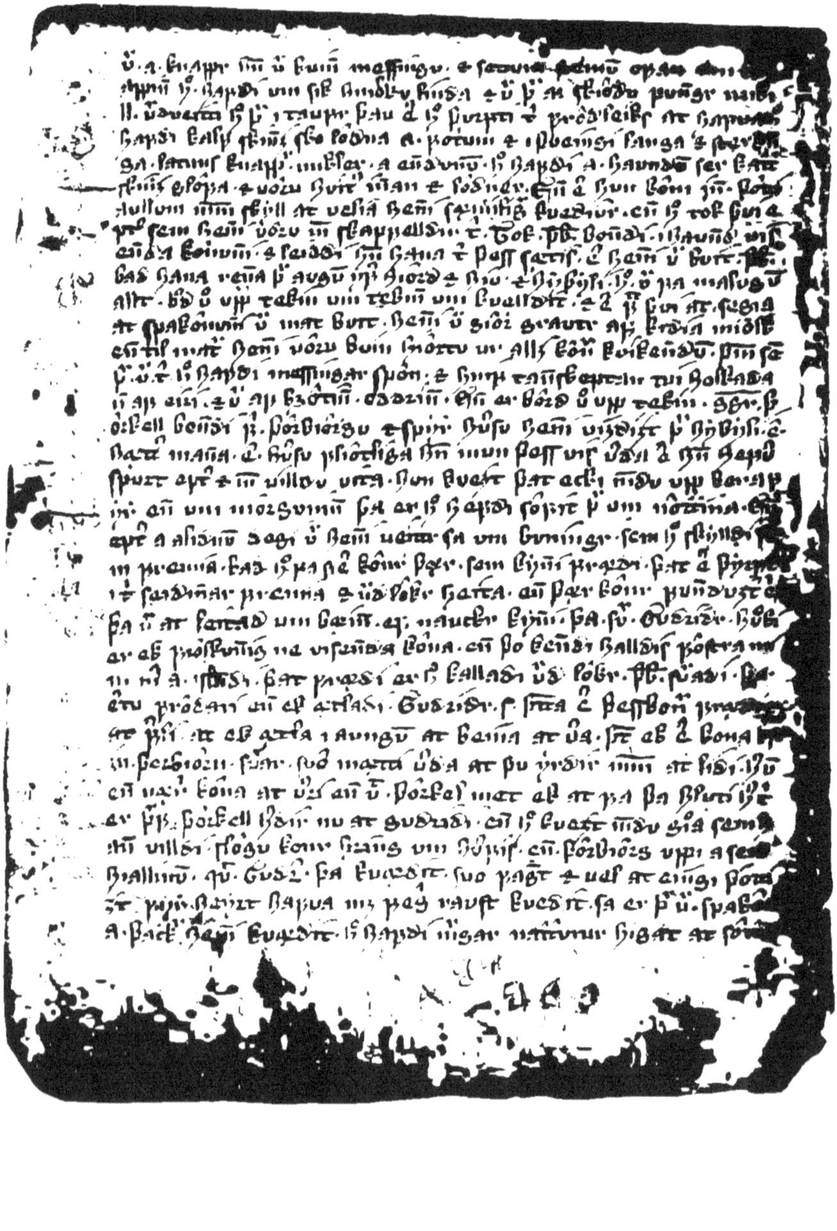

[AM. 557, 4to, p. 29 *b*.] EIRÍKS SAGA RAUÐA.—6.

var á knappr; hann var búinn messingu, ok settr[1] steinum ofan um kn-appinn. Hon hafði um sik hnjóskulinda, ok var þar á skjóðupungr miki-ll; varðveitti hon þar í taufr þau, er hon þurfti til fróðleiks at hafa. Hon hafði kálfskinns-skó loðna á fótum, ok í þvengi langa ok sterkli-ga, látúnsknappar miklir á endunum. Hon hafði á hǫndum sér katt-skinns-glófa, ok váru hvítir innan ok loðnir. En er hon kom inn, þótti ǫllum mǫnnum skylt[2] at velja henni sœmiligar kveðjur. En hon tók því e-ptir sem henni váru menn skapfeldir til. Tók Þorkell bóndi í hǫnd vís-endakonunni, ok leiddi hann hana til þess sætis, er henni var búit. Þorkell bað hana renna þar augum yfir hjǫrð ok hjú ok hýbýli. Hon var fámálug um allt. Borð váru upp tekin[3] um kveldit, ok er frá því at segja at spákonunni var matbúit. Henni var gǫrr grautr af kiðjamjólk, en til matar henni váru búin hjǫrtu ór allskonar kvikendum, þeim sem þar váru til. Hon hafði messingarspón ok kníf[4] tannskeptan, tvíholkaða-n af eiri, ok var af brotinn oddrinn. En er borð váru upp tekin, gengr Þ-orkell bóndi fyrir Þorbjǫrgu, ok spyrr hversu henni virðisk[5] þar hýbýli eða hættir manna, eða hversu fljótliga hann mun þess víss verða, er hann hefir spurt eptir, ok menn vildu vita. Hon kvezk þat ekki mundu upp bera f-yrr en um morgininn[6], þá er hon hefði sofit þar um nóttina. En eptir á áliðnum degi var henni veittr sá umbúningr, sem hon skyldi se-iðinn[7] fremja. Bað hon fá sér konur þær, sem kynni frœði þat, er þyrft-i til seiðinn at fremja[8], ok varðlokkur[9] heita; en þær konur fundusk eigi. Þá var at leitat um bœinn, ef nǫkkur kynni. Þá svarar Guðríðr: 'Hvárki em[10] ek fjǫlkunnig né vísenda kona, en þó kendi Halldís, fóstra mí-n, mér á Íslandi, þat frœði, er hon kallaði varðlokkur[9].' Þorbjǫrg svaraði: 'Þá ertu fróðari en ek ætlaða.' Guðríðr segir: 'Þetta er þess konar frœði ok atferli, at ek ætla í ǫngum atbeina at vera, því at ek em[10] kona krist-in.' Þorbjǫrg[11] svarar: 'Svá mætti verða, at þú yrðir mǫnnum at liði hér um, en værir kona [eigi] at verri; en við Þorkel met ek at fá þá hluti hér til, er þarf.' Þorkell herðir nú at Guðríði, en hon kvezk mundu gǫra sem h-ann vildi. Slógu konur hring umhverfis, en Þorbjǫrg uppi á seið-hjallinum. Kvað Guðríðr þá kvæðit svá fagrt ok vel, at engi þótti-isk fyrr heyrt hafa með fegri raust kveðit, sá er þar var. Spákon-a þakkar henni kvæðit; 'hon hafði margar náttúrur hingat at sótt, ok

[1] MS. settum. [2] MS. skyll. [3] MS. upp tekin um tekin*n*. [4] MS. knif. [5] MS. vizdizt.
[6] MS. morgvnin*n*. [7] MS. se in, apparently a clerical omission. [8] MS. seidin*n*ar fremia.
[9] MS. vard lokr. [10] MS. er. [11] MS. þorbjǫrn.

[AM. 557, 4to, p. 30.] EIRÍKS SAGA RAUDA—7.

1. þótti fagrt[1] at heyra þat er kveðit var, er áðr vildi frá oss snúa-
2. sk, ok oss øngva hlýðni veita. En mér eru nú margir þeir hlutir a-
3. uðsýnir, er áðr var bæði ek ok aðrir dulðir. En ek kann þat at
4. segja, at hallæri þetta mun ekki haldask lengr, ok mun batna
5. árangr sem várar. Sóttarfar þat, sem lengi hefir legit, mun batna v-
6. ánu bráðara. En þér, Guðríðr, skal ek launa í hǫnd liðsinni þat, se-
7. m oss hefir af [þér] staðit, því at þín forlǫg eru mér nú ǫll glǫggsæ. Þat
8. muntu gjaforð fá hér á Grœnlandi, er sœmiligast er til, þó at þér ver-
9. ði þat eigi til langæðar, því at vegir þínir liggja út til Íslands, ok mun þar ko-
10. ma frá þér ættbogi bæði mikill ok góðr, ok yfir þínum ættkvíslum m-
11. un skína bjartr geisli; enda far nú vel ok heil, dóttir mín!' Síðan ge-
12. ngu menn at vísenda-konunni, ok frétti hverr eptir því sem mest forvitni var á.
13. Var hon ok góð af frásǫgnum; gekk þat ok lítt í tauma, sem hon [sagði]. Þessu næst var k-
14. omit eptir henni af ǫðrum bœ, ok fór hon þá þangat. Var sent eptir Þorbirni, þ-
15. ví at hann vildi eigi heima vera meðan slík heiðni var framin[2]. Veð-
16. rátta[3] batnaði skjótt, þegar er vára tók, sem Þorbjǫrg hafði sagt. B-
17. ýr Þorbjǫrn skip sitt, ok ferr unz hann kemr í Brattahlíð. Tekr Eiríkr við
18. honum báðum hǫndum, ok kvað þat vel, er hann var þar kominn. Var Þorbjǫrn með honum um
19. vetrinn, ok skuldalið hans. Eptir um várit gaf Eiríkr Þorbirni land á Stok-
20. kanesi, ok var þar gǫrr sœmiligr bœr, ok bjó hann þar síðan. Eiríkr átti þá ko-
21. nu, er Þjóðhildr hét, ok tvá sonu; hét annarr Þorsteinn, en annarr Leifr. Þ-
22. eir váru báðir efniligir menn; var Þorsteinn heima með fǫður sínum, ok var eigi þá s-
23. á maðr á Grœnlandi, er jafnmannvænn þótti sem hann. Leifr hafði
24. siglt til Noregs; var hann þar með Ólafi konungi Tryggvasyni. En er Leifr sigldi
25. af Grœnlandi um sumarit, urðu þeir sæhafa til Suðreyja. Það-
26. an byrjaði þeim seint, ok dvǫlðusk þar lengi um sumarit. Leifr
27. lagði hug á konu þá, er Þórgunna hét. Hon var kona ættstór. Þat sá
28. Leifr, at hon mundi kunna fleira en fátt eitt; en er Leifr sigldi á
29. brott,[4] beiddisk Þórgunna at fara með honum. Leifr spurði hvárt þat v-
30. æri nǫkkut vili frænda hennar. Hon kvezk ekki at því fara. Leifr
31. kvezk eigi kunna at gǫra hertekna svá stórættaða konu í ókunn-
32. u landi; 'en vér liðfáir.' Þórgunna mælti: 'Eigi er víst, at þér þikki
33. því betr ráðit.' 'Á þat mun ek hætta,' sagði Leifr. 'Þá segi
34. ek þér,' sagði Þórgunna, 'at ek fer eigi einsaman, ok mun ek vera

[1] MS. fagvrt. [2] MS. framan. [3] MS. vedradtta. [4] MS. bvrt.

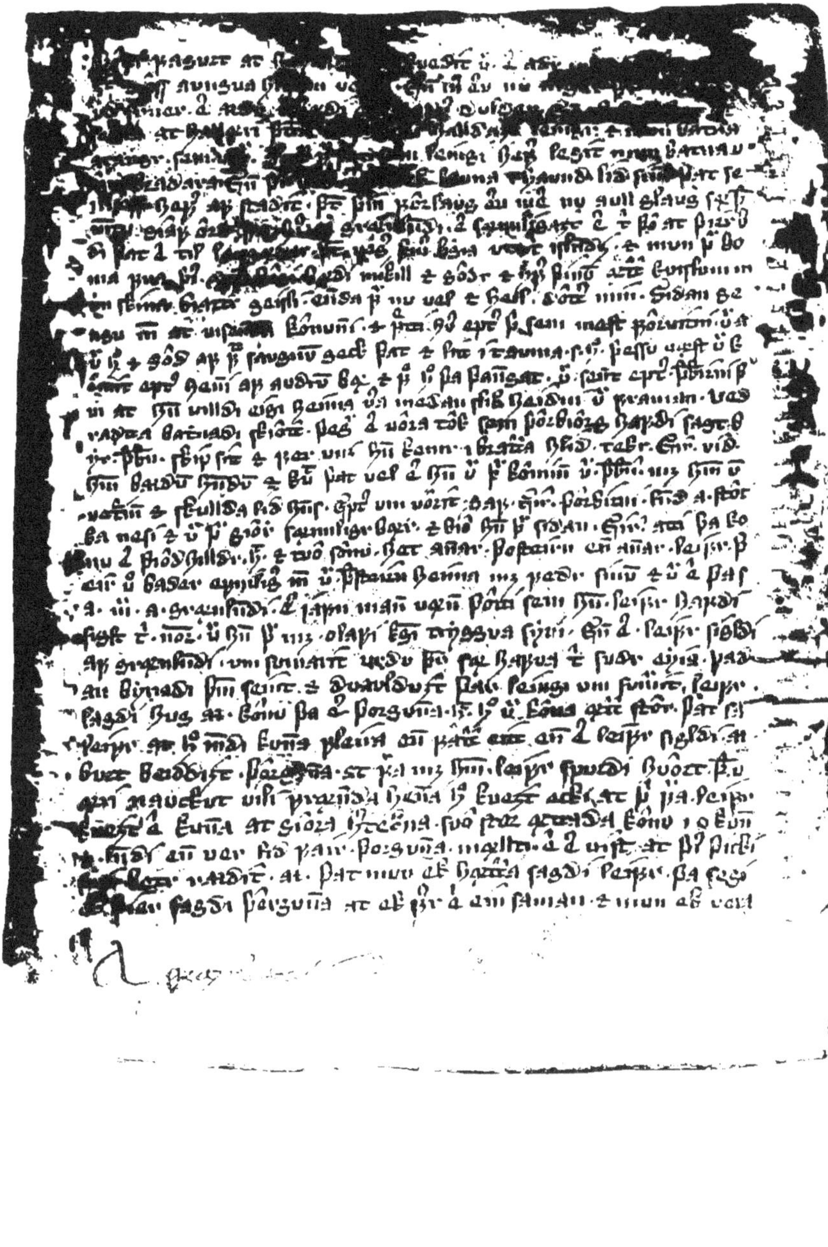

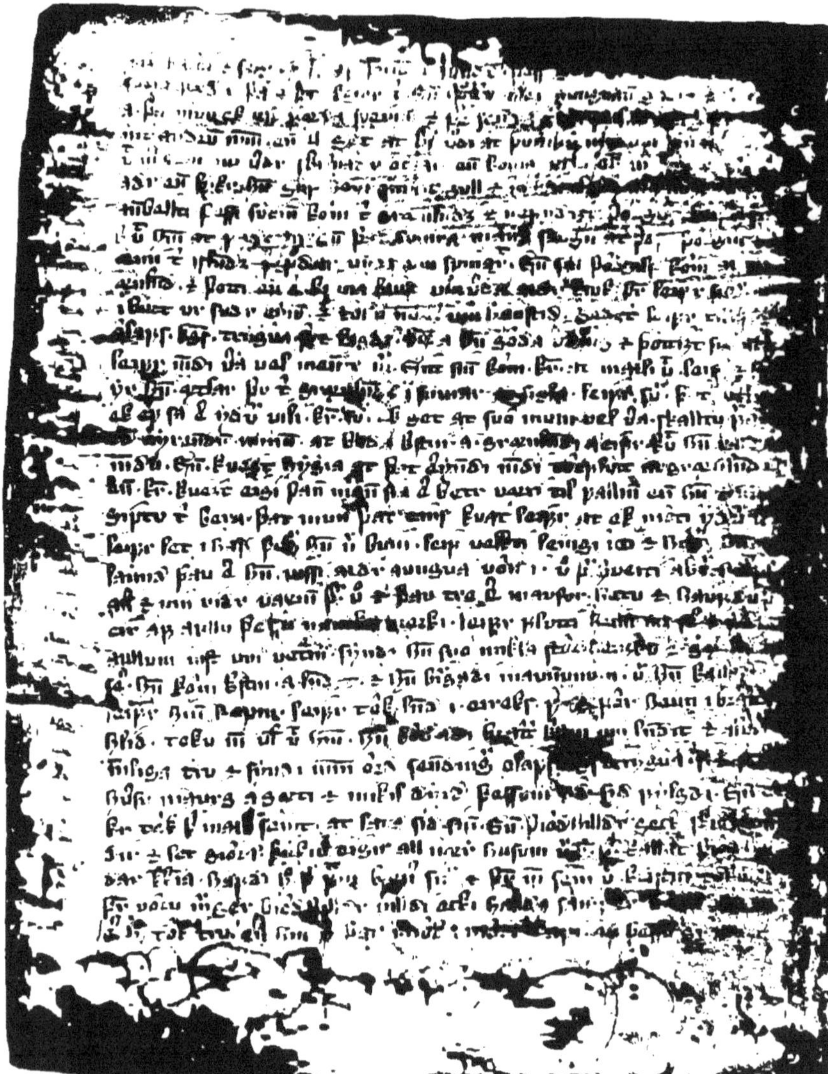

[AM. 557, 4to, p. 30 *b*.] EIRÍKS SAGA RAUÐA—8.

með barni, ok segi ek þat af þínum vǫldum. Þess get ek ok, at ek muni[1] svein fœða, þá er þar kemr til. En þóttú vilir øngvan gaum at gef-[1]a, þá mun ek upp fœða sveininn, ok þér senda til Grœnlands, þegar fara má[1] með ǫðrum mǫnnum. En ek get, at þér verði at þvílíkum nytjum sonareignin[1] við mér, sem nú verðr skilnaðr okkar til[1]; en koma ætla ek til Grœnlands[1] áðr en lýkr.' Hann gaf henni fingrgull, ok mǫttul grœnlenzkan ok t-[1]annbelti. Þessi sveinn kom til Grœnlands, ok nefndisk Þorgils. Leifr tó-k við honum at faðerni; en þat [er] sumra manna sǫgn, at þessi Þorgils k-œmi til Íslands í Fróðárundr um sumarit. En sjá Þorgils kom á Gr-œnland, ok þótti enn eigi kynjalaust um verða, áðr lauk. Þeir Leifr sigldu í brott ór Suðreyjum, ok tóku Noreg um haustit. Rézk Leifr til hirðar Óláfs konungs Tryggvasonar, ok lagði konungr á hann góða virðing, ok þóttisk sjá at Leifr mundi vera vel mentr maðr. Eitt sinn kom konungr at máli við Leif, ok sp-yrr hann: 'Ætlar þú til Grœnlands í sumar at sigla?' Leifr svarar: 'Þat vilda[2] ek, ef sá er yðvarr vili.' Konungr svarar: 'Ek get, at svá muni vel vera. Skaltu fara m-eð ørindum mínum, at boða kristni á Grœnlandi.' Leifr kvað hann ráða mundu, en kvezk hyggja, at þat ørindi mundi torflutt á Grœnlandi. En konungr kvezk eigi þann mann sjá, er betr væri til fallinn en hann, 'ok muntu giptu til bera.' 'Þat mun því at eins,' kvað Leifr, 'at ek njóta[3] yðvar við.' Leifr lét í haf, þegar hann var búinn. Leif velkti lengi úti, ok hitti hann á lǫnd þau, er hann vissi áðr øngva ván í. Váru þar hveitiakrar sjálfs-ánir, ok vínviðr vaxinn. Þar váru ok þau tré, er mǫsur[r][4] hétu, ok hǫfðu þ-eir af ǫllu þessu nǫkkur merki. Leifr flutti heim með sér, ok fekk ǫllum vist um vetrinn[5]. Sýndi hann svá mikla stórmensku ok gœzku af sér, [er] hann kom kristni á landit, ok hann bjargaði mǫnnunum; var hann kallaðr Leifr hinn heppni. Leifr tók land í Eiríksfirði, ok fór hann heim í Bratta-hlíð. Tóku menn vel við honum. Hann boðaði brátt kristni um landit, ok alme-nniliga trú, ok sýndi mǫnnum orðsendingar Óláfs konungs Tryggvasonar ok segir hversu mǫrg ágæti ok mikil dýrð þessum sið[6] fylgði. Eirí-kr tók því máli seint, at láta sið sinn. En Þjóðhildr gekk skjótt un-dir, ok lét gøra kirkju eigi allnær húsum. Var þat hús kallat Þjóðhil-darkirkja. Hafði hon þar fram bœnir sínar, ok þeir menn sem við kristni tóku, en þeir váru margir. Þjóðhildr vildi ekki halda samfarir við Eirík, síðan er hon tók trú, en honum var þat mjǫk í móti skapi. Af þessu gørðisk

[1] The words and syllables thus marked are not clearly legible in the vellum.
[2] MS. vildi.
[3] MS. nioti.
[4] MS. mavsvr.
[5] The scribe has apparently omitted a line after merki, the reference in this sentence being clearly to the ship-wrecked mariners.
[6] Repeated in MS.

[AM. 557, 4to, p. 31.] EIRÍKS SAGA RAUÐA—9.

orð mikit, at hann mundi leita lands þess, er Leifr hafði fundit. Var þar formaðr [1] at [1] Þorsteinn [1] Eiríksson, góðr maðr ok fróðr, ok vinsæll. Eiríkr var ok til beðinn, ok trúðu menn [1] því, at hans gæfa mundi framast vera ok forsjá. Hann var þá við [2], er vinir hans fýstu hann til. Bjoggu þeir skip þat síðan, er Þorbjǫrn hafði út haft, ok váru til ráðnir tuttugu menn. Hǫfðu þeir fé lítit, en mest vápn ok vistir. Þann morgin er Eiríkr fór heiman tók hann kistil, ok var þar í gull ok silfr; fal hann þat fé, ok fór síðan leiðar sinnar; ok er hann var skamt á leið kominn, fell hann af baki, ok braut rif sín, ok lesti ǫxl sína, ok kvað við: 'a iai!' Af þessum atburð sendi hann konu sinni orð, at hon tœki féit á brott, þat [3] er hann hafði fólgit; lét þess hafa at goldit, er hann hafði féit fólgit. Síðan sigldu þeir út ór Eiríksfirði með gleði, ok þótti vænt um sitt ráð. Þá velkði lengi út í hafi, ok kvámu ekki á þær sæin [4] slóðir, [er] þeir vildu. Þeir kvámu í sýn við Ísland, ok svá hǫfðu þeir fugl af Írlandi. Reiddi þá skip þeira um haf innan. Fóru aptr um haustit, ok váru mœddir ok mjǫk þrekaðir, ok kvámu við sjálfan Eiríksfjǫrð. 'Kátari váru þér í sumar, er þér fóruð út ór [5] firðinum, en nú eru þér, ok eru nú þó mǫrg góð at.' Þorsteinn mælti: 'Þat er þó hǫfðingligt bragð, at sjá nǫkkut ráð fyrir þeim mǫnnum, sem nú eru ráðlausir, ok fá þeim vistir.' Eiríkr svarar: 'Skal þeim orð um þetta fara [6] ǫll.' [7] um þeim er eigi hǫfðu áðr vistir, með þeim feðgum. Síðan tóku þeir land, ok fóru heim. [Guðríði Þorbjarnardóttur. Var því m-[7]

Nú er frá því at segja, at Þorsteinn Eiríksson vakði bónorð við áli vel svarat, bæði af henni, ok svá af fǫður hennar; ok er þetta at ráðum gǫrt, at Þorsteinn gekk at eiga Guðríði, ok var brúðkaupit í Brattahlíð um haustit. Fór sú veizla vel fram, ok var mjǫk fjǫlmennt. Þorsteinn átti bú í Vestribygð á bœ þeim, er í Lýsufirði heitir. Sá maðr átti [1] þar helming í búi, er Þorsteinn hét; Sigríðr hét kona hans. Fór Þorsteinn [1] í Lýsufjǫrð. Fór Þorsteinn í Lýsufjǫrð [8] ok [þau] Guðríðr bæði. Var þar vel við þeim tekit. Váru þau þar um vetrinn [9]. Þat gǫrðisk þar til tíðinda, at sótt kom í bœ þeira, er lítit var af vetri. Garði hét þar verkstjóri; hann var óvinsæll maðr; hann tók fyrst sótt, ok andaðisk. Síðan var skamt at [1] bíða, at hverr tók sótt at ǫðrum, ok ǫnduðusk. Þá tók sótt Þorsteinn Eiríksson, ok Sigríðr, kona Þorsteins; ok eitt kveld fýstisk hon at ganga til garðs þess, er stóð gegnt útidyrum. Guðríðr fylgði, ok sátu þær í mót durunum; þá kvað Sigríðr, 'o!' Guðríðr mælti: Vit hǫfum farit óhyggiliga, ok áttu ǫngvan stað við, at í kalt veðr koma [10], ok fǫrum inn sem skjótast. Sigríðr svarar: 'Eigi fer ek at svá búnu. Hér er [1] liðit allt hit [11] dauða fyrir dyrunum, ok þar í sveit kenni ek Þorstein bónda þinn, ok kenni ek mik, ok er slíkt hǫrmung at sjá;' ok er þetta leið

[1] The words and syllables so marked are not clearly decipherable.

[2] The passage between þá and við is not decipherable in the vellum, and the paper copies are not agreed in their readings. The Kall. Coll. [Royal Library, Copenhagen,] 616, 4to, New Roy. Coll. 1697, 4to, AM. 563 *b*, 4to, 401, fol. [amended], Rask Coll. 30, have 'var hann brátt þessa fúss;' Thott. Coll. 984 *a*, fol. and 1776, 4to [Royal Library, Copenhagen], New Roy. Coll. 1714, 4to, AM. 931, 4to, 770 *b*, 4to, 932, 4to, 401, fol., have 'var hann skipsþurfi við.'

[3] MS. apparently þau. [4] *sic.* [5] MS. vrvt.

[6] There is an omission or clerical blunder here which can only be rectified by free emendation.

[7] The bracketed passage belongs to the end of line 22.

[8] Apparently a clerical repetition.

[9] MS. vinturinn. [10] This sentence as it stands is unintelligible. [11] MS. vid.

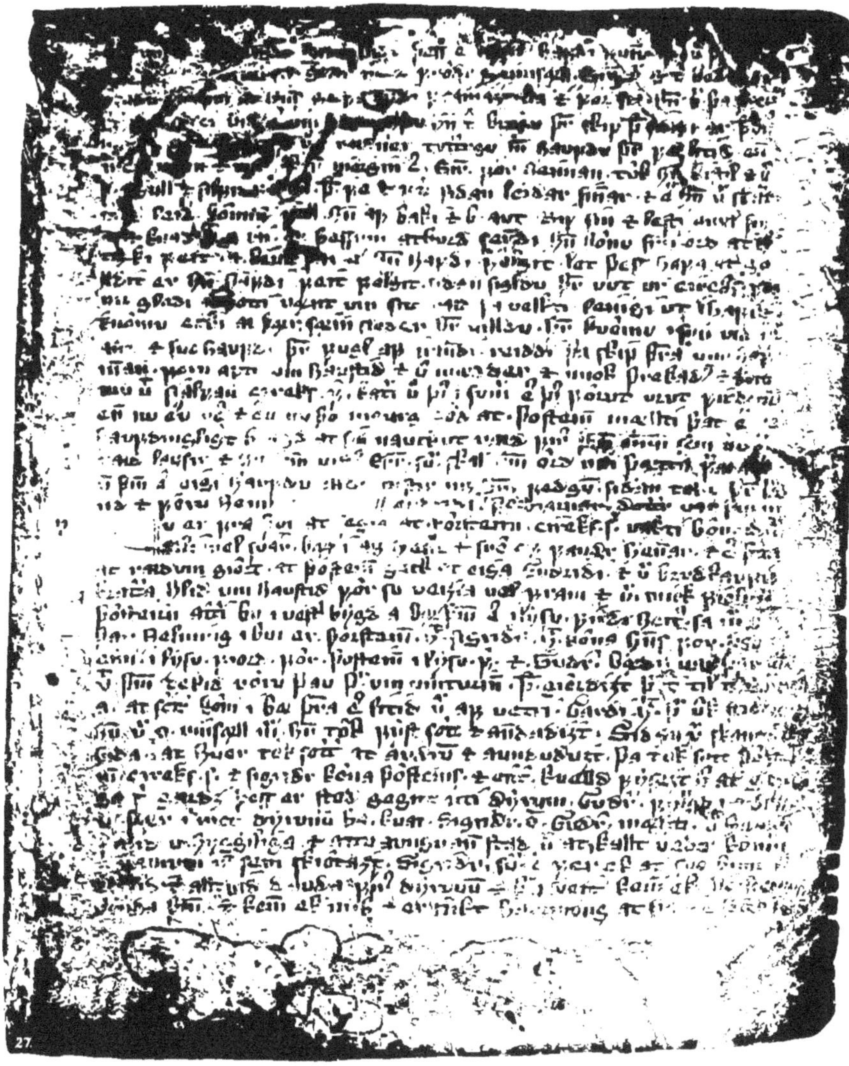

27.

[illegible] vil [illegible] v ꝥ e vestrdum [illegible]
[illegible] hafnar [illegible] ok vilia leita [illegible]
[illegible] morgum [illegible] hauste [illegible] giort [illegible]
dag eptir [illegible] at [illegible] ok leiddi. Þorsteinn [illegible] varð ok [illegible]
[illegible] Þorsteinn at [illegible] vm veizlu [illegible] Þorsteinn [illegible]
na sinu [illegible] at hann [illegible] ok hus. ok sagði suo at [illegible]
husfreyia villdi [illegible] a [illegible] ok villdi undir [illegible]
[illegible] Þorsteinn [illegible] Þorsteinn tok [illegible]
[illegible] ok sagði [illegible] Þorsteinn [illegible]
[illegible] dag [illegible] Þorsteinn bað Guðriði leggiaz niðr ok sofa [illegible]
hann kvaz vaka mundu um nottina [illegible] Guðriðr [illegible]
[illegible] ok [illegible] leið a nottina reistiz hann upp. Þorsteinn [illegible]
[illegible] Þangat [illegible] ok kvaz vilia mæla við hana
Guð vill at [illegible]
[illegible] Þorsteinn gengr a fund Guðriðar ok vakti hana ok bað hana [illegible]
[illegible] ok [illegible] Þorsteinn [illegible]
[illegible] at hann vill [illegible]
[illegible] at [illegible]
[illegible]
[illegible] mikla [illegible]
[illegible] at hann [illegible]
[illegible] Guðriðr [illegible] Þorsteinn [illegible]
[illegible]
[illegible] ok sagði [illegible] mikla [illegible]
[illegible] ok [illegible] ok sagði [illegible] at [illegible]
[illegible] Grænlandi [illegible]
[illegible] kristni [illegible] at [illegible]
[illegible]
[illegible]
[illegible] Guðriðr [illegible]
[illegible] ok [illegible]
[illegible] Grænlandi [illegible]
[illegible]
[illegible] Guðriðr [illegible]
[illegible] kristni [illegible] at [illegible]
[illegible]
[illegible]
[illegible] ok [illegible]

[AM. 557, 4to, p. 31 *b*.] EIRÍKS SAGA RAUÐA—10.

af, mælti hon[1]: 'Nú sé ek eigi liðit.' Var þá ok verkstjórinn horfinn[2], er henni þótti áðr hafa svipu í hendi, ok vilja berja liðit. Síðan gengu þær inn, ok áðr morgunn kœmi, var hon ǫnduð, ok var gǫr kista at líkinu. Ok þann sama dag ætluðu menn út at róa, ok leiddi Þorsteinn þá til vara, ok í annan lit fór hann at sjá um veiðiskap þeira. Þá sendi Þorsteinn Eiríksson nafna sínum orð, at hann kœmi til hans, ok sagði svá, at þar var varla kyrt, ok húsfreyja vildi fœrask á fœtr, ok vildi undir klæðin hjá honum, ok er hann kom inn, var hon komin á rekkjustokkinn hjá honum. Hann tók hana hǫndum, ok lagði bolǫxi fyrir brjóstit. Þorsteinn Eiríksson andaðisk nær dagsetri. Þorsteinn bað Guðríði leggjask niðr ok sofa; en hann kvezk vaka mundu um nóttina yfir líkunum. Hon gǫrir svá. Guðríðr sofnar brátt, ok er skamt leið á nóttina, reistisk hann upp, Þorsteinn, ok kvezk vilja at Guðríðr væri þangat kǫlluð, ok kvezk vilja mæla við hana; 'Guð vill at þessi stund sé mér gefin til leyfis ok umbóta míns ráðs.' Þorsteinn gengr á fund Guðríðar, ok vakði hana, ok bað hana signa sik, ok biðja sér guð hjálpa: 'Þorsteinn Eiríksson hefir mælt við mik, at hann vill finna þik. Sjá þú nú ráð fyrir, hvárskis kann ek fýsa.' Hon svarar: 'Vera kann, at þetta sé ætlat[3] til nǫkkurra hluta þeira, sem síðan eru í minni hafðir, þessi hinn undarligi hlutr, en ek vænti, at guðs gæzla mun yfir mér standa. Mun ek á hætta með guðs miskunn at mæla við hann, því at ek má nú ekki forðask mein til mín. Vil ek síðr at hann gangi[4] víðara. En mik grunar, at þat sé at ǫðrum kosti.' Nú fór Guðríðr, ok hitti Þorsteinn, ok sýndisk henni sem hann feldi tár; ok mælti í eyra henni nǫkkur orð hljótt, svá at hon ein vissi, ok sagði at þeir menn væri sælir, er trúna heldu vel, ok henni fylgði miskunn[5] ok hjálp, ok sagði þó, at margir heldi hana illa; 'er þat engi háttr, sem hér hefir verit á Grœnlandi, síðan kristni var hér, at setja menn niðr í óvígða[6] mold við lítla yfirsǫngva. Vil ek mik láta flytja til kirkju ok aðra þá menn, sem hér hafa andazk, en Garða vil ek láta brenna á báli sem skjótast, því at hann veldr ǫllum aptrgǫngum þeim, sem hér hafa orðit[7] í vetr.' Hann sagði henni ok um sína hagi, ok kvað hennar forlǫg mikil mundu verða. En hann bað hana varask at giptask grœnlenzkum manni; bað hann ok at hon legði fé þeira til kirkju, eða gefa þat fátœkum mǫnnum, ok þá hneig hann aptr í ǫðru [sinni]. Sá hafði háttr verit á Grœnlandi, síðan kristni kom út þangat, at menn váru grafnir þar á bœjum[8], er menn ǫnduðusk[9], í óvígðri[10] moldu; skyldi þar setja staur upp af brjósti[11] en síðan, er kennimenn kvámu til, þá skyldi kippa upp staurinum, ok hella þar í vígðu vatni, ok veita þar

[1] MS. *hon* mælti. [2] Repeated in MS. [3] MS. ætla. [4] MS. ganga. [5] MS. myskyn*n*. [6] MS. vigda. [7] MS. vordit. [8] MS. bœnv*m*. [9] MS. aunduzt. [10] MS. vigri. [11] MS. bristi.

[AM. 557, 4to, p. 32.] EIRÍKS SAGA RAUDA—11.

yfirsǫngva, þótt þat væri miklu síðar. Líkin váru fœrð til kirkju í Eiríksfjǫrð, ok veittir yfirsǫngvar af kennimǫnnum. Eptir þat andaðisk Þorbjǫrn; bar þá féit allt undir Guðríði. Tók Eiríkr við henni, ok sá vel um kost hennar.

[M]aðr hét Þorfinnr karlsefni, son Þórðar hesthǫfða, er bjó norðr í Reyninesi í Skagafirði, er nú er kallat. Karlsefni var ættgóðr maðr, ok vel auðigr at fé. Þórunn hét móðir hans. Hann var í kaupferðum ok þótti fardrengr góðr. Eitt sumar býr Karlsefni skip sitt, ok ætlaði til Grœnlands. Rézk til ferðar með honum Snorri Þorbrandsson[1] ór Álptafirði, ok váru XL manna með þeim. Maðr hét Bjarni Grímólfsson, breiðfirzkr maðr; annarr hét Þórhallr Gamlason, austfirzkr[2] maðr. Þeir bjoggu skip sitt samsumars sem Karlsefni, ok ætluðu til Grœnlands. Þeir váru á skipi XL manna. Láta þeir í haf fram tvennum skipum, þegar þeir eru búnir. Eigi var um þat getit, hversu langa útivist þeir hǫfðu. En frá því er at segja, at bæði þessi skip kvámu í Eiríksfjǫrð um haustit. Eiríkr reið til skips, ok aðrir landsmenn, ok tóksk með þeim greiðlig kaupstefna. Buðu stýrimenn Guðríði at hafa slíkt af varninginum, sem hon vildi. En Eiríkr sýndi mikla stórmensku af sér í móti, því at hann bauð þessum skipverjunum báðum heim til sín til vetrvistar í Brattahlíð. Þetta þágu kaupmenn, ok fóru með Eiríki. Síðan var fluttr heim varningr þeira í Brattahlíð; skorti þar eigi góð ok stór útibúr at varðveita í; líkaði kaupmǫnnum vel með Eiríki um[3] vetrinn. En er dró at jólum, tók Eiríkr at verða óglaðari en[4] hann átti vanda til. Eitt sinn kom Karlsefni at máli við Eirík, ok mælti: 'Er [þér] þungt, Eiríkr? Ek þikkjumk finna, at þú ert nǫkkuru fálátari en verit hefir, ok þú veitir oss með mikilli rausn, ok eru vér skyldir at launa þér eptir því sem vér hǫfum fǫng á. Nú segðu hvat ógleði þinni veldr.' Eiríkr svarar: 'Þér þiggið vel ok góðmannliga. Nú leikr mér þat eigi í hug, at á yðr hallisk um vár viðskipti; hitt er heldr, at mér þikkir illt, ef at er spurt, at þér hafið verit hér svá jólin þessi, er nú koma í hǫnd.' Karlsefni svarar: 'Þat mun ekki á þá leið, vér hǫfum á skipum várum malt ok mjǫl ok korn, ok er yðr heimilt at hafa af slíkt sem þér vilið, ok gǫrið veizlu slíka, sem stórmensku ber til;' ok þat þiggr hann. Var þá búit til jólaveizlu, ok varð hon svá skǫrulig, at menn þóttusk trautt slíka rausnarveizlu sét hafa. Ok eptir jólin vekr Karlsefni við Eirík um ráðahag við Guðríði, er honum leizk sem þat mundi á hans forræði; en honum leizk kona fríð ok vel kunnandi. Eiríkr svarar; kvezk vel mundu undir taka hans mál, en kvað hana góðs gjaforðs verða; 'er þat ok líkligt, at hon fylgi sínum forlǫgum,' þó at hon væri honum gefin; ok kvað góða frétt af honum koma.

[1] MS. þorbiazr son.
[2] MS. austfizdzkr.
[3] Repeated in MS.
[4] MS. ugladr er.

[illegible]
[illegible] vetrar [illegible] eptir [illegible]
[illegible] Eir. [illegible] hann ok sá vel um hennar hag
[illegible] Þorfinnr karlsefni son Þórðar hestshaufða er bjó norðr í Reynines í Skagafirði er nú er kallat. Karlsefni var maðr góð-
ættaðr ok vel auðigr at fé. Þórunn hét móðir hans. Hann var í kaupferðum ok þótti drengr góðr. Annat sumar bjó Karlsefni skip sitt ok ætlaði til
Grænlands. Ræðst til ferðar með honum Snorri Þorbrandsson [illegible]
ok voru xl. manna með þeim. Maðr hét Bjarni Grímólfsson [illegible] annar hét Þórhallr Gamlason austfirzkr. Þeir bjuggu skip sitt it sama sumar sem Karlsefni ok ætluðu til Grænlands. Þeir voru á skipi xl. manna
[illegible] í haf [illegible] tveimr skipum [illegible]
[illegible]
[illegible] báðum þessum skipum [illegible] um haustit. Eir. reið
til skips ok aðrir landsmenn ok tóksk með þeim greiðlig kaupstefna
[illegible] Guðríði at hafa [illegible] af varningi sem hon vildi. En Eir. [illegible] stórmennsku af sér í móti. Bauð hann báðum þessum skipshöfnum [illegible] til sín [illegible]
[illegible] kaupmenn ok fara með Eir. Síðan [illegible]
[illegible] í Brattahlíð. Skorti þar eigi góð ok stór [illegible]
[illegible] kaupmönnum vel með Eir. um vetrinn. En er
[illegible] at jólum tók Eir. at verða [illegible]
[illegible] Karlsefni [illegible] Eir. [illegible]
[illegible]
[illegible]
[illegible]
[illegible]
[illegible]
[illegible]
[illegible]
[illegible]
[illegible]
[illegible]
[illegible]
[illegible]
[illegible]
[illegible]
[illegible]

ru er veizla mikil við hæfi ok lét h(ann) þat fara með sam(þykki) Eir(íks). villdi
hann ok er nu ekki at lengja um þat. at þessi ráð tókusk ok var þá gert aukin ok gjört brúðlaup. gleði mikil var í Brattahlíð um vetrinn. þ(ar) teflu miklar umræður um vetrinn í Brattahlíð at þ(eir) voru
mjök teflt uppi hafðr ok sagna skemtan ok mart þat er til hýbýlis
bóta mátti verða. Töluðu þ(eir) Karlsefni ok Snorri at leita Vínlands ok töluðu m(enn) mart um þ(at). En þar lauk svá at þ(eir) Karlsefni ok Snorri bjuggu skip sitt ok ætluðu at leita Vínlands um sumarit. Til þeirar ferðar réðusk þ(eir) Bjarni ok Þórhallr með skip sitt
ok þat föruneyti er þ(eim) hafði fylgt. Maðr h(ét) Þorvalldr. h(ann)
var mágr Eir(íks) rauða. Þórhallr var kallaðr veiðimaðr. h(ann) hafði
lengi verit í veiðiferðum með Eir(íki) um sumrum ok hafði h(ann)
margar varðveizlur. Þórhallr v(ar) mikill vexti svartr ok þursligr. h(ann)
v(ar) hljóðr við alla. vandr í skapi. hljóðlyndr. jafnan illorðr. h(ann)
eggjaði jafnan Eirík ins verra. ok þó at m(enn) hafði vinátt(u) við h(ann)
hann var illa kristinn. h(ann) hafði lítt vid ..... trú blandazk síðan h(on) kom
á Grænland. Þórhallr v(ar) lítt vinsæll af mörgum. en þá hafði
Eir(íkr) lengi tal af hin(um) haft. h(ann) v(ar) á skipi með Þ(or)v-
alldi. ok h(ann) v(ar) víða kunnigr í óbyggðum. Þ(eir) höfðu þat skip er Þorbjörn hafði út þangat. ok réðusk til ferðar með Karlsefni ok váru þar flestir grænlenzkir menn á. á skipum þeira var fjórir tigir manna ok hundraðs. Sigldu þ(eir) undan til Ve-
stribyggðar ok til Bjarneyja. Sigldu þ(eir) þaðan undan no-
rðanveðri. váru þ(eir) úti tvau dægr. þá fundu þ(eir)
land ok reru fyrir á bátum ok könnuðu landit ok fundu þar hellur margar ok svá stórar at tveir menn máttu vel spyrnast í iljar.
melrakkar váru þ(ar) margir. Þ(eir) gáfu nafn landinu ok kölluðu Helluland. þá sigldu þ(eir) norðanveðr tvau dægr ok var þá land fyrir þ(eim)
ok var á mörk mikil ok dýr mörg. ey lá í landsuðr und-
an landinu ok fundu þ(eir) þar bjarndýr ok kölluðu Bjarney. en
landit kölluðu þ(eir) Markland þ(ar) er mörkin var. þá er liðin váru tvau dægr. sá þ(eir) land. ok þ(eir) sigldu undir landit. Þ(ar) var nes er þ(eir)
kómu at. Þ(eir) beittu með landinu ok létu landit á stjórnborða.
þ(ar) var öræfi ok strandir langar ok sandar. Fara þ(eir) á bátum til
lands ok fundu á nesinu kjöl af skipi ok kölluðu þ(ar) Kjalarnes. Þ(eir) kalla ok nafn strandirnar ok kölluðu Furðustrandir. Þ(ví) at langt v(ar) með at sigla. þá gerðisk vágskorit landit ok heldu þ(eir)
þeir skipunum at vágunum. Þat v(ar) þá er Óláfr konungr Tryggva-
sonr ok h(ann) bað h(ann) boða kristni á Grænlandi ok

[AM. 557, 4to, p. 32 *b*.] EIRÍKS SAGA RAUÐA—12.

Nú er vakit mál við hana, ok lét hon þat sitt ráð, sem Eiríkr vildi fyrir sjá; ok er nú ekki at lengja um þat, at þessi ráð tókusk, ok var þá veizla aukin, ok gǫrt brullaup. Gleði mikil var í Brattahlíð um vetrinn. Á því léku miklar umrœður um vetrinn[1] í Brattahlíð[2], at þar váru mjǫk tǫfl uppi hǫfð ok sagnaskemtan, ok margt þat, er til hýbýlabótar mátti vera. Ætluðu þeir Karlsefni ok Snorri at leita Vínlands, ok tǫluðu menn margt um þat. En því lauk svá, at þeir Karlsefni ok Snorri bjoggu skip sitt, ok ætluðu at leita Vínlands um sumarit. Til þeirar ferðar réðusk þeir Bjarni ok Þórhallr, með skip sitt, ok þat fǫruneyti, er þeim hafði fylgt. Maðr hét Þorvaldr; hann var mágr Eiríks rauða. Þórhallr var kallaðr veiðimaðr; hann hafði lengi verit í veiðifǫrum með Eiríki um sumrum, ok hafði hann margar varðveizlur. Þórhallr var mikill vexti, svartr ok þursligr; hann var heldr við aldr, ódæll í skapi, hljóðlyndr, fámálugr hversdagliga, undirfǫrull, ok þó atmælasamr, ok fýstisk jafnan hins verra. Hann hafði lítt við trú blandazk, síðan hon kom á Grœnland. Þórhallr var lítt vinsældum horfinn, en þó hafði Eiríkr lengi tal af honum haldit. Hann var á skipi með þeim Þorvaldi, því at honum var víða kunnigt í óbygðum. Þeir hǫfðu þat skip, er Þorbjǫrn hafði út þangat, ok réðusk til ferðar með þeim Karlsefni, ok váru þar flestir grœnlenzkir menn á. Á skipum þeira var fjǫrutigi manna annars hundraðs. Sigldu þeir undan síðan til Vestribygðar[3], ok til Bjarneyja. Sigldu þeir undan Bjarneyjum, norðanveðr. Váru þeir úti tvau dœgr; þá fundu þeir land ok reru fyrir á bátum, ok kǫnnuðu landit, ok fundu þar hellur margar, ok svá stórar, at tveir menn máttu vel spyrnask í iljar: melrakkar váru þar margir. Þeir gáfu nafn landinu, ok kǫlluðu Helluland. Þá sigldu þeir norðanveðr tvau dœgr, ok var þá land fyrir þeim, ok var á skógr mikill, ok dýr mǫrg; ey lá í landsuðr undan landinu, ok fundu þeir þar bjarndýr, ok kǫlluðu Bjarney. En landit kǫlluðu þeir Markland, þar er skógrinn[4] [var]. Þá er liðin váru tvau dœgr, sjá þeir land, ok þeir sigldu undir landit; þar var nes, er þeir kvámu at. Þeir beittu með landinu, ok létu landit á stjórnborða; þar var ǫrœfi, ok strandir langar ok sandar. Fara þeir á bátum til lands, ok fengu kjǫl[5] af skipi, ok kǫlluðu þar Kjalarnes. Þeir gáfu ok nafn strǫndunum, ok kǫlluðu Furðustrandir, því at langt var með at sigla. Þá gǫrðisk vágskorit landit, ok heldu[6] þeir skipunum at vágunum. Þat var þá, er Leifr var með Óláfi konungi Tryggvasyni, ok hann bað hann boða kristni á Grœnlandi, ok

[1] MS. vetvrin*n*.

[2] This sentence appears to have been interpolated here by a clerical blunder; it belongs properly to line 6, before 'Ætluðu þeir Karlsefni,' &c.

[3] New Roy. Coll. Copenhagen, No. 1714, 4to, AM. 931, 4to, 563 *b*, 4to, 401 fol. (amended), 932, 4to, Rask Coll. 30 and 36, have 'til vestri óbygðar.'

[4] MS. skogvrin*n*.

[5] MS. skiol.

[6] 'ok helldu' repeated in MS.

[AM. 557, 4to, p. 33.] EIRÍKS SAGA RAUÐA—13.

þá gaf konungr honum tvá menn skozka, hét karlmaðrinn Haki, en konan Hækja. Konungr bað Leif taka til þessara manna, ef hann þyrfti skjótleiks við, því at þau váru dýrum skjótari. Þessa menn fengu þeir Leifr[1] ok Eiríkr til fylgðar við Karlsefni. En er þeir hǫfðu siglt fyrir Furðustrandir, þá létu þeir ena skozku menn á land, ok báðu þau hlaupa í suðrátt, ok leita landskosta, ok koma aptr áðr þrjú dœgr væri liðin. Þau váru svá búin, at þau hǫfðu þat klæði, er þau kǫlluðu biafal, þat var svá gǫrt, at hattrinn[2] var á upp, ok opit at hliðum, ok engar ermar á, ok knept í milli fóta; helt þar saman knappr ok nezla, en ber váru [þau] annarsstaðar. Þeir kǫstuðu akkerum, ok lágu þar þessa stund, ok er þrír dagar váru liðnir, hljópu þau af landi ofan, ok hafði annat þeira í hendi vínber[3], en annat hveiti sjálfsáit. Sagði Karlsefni at þau þóttusk[4] fundit hafa landskosti góða. Tóku þeir þau á skip sitt, ok fóru leiðar sinnar, þar til er varð fjarðskorit. Þeir lǫgðu skipunum inn á fjǫrðinn; þar var ey ein út fyrir, ok váru þar straumar miklir[5], ok um eyna; þeir kǫlluðu hana Straumsey. Fugl var þar svá margr, at trautt mátti fœti niðr koma í milli eggjanna. Þeir heldu inn með firðinum, ok kǫlluðu hann Straumsfjǫrð, ok báru farminn af skipunum, ok bjoggusk þar um. Þeir hǫfðu með sér allskonar fé, ok leituðu sér þar landsnytja. Fjǫll váru þar, ok fagrt var þar um at litask. Þeir gáðu enskis nema at kanna landit. Þar váru grǫs mikil. Þar váru þeir um vetrinn, ok gǫrðisk vetr mikill, en ekki fyrir unnit, ok gǫrðisk illt til matarins, ok tókusk af veiðarnar[6]. Þá fóru þeir út í eyna, ok væntu at þar mundi gefa nǫkkut af veiðum eða rekum. Þar var þó lítit til matfanga, en fé þeira varð þar vel. Síðan hétu þeir á guð, at hann sendi þeim nǫkkut til matfanga, ok var eigi svá brátt við látit, sem þeim var annt til. Þórhallr hvarf á brott, ok gengu menn at leita hans; stóð þat yfir þrjú dœgr í samt. Á hinu fjórða dœgri fundu þeir Karlsefni ok Bjarni[7], hann Þórhall á hamargnípu einni; hann horfði í lopt upp, ok gapti hann bæði augum ok munni ok nǫsum, ok klóraði sér, ok klýpti sik, ok þulði nǫkkut. Þeir spurðu hví[8] hann væri þar kominn. Hann kvað þat ǫngu skipta; bað hann þá ekki þat undrask; kvezk svá lengst lifat hafa at þeir þurftu ekki ráð fyrir honum at gǫra. Þeir báðu hann fara heim með sér. Hann gǫrði svá. Lítlu síðar kom þar hvalr, ok drifu menn til, ok skáru hann, en þó kendu menn eigi hvat hval þat var. Karlsefni kunni mikla skyn á hvalnum, ok kendi hann þó eigi. Þenna hval suðu matsveinar, ok átu af, ok varð þó ǫllum illt af. Þá gengr Þórhallr at, ok mælti: 'Var eigi svá, at hinn rauðskeggjaði varð drjúgari en Kristr yðvarr? Þetta hafða

[1] MS. leifi. [2] MS. hatturinn. [3] MS. apparently vinker. [4] MS. þottizt. [5] MS. mikli. [6] MS. veidimar. [7] MS. bjarnadi. [8] MS. þvi.

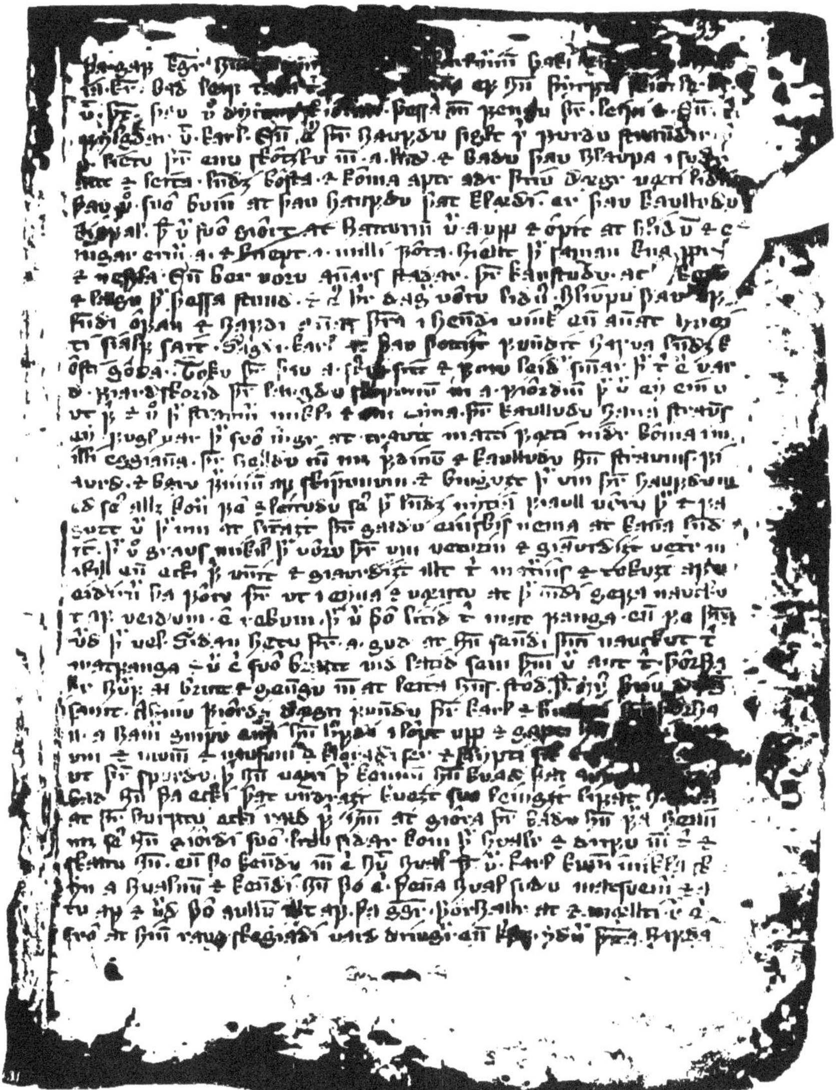

[illegible] skap [illegible] ok [illegible] um þor [illegible]
[illegible] ok [illegible] vildu [illegible]
[illegible] ok [illegible]
[illegible] ok [illegible] um [illegible]
[illegible] ok [illegible] af [illegible]
[illegible] ok [illegible] //   // [illegible]
[illegible] um [illegible] ok [illegible] Þorhallr [illegible]
[illegible] ok [illegible]
[illegible] ok [illegible]
[illegible] ok [illegible]
[illegible] Þorhallr [illegible] ok [illegible]
[illegible]
Þorhallr [illegible] ok [illegible]
[illegible]
[illegible]
[illegible]
[illegible]
[illegible]
[illegible]
[illegible]
[illegible]
[illegible] ok [illegible]
[illegible] ok [illegible] vildu [illegible]
[illegible] ok [illegible] ok [illegible]
[illegible] ok [illegible] Þorhallr [illegible] //
[illegible] ok [illegible] ok [illegible]
[illegible] ok [illegible]
[illegible] ok [illegible] ok [illegible]
[illegible] ok [illegible]
[illegible] ok [illegible]
[illegible]
[illegible]
[illegible] ok [illegible]
[illegible] ok [illegible]
[illegible] ok [illegible] ok [illegible]
[illegible] ok [illegible]
[illegible] ok [illegible]
[illegible] ok [illegible]
[illegible]
[illegible] ok [illegible] ok [illegible]
[illegible]
[illegible]

[AM. 557, 4to, p. 33 *b*.] EIRÍKS SAGA RAUÐA.—14.

ek nú fyrir skáldskap minn, er ek[1] orta um Þór fulltrúann; sjaldan hefir hann mér brugðizk.' Ok er menn vissu þetta vildu øngvir nýta, ok kǫstuðu fyrir bjǫrg ofan, ok sneru sínu máli til guðs miskunnar. Gaf þeim þá út at róa, ok skorti þá eigi birgðir. Um várit fara þeir inn í Straumsfjǫrð, ok hǫfðu fǫng af hvárutveggja landinu, veiðar af meginlandinu, eggver ok útróðra af sjónum. [iðimaðr fara[2]

[N]ú rœða þeir um ferð sína ok hafa tilskipan. Vill Þórhallr venorðr um Furðustrandir, ok fyrir Kjalarnes, ok leita svá Vínlands; en Karlsefni vill fara suðr fyrir land ok fyrir austan, ok þikkir land því meira, sem suðr er meir, ok þikkir honum þat ráðligra, at kanna hvártveggja. Nú býsk Þórhallr út undir eyjum, ok urðu [eigi] meir í ferð með honum en níu menn. En með Karlsefni fór annat liðit þeira. Ok einn dag, er Þórhallr bar vatn á skip sitt, þá drakk hann, ok kvað vísu þessa: 'Hafa kváðu mik meiðar málmþings, er ek kom hingat, mér samir lítt fyrir lýðum lasta, drykk inn bazta. Bílds hattar[3] verð ek byttu beiðitýr at reiða, heldr er svá at ek krýp at keldu; komat[4] vín á grǫn mína.' Láta þeir út síðan, ok fylgir Karlsefni þeim undir eyna. Áðr þeir drógu seglit upp, kvað Þórhallr vísu: 'Fǫrum aptr þar er ærir eru, sandhimins, landar, látum val kanna kæti knarrar skreið hin breiðu; meðan bilstyggvir byggja bellendr, ok hval vella, laufa veðrs, þann er leyfir lǫnd á Furðustrǫndum!' Síðan skilðu þeir, ok sigldu norðr fyrir Furðustrandir ok Kjalarnes, ok vildu beita þar fyrir vestan; kom þá veðr á móti þeim, ok rak þá upp við Írland, ok váru þar mjǫk þjáðir ok barðir. Þá lét Þórhallr líf sitt.

Karlsefni fór suðr fyrir land, ok Snorri ok Bjarni, ok annat lið þeira. Þeir fóru lengi, ok til þess, er þeir kvámu at á þeiri, er fell af landi ofan ok í vatn, ok svá til sjóvar. Eyjar váru þar miklar fyrir ár-ósinum, ok mátti eigi komask inn í ána nema at háflœðum. Sigldu þeir Karlsefni þá til ár-óssins, ok kǫlluðu í Hópi landit. Þar fundu þeir sjálfsána hveitiakra, þar sem lægðir váru, en vínviðr allt þar sem holta kendi. Hverr lœkr var þar fullr af fiskum. Þeir gǫrðu þar grafir, sem landit mœttisk, ok flóðit gekk efst, ok er út fell, váru helgir fiskar í grǫfunum. Þar var mikill fjǫlði dýra á skógi með ǫllu móti. Þeir váru þar hálfan mánuð, ok skemtu sér, ok urðu við ekki varir. Fé sitt hǫfðu þeir með sér. Ok einn morgin snemma, er þeir lituðusk um, sá þeir níu húðkeipa, ok var veift trjánum af skipunum, ok lét því líkast í sem í hálmþustum, ok ferr sólarsinnis. Þá mælti Karlsefni: 'Hvat mun þetta tákna?' Snorri svarar honum: 'Vera kann at[5] þetta sé friðartákn, ok tǫkum skjǫld hvítan, ok berum í mót.' Ok svá

[1] a is inserted in the MS. after ek, apparently a clerical error. [2] The bracketed words belong to the end of line 7.
[3] MS. hattr. [4] MS. komit. [5] MS. a.

[AM. 557, 4to, p. 34.] EIRÍKS SAGA RAUÐA—15.

gørðu þeir. Þá reru hinir í mót, ok undruðusk þá, ok gengu þeir á land. Þ-eir váru smáir menn ok illiligir, ok illt hǫſðu þeir hár á hǫſði; eygðir vá-ru þeir mjǫk ok breiðir í kinnunum. Ok dvǫlðusk þar um stund ok undruðusk; reru síðan í brott, ok suðr ſyrir nesit. Þeir hǫſðu gǫrt bygðir sínar upp ſrá vatninu, ok váru sumir skálarnir nær meginlandinu, en sumir nær vatni-nu. Nú váru þeir þar þann vetr. Þar kom alls engi snjár, ok allr fénaðr gekk þar úti sjálſala. [húðkeipa reri sunnan ſyrir nesit [1], En er vára tók, geta þeir at líta, einn morgin snemma, at ſjǫlði svá margir sem kolum væri sáit, ok var þá [2] veiſt á hverju skipi tr-jánum. Þeir brugðu þá skjǫldum upp, ok tóku kaupstefnu sín á mill-um, ok vildi þat ſólk helzt kaupa rautt klæði, þeir vildu ok kaup-a sverð ok spjót, en þat bǫnnuðu þeir Karlseſni ok Snorri. Þeir hǫſðu óſǫlv-an belg ſyrir klæðit, ok tóku spannarlangt klæði ſyrir belg, ok bundu um hǫſuð sér; ok ſór svá um stund; en er minka tók klæðit, þá skáru þeir í sundr svá at eigi var breiðara en þvers fingrar breitt. Gáſu þeir Sk-rælingar jaſnmikit ſyrir eða meira. Þat bar til, at griðungr hljóp ór skógi, er [3] þeir Karlseſni áttu, ok gall hátt við. Þeir ſælask við, Skrælingar, ok hlaupa ú-t á keipana, ok reru suðr ſyrir land. Varð þá ekki vart við þá þrjár vikur í samt. En er sjá stund var liðin, sjá þeir sunnan ſara mikinn ſjǫ-lða skipa Skrælinga, svá sem straumr stœði; var þá veiſt trjánum ǫllum rangsœlis, ok ýla allir Skrælingar há-tt upp. Þá tóku þeir rauða skjǫldu ok báru í mót. Gengu þeir þá sa-man ok bǫrðusk; varð þar skothríð hǫrð. Þeir hǫſðu ok valslǫ-ngur, Skrælingar. Þat sjá þeir Karlseſni ok Snorri, at þeir fœrðu upp á stǫng-um, Skrælingarnir, knǫtt mikinn, ok blán at lit, ok ſló upp á land y-ſir liðit, ok lét illiliga við, þar er niðr kom. Við þetta sló ótta miklum yſir Karlseſni ok á lið hans, svá at þá ſýsti enskis annars, en ha-lda undan, ok upp með ánni, ok til hamra nǫkkurra; veittu þeir þar viðtǫku harða. Freydís kom út, ok sá er þeir heldu undan. Hon kallaði: 'Hví [4] renni þér undan, slíkum auvirðis [5] mǫnnum, svá gildir menn, er mér þætti líkligt at þér mættið drepa þá svá sem búſé; ok eſ ek heſða vápn, þætti mér sem ek munda betr berjask en einnhverr yðvar.' Þeir gáſu ǫngvan gaum hvat sem hon sagði. Freydís vildi ſylgja þeim, ok varð hon heldr sein, því at hon var eigi heil; gekk hon þá eptir þeim í skóginn; en [6] Skrælingar sœkja at henni. Hon ſann ſyrir sér mann dauðan, Þorbrand Snorrason, ok stóð hellu-steinn í hǫſði honum; sverðit lá hjá honum, ok hon tók þat upp, ok býsk at verja sik með. Þá koma Skrælingar at henni; hon tekr brjóst-it upp ór serkinum, ok slettir á sverðit; þeir ſælask við, ok hlaupa undan,

[1] The bracketed words belong to the end of line 8. [2] MS. þo, i.e. þó. [3] MS. enn. [4] MS. þvi. [5] MS. v virdis, i.e. ú-virðis. [6] MS. er.

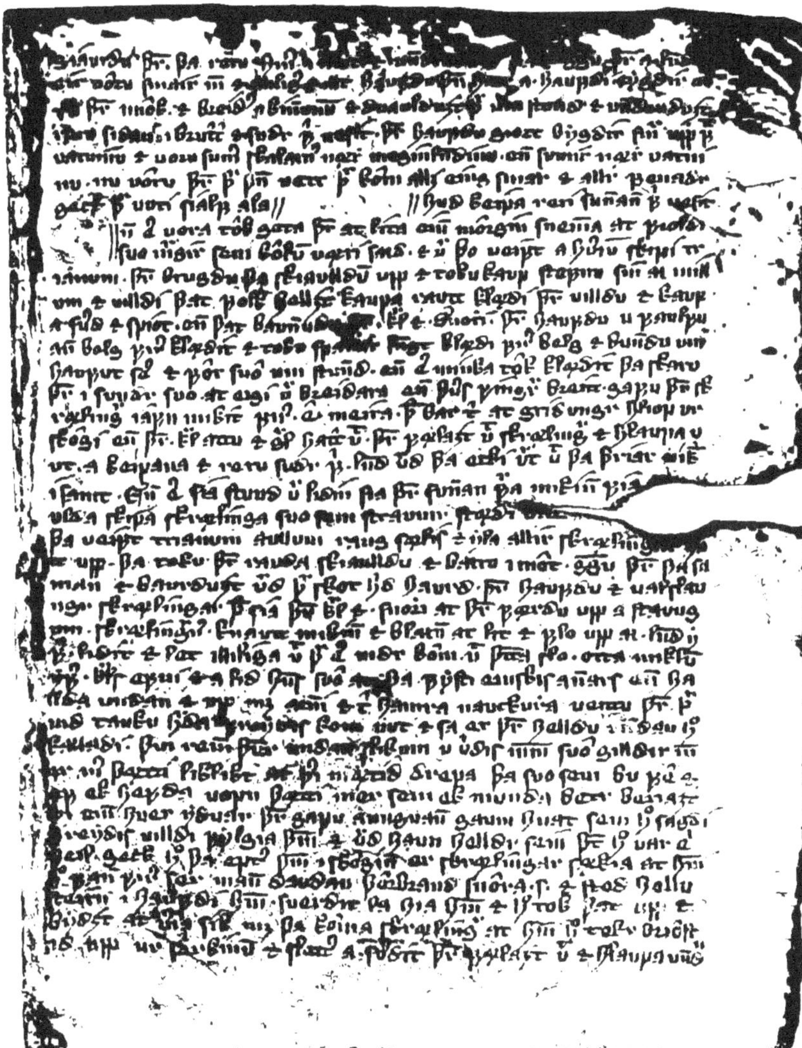

ok a skip sin ok hallda a brott. fr. karl ...a heima ok ... [illegible]
heiman. tveir m̄ pollu af. karli. an ... af fraklingu. an ...
.... fr. opinbert. ... fara fr. nu t budar sinar ok i huga ... ...
hin ... at hin ... Ambin sinnt ... nu ... ...
m̄ ... hafua ... ar ... skipunum ... Epi ... ... [illegible]
hafua ... fulfinng. fr. frakling ... ... ok ... ... ok ...
... hin ... hio i ... ... hin ...
... uitt ar a ... vid ... ok ... ... fr. ...
... ... gedir at par ... ... u ...
ok ... a liggia. en fr. ar vm hugu. ... fr. a ... ok ...
... ... Sighu. fr. nordr ... ...
... i ... ... ok ... ...
... ... fr. ... at fr. ... ... fr.
... ... fr. ... ... ok ... ... ok fr. ...
u ... at ... ...
ar ... ... fr. i ... ... ok ar ... Alla ...
ar ... ... ok ... hafui ... ...
ok ... manna ... ... ok hafui a ... ... En fr. karl ok ...
[illegible] ... hauþdu ... ... manna ok ... ...
... hafui. en ... tuo ... ok ... ...
[illegible] ... ...
... en ... ... ok ... fr. nordr ... ... ok ...
... ... ok u ... a ... ...
... en ok ar fr. ... ... opan ...
... ok i ... fr. ... i ... ok ... ...
... u ... morgin ... fr. karl ... opan ... ...
inn suo sem ... ... ok ... fr. ... ... ok u ...
en ... ok ... opan ... sem fr. ... ...
... ...
... ... a ... ok nordr ... ok ... ...
... a. ... ...
fr. ... ... ok ... ... ok ... sem ...
... ... fr. ...
... ... en ... ... all ... ...
u en ... [illegible] opan ok ... en ... ...
ar. [illegible] ... ... fr. ... ... i ... ok
nordr ... [illegible] ... ... en ... ... fr. ... a
... ... fr. ... at ... ...
ar i ... ... ok er ... ... fr. ... ok u i ... ...

[AM. 537, 4to, p. 34 *b*.] EIRÍKS SAGA RAUDA—16.

ok á skip ſín, ok heldu á brottu. Þeir Karlsefni ſinna hana, ok loſa[1] happ hennar. Tveir menn ſellu aſ Karlsefni, en ſjórir aſ Skrælingum, en þó urðu þeir oſrliði bornir. Fara þeir nú til búða sinna, ok ſhuga hvat ſjǫlmenni þat var, er at þeim sótti á landinu; sýnisk þeim nú, at þat eina mun liðit haſa verit, er á skipunum kom, en annat liðit mun haſa verit þversýningar. Þeir Skrælingar ſundu ok mann dauðan, ok lá øx hjá honum; einn þeira hjó í stein, ok brotnaði øxin; þótti honum þá øngu nýt er eigi stóð við grjótinu, ok kastaði niðr. Þeir þóttusk nú sjá, þótt þar væri landskostir góðir, at þar mundi jaſn óſriðr ok ótti á liggja, aſ þeim[2] er ſyrir bjoggu. Bjoggusk þeir á brott, ok ætluðu til síns lands. Sigldu þeir norðr ſyrir, ok ſundu ſimm Skrælinga í skinnhjúpum soſanda, ok hǫſðu með sér skrokka[3] ok í dýramerg dreyra blandinn. Virtu þeir svá, at þeir mundu gørvir aſ landinu. Þeir drápu þá. Síðan ſundu þeir nes eitt ok ſjǫlða dýra, ok þann veg[4] var nesit at sjá, sem mykiskán væri, aſ því at dýrin lágu þar um vetrna. Nú koma þeir í Straumsſjǫrð, ok er þar allskonar [gnóttir]. Er þat sumra manna sǫgn, at þau Bjarni ok Freydís haſi þar eptir verit, ok tíu tigir manna með þeim, ok haſi eigi farit lengra. En þeir Karlsefni ok Snorri hǫſðu suðr farit, ok XL manna, ok haſði eigi lengr verit í Hópi, en vart tvá mánaði[5], ok haſði hit sama sumar aptr komit. Karlsefni ſór á einu skipi, at leita Þórhalls, en liðit var eptir, ok ſóru þeir norðr ſyrir Kjalarnes, ok berr þá ſyrir vestan ſram, ok var landit á bakborða þeim. Þar váru eyðimerkr einar; ok er þeir hǫſðu lengi ſarit, ſellr á aſ landi oſan ór austri ok í vestr. Þeir lágu inn í árósinum, ok lágu við hinn syðra bakkann. Þat var einn morgin, sjá þeir Karlsefni ſyrir oſan rjóðrit ſlekk nǫkkurn, svá sem glitaði við þeim, ok œptu þeir á. Þat hrœrðisk, ok var þat Einſœtingr, ok skýzk oſan þangat sem þeir lágu, Þorvaldr, son Eiríks hins rauða; þá mælti Þorvaldr[6]: 'Gott land hǫſum vér ſengit.' Þá hleypr Einſœtingrinn á brott, ok norðr aptr, ok skaut áðr í smáþarma á Þorvaldi. Hann dró út ǫrina; þá mælti Þorvaldr: 'Feitt er um ístruna.' Þeir hljópu[7] eptir Einſœtingi, ok sá[8] hann stundum, ok þótti sem hann leitaði undan; hljóp hann út á vág einn. Þá hurſu þeir aptr. Þá kvað einn maðr kviðling þenna: 'Eltu seggir, allsatt var þat, einn Einſœting oſan til strandar; en kynligr maðr kostaði rásar hart of stopi; heyrðu Karlsefni!' Þeir ſóru þá í brott, ok norðr aptr, ok þóttusk sjá Einſœtingaland. Vildu þeir þá eigi lengr hætta liði sínu. Þeir ætluðu at kanna ǫll ſjǫll, þau er í Hópi váru, ok er þeir ſundu. Fóru þeir aptr, ok váru í Straumsſirði

[1] MS. loſ. [2] MS. *enn þeir*. [3] skokka? [4] MS. vag. [5] MS. manadu.

[6] There is an obvious clerical confusion here, as also in the following passage, which, except in arrangement, conforms to the similar passage in þsK. [7] MS. hlippn. [8] MS. san.

[AM. 557, 4to, p. 35.] EIRÍKS SAGA RAUÐA—17.

1. hinn þriðja vetr[1]. Gengu menn þá mjǫk sleitum; sóttu [þeir] er kvánlausir váru í hen-
2. dr þeim, er kvángaðir váru. Þar kom til hit fyrsta haust Snorri, son Karlsefnis, ok var þar
3. þann, er þeir fóru á brott; hǫfðu þeir sunnanveðr[2] ok hittu Markland, ok fun-
4. du Skrælinga fimm, var einn skeggjaðr, ok tvær konur, bǫrn tvau. Tóku
5. þeir Karlsefni til sveinanna, en hitt komsk undan, ok sukku í jǫrð niðr. E-
6. n sveinana hǫfðu þeir með sér, ok kendu þeim mál, ok váru skírðir. Þeir n-
7. efndu móður sína Vætilldi ok Uvægi[3]. Þeir sǫgðu at konungar stjórnuðu
8. Skrælingalandi. Hét annarr Avalldamon, en annarr hét Valldidida. Þeir kv-
9. áðu þar engi hús, ok lágu menn í hellum eða holum. Þeir sǫgðu land þar ǫ-
10. ðrumegin gagnvart sínu landi, ok gengu menn þar í hvítum klæðum, ok œ-
11. pðu hátt, ok báru stangir, ok fóru með flíkr. Þat ætla menn Hvítramannaland.
12. Nú kómu þeir til Grœnlands, ok eru með Eiríki rauða um vetrinn. Þá Bja-
13. rna Grímólfsson bar í Grœnlandshaf, ok kómu[4] í maðkasjá; fundu þeir
14. ei fyrr en skipit gørisk maðksmogit undir[5] þeim. Þá tǫ-
15. luðu þeir um hvert ráð þeir skyldu taka. Þeir hǫfðu eptirbát þann,
16. er bræddr var seltjǫru; þat segja menn, at skelmaðkrinn smjúgi eigi þat tré
17. er seltjǫrunni er brætt. Var þat flestra manna sǫgn og tillaga, at skipa m-
18. ǫnnum bátinn, svá sem hann tœki upp. En er þat var reynt, þá tók bá-
19. trinn eigi meirr upp en helming manna. Bjarni mælti þá, at menn skyldi
20. fara í bátinn, ok skyldi þat fara at hlutfǫllum, en eigi at mannvirðing-
21. um[6]. En hverr þeira manna vildi fara í bátinn, sem þar váru; þá mátti hann eigi við ǫ-
22. llum taka. Fyrir því tóku þeir þetta ráð, at hluta menn í bátinn ok af k-
23. aupskipinu[7]. Hlutaðisk þar svá til, at Bjarni hlaut at fara í bátinn ok n-
24. ær helmingr manna með[8] honum. Þá gengu þeir af skipinu, ok í bátinn, er til
25. þess hǫfðu hlotizk. Þá er menn váru komnir í bátinn, mælti einn ungr maðr
26. íslenzkr, sá er verit hafði fǫrunautr Bjarna: 'Ætlar þú, Bjarni, at skiljask hér við
27. mik?' Bjarni svarar: 'Svá verðr nú at vera.' Hann segir: 'Svá með því, at þú hézk mér
eigi því,
28. þá er ek fór með þér af Íslandi frá búi fǫður míns.' Bjarni segir: 'Eigi sé ek hér
29. þó annat ráð til; eða svara, hvat leggr þú hér til ráðs.' Hann segir: 'Sé ek ráðit
30. til, at vit skiptumsk í rúmunum, ok farir þú hingat en ek mun þan-
31. gat[9].' Bjarni svarar: 'Svá skal vera. Ok þat sé ek, at þú vinnr gjarna til lífs, ok þikkir
32. mikit fyrir at deyja.' Skiptusk þeir þá í rúmunum. Gekk þessi maðr í b-
33. átinn, en Bjarni[10] upp í skipit; ok er þat sǫgn manna, at Bjarni létisk þar í
34. maðkahafinu, ok þeir menn, sem í skipinu váru með honum. En bátrinn ok
35. þeir, er þar váru á, fóru leiðar sinnar, til þess er þeir tóku land,
36. ok sǫgðu þessa sǫgu síðan. [fór hann heim til[11]
37. Annat sumar eptir fór Karlsefni til Íslands, ok Snorri með honum, ok
38. bús síns í Reynines. Móður hans þótti sem hann hefð-
39. i lítt til kostar tekit, ok var hon eigi heim[a] þar hinn fyrsta vetr; ok er hon

[1] MS. vintr.
[2] er þeir fóru á brott may belong to this clause; there is, in any reading, an obvious error in the preceding words.
[3] fǫður should, perhaps, be supplied before Uvægi, as in þsK. [4] MS. kom. [5] MS. undir vndi.
[6] MS. mannvirdinvm. [7] MS. erroneously kavpskipvnvm. [8] MS. með með. [9] MS. þanat.
[10] MS. biarna. [11] The bracketed words belong to the end of line 37.

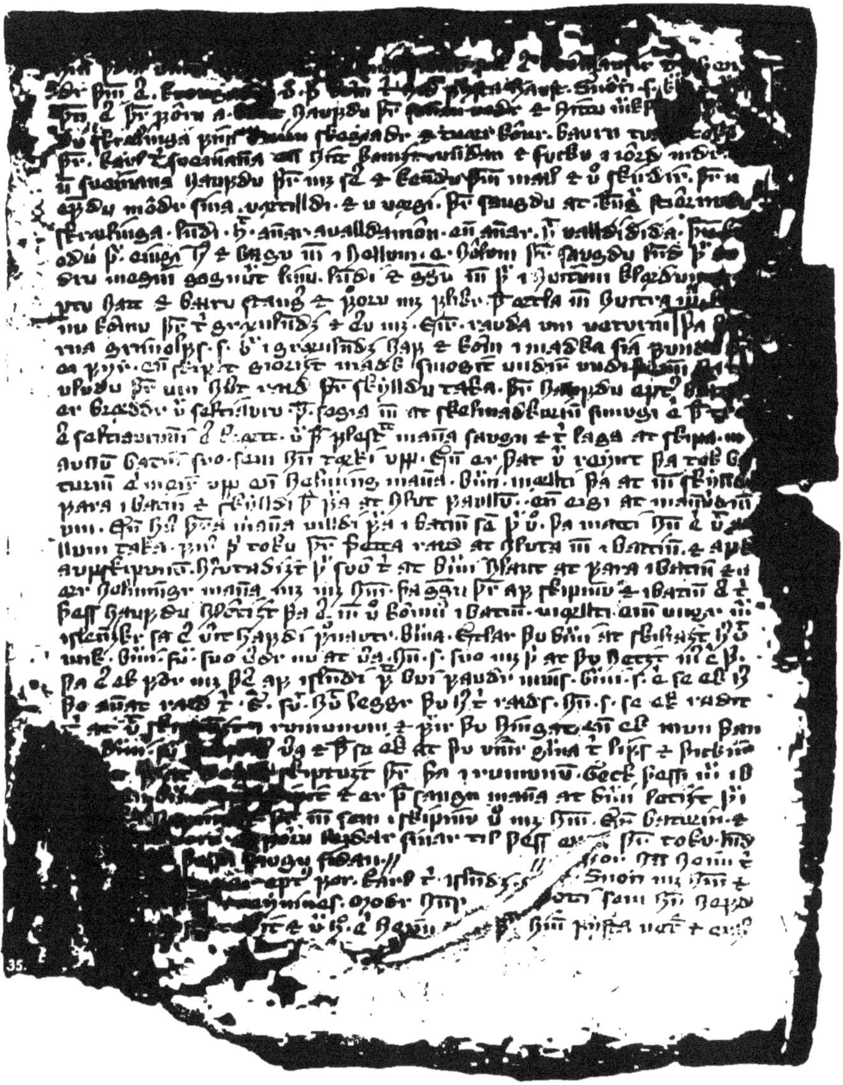

35.

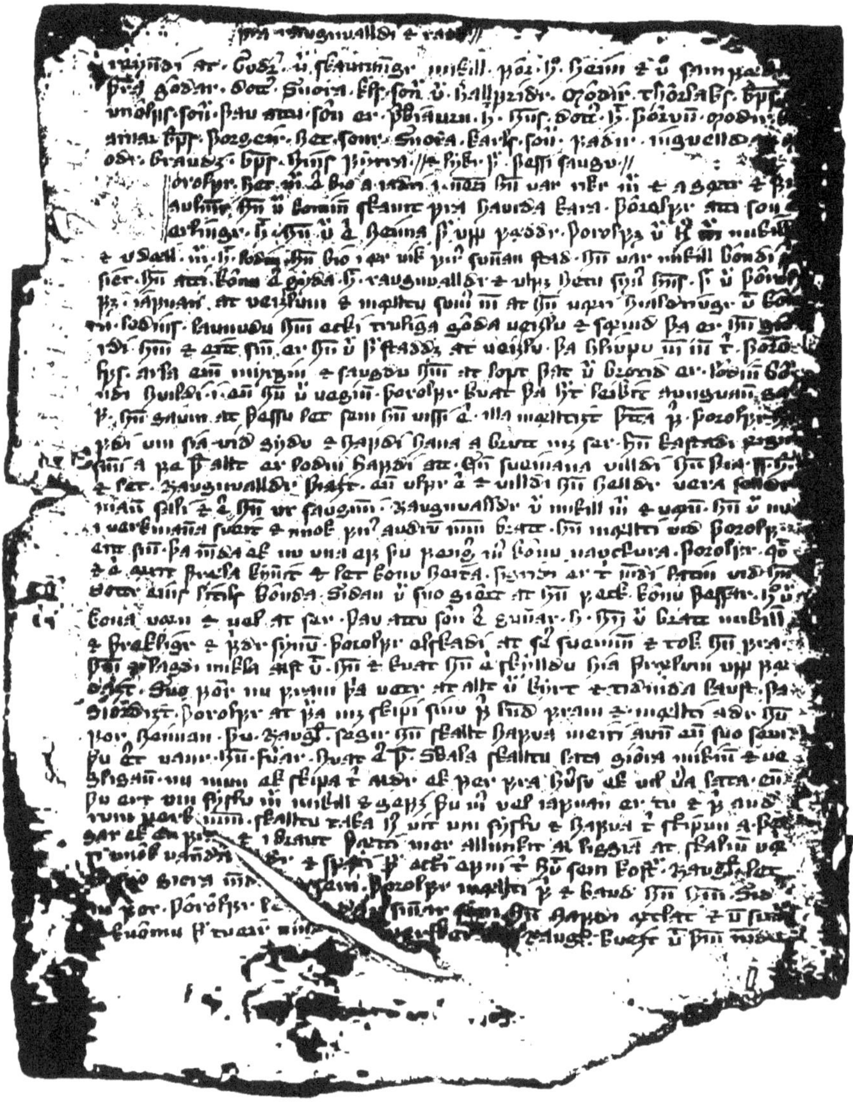

[AM. 557, 4to, p. 35 *b*.] EIRÍKS SAGA RAUDA—18.

reyndi at Guðríðr var skǫrungr mikill, fór hon heim, ok váru samfarar[1] þeira góðar. Dóttir Snorra Karlsefnissonar var Hallfríðr, móðir Thorlaks[2] biskups Runólfssonar; þau áttu son, er Þorbjǫrn hét. Hans dóttir hét Þórunn, móðir Bjarnar biskups. Þorgeirr hét sonr Snorra Karlsefnissonar, faðir Ingveldar, móður Brands biskups hins fyrra. Ok lýkr þar þessi sǫgu.

[1] MS. samfædr. [2] MS. *sic.*

[FLATEYJARBÓK, Column 221 *b*.] EIRÍKS ÞÁTTR RAUÐA—I.

Þorvaldr hét maðr, **Þáttr Eiríks rauða. Capitulum.** son Ósvalds Úlfssonar, Øxna-Þórissonar. Þorvaldr ok Ei-

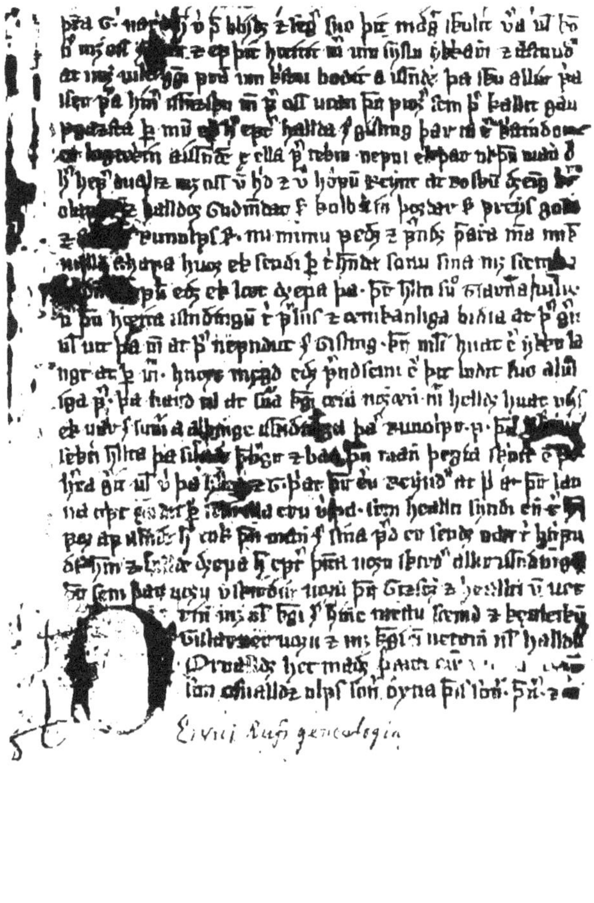

Eirici Rufi genealogia

hinn rauði son h's · þ af iadri t ıſldz f viga ſak' þa v' vıda
bygt ıſld ſettız buıgu þıoðhılldar ... a hornſtrond' · þar andadız
... · ... · ... þa ... hıllð ... ... z ... bygu
... þa ... hın ... dalſkı ... ... þa noʀð' z bıo
a ... hıt ... ſon ... · z ... h' leıpr en
... ... ſauꝛ z holmgaungu ... ... b'
... ... h ... t' ... · ꝩ · z bıo ſ ... ... h' le
... ... ſ ... z ... h ... t · ... af ... z
... ... ſ ... ... · ... ... ar
... z ... z ... ... · ꝩ · z ... ...
ſon · ... ... z ... ...
... ... a ... ...
en er h ... ...
... h ... ... er ... ſon ... ...
er ... ... er h ... ... · ... h ...
er ... ... h ... ... · ... · ... ...
... ... h ... ... z ... ... h ... ...
... ... h ... ... h ... ...
... ... h ... ...
... ... h ... ... h t ... · ꝩ · z
... ... h ... ... ſ ... ... z ...
... ... · h ... ... ſ holmu ... ...
... ... h t ... z kom ... ... ſ ... · ꝩ · h
... ... h ... ... h ... ...
... ...
... ... h ... ... h bıo ſ ... ...
... ...
... ... þa ... ... · ꝩ · z ...
ꝩ · en ... ...
... ...

[FLATEYJARBÓK, Column 222.] EIRÍKS ÞÁTTR RAUÐA—2.

ríkr hinn rauði, son hans, fóru af Jaðri til Íslands, fyrir víga sakir. Þá var víða bygt Ísland. Þeir bjoggu fyrst at Drǫngum á Hornstrǫndum. Þar andaðisk Þorvaldr. Eiríkr fekk þá Þórhildar, dóttur Jǫrundar ok Þorbjargar knarrarbringu, er þá átti Þorbjǫrn hinn haukdœlski. Rézk Eiríkr þá norðan, ok bjó á Eiríksstǫðum hjá Vatnshorni. Son Eiríks ok Þórhildar hét Leifr. En eptir víg Eyjúlfs saurs ok Hólmgǫngu-Hrafns var Eiríkr gǫrr brott ór Haukadal; fór hann vestr til Breiðafjarðar, ok bjó í Øxney á Eiríksstǫðum. Hann léði Þorgesti setstokka, ok náði eigi [þá er] hann kallaði til. Þaðan af gǫrðusk deilur ok bardagar með þeim Þorgesti, sem segir í sǫgu Eiríks. Styrr Þorgrímsson veitti Eiríki at málum, ok Eyjúlfr ór Svíney ok synir Brands ór Álptafirði, ok Þorbjǫrn Vífilsson. En Þorgestlingum veittu synir Þórðar gellis ok Þorgeirr ór Hítardal; Eiríkr varð sekr á Þórsnes-þingi. Bjó Eiríkr skip sitt [til] hafs, í Eiríksvági; en er hann var búinn, fylgðu þeir Styrr honum út um eyjar. Eiríkr sagði þeim, at hann ætlaði at leita lands þess, er Gunnbjǫrn, son Úlfs kráku, sá, er [hann] rak vestr um haf, þá er hann fann Gunnbjarnarsker; kvezk hann aptr mundu leita til vina sinna, ef hann fyndi landit. Eiríkr sigldi undan Snæfellsjǫkli. Hann fann landit, ok kom utan at því, þar sem hann kallaði Miðjǫkul; sá heitir nú Bláserkr. Hann fór þá þaðan suðr með landinu, at leita ef þaðan væri byggjanda landit. Hann var hinn fyrsta vetr í Eiríksey, nær miðri hinni eystri bygð; um várit eptir fór hann til Eiríksfjarðar, ok tók sér þar bústað. Hann fór þat sumar í hina vestri úbygð, ok gaf víða ǫrnefni. Hann var annan vetr í Hólmum við Hrafnsgnípu. En hit þriðja sumarit fór hann til Íslands, ok kom skipi sínu í Breiðafjǫrð. Hann kallaði landit, þat er hann hafði fundit, Grœnland, því at hann kvað þat mundu fýsa menn þangat, er landit héti vel. Eiríkr var á Íslandi um vetrinn; en um sumarit eptir fór hann at byggja landit. Hann bjó í Brattahlíð í Eiríksfirði. Svá segja fróðir menn at á því sama sumri, er Eiríkr rauði fór at byggja Grœnland, þá fór hálfr fjórði tǫgr skipa ór Breiðafirði ok Borgarfirði, en fjórtán kvámusk út þangat; sum rak aptr, en sum týndusk. Þat var XV vetrum fyrr en kristni var lǫgtekin á Íslandi. Á

[FLATEYJARBÓK, Column 222 *b*.] EIRÍKS ÞÁTTR RAUÐA—3.

því sama sumri fór utan Friðrekr biskup ok Þorvaldr Koðránsson. Þessir menn námu land á Grœnlandi, er þá fóru út með Eiríki: Herjúlfr Herjúlfsfjǫrð, hann bjó á Herjúlfsnesi; Ketill Ketilsfjǫrð; Hrafn Hrafnsfjǫrð; Sǫlvi Sǫlvadal; Helgi Þorbrandsson Álptafjǫrð; Þorbjǫrn glóra Siglufjǫrð; Einarr Einarsfjǫrð; Hafgrímr Hafgrímsfjǫrð ok Vatnahverfi; Arnlaugr Arnlaugsfjǫrð; en sumir fóru til Vestribygðar. **Leifr heppni var skírðr.** Þá er sextán vetr váru liðnir frá því er Eiríkr rauði fór at byggja Grœnland, þá fór Leifr, son Eiríks, utan af Grœnlandi til Noregs. Kom hann til Þrándheims um haustit, þá er Óláfr konungr Tryggvason var kominn norðan af Hálogalandi. Leifr lagði skipi sínu inn til Niðaróss, ok fór þegar á fund Óláfs konungs. Boðaði konungr trú honum sem ǫðrum heiðnum mǫnnum, er á hans fund kómu. Gekk konungi þat auðveldliga við Leif; var hann þá skírðr ok allir skipverjar hans. Var Leifr með konungi um vetrinn vel haldinn. **Bjarni leitaði Grœnlands.** Herjúlfr var Bárðarson, Herjúlfssonar; hann var frændi Ingólfs landnámamanns. Þeim Herjúlfi gaf Ingólfr land á milli Vágs ok Reykjaness. Herjúlfr bjó fyrst á Drepstokki; Þorgerðr hét kona hans, en Bjarni son þeira, ok var hinn efniligsti maðr. Hann fýstisk utan þegar á unga aldri. Varð honum gott bæði til fjár ok mannvirðingar, ok var sinn vetr hvárt utan lands eða með fǫður sínum. Brátt átti Bjarni skip í fǫrum; ok hinn síðasta vetr, er hann var í Noregi, þá brá Herjúlfr til Grœnlandsferðar með Eiríki, ok brá búi sínu. Með Herjúlfi var á skipi suðreyskr maðr kristinn, sá er orti Hafgerðingar drápu; þar er þetta stef í: 'Mínar biðr ek múnkareyni meinalausan fara beina heiðis haldi hattar foldar hallar dróttinn yfir mér stalli.' Herjúlfr bjó á Herjúlfsnesi; hann var hinn gǫfgasti maðr. Eiríkr rauði bjó í Brattahlíð; hann var þar með mestri virðingu, ok lutu allir til hans. Þessi váru bǫrn Eiríks: Leifr, Þorvaldr ok Þorsteinn, en Freydís hét dóttir hans; hon var gipt þeim manni, er Þorvarðr hét, ok bjoggu þau í Gǫrðum, þar sem nú er biskupsstóll. Hon

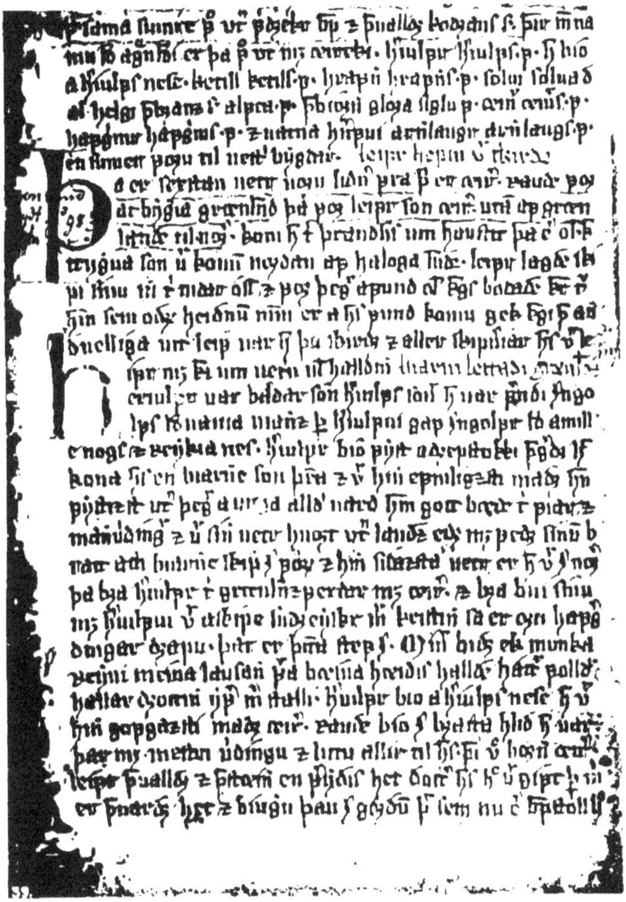

lutavie mikill en þuarnk var litil mn var hn mjog gefin t pred
hcuirsit vatt polb at guardi þ þin tima · þ sama sum ko · beartie
skipi sinu a eyrar er pad hr hepde byrt sighlt um vorit · þan
utende pottu biarna mikil z vilde e ba ep skipe sinu þa sjn
du haseta hr huart er h barnast þ en h sutr · at h ætlade at
hallar bonentu sinie z pigkar padg sinu ꝛ liter vist z vil ek h
allan skipinu til gnlds ep þ uilr m pylgd vierra ullir quod
vzt hr radu pylgia vilia þa mn · biarne v uitulg inu þible
uoz þd þatt sem ætinge uoz hep komit þ gnlds hap en þo hal
lm þr nu þ hap bep þr v buner z siglðu þina daga þar t e lndr
uar uturinr en þa tok ap byruna z lagðr at norænuir z þoku
z vissu þr e huert at þr þ z stepm þ mrgu dagrn · ept þ sa þr
sol lid z matthu þa dela ætt umdi nu segl z sigla þna dagr
tiðs þr sa lð z ræddu um mz ser huar lð þra mu ua e.B. bue
tat hyggia at þ mdi e gnld þr spyria huart h vill sigla at þessu
lði eða e · þ e mit raad at sigla þ nand at lðn z suo ga þr ok
sia þ brat at lðit var ofiallott z skogi vaxit z smar haedir
a lðinu z letu lðit a bakborda z letu skautr horpa a lðs sidu
sigla þr nu dagr ad þr sa lðd anat · þr spyria huart B · et
lade þ en gnld · h q e hellds ætla þetta gnld en hr þyria · þui
at iokla eru mjog mikla sagdr a gnldi þr nalgadust brat
þetta lnd z sa þ uar slett lnd z vidi uaxit · þa tok ahr byr þ þ þa a
ræddu hasetar þ et þ þotti þ rad at taka þ lnd en · B · vill þ e
þr · þotti zest bæde biurgud vid z vatn at engu e m þ þ obirg
ser · B · en þo pecs h ap þm nokkut amæli ap hasetu sinu h bad
þa vinda segl z suo v gt z sem þrsa stapni pra lde z sigla
hap vtsynings byr þria dagr z sa þa lðit þ et e þ lð uar h
att z fiallott z iokull a · þr spyria þa ep huarne vilde at
lata þar en h q e þ vilia · þuiat m lrzst þat lð ogagnuarlige
mr logdu þr e segl sia hallda mz lðinu þra z sa at þ v eiland

[FLATEYJARBÓK, Column 223.] EIRÍKS ÞÁTTR RAUÐA—4.

[var] svarri mikill, en Þorvarðr var lítilmenni. Var hon mjǫk gefin til fjár. Heiðit var fólk á Grœnlandi í þann tíma. Þat sama sumar kom Bjarni skipi sínu á Eyrar, er faðir hans hafði brott siglt um várit. Þau tíðindi þóttu Bjarna mikil, ok vildi eigi bera af skipi sínu. Þá spurðu hásetar hans, hvat er hann bærisk fyrir, en hann svarar, at hann ætlaði at halda siðvenju sinni, ok þiggja at fǫður sínum vetrvist; 'ok vil ek halda skipinu til Grœnlands, ef þér vilit mér fylgð veita.' Allir kváðusk hans ráðum fylgja vilja. Þá mælti Bjarni: 'úvitrlig mun þikkja vár ferð, þar sem engi várr hefir komit í Grœnlandshaf.' En þó halda þeir nú í haf, þegar þeir váru búnir, ok sigldu þrjá daga, þar til er landit var vatnat; en þá tók af byrina, ok lagði á norrœnur ok þokur, ok vissu þeir eigi hvert at þeir fóru, ok skipti þat mǫrgum dœgrum. Eptir þat sá þeir sól[1] ok máttu þá deila ættir; vinda nú segl, ok sigla þetta dœgr áðr þeir sá land, ok rœddu um með sér, hvat landi þetta mun vera. En Bjarni kvezk hyggja, at þat mundi eigi Grœnland. Þeir spyrja, hvárt hann vill sigla at þessu landi eða eigi; 'Þat er mitt ráð, at sigla í nánd við landit.' Ok svá gǿra þeir ok sá þat brátt, at landit var ófjǫllótt, ok skógi vaxit, ok smár hæðir á landinu, ok létu landit á bakborða, ok létu skaut horfa á land. Síðan sigla þeir tvau dœgr, áðr þeir sá land annat. Þeir spyrja hvárt Bjarni ætlaði þat enn Grœnland. Hann kvazk eigi heldr ætla þetta Grœnland en hit fyrra; 'því at jǫklar eru mjǫk miklir sagðir á Grœnlandi.' Þeir nálguðusk brátt þetta land, ok sá þat vera slétt land ok viði vaxit. Þá tók af byr fyrir þeim. Þá rœddu hásetar þat, at þeim þótti þat ráð, at taka þat land, en Bjarni vill þat eigi. Þeir þóttusk bæði þurfa við ok vatn. 'At ǿngu eru þér því óbirgir,' segir Bjarni. En þó fekk hann af því nǫkkut ámæli af hásetum sínum. Hann bað þá vinda segl, ok svá var gǿrt, ok settu framstafn frá landi; ok sigla í haf útsynnings byr þrjú dœgr, ok sá land it þriðja; en þat land var hátt ok fjǫllótt ok jǫkull á. Þeir spyrja þá, ef Bjarni vildi at landi láta þar; en hann kvazk eigi þat vilja; 'því at mér lízk þetta land ógagnvænligt.' Nú lǫgðu þeir eigi segl sitt, halda með landinu fram, ok sá, at þat var eyland;

[1] MS. has sia [i.e. sjá] after sól.

[FLATEYJARBÓK, Column 223 *b*.] EIRÍKS ÞÁTTR RAUÐA—5.

settu enn staſn við því landi, ok heldu í haſ hinn sama byr; en veðr óx í hǫnd, ok bað Bjarni þá svipta, ok eigi sigla meira en bæði dygði vel skipi þeira ok reiða. Sigldu nú ſjogur dœgr; þá sá þeir land hit ſjórða. Þá spurðu þeir Bjarna, hvárt hann ætlaði þetta vera Grœnland eða eigi. Bjarni svarar: 'Þetta er líkast því, er mér er sagt frá Grœnlandi, ok hér munu vér at landi halda.' Svá gøra þeir, ok taka land undir einhverju nesi at kveldi dags, ok var þar bátr á nesinu; en þar bjó Herjúlſr, ſaðir Bjarna, á því nesi, ok aſ því heſir nesit naſn tekit, ok er síðan kallat Herjúlſsnes. Fór Bjarni nú til ſǫður síns, ok hættir nú siglingu, ok er með ſǫður sínum meðan Herjúlſr liſði, ok síðan bjó hann þar eptir ſǫður sinn.

sitiu en skipin v þau lði ⁊ hellðu ſ hap hm ſama byr. en ve
ðr by ſ hnð ⁊ hað. B. þa ſnpeit ⁊ ec ſigla mætta en borðe ðy
gðe ut ſkipin þra ⁊ rendu ſiglðu nu ptogniv dægr þa ſa þt lnð
hit ptoyðu þa ſpurðu þr. B. hvort h̅ ætlaðe þra vera gulð ecc
B. ſuðr þra ev likazt þ er vn ætlaðr pra gulði ⁊ h̅ m v ar lði
hallaz ſiþ gð þr ⁊ tala lð unð ærnlhm neſe at buella dægr
⁊ uatr þar batr aueſmn en þar bio hiulpr prð. B. atþ neſi
⁊ atþ h̅ hęþ neſe napn tokr ⁊ en ſiðan kallar hiulpſ nes þ
B. nu til pandun liuſ. ⁊ hava nu ſiglinga ⁊ er mz podur ſint
meða heriulpr lipðe ⁊ ſiðan bio h̅ þar ep̅t. þ. ſln.

rnaðoðr het ſon eitres blodeyar
⁊ gunnhr hapðe vit ı neſte londu ſuðr plyðe ſuð
þ hab ı. en aþn ſunnr ſem nue pra lage þa ol.
kr. t. lon hapðe pryða nett radit nor. ko guðr. kc
til nor mz nioga h̅ ſkip ⁊ mikit lið. en e h̅ ko ı ſkuon v nor
þa ſtepnde ſuðr mz ſnde pangat e hin v nune uon ol kr ſig
tar h̅ auſtr til vikonnar. en þeg h̅ ko til lðz tok h̅ at hia ob
heim und ſig lðz polbar en heruði ſto uid toku en e lðz
m ſa at hic mikill mu̅ komi ahendr þ þa leitoðu þr ſe goða
⁊ ſatta ⁊ buðu ſigi at þing bod ſkyllðu pra um lðit. ſogðu at
þr ect villðu uatna hin undr toku hellðr en pala hinar ok
ſtepna t pinluiit þing at taka h̅ til kgs uoin þar nilkt a l
dung porit mz þing bod þı vıı ulmne brapðe ku þa vilia
gialldr ⁊ mz ſu bidanðe ſkyllðe vra en bændr þegu hellðr þin.
boſt at bua ſigi ſua lengi vartellur ſem h̅ þyrpin ⁊ þing
boð gat up gudl. ko tok þn bott at hn þey ymſ lðtr en uei
⁊ſlum em lið ſuc en ſunn garth ſkipa hi. þr. kr. pronn ⁊
hyrmngr magar ol kgs. uoru ſkipað ep hr halpu hop
ðmgrar up alla vikina þa er ol. kr. uar norðr ı lði ſeti
an bændr þm eoð mykla ſkiorn e þingboð g... ⁊ letu ſeg

blriit at dagueiðū en at uarueroū v̄ omelit ꝺgubbar. en
er ꝩſ. uoꝛu uaꝛ̄ þa hapðe h̄ cc. mā. allð poꝛ h̄ petrūdar e
m; xx. ſeſſu alſkipaða. ert. am lkarð nyklo tuncugat ok
h̄ kuin at kuma eiti z þo mikil at þui h̄t hapðe h̄ ſuib
ing eꝛ leiðangur ilepiu z v̄ þar a cc. mā eꝛ macir.
hapðe m; ſ̄ xxx. ſkeða z vin pirā miar mā h̄ ardaðe þr
œluin ſinū dag ſueib z gap þ liðen ſkunð z lopt at ſir yrie
ſen ū rokkr eꝛ um narar. h̄ gap þ aber ſua at ſa ſ koꝛin z
pœna borttni t peðu ſer. h̄ laga aluti þra v̄e z lauin. z le
yttu nidr lig t prelſis m; þ ſe keipri cuit. ſ maar men e
lenſingiū ſinū ſkipaðe h̄ z ſuð puk en ſinui t andard pe pā
gā. ſum ruiððu niker z gāu ſ ter z ollū bo h̄ til nokkur ſþr
Aſt er
nu þu uarit at biarne hſulpi ſ ko vīt
ap gulude apuud aru z z nt z v̄ him vt
ſiga biarnie þ paū ſinū e h̄ hapðe lond
ſer z þom m̄ h̄ var hapða v peꝛoui e h̄n
hapðe eꝛ at ſegia ap þ ſuðū z pet h̄ ap þ nokkur ami
biarnie gaat hirð maðr z z pe vt t gulude v̄ ſuant epr
vað nu mikil vin rað vin ſuat leiðan. lepr ſ aru. rau
ðr eꝛ beaua lifið pes e pirið biarna hſulpſ ſon z keipre
ſkip at ſim z reð til halſeia ſua at ſe v̄ halpe pioðe toꝛr
mā ſam. lepr baa gū pað ur aru. at h̄ mā eꝛ þ ya pos
ſite. aeſu tallraſt halða undan buerat þa va hingi z alla
z buerat numi niega v̄ noſe auſtu e v̄. lepr q̄ h̄ en mau
mett hell ſtira ap þ nū oū z þāl lee aru epr z z raðs h
eima þa e ſir eru at þui buī z v̄ þa ſkatnir at þa t ſkipiſ

Þat er **Hér hefr Grœnlendinga þátt. Capitulum.** nú þessu næst, at Bjarni Herjúlſsson kom utan aſ Grœnlandi á ſund Eirſks jarls, ok tók jarl við honum vel. Sagði Bjarni frá ſerðum sínum, er hann haſði lǫnd sét, ok þótti mǫnnum hann verit haſa úſorvitinn, er hann haſði ekki at segja aſ þeim lǫndum, ok ſekk hann aſ því nǫkkut ámæli. Bjarni gørðisk hirðmaðr jarls, ok ſór út til Grœnlands um sumarit eptir. Var nú mikil umrœða um landaleitan. Leiſr, son Eirſks rauða ór Brattahlíð, ſór á ſund Bjarna Herjúlſssonar, ok keypti skip at honum, ok réð til háseta, svá at þeir váru hálſr ſjórði tøgr manna saman. Leiſr bað sinn ſǫður Eirſk, at hann mundi enn ſyrir vera ſǫrinni. Eirſkr talðisk heldr undan; kvezk þá vera hniginn í aldr, ok kvezk minna mega við vási ǫllu en var. Leiſr kveðr hann enn mundu mestri heill stýra aſ þeim ſrændum; ok þetta lét Eirſkr eptir Leiſi, ok ríðr heiman, þá er þeir eru at því búnir, ok var þá skamt at ſara til skipsins.

[FLATEYJARBÓK, Column 282.] GRŒNLENDINGA ÞÁTTR—7.

Drepr hestrinn fœti, sá er Eiríkr reið, ok fell hann af baki, ok lestisk fótr hans. Þá mælti Eiríkr: 'Ekki mun mér ætlat at finna lǫnd fleiri en þetta, er nú byggjum vér; munum vér nú ekki lengr fara allir samt.' Fór Eiríkr heim í Brattahlíð, en Leifr rézk til skips ok félagar hans með honum; hálfr fjórði tøgr manna. Þar var suðrmaðr einn í ferð, er Tyrker hét. Nú bjoggu þeir skip sitt, ok sigldu í haf, þá [er] þeir váru búnir; ok fundu þá þat land fyrst, er þeir Bjarni fundu síðast. Þar sigla þeir at landi, ok kǫstuðu[1] akkerum, ok skutu báti, ok fóru á land, ok sá þar eigi gras; jǫklar miklir váru allt hit efra, en sem ein hella væri allt til jǫklanna frá sjónum, ok sýndisk þeim þat land vera gœðalaust. Þá mælti Leifr: 'Eigi er oss nú þat orðit um þetta land sem Bjarna, at vér hafim eigi komit á landit. Nú mun ek gefa nafn landinu, ok kalla Helluland.' Síðan fóru þeir til skips. Eptir þetta sigla þeir í haf, ok fundu land annat. Sigla enn at landi, ok kasta akkerum; skjóta síðan báti, ok ganga á landit. Þat land var slétt, ok skógi vaxit, ok sandar hvítir víða, þar sem þeir fóru, ok ósæbratt. Þá mælti Leifr: 'Af kostum[2] skal þessu landi nafn gefa[3], ok kalla Markland.' Fóru síðan ofan aptr til skips sem fljótast. Nú sigla þeir þaðan í haf landnyrðings-veðr, ok váru úti II dœgr áðr þeir sá land, ok sigldu at landi, ok kómu at ey einni, er lá norðr af landinu, og gengu þar upp, ok sásk um, í góðu veðri, ok fundu þat at dǫgg var á grasinu ok varð þeim þat fyrir[4], at þeir tóku hǫndum sínum í dǫggina[5], ok brugðu í munn sér, ok þóttusk ekki jafnsœtt kent hafa, sem þat var. Síðan fóru þeir til skips síns, ok sigldu í sund þat, er lá milli eyjarinnar, ok ness þess, er norðr gekk[6] af landinu; stefndu í vestrætt fyrir nesit. Þar var grunnsævi mikit at fjǫru-sjóvar, ok stóð þá uppi skip þeira, ok var þá langt til sjóvar at sjá frá skipinu. En þeim var svá mikil forvitni á, at fara til landsins, at þeir nentu eigi þess at bíða, at sjór felli undir skip þeira, ok runnu til lands þar er á ein fell ór vatni einu. En þegar sjór fell undir skip þeira, þá tóku þeir bátinn, ok reru til skip-

[1] MS. kostude. [2] MS. kustum! [3] MS. gef. [4] varð þeim þat fyrir repeated in MS. [5] MS. dǫgina. [6] MS. gek.

[illegible] slonu ȝ [illegible] epyng [illegible]
[illegible] pāa luo se b · ar u̅ lid [illegible]
[illegible] indiuy ȝ balla lid [illegible]
[illegible] þr s̄ hæþ ȝ purpdu [illegible]
[illegible] laan hære ȝ oga [illegible]
[illegible] þær se [illegible]
[illegible] godes [illegible]
[illegible] laan þ þr t lbips lini t ligi
[illegible] ȝ hest þest er noȝt god
[illegible] þær ne was [illegible]
[illegible] þe lang [illegible]
[illegible] ne sio [illegible] poȝuerin [illegible]
[illegible] þest ar bæn ar sicȝ pelle [illegible]
[illegible] acunu [illegible]
[illegible] t lbip

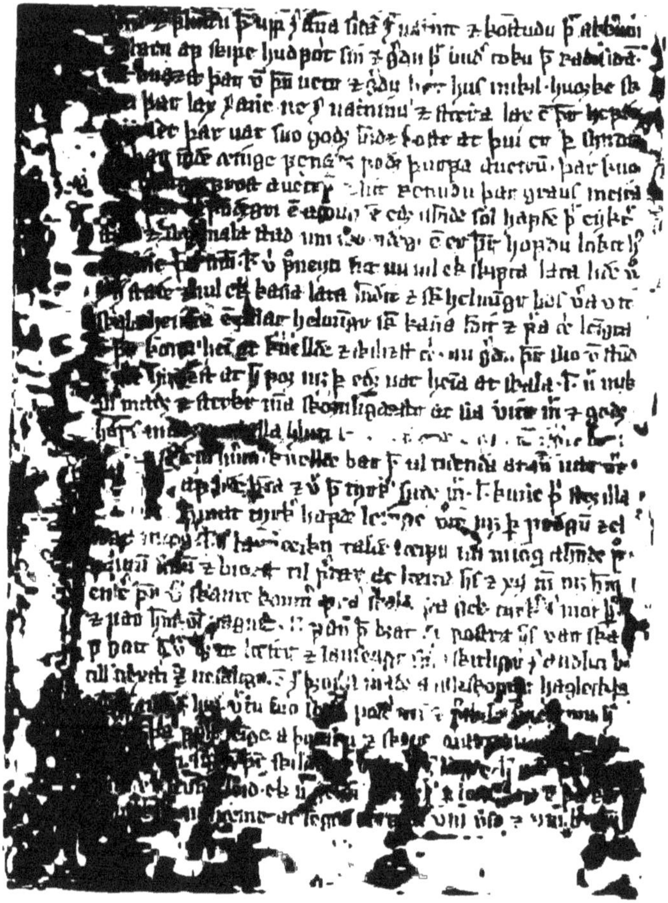

[FLATEYJARBÓK, Column 282 *b*.] GRŒNLENDINGA ÞÁTTR—8.

sins, ok fluttu þat upp í ána, síðan í vatnit, ok kǫstuðu þar akkerum, ok báru af skipi húðfǫt sín, ok gørðu þar búðir; tóku þat ráð síðan at búask þar um þann vetr, ok gørðu þar hús mikil. Hvárki skorti þar lax í ánni né í vatninu, ok stœrra lax en þeir hefði fyrr sét. Þar var svá góðr landskostr, at því er þeim sýndisk, at þar mundi engi fénaðr fóðr þurfa á vetrum. Þar kvámu engi frost á vetrum, ok lítt rénuðu þar grǫs. Meira var þar jafndœgri en á Grœnlandi eða Íslandi: sól hafði þar eyktarstað ok dagmálastað um skammdegi. En er þeir hǫfðu lokit húsgørð sinni, þá mælti Leifr við fǫruneyti sitt: 'Nú vil ek skipta láta liði váru í II staði, ok vil ek kanna láta landit, ok skal helmingr liðs vera við skála heima, en annarr helmingr skal kanna landit, ok fara eigi lengra en þeir komi heim at kveldi, ok skilisk eigi.' Nú gørðu þeir svá um stund. Leifr gørði ýmist, at hann fór með þeim eða var heima at skála. Leifr var mikill maðr ok sterkr, manna skǫruligastr at sjá, vitr maðr ok góðr hófsmaðr um alla hluti.

Leifr hinn heppni fann menn í skeri á hafi.

Á einhverju kveldi bar þat til tíðinda, at manns var vant af liði þeira, ok var þat Tyrker suðrmaðr. Leifr kunni því stórilla, því at Tyrker hafði lengi verit með þeim feðgum, ok elskat mjǫk Leif í barnœsku. Talði Leifr nú mjǫk á hendr fǫrunautum sínum, ok bjósk til ferðar at leita hans, ok XII menn með honum. En er þeir váru skamt komnir frá skála, þá gekk Tyrker í mót þeim, ok var honum vel fagnat. Leifr fann þat brátt, at fóstra hans var skapgott. Hann var brattleitr ok lauseygr, smáskitligr í andliti, lítill vexti, ok vesalligr[1], en íþróttamaðr á allskonar hagleik. Þá mælti Leifr til hans: 'Hví vartu svá seinn, fóstri minn, ok fráskili fǫruneytinu?' Hann talaði þá fyrst lengi á þýzku, ok skaut marga vega augunum, ok gretti sik; en þeir skildu eigi hvat er hann sagði. Hann mælti þá á norrœnu, er stund leið: 'Ek var genginn eigi miklu lengra en þit; kann ek nǫkkur nýnæmi at segja. Ek fann vínvið ok vínber.' Mun

[1] MS. uesaligr.

[FLATEYJARBÓK, Column 283.] GRŒNLENDINGA ÞÁTTR—9.

þat satt, fóstri minn?' kvað Leifr. 'At vísu er þat satt,' kvað hann, 'því at ek var þar fœddr, er hvárki skorti vínvið né vínber.' Nú sváfu þeir af þá nótt; en um morguninn mælti Leifr við háseta sína: 'Nú skal hafa tvennar sýslur fram, ok skal sinn dag hvárt lesa vínber eða hǫggva vínvið, ok fella mǫrkina, svá at þat verði farmr til skips míns.' Ok þetta var ráðs tekit. Svá er sagt, at eptirbátr þeira var f-yldr af vínberjum. Nú var hǫggvinn farmr á skipit; ok er várar, þá b-joggusk þeir, ok sigldu brott, ok gaf Leifr nafn landinu eptir land-kostum, ok kallaði Vínland. Sigla nú síðan í haf, ok gaf þeim vel byri þar til er þeir sá Grœnland, ok fjǫll undir jǫklum; þá tók einn maðr til máls, ok mælti við Leif: 'Hví stýrir þú svá mjǫk undir veðr skipinu?' Leifr svarar: 'Ek hygg at stjórn minni, en þó enn at fleira, eða hvat sjái þér til tíðinda?' Þeir kváðusk ekki sjá þat er tíðindum sætti. 'Ek veit eigi,' segir Leifr, 'hvárt ek sé skip eða sker.' Nú sjá þeir, ok kváðu sker vera. Hann sá því framar en þeir, at hann sá menn í skerinu. 'Nú vil ek, at vér bei-tim undir veðrit,' segir Leifr, 'svá at (vér) náim til þeira, ef menn eru þurftugir at ná várum fundi, ok er nauðsyn á at duga þeim; en með því at þeir sé eigi friðmenn, þá eigum vér allan kost undir oss, en þeir ekki undir sér.' Nú sœkja þeir undir skerit, ok lægðu [segl] sitt, kǫstuðu akkeri, ok sku-tu litlum báti ǫðrum, er þeir hǫfðu með sér. Þá spurði Tyrker, hverr þar réði fyrir liði. Sá kvezk Þórir heita, ok vera norrœnn maðr at kyni; 'eða hvert er þitt nafn?' Leifr segir til sín. 'Ertu son Eiríks rau-ða ór Brattahlíð?' segir hann. Leifr kvað svá vera. 'Nú vil ek,' segir Leifr, 'bjóða yðr ǫllum á mitt skip, ok fémunum þeim, er skipit má við taka.' Þeir þ-águ þann kost, ok sigldu síðan til Eiríksfjarðar með þeim farmi, þar til er þeir kómu til Brattahlíðar. Báru farminn af skipi; síðan bau-ð Leifr Þóri til vistar með sér, ok Guðríði, konu hans, ok III mǫnnum ǫðrum, en fekk[1] vistir ǫðrum hásetum, bæði Þóris ok sínum félǫgum. Leifr tók XV menn ór skerinu. Hann var síðan kallaðr Leifr hinn heppni[2]. Leifi varð n-ú bæði gott til fjár ok mannvirðingar. Þann vetr kom sótt mik-

[1] MS. fek. [2] MS. hepni.

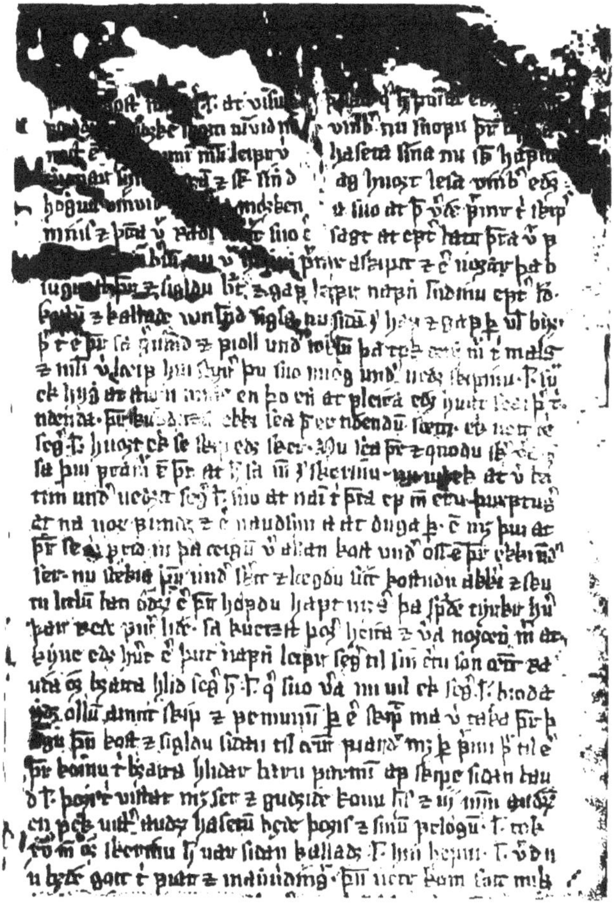

il s lid þrir z audaurett. h pos z mikill hlun[illegible] lit hi [illegible] ue
tu audlaust z aur [illegible] iuu v um vaedi mikil v [illegible]
pos l z þann þorualldr [illegible] hi op v ui[illegible] kaniar hapa [illegible]
[illegible] linda þat mli. [illegible] ut þou þu [illegible] þaira m; skip [illegible] lrod [illegible]
þu uill til vinlonde z iul ek þo at [illegible] þann [illegible]
[illegible] er þos dan i leermu z suo uar geert [illegible]
N[illegible] biozt þu til þrar þaar m; [illegible]
brodur sins [illegible] buigu þar skip sitt z hell [illegible] hap [illegible]
aringe [illegible] sogu v [illegible] þra [illegible] e þr koma i vinlond [illegible]
[illegible] budir z biugou [illegible] skip sitt z [illegible] þar [illegible] ab
[illegible] til [illegible] en v [illegible] þr [illegible] ab
a skip sitt z [illegible]
[illegible] linda z [illegible] linderett linda [illegible]
[illegible] z [illegible] mille [illegible] z [illegible] z hu[illegible] [illegible] v ei
[illegible] z [illegible] pundu [illegible] ma [illegible]
[illegible] en s [illegible] pundu [illegible] halm
[illegible] pundu þr [illegible] z [illegible] z quonu
til [illegible] at [illegible] en at [illegible] þa [illegible]
[illegible] z [illegible] þa [illegible] at [illegible] land
[illegible] z [illegible] þa [illegible] z [illegible] imad [illegible]
[illegible] þar lange [illegible] z [illegible] þa [illegible]
þu [illegible] tu uil ek [illegible]
[illegible] z [illegible] þr [illegible]
[illegible] z [illegible] z [illegible]
er þar [illegible] z at [illegible] er þat [illegible]
[illegible] þa [illegible] þr [illegible] z [illegible]
[illegible] z [illegible] þar [illegible] alla [illegible]
[illegible] þa h er [illegible] z h [illegible]
[illegible] z [illegible] z [illegible]
[illegible] z [illegible] þar [illegible] iij z iij [illegible] þa [illegible]

[FLATEYJARBÓK, Column 283 *b*.] GRŒNLENDINGA ÞÁTTR—10.

il í lið Þóris, ok andaðisk hann Þórir ok mikill hluti liðs hans. Þann vetr andaðisk ok Eiríkr rauði. Nú var umrœða mikil um Vínlandsfǫr Leifs, ok þótti Þorvaldi, bróður hans, of úvíða kannat hafa verit landit. Þá mælti Leifr við Þorvald: 'Þú skalt fara með skip mitt, bróðir, ef þú vill til Vínlands, ok vil ek þó, at skipit fari áðr eptir viði þeim, er Þórir átti í skerinu.' Ok svá var gert. **Þorvaldr fór til Vínlands.** Nú bjósk Þorvaldr til þeirar ferðar með XXX manna, með umráði Leifs, bróður síns. Síðan bjoggu þeir skip sitt, ok heldu í haf ok er engi frásǫgn um ferð þeira, fyrr en þeir koma til Vínlands til Leifsbúða, ok bjoggu þar um skip sitt, ok sátu um kyrt þann vetr, ok veiddu fiska til matar sér. En um várit mælti Þorvaldr, at þeir skyldu búa skip sitt, ok skyldi eptirbátr skipsins, ok nǫkkurir menn með, fara fyrir vestan landit, ok kanna þar um sumarit. Þeim sýndisk landit fagrt ok skógótt, ok skamt milli skógar ok sjóvar, ok hvítir sandar. Þar var eyjótt mjǫk, ok grunnsævi mikit. Þeir fundu hvergi manna vistir né dýra, en í eyju einni vestarliga fundu þeir kornhjálm af tré. Eigi fundu þeir fleiri mannaverk, ok fóru aptr, ok kvámu til Leifsbúða at hausti. En at sumri ǫðru fór Þorvaldr fyrir austan með kaupskipit, ok hit nyrðra fyrir landit. Þá gørði at þeim veðr hvasst fyrir andnesi einu, ok rak þá þar upp, ok brutu kjǫlinn undan skipinu, ok hǫfðu þar langa dvǫl, ok bœttu skip sitt. Þá mælti Þorvaldr við fǫrunauta sína: 'Nú vil ek at vér reisim hér upp kjǫlinn á nesinu, ok kallim Kjalarnes[1],' ok svá gørðu þeir. Síðan sigla þeir þaðan í braut, ok austr fyrir landit, ok inn í fjarðarkjapta þá, er þar váru næstir, ok at hǫfða þeim, er þar gekk fram; hann var allr skógi vaxinn. Þá leggja þeir fram skip sín í lægi, ok skjóta bryggjum á land, ok gengur Þorvaldr þar á land upp með alla fǫrunauta sína. Hann mælti þá: 'Hér er fagrt, ok hér vilda ek bœ minn reisa;' ganga síðan til skips, ok sjá á sandinum inn frá hǫfðanum III hæðir, ok fóru til þangat, ok sjá þar húðkeipa III, ok III menn undir hverjum. Þá skip-

[1] MS. kialnar nes.

[FLATEYJARBÓK, Column 284.] GRŒNLENDINGA ÞÁTTR—II.

tu þeir liði sínu, ok hǫfðu hendr á þeim ǫllum, nema einn komsk í braut með keip sinn. Þeir drepa hina VIII, ok ganga síðan aptr á hǫfðann, ok sjásk þar um, ok sjá inn í fjǫrðinn hæðir nǫkkurar, ok ætluðu þeir þat vera bygðir. Eptir þat sló á þá hǫfga svá miklum, at þeir máttu eigi vǫku halda, ok sofna þeir allir. Þá kom kall yfir þá, svá at þeir vǫknuðu allir. Svá segir kallit: 'Vaki þú Þorvaldr ok allt fǫruneyti þitt, ef þú vill líf þitt hafa, ok far þú á skip þitt, ok allir menn þínir, ok farið frá landi sem skjótast.' Þá fór innan eptir firðinum útal húðkeipa, ok lǫgðu at þeim. Þorvaldr mælti þá: 'Vér skulum fœra út á borð vígfleka, ok verjask sem bezt, en vega lítt í mót.' Svá gøra þeir, en Skrælingar skutu á þá um stund, en flýja síðan í brott[1] sem ákafast, hverr sem mátti. Þá spurði Þorvaldr menn sína, ef þeir væri nǫkkut sárir. Þeir kváðusk eigi sárir vera. 'Ek hefir fengit sár undir hendi,' segir hann, 'ok fló ǫr milli skipborðsins ok skjaldarins undir hǫnd mér, ok er hér ǫrin; en mun mik þetta til bana leiða. Nú ræð ek, at þér búið ferð yðra sem fljótast aptr á leið en[2] þér skulut fœra mik á hǫfða þann, er mér þótti byggiligastr[3] vera; má þat vera, at mér hafi satt á munn komit, at ek muni þar búa á um stund. Þar skulu þér mik grafa, ok setja krossa at hǫfðum mér ok at fótum, ok kallið þat Krossanes jafnan síðan.' Grœnland var þá kristnat, en þó andaðisk Eiríkr rauði fyrir kristni. Nú andaðisk Þorvaldr, en þeir gørðu allt eptir því sem hann hafði mælt, ok fóru síðan, ok hittu þar fǫrunauta sína, ok sǫgðu hvárir ǫðrum slík tíðindi sem vissu, ok bjoggu[4] þar þann vetr, ok fengu sér vínber ok vínvið til skipsins. Nú búask [þeir] þaðan um várit eptir til Grœnlands, ok kvámu skipi sínu í Eiríksfjǫrð ok kunnu Leifi at segja mikil tíðindi.

Þorsteinn Eiríksson andaðisk í Vestribygð. Þat hafði gørzk til tíðinda meðan á Grœnlandi, at Þorsteinn í Eiríksfirði hafði kvángask, ok fengit Guðríðar Þorbjarnardóttur, er átt hafði Þórir austmaðr, er fyrr var frá sagt. Nú fýstisk Þorsteinn Eiríksson at fara til Vínlands eptir líki Þorvalds, bróður síns, ok

[1] MS. burt. [2] en is repeated in the MS. [3] MS. byggiligazst. [4] biugg.

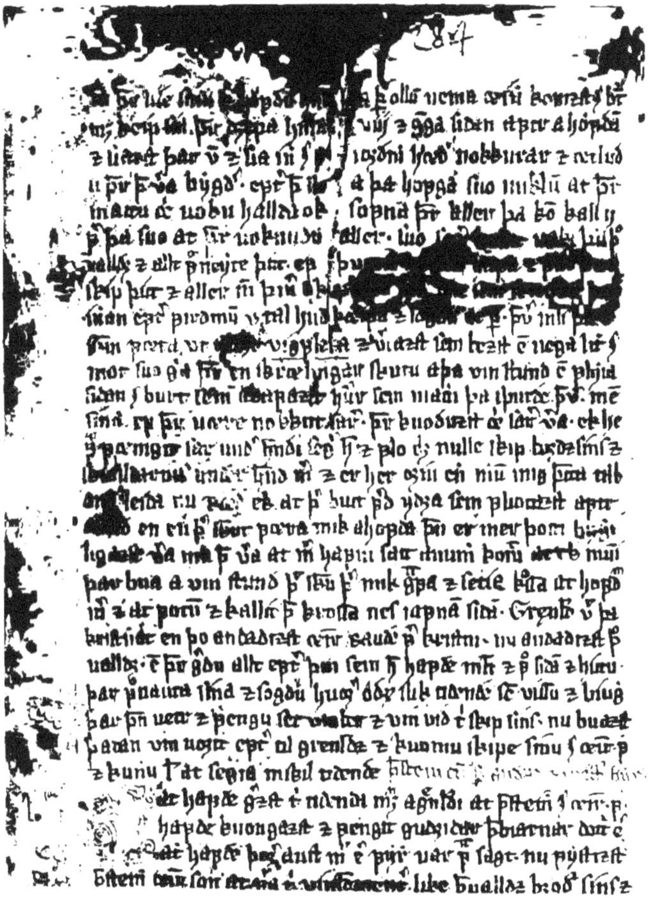

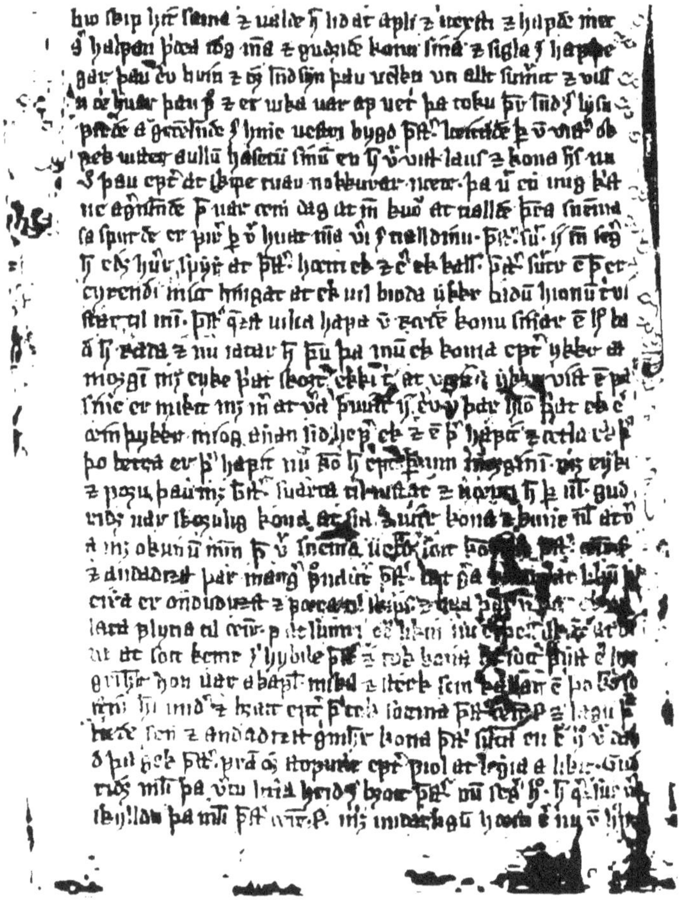

[FLATEYJARBÓK, Column 281 *b*.] GRŒNLENDINGA ÞÁTTR—12.

bjó skip hit sama, ok valdi hann lið at afli ok vexti, ok hafði með sér hálfan þriðja tøg manna, ok Guðríði konu sína; ok sigla í haf, þegar þau eru búin, ok ór landsýn. Þau velkði úti allt sumarit, ok vissu eigi hvar þau fóru; ok er vika var af vetri, þá tóku þeir land í Lýsufirði á Grœnlandi, í hinni vestri bygð. Þorsteinn leitaði þeim um vistir, ok fekk vistir ǫllum hásetum sínum, en hann var vistlaus, ok kona hans. Nú váru þau eptir at skipi tvau nǫkkurar nætr. Þá var enn ung kristni á Grœnlandi. Þat var einn dag, at menn kvámu at tjaldi þeira snemma. Sá spurði, er fyrir þeim var, hvat manna væri í tjaldinu. Þorsteinn svarar: 'II menn,' segir hann, 'eða hverr spyrr at?' 'Þorsteinn heiti ek ok er kallaðr Þorsteinn svartr; en þat er ørindi mitt hingat, at ek vil bjóða ykkr báðum hjónum til vistar til mín.' Þorsteinn kvezk vilja hafa umræði konu sinnar, en hon bað hann ráða, ok nú játar hann þessu. 'Þá mun ek koma eptir ykkr á morgin með eyki, því at [mik] skortir ekki til at veita ykkr vist, en fásinni er mikit með mér at vera, því at II eru vit þar hjón, því at ek er einþykkr mjǫk. Annan sið hefir ek ok en þér hafið, ok ætla ek þann þó betra, er þér hafið.' Nú kom hann eptir þeim um morgininn með eyki, ok fóru þau með Þorsteini svarta til vistar, ok veitti hann þeim vel. Guðríðr var skǫrulig kona at sjá, ok vitr kona, ok kunni vel at vera með ókunnum mǫnnum. Þat var snemma vetrar, sótt kom í lið Þorsteins Eiríkssonar, ok andaðisk þar margir fǫrunautar [hans]. Þorsteinn bað[1] gøra kistur at líkum þeira, er ǫnduðusk, ok fœra til skips, ok búa þar um; 'því at ek vil láta flytja til Eiríksfjarðar at sumri, ǫll líkin.' Nú er þess skamt at bíða, at sótt kemr í hýbýli Þorsteins, ok tók kona hans sótt fyrst, er hét Grímhildr. Hon var ákafliga mikil, ok sterk sem karlar[2], en þó kom sóttin henni undir; ok brátt eptir þat tók sóttina Þorsteinn Eiríksson, ok lágu þau bæði senn; ok andaðisk Grímhildr, kona Þorsteins svarta. En er hon var dauð, þá gekk Þorsteinn fram ór stofunni eptir fjǫl, at leggja á líkit. Guðríðr mælti þá: 'Vertu lítla hríð í brott, Þorsteinn minn,' segir hon. Hann kvað svá vera skyldu. Þá mælti Þorsteinn Eiríksson: 'Með undarligum hætti er nú um húsfr-

[1] MS. bat. [2] MS. kallar.

[FLATEYJARBÓK, Column 285.] GRŒNLENDINGA ÞÁTTR—13.

1. eyju[1] vára[2], því at nú ǫrglask hon upp við ǫlnboga, ok þokar fótum sí-
2. num frá stokki, ok þreifar til skúa sinna; ok í því kom Þorsteinn bóndi inn,
3. ok lagðisk Grímhildr niðr í því, ok brakaði þá í hverju tré í stofunni.
4. Nú gørir Þorsteinn kistu at líki Grímhildar, ok fœrði í brott, ok bjó um. Hann var bæ-
5. ði mikill maðr ok sterkr, ok þurfti hann þess alls, áðr hann kom henni brott[3] af
6. bœnum. Nú elnaði sóttin Þorsteini Eiríkssyni, ok andaðisk hann. Guðríðr kon-
7. a hans, kunni því lítt. Þá váru þau ǫll í stofunni. Guðríðr hafði setit
8. á stóli frammi fyrir bekknum, er hann hafði legit [á], Þorsteinn bóndi hennar. Þá tó-
9. k Þorsteinn bóndi Guðríði af stólinum í fang sér, ok settisk í bekkinn ann-
10. an með hana, gegnt líki Þorsteins, ok talði um fyrir henni marga vega, ok huggaði
11. hana, ok hét henni því, at hann mundi fara með henni til Eiríksfjarðar, með líki Þorsteins, bónda hennar,
12. ok fǫrunauta hans; 'ok svá skal ek taka hingat hjón fleiri,' segir hann, 'þér til
13. hugganar ok skemtanar.' Hon þakkaði honum. Þorsteinn Eiríksson settisk þá upp,
14. ok mælti: 'Hvar er Guðríðr?' III tíma mælti hann þetta, en hon þagði. Þá mælti hon við
15. Þorstein bónda: 'Hvárt skal ek svǫr veita hans máli eða eigi?' Hann bað hana eigi
16. svara. Þá gekk Þorsteinn bóndi yfir gólfit, ok settisk á stólinn, en Guðríðr sat í kn-
17. jám honum, ok þá mælti Þorsteinn bóndi: 'Hvat viltu, nafni?' segir hann. Hann svarar, er stun-
18. d leið: 'Mér er annt til þess, at segja Guðríði forlǫg sín, til þess at
19. hon kunni þá betr andláti mínu; því at ek er kominn til góðra hvíl-
20. dastaða. En þat er þér at segja, Guðríðr, at þú munt gipt vera íslenzkum manni,
21. ok munu langar vera samfarar ykkrar, ok mart manna mun frá ykkr
22. koma, þroskasamt, bjart ok ágætt, sœtt ok ilmat vel. Munu þit
23. fara af Grœnlandi til Noregs, ok þaðan til Íslands, ok gøra bú á Íslandi. Þar munu þit le-
24. ngi búa, ok muntu honum lengr lifa. Þú munt utan fara, ok ganga suðr, ok
25. koma út aptr til Íslands til bús þíns, ok þá mun þar kirkja reist vera,
26. ok muntu þar vera ok taka nunnuvígslu, ok þar muntu andask.' Ok þá
27. hnígr Þorsteinn aptr, ok var búit um lík hans, ok fœrt til skips. Þorsteinn bóndi

[1] MS. husfr-eiu. [2] MS. uorrar. [3] MS. burt.

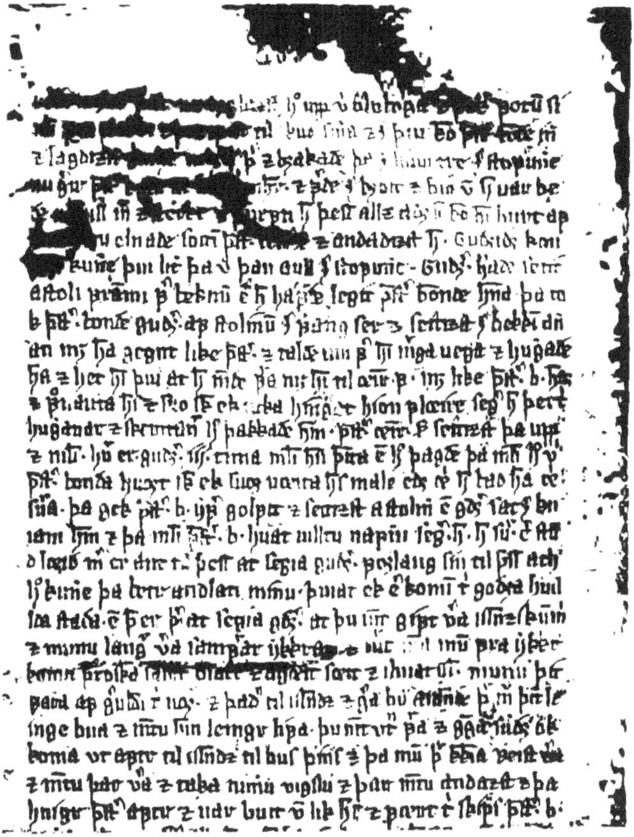

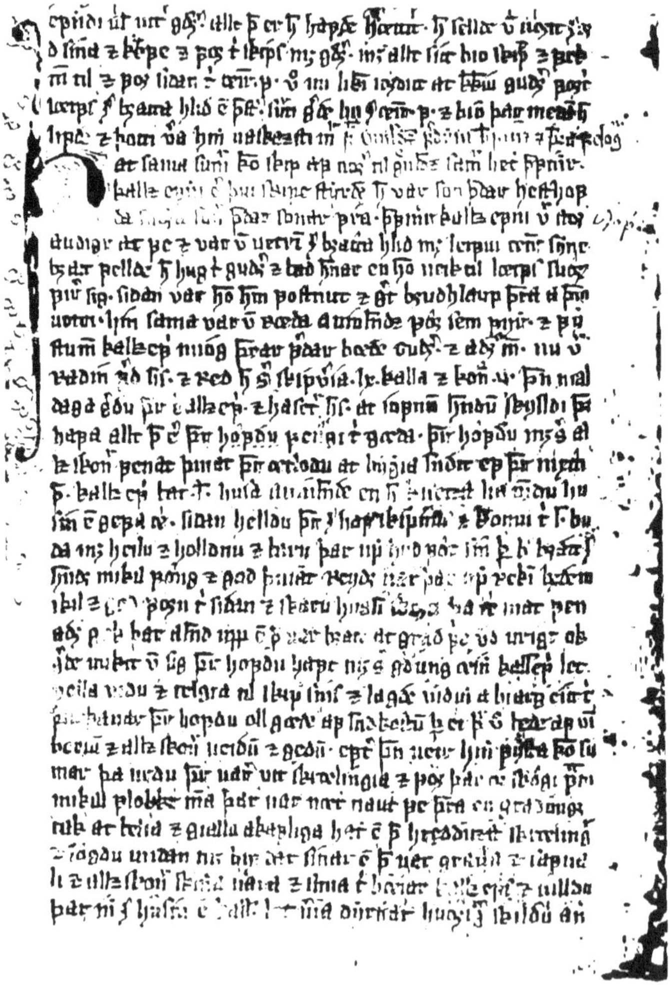

epı̄dı ut ut gds alle þ er h hafþe ħornır · h sellar v uısır ȝ a
d lına ȝ kepe ȝ poſ t lepſ m; gds · m; alle ſıa bıo lepþ ȝ pıeb
m tıl ȝ poſ lıdan ē eırıp · v ıııı lıbı ıoydır at bēu guds poſt
lærpſ ſ hramt hlıd ē pſt · ſum gıa hıı ſ eırıp · ȝ bıo þetg meaþ h
lıpa ȝ komı va hm uelkeaftı m ... ſkıp dog
at ſama ſum ko lep ep naſ tıl guds ſem het þenir ·
halla ... ſtırǽ h var ſon þorar hetthop
... þorar ſonar pıa · þenir halla epı v ſtor
audıgr at þe ȝ var v uetrı ſ hramt hlıd m; lærpu eın ſıgı
hrır pellar h hug t guds ȝ bad ſnar en ho uılı al lærpſ ſıag
pıu ſıp · ſıdan var ho hm poſtnut ȝ gıt brudhlaup þett at þın
uetr · hın ſama var v eeda a ua kıde poſ ſem pıır · ȝ þ
ſtum hallz epı mıog þrar þaar hert guds · ȝ ady m · nu v
vedın ... ſıſ · ȝ red h ſı ſkıp vıa · lx · halla ȝ kon · vı · þn mal
daga ... þır ı allz ep · ȝ haſer hſ · at ſopnu ... ſkyldı þa
hepa alle þ ē þr hopdu perıat t gera · þır hopdu m; ſ al
lz ſkon pendar pıner þr atlodu at lıngıa ſıdar ep þr nıeth
þ · hallz ep bar · t · hula ... en h ... hın ...
ſın ē gepa ... ſıdan hellau þr ſ hap ... ȝ komu t ... bu
da m; helu ȝ hollanu ȝ bıru þar upp ... ſın ... hrapa ſ
ſnıdr mıbıl pomg ȝ pad þıuar · Reyd ... þa ... upp rekı hram
ıbıl ȝ ... poſn t ſıdan ȝ ſkaru hıaſt ... ha ... mar pen
adr p ... bar a kıd upp ē p var brat · at grad pe vs ıııgr ob
... mıkıt v ſıg þır hopdu hıpe m; s ... ung ... hallz ep ler
... ȝ ... tıl ſkıp ... ȝ lagar ... a bıang ... t
... þır hopdu oll gerve up ... er ... v ... vı
berıu ȝ allz ſkon ... ȝ ged · ep ... hın ... ko ſu
mar þa ... þır uar vıt ſkıalıngıa ȝ poſ þar ... þın
mıbıll plob ... þar uar nart nauı pe þın en ...
tılb at beıa ȝ gıella ... h ... ē þ heradınt ſkıalıng
... ſagdu ... ē þ uer ... ȝ ...
lı ȝ allz ſkon ... ȝ lına t ... hallz ep ȝ ... ıılla
þar m ſ hıaſt ... m ... dıırkar hugıı ſ ſkıldu an

[FLATEYJARBÓK, Column 285 *b*.] GRŒNLENDINGA ÞÁTTR—14.

efndi vel við Guðríði allt þat, er hann hafði heitit. Hann seldi um várit jǫrð sína ok kvikfé, ok fór til skips með Guðríði, með allt sitt; bjó skipit, ok fekk menn til, ok fór síðan til Eiríksfjarðar. Váru nú líkin jǫrðut at kirkju. Guðríðr fór til Leifs í Brattahlíð, en Þorsteinn svarti gørði bú í Eiríksfirði, ok bjó þar meðan hann lifði, ok þótti vera hinn vaskasti maðr.

Fra Vinlandsferðum Þorfinns ok þeira fǫlǫgum.

Þat sama sumar kom skip af Noregi til Grœnlands. Sá maðr hét Þorfinnr Karlsefni, er því skipi stýrði. Hann var son Þórðar hesthǫfða, Snorrasonar, Þórðarsonar frá [Hǫfða]. Þorfinnr karlsefni var stórauðigr at fé, ok var um vetrinn í Brattahlíð með Leifi Eiríkssyni. Brátt feldi hann hug til Guðríðar, ok bað hennar, en hon veik til Leifs svǫrum fyrir sik. Síðan var hon honum fǫstnuð, ok gørt brúðhlaup þeira á þeim vetri. Hin sama var umrœða á Vínlandsfǫr sem fyrr, ok fýstu menn Karlsefni mjǫk þeirar ferðar, bæði Guðríðr ok aðrir menn. Nú var ráðin ferð hans, ok réð hann sér skipverja, LX karla ok konur V. Þann máldaga gørðu þeir Karlsefni ok hásetar hans, at jǫfnum hǫndum skyldi þeir hafa allt þat, er þeir hǫfðu fengit[1] til gœða. Þeir hǫfðu með sér allskonar fénað, því at þeir ætluðu at byggja landit, ef þeir mætti þat. Karlsefni bað Leif húsa á Vínlandi, en hann kvezk ljá mundu húsin, en gefa eigi. Síðan heldu þeir í haf skipinu, ok kómu til Leifsbúða með heilu ok hǫldnu, ok báru þar upp húðfǫt sin. Þeim bar brátt í hendr mikil fǫng ok góð: því at reyðr var þar upp rekin, bæði mikil ok góð; fóru til síðan, ok skáru hvalinn. Skorti þá eigi mat. Fénaðr gekk þar á land upp; en þat var brátt at graðfé varð úrigt, ok gørði mikit um sik. Þeir hǫfðu haft með sér graðung einn. Karlsefni lét fella viðu, ok telgja til skipsins, ok lagði viðinn á bjarg eitt til þurkanar. Þeir hǫfðu ǫll gœði af landkostum þeim, er þar váru, bæði af vínberjum ok allskonar veiðum ok gœðum. Eptir þann vetr hinn fyrsta kom sumar; þá urðu þeir varir við Skrælingja, ok fór þar ór skógi fram mikill flokkr manna. Þar var nær nautfé þeira, en graðungr tók at belja, ok gjalla ákafliga hátt; en þat hræddusk Skrælingar, ok lǫgðu undan með byrðar sínar, en þat var grávara ok safali, ok allskonar skinnavara, ok snúa til bœjar Karlsefnis, ok vildu þar inn í húsin, en Karlsefni lét verja dyrnar. Hvárigir skilðu ann-

[1] More correctly, er þeir fengi.

[FLATEYJARBÓK, Column 286.] GRŒNLENDINGA ÞÁTTR—15.

ars mál. Þá tóku Skrælingjar ofan bagga[1] sína, ok leystu, ok buðu þeim, ok vildu vápn helzt fyrir; en Karlsefni bannaði þeim at selja vápnin, ok nú l-eitar hann ráðs með þeim hætti, at hann bað konur bera út búnyt at þeim, ok þe-gar er þeir sá búnyt, þá vildu þeir kaupa þat, en ekki annat. Nú var s-ú kaupfǫr Skrælingja, at þeir báru sinn varning í brott í mǫg-um sínum, en Karlsefni ok fǫrunautar hans hǫfðu eptir bagga þeira ok sk-innavǫru; fóru þeir við svá búit í brott[2]. Nú er frá því at segja, at Karlsefni lætr gøra skíðgarð ramligan um bœ sinn, ok bjoggusk þar um. Í þann tíma fœddi Guðríðr sveinbarn, kona Karlsefnis, ok hét sá sveinn S-norri. Á ǫndverðum ǫðrum vetri kvámu Skrælingjar til móts við þá, ok váru m-iklu fleiri en fyrr, ok hǫfðu slíkan varnað sem fyrr. Þá mælti Karlsefni við konur: 'Nú skulu þér béra út slíkan mat sem fyrr var rífas-tr, en ekki annat;' ok er þeir sá þat þá kǫstuðu þeir bǫggunum sínum inn yfir skíðgarðinn. En Guðríðr sat í dyrum inni með vǫggu Snorra, sonar síns, þá bar skugga í dyrrin, ok gekk þar inn kona í svǫrtum námkyrtli heldr lág, ok hafði dregil um hǫfuð, ok ljósjǫrp á hár, fǫlleit[3] ok mjǫk eygð, svá at eigi hafði jafnmikil augu sét í einum manns-hausi. Hon gekk þar at, er Guðríðr sat, ok mælti: 'Hvat heitir þú?' se-gir hon. 'Ek heiti Guðríðr, eða hvert er þitt heiti?' 'Ek heiti Guðríðr,' segir hon. Þá rétti Guðríðr húsfreyja hǫnd sína til hennar, at hon sæti hjá henni, en þat bar allt saman, at þá heyrði Guðríðr brest mikinn, ok var þá k-onan horfin, ok í því var ok veginn einn Skrælingja af einum húskarli Karlsefnis, því at hann hafði viljat taka vápn þeira. Ok fóru nú í brott sem tíðast, en klæði þeira lágu þar eptir ok varningr. Engi maðr hafði konu þessa sét utan Guðríðr ein. 'Nú munum vér þurfa til ráða at t-aka,' segir Karlsefni, 'því at ek hygg at þeir muni vitja vár hit þriðja sinni með úfriði ok fjǫlmenni. Nú skulum vér taka þat ráð, at X menn fari fram á nes þetta, ok sýni sik þar, en annat lið várt skal fara í skóg, ok hǫ-ggva þar rjóðr fyrir nautfé váru, þá er liðit kemr fram ór skógi-num. Vér skulum ok taka griðung várn, ok láta hann fara fyrir oss.' En þar

[1] MS. bakka. [2] MS. burt. [3] MS. folleit.

ørſ mal· þa tolu ſtrællingiar oꝼ [illegible] ſma ⁊ leyſtu ⁊ buðu þr
⁊ villdu uopn hellzt þ e̅ balld ep [illegible] þ at ſelia uopn̄ ꝼauſt
att h̅ ꝛaðſ m; þ hann at; h̅ bað kon̅ bera ut bunyt at þ ⁊ þe
gar er þr ſa bunyt þa villdu þr kaupa þ e̅ ecki annat nu/ u̅ſ
u kaup þꝛ ſtrælingia at þr baru ſin̅ vaning j burt / mog
u̅ ſin̅u· en balld ep ⁊ þm̅ ꝼundar h̅ſ hoꝼðu ept leg̅it ſiu / a ⁊ ſt
ma ugu þ þr u̅ ſtoðbunt j bunt j hu er þa þ at ſe / gua at
balld· lett gia ſkiðgarð ꝛaml; gan um bæ ſin ⁊ bug [illegible] uarþ þ u̅
j þn tima það de guð· ſun ſi kari kona balld· ⁊ het [illegible] ſo ſuein̄ s
noꝛe a aundu u̅du̅ oðr uet þa kuð ſkrſt· e̅ ſtoꝛ [illegible] ⁊ u̅ þa ⁊ u̅m
gðu pleaue e̅ þiſi· ⁊ hoꝼðu ſkad. u̅nir ſe þat [illegible] þa nu balld· u̅
konnt nu ſkn þer ber a ut ſliku mat ſem [illegible] þrir ua̅r ep̅te
ſte en ecki annat ⁊ er þr ſa þ j a konu [illegible] mu̅ ſmu̅ m̅
yþ ſkuð gani en guð· ſun j an̅ mc m; no [illegible] ſon ſmſ
þa bar ſkapa j dyrin ⁊ gek þar m̅ kona [illegible] na· þrurth n
hellz lag ⁊ haꝼðe ðregil um hoꝼut ⁊ [illegible] þo [illegible]
⁊ miog eygð ſuo at e̅ haꝼðe ſeð m̅ ſlik [illegible] ſer [illegible] m̅
hauſe hon gek þar at er guð· ſat ⁊ m̅ huat heitr þu ſe
g̅ h̅ ek heiti guð· eða hue̅ e̅ þitt heiti ek heiti guð· ſeg h̅
þa rett guð· huſpreyia h̅ne ſma til hinar at h̅ ſeti hia h̅i e̅
þ bar allt ſaman at þa heyrðe guð· brest mikinn ⁊ uar þa k
onan hoꝛꝼin ⁊ j þui u̅ ⁊ ueginn ein ſkrſ· aꝼ ꝼenu̅ h̅ balld·
balld· þotte h̅ haꝼa ꝼunda tekit uopn þra ⁊ þ m; j broꝛt ſe
oꝛðz en blaðr þra lagu þar ept ⁊ u̅nig ꝼenge m̅ haꝼa
konu þa ſer ut en guð· ein· nu mun̅ u̅ þurꝼa r̅ aðða at t
el a ſeg balld· þat ek hyg at þr munu uitia uor h̅a þriða
ſinn m; uꝼ ⁊ þialm̅· nu ſkm̅ u̅ taka þ r̅að at· x· m̅ þr þa
a ueſ þetta ⁊ ſyne ſig þ̅ en annat lið ſkal ꝼara j ſkog ⁊ h̅o
gua þan ꝛioðr þ naut þe u̅ þa er liða kemr· þra oꝼ ſkogi
nu̅ u̅ er ſkm̅ ⁊ taka gudung uopn̄ ⁊ lata h̅ þa þ oſ e̅ þ

v̄ ſuo hættr e̊ þuınas ſıra ·ıaır cerlads at ueıtn ııeır ·audsu
megı en skogr a ariaın ueg nu ů ḟı ꝛad hoþa c̄ balle eþl
agde tıl · nu · komu ſkıṗ · ſ ḟn ſtad c̄ balt · haþa ærlar ı hır
tıga nu uar þar bardage ꝛ þell þıollæ aþ lıðı ſkıṗ · eın
m̄ uar mıkıll ꝛ uarı ſ lıð ſkıṗ ꝛ komı ḃll · ſe h ıııðr v̄a hoþð
ınge ſıra nu haþðı ærın ḃod ſkıṗ · tekıt uþ eyı eına ꝛ lett
a um ſtund ꝛ ueıdðr at þelage ſınū ꝛ hıo tıl hſ ſu þell þeıꝛ
taucs þa tok ſa hın mıkle maðr vıt oꝛmıc ꝛ lett a v̄ ſtund
ꝛ næſþ hı ſıdan a ſıonı ſem lengſt mættı h c̄ ſtað þlyıe ḟe
a skogın ſuo hın · ſe þatt ma · n ꝛ lyker þar nu ſıra v ſkıpt ·
v̄ ſıt ḃll þar ſkıṗ uerı alla c̄ at voꝛı þa lyſc ḃll · at h ull c̄ ḃ
v̄a lengıa ꝛ uıll þat ı gıalde nu bua ſr ḃd ſına ꝛ hoþðu ḃ
an mıoꝛ gæte ſ v̄ınnıte ꝛ bū ꝛ ſkına v̄ nu ſıgla ſr ſ ha
þ ꝛ kuomu ı æıt · þ · ſkıþe ſınu heılu ꝛ v̄ ḃ vın ueın ..

Þv tekſt vıııcetta at nyın vın vınſæ ḃd lec ..
þat ſu ḃd þıḱ ... god tıl þıar ꝛ ùdıng · ſ ſame ..
ko ſkıp aþ nor tıl gıalde er ḃll · ko aþ vılıe ḃ ſkıþe ſt .
yrau · ſpedı ſ helgı · ꝛ ḃın hoge ꝛ ſ ḟn uerı a gıalde ſr ſkıṗ · v̄ ſıl
cnaſk at kyne ꝛ oſ aulſ þıoðū · þat c̄ nu c̄ at taka at ḃre
ydu ar .. a · gd ḃd ſına heım er gardū ꝛ ḃor ı ... v̄ þa
ſkıṗ helga ꝛ þrıbyga ꝛ bradar þa at ḃe ḃarı ı vılıe ın ḃſo
ſt ſını ꝛ haþa holmıg ... allra v̄ hıa ſına c̄ ḃ þegızt nuꝫ
a ... ſr ḃ ſſıın ḃor lı a þınıd · ſ · broðır ſınſ ꝛ at h ga ḃuı ſı·
h þau c̄ ſ h · haþa gıa lett aumke en h lu · hımu lanıt kne
ꝛſt lıd ... huſ en geþıt ce · la v̄ ıııdlaagı ınꝫ ḃ ḃll · at þıe
ȳdıſe at .. ſkyldu haþa ... ıııa a ſkeþe ꝛ konıng
u ... c̄ þrcȳd · ſ lıd aþ ḃ ḃeg ꝛ haþet · v · ıı ſ ... ꝛ legıı
dı ḃ ꝛ ıırdu ſr · ſkıṗ er ... v̄ þa · vır c̄ ſr komu ı vılaꝛ · nu
lenı þau ſ hıaþ ꝛ hoþðu ı ḃell ınn ... at þau ınn ſaþſe
at haþa er ſuo mılle v̄at ꝛ ſıt v̄ lıtıll ... e ko komu ſr ſkıṗ ·

[FLATEYJARBÓK, Column 286 *b*.] GRŒNLENDINGA ÞÁTTR—16.

var svá háttat, er fundr þeira var ætlaðr, at vatn var ǫðrumegin, en skógr á annan veg. Nú váru þessi ráð hǫfð, er Karlsefni lagði til. Nú kómu Skrælingjar í þann stað, er Karlsefni hafði ætlat til bardaga. Nú var þar bardagi, ok fell fjǫlði af liði Skrælingja. Einn maðr var mikill ok vænn í liði Skrælingja, ok þótti Karlsefni sem hann mundi vera hǫfðingi þeira. Nú hafði einn þeira Skrælingja tekit upp øxi eina, ok leit á um stund, ok reiddi at félaga sínum, ok hjó til hans; sá fell þegar dauðr. Þá tók sá hinn mikli maðr við øxinni, ok leit á um stund, ok varp henni síðan á sjóinn sem lengst mátti hann; en síðan flýja þeir á skóginn, svá hverr sem fara mátti, ok lýkr þar nú þeira viðskiptum. Váru þeir Karlsefni þar þann vetr allan, en at vári þá lýsir Karlsefni, at hann vill eigi þar vera lengr, ok vill fara til Grœnlands. Nú búa þeir ferð sína, ok hǫfðu þaðan mǫrg gœði í vínviði ok berjum ok skinnavǫru. Nú sigla þeir í haf, ok kvámu til Eiríksfjarðar skipi sínu heilu, ok váru þar um vetrinn.

Freydís lét drepa brœðr

Nú teksk umrœða at nýju um Vínlandsferð, því at sú ferð þykkir bæði góð til fjár ok virðingar. Þat sama sumar kom skip af Noregi til Grœnlands, er Karlsefni kom af Vínlandi. Því skipi stýrðu brœðr II, Helgi ok Finnbogi, ok váru þann vetr á Grœnlandi. Þeir brœðr váru íslenzkir at kyni, ok ór Austfjǫrðum. Þar er nú til at taka, at Freydís Eiríksdóttir gørði ferð sína heiman ór Gǫrðum, ok fór til fundar við þá brœðr Helga ok Finnboga, ok beiddi þá, at þeir fœri til Vínlands með farkost sinn, ok hafa helming gœða allra við hana, þeira er þar fengisk. Nú játtu þeir því. Þaðan fór hon á fund Leifs bróður síns, ok [bað], at hann gæfi henni hús þau, er hann hafði gøra látit á Vínlandi. En hann svarar hinu sama, kvezk ljá mundu hús, en gefa eigi. Sá var máldagi með þeim Karlsefni ok Freydísi, at hvárir skyldu hafa XXX vígra manna á skipi, ok konur um fram; en Freydís brá af því þegar, ok hafði V mǫnnum fleira, ok leyndi þeim, ok urðu þeir brœðr eigi fyrri við þá varir, en þeir kómu til Vínlands. Nú létu þau í haf, ok hǫfðu til þess mælt áðr, at þau mundi samflota hafa, ef svá vildi verða, ok þess var lítill munr, en þó kómu þeir brœðr

[FLATEYJARBÓK, Column 287.] GRŒNLENDINGA ÞÁTTR—17.

nǫkkuru fyrri, ok hǫfðu uppborit fǫng sín til húsa Leifs. En er Freydís kom at landi, þá ryðja þeir skip sitt, ok bera upp til húss fǫng sín. Þá mælti Freydís: 'Hví báru þér inn hér fǫng yðr?' 'Því at vér hugðum,' segja þeir, 'at haldask muni ǫll ákveðin orð með oss.' 'Mér léði Leifr húsanna,' segir hon, 'en eigi yðr.' Þá mælti Helgi: 'Þrjóta mun okkr brœðr illsku við þik.' Báru nú út fǫng, ok gørðu sér skála, ok settu þann skála firr sjónum á vatnsstrǫndu, ok bjoggu vel um. En Freydís lét fella viðu til skips síns. Nú tók at vetra, ok tǫluðu þeir brœðr, at takask mundu upp leikar, ok væri hǫfð skemtan. Svá var gørt um stund, þar til er menn bárusk verra í milli, ok þá gørðisk sundrþykki með þeim, ok tókusk af leikar, ok øngvar gørðusk kvámur milli skálanna, ok fór svá fram lengi vetrar. Þat var einn morgin snemma at Freydís stóð upp ór rúmi sínu, ok klæddisk, ok fór eigi í skóklæðin; en veðri var svá farit, at dǫgg var fallin mikil. Hon tók kápu bónda síns, ok fór í, en síðan gekk hon til skála[1] þeira brœðra, ok til dyra, en maðr einn hafði út gengit litlu áðr, ok lokit hurð aptr á miðjan klofa. Hon lauk upp hurðinni, ok stóð í gáttum stund þá ok þagði; en Finnbogi lá innstr í skálanum, ok vakði. Hann mælti: 'Hvat viltu hingat, Freydís?' Hon svarar: 'Ek vil at þú standir upp, ok gangir út með mér, ok vil ek tala við þik.' Svá gørir hann. Þau ganga at tré, er lá undir skálaveggінum, ok settusk[2] þar niðr. 'Hversu líkar þér?' segir hon. Hann svarar: 'Góðr þikki[3] mér landskostur, en illr þikki[3] mér þústr sá, er vár í milli er, því at ek kalla ekki hafa til orðit.' 'Þá segir þú sem er,' segir hon, 'ok svá þikki[3] mér; en þat er ørindi[4] mitt á þinn fund, at ek vildi kaupa skipum við ykkr brœðr, því at þit hafit meira skip en ek, ok vilda ek í brott heðan.' 'Þat mun ek láta gangask,' segir hann, 'ef þér líkar þá vel.' Nú skilja þau við þat. Gengr hon heim, en Finnbogi til hvílu sinnar. Hon stígr upp í rúmit kǫldum fótum, ok vaknar hann Þorvarðr við, ok spyrr hví at hon væri svá kǫld ok vát. Hon svarar með miklum þjósti: 'Ek var gengin,' segir hon, 'til þeira brœðra, at fala skip at þeim, ok vilda ek kaupa meira skip; en þeir urðu við þat svá illa,

[1] gekk hon til skála repeated in MS. [2] MS. settizst. [3] MS. þikí.
[4] MS. eyre*n*de.

nokkuru þyrre ⁊ hlopu up þeir þaung sin i huita lerpt ok [illegible]
gerdu kom at hende þa syndia þeir skip sitt ⁊ bru up i hin þaung
sin þa uilu þreyđu hui beru þeir m her þaung nu þuiat v l. ug
dū legia þr at hallagert muni all akuedi gđ m; oll. in leit
s. husaria seg ho en at [illegible] þa m; helgi biorn mn olkr þr. ill
⁊ sku vit þig beru nu vt þaung ⁊ gerdu ser skala ⁊ letru
þn skala þir lionū au[illegible]stronda ⁊ biugu ill v e þr. ler
þtlla vidu til skips sins. [illegible] uenia ⁊ toludu þr. þr
at [illegible] mundu up. lonbar ⁊ vi hopa skemū suo vel gr
vm stund þar i e m [illegible] [illegible] skulle ⁊ þa gerast sunde
þykke m; þ ⁊ [illegible] lonb[illegible] gerast buoin inulle
[illegible] ⁊ þos suo þia lengje uetr. [illegible] eun morgin skica
at þr. [illegible] upp [illegible] [illegible] sinu ⁊ [illegible] ⁊ þos [illegible] s skolls eđ
en [illegible] uar suo þauit at dag [illegible] þalli [illegible]. h tok [illegible]
bonda sins ⁊ þos [illegible] sine yck h i skala [illegible] h til skala þr.
þr. ⁊ til [illegible] en [illegible] eni hapde vt [illegible] [illegible] ⁊ loker hurđ
[illegible] a midian elopa h lauk upp hurdine ⁊ [illegible] [illegible] stund
þa ⁊ þagde en þrusboga la [illegible] s skalanū ⁊ [illegible] miki
huat uillter hinger þr. h [illegible] ek uil at þu standr up ⁊ gang
vt m; m ⁊ uil ek tala vit þig suo [illegible] h þau [illegible] at tre er
la und skala [illegible] ⁊ settust þar [illegible] h [illegible] liker þ seg h h [illegible]
gođ; [illegible] m [illegible] kostur en illr [illegible] ni [illegible] e [illegible] s miki e
þat ek [illegible] [illegible] hapa t [illegible]. þa seg þu se e seg h ⁊ suo þ
[illegible] en þ e [illegible] [illegible] [illegible] [illegible] ek vilde kaupa skipi
vit [illegible] þr. þuiat þer hapet meira skip e ek ⁊ villta ek i be
[illegible] þ mu ek lond gangast seg h ep þ [illegible] þa vt. nu skalia þ
v þ [illegible] h het e [illegible] til [illegible] [illegible] h stigr upp s [illegible] [illegible]
[illegible] ⁊ [illegible] h [illegible] v ⁊ [illegible] h at h vi suo [illegible] ⁊ v [illegible]
ho su. m; [illegible] [illegible]. ek uar [illegible] seg h til [illegible]. þr. [illegible]
up at þ ⁊ [illegible] [illegible] e [illegible] [illegible]

at þr̄ hofdu mıkıt z lokıt landı. ē þu ueızt ın ... hıkr uılldı bck
a ... mıtır ... ne þınar z mıt ek þ̄ tıl þıña at ek er
þ̄ hıarta ap ... z mu̅ ek ... skılıat ū þıg ut þu hepır þa z
mı ... h̄ ek atoluır hınar z bıd m̄ up standa ...
mıt uopın sín z sua ... þr̄ z þa pegar t̄ skala þra ...
... nı at ꝥ sopundū z toku þa z pœrdu þ̄ bond z leıddu s
ut hūn sem bundır u̅ en. þr̄. let drepa hūn se ut kom nu u̅
þar allır kallar drepnır. ē konur uoru epť z uıllde engı þær d
repa þa. nu. þr̄. þat ... þ̄ hınd ... uar ... nu ... h̄
at konū ꝥ u. er þar ... ok ... ap ... nu þ̄ þau tıl ...
la sínſ epť þ̄ ... z ... þr̄. þottıst all
... hapa uındat z mıt ū pelaga sína ep oll ...
at koma tıl grænlandz ... þa ... mān ... ap ...
seg̃ þra þessū athurdū. nu ... ū ꝥ ... at þau bu̅ h̄ ...
t̄ þa er ū ... þ̄ ... nu ... þr̄ ... ūt ...
er þr̄ ... hopdu at ... ꝥ ollū ... ē þau mau̅ t̄ ...
... ... hap z urdu ... þa z komu ... p.
... sınu ınēma sínſ. nu ū þ̄ ... þ̄ z hapa ...
... t̄ hapſ z bıd ... z e ... at ...
... skıp ... hapa ap ... ē þ̄ e ... ...

Freydıſ for nu t̄ buı sínſ þar þ̄ hapde ... ı ...
... h̄ pekk mıkın ... ollu ... sína ... h̄
uıllde leyna ... sínū ... h̄ nu t̄ buı sınu ē
urdu allır ... hallom ... at pegðe ... ...
... at ... kemr ... ... nu ... ...
... z ... ... sagt allt ... ... m̄ ap ... þ̄ra
þr̄. z ... þa ... ū ... at ... ... z ū.
... ... sogu þra ... ek sep ... at ... þ̄ at ū þr̄. sy
... sem ... ū ... ē ... mu̅ ok ꝥ ... at þra ap ...
... ... at ... nu ... þ̄ ... þra ... kom ū þa

[FLATEYJARBÓK, Column 287 *b*.] GRŒNLENDINGA ÞÁTTR—18.

at þeir bǫrðu mik, ok léku sárliga; en þú, vesæll maðr, munt hvárki vilja reka minnar[1] skammar né þinnar, ok mun ek þat nú finna, at ek er í brottu af Grœnlandi, ok mun ek gøra skilnað við þik, utan þú hefnir þessa.' Ok nú stóðsk hann eigi átǫlur hennar, ok bað menn upp standa sem skjótast, ok taka vápn sín; ok svá gøra þeir, ok fara þegar til skála þeira brœðra, ok gengu inn at þeim sofǫndum[2] ok tóku þá, ok fœrðu í bǫnd, ok leiddu svá út hvern sem bundinn var, en Freydís lét drepa hvern sem út kom. Nú váru þar allir karlar[3] drepnir, en konur váru eptir, ok vildi engi þær drepa. Þá mælti Freydís: 'Fái mér øxi í hǫnd.' Svá var gørt; síðan vegr hon at konum þeim V, er þar váru, ok gekk af þeim dauðum. Nú fóru þau til skála síns eptir þat it illa verk, ok fannsk þat eitt á, at Freydís þóttisk allvel hafa umráðit, ok mælti við félaga sína: 'Ef oss verðr auðit, at koma til Grœnlands,' segir hon, 'þá skal ek þann mann ráða af lífi, er segir frá þessum atburðum. Nú skulu vér þat segja, at þau búi hér eptir, þá er vér fórum í brott.' Nú bjoggu þeir skipit snemma um várit, þat er þeir brœðr hǫfðu átt, með þeim ǫllum gœðum, er þau máttu til fá ok skipit bar; sigla síðan í haf, ok urðu vel reiðfara, ok kómu í Eiríksfjǫrð skipi sínu snemma sumars. Nú var þar Karlsefni fyrir, ok hafði albúit skip sitt til hafs, ok beið byrjar, ok er þat mál manna, at eigi mundi auðgara skip gengit hafa af Grœnlandi, en þat er hann stýrði. **Frá Freydísi.** Freydís fór nú til bús síns, því at þat hafði staðit meðan úskatt. Hon fekk mikin feng fjár ǫllu fǫruneyti sínu, því at hon vildi leyna láta údáðum sínum. Sitr hon nú í búi sínu. Eigi urðu allir svá haldinorðir, at þegði yfir údáðum þeira eða illsku, at eigi kœmi upp um síðir. Nú kom þetta upp um síðir fyrir Leif, bróður hennar, ok þótti honum þessi saga allill. Þá tók Leifr III menn af liði þeira Freydísar, ok píndi þá [til] sagna[4] um þenna atburð allan jafnsaman, ok var með einu móti sǫgn þeira. 'Eigi nenni ek,' segir Leifr, 'at gøra þat at við Freydísi systur mína, sem hon væri verð, en spá mun ek þeim þess, at þeira afkvæmi mun lítt at þrifum verða.' Nú leið þat svá fram, at øngum þótti um þau

[1] MS. mitar minnar. [2] MS. sofundum. [3] MS. kallar. [4] MS. sagn*ara*?

[FLATEYJARBÓK, Column 288.] GRŒNLENDINGA ÞÁTTR—19.

þau[1] vert þaðan í frá, nema ills. Nú [er] at segja frá því er Karlsefni býr skip sitt, ok sigldi í haf. Honum fórsk vel, ok kom til Noregs með heilu ok hǫldnu, ok sat þar um vetrinn, ok seldi varning sinn, ok hafði þar gott yfirlæti, ok þau bæði hjón, af hinum gǫfgustum mǫnnum í Noregi. En um várit eptir bjó hann skip sitt til Íslands, ok er hann var albúinn, ok skip hans lá til byrjar fyrir bryggjunum, þá kom þar at honum suðrmaðr einn, ættaðr af Brimum ór Saxlandi. Hann falar at Karlsefni húsasnotru hans. 'Ek vil eigi selja,' sagði hann. 'Ek mun gefa þér við hálfa[2] mǫrk gulls,' segir suðrmaðr. Karlsefni þótti vel við boðit, ok keyptu síðan. Fór suðrmaðr í brott[3] með húsasnotruna, en Karlsefni vissi eigi hvat tré var; en þat var mǫsurr[4], kominn af Vínlandi. Nú siglir Karlsefni í haf, ok kom skipi sínu fyrir norðanland í Skagafjǫrð, ok var þar upp sett skip hans um vetrinn; en um várit keypti hann Glaumbœjarland, ok gørði bú á, ok bjó þar meðan hann lifði, ok var hit mesta gǫfugmenni, ok er mart manna frá honum komit ok Guðríði, konu hans, ok góðr ættbogi. Ok er Karlsefni var andaðr tók Guðríðr við bús varðveizlu ok Snorri, son hennar, er fœddr var á Vínlandi; ok er Snorri var kvángaðr, þá fór Guðríðr utan, ok gekk suðr, ok kom út aptr til bús Snorra, sonar síns, ok hafði hann þá látit gøra kirkju í Glaumbœ. Síðan varð Guðríðr nunna ok einsetukona, ok var þar meðan hon lifði. Snorri átti son þann, er Þorgeirr hét, hann var faðir Ingveldar, móður Brands biskups. Dóttir Snorra Karlsefnissonar hét Hallfríðr; hon var móðir Runólfs, fǫður Þorláks biskups. Bjǫrn hét son Karlsefnis og Guðríðar; hann var faðir Þórunnar, móður Bjarnar biskups. Fjǫlði manna er frá Karlsefni komit, ok er hann kynsæll maðr orðinn, ok hefir Karlsefni fyrst sagt allra manna atburði um farar þessar allar, er nú er nǫkkut orði á komit.

[1] Þau repeated in MS. [2] MS. half. [3] MS. burt. [4] MS. mausurr.

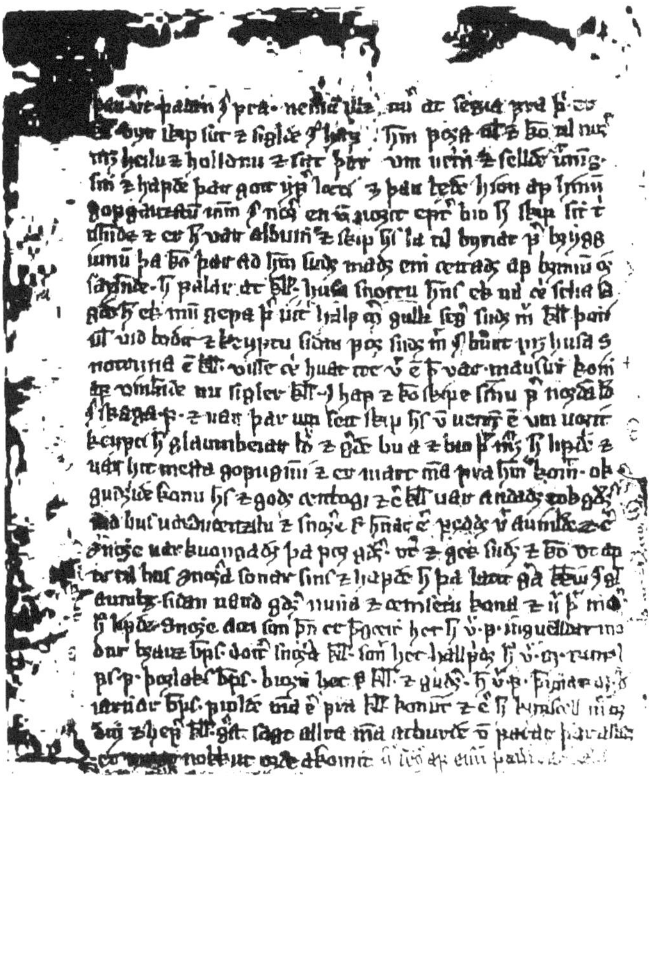

NOTES.

(1) It has been claimed that the Icelandic discovery attained a practical result through the imparting of information to those to whom the discovery of America has been generally ascribed, and notably to Columbus and the Cabots. The tendency to qualify Columbus' fame as the original discoverer dates from the time of Ortelius [1], while the effort to show that his first voyage was influenced by information which he received from Icelandic sources was, perhaps, first formulated *in extenso* within the present century [2]. The theory that Columbus obtained definite information from Icelandic channels rests, after all, upon the following vague letter, which is cited by Columbus' son in the biography of his father, as follows:

'In the month of February, of the year 1477, I sailed one hundred leagues beyond the island of Tile, the southern portion of which is seventy-three degrees removed from the equinoctial, and not sixty-three, as some will have it; nor is it situated within the line which includes Ptolemy's west, but is much further to the westward; and to this island, which is as large as England, the English come with their wares, especially those from Bristol. And at the time when I went thither the sea was not frozen, although the tides there are so great that in some places they rose twenty-six fathoms, and fell as much. It is, indeed, the fact that that Tile, of which Ptolemy makes mention, is situated where he describes it, and by the moderns this is called Frislanda [3].'

John and Sebastian Cabot are supposed, by similar theorists, to have derived knowledge

[1] '"Christophe Colombe," dit Ortélius, "a seulement mis le Nouveau-Monde en rapport durable de commerce et d'utilité avec l'Europe." [Theatr. Orbis terr. éd. 1601, pp. 5 et 6.] Ce jugement est beaucoup trop sévère. D'ailleurs l'opinion du géographe n'était point basée sur l'expédition au Vinland dont il ne fait aucunement mention, peut-être parce que les ouvrages d'Adam de Brême ne furent imprimés qu'en 1579, mais sur les voyages de Nicolo et Antonio Zeni [1388–1404], dont, pour le moins, la localité est restée problématique.' Alex. v. Humboldt, Examen critique, Paris, 1837, vol. ii. p. 120.

[2] Finn Magnusen, 'Om de Engelskes Handel og Færd paa Island i det 15de Aarhundrede, især med Hensyn til Columbus's formentlige Reise dertil i Aaret 1477,' in Nord. Tidskr. for Oldkyndighed, Copenh. 1833. pp. 112–169.

[3] I have not been able to find that the original of this letter is in existence. The quotation is made from the Italian edition of the Biography, entitled: Historie Del. S. D. Fernando Colombo; nelle quali s' ha particolare, & vera relatione della vita, & de' fatti dell' Ammiraglio D. Christoforo Colombo, suo padre, * * nuouamente di lingua Spagnuola tradotta nell Italiana dal S. Alfonso Vlloa, Venice, 1571. On page 9 of this book, the letter is thus printed: 'Jo nauigai l' anno MCCCCLXXVII nel mese di Febraio oltra Tile isola cento leghe, la cui parte Australe è lontana dall' Equinottiale settantatre gradi, & non sessantatre, come alcuni vogliono: ne giace dentro della linea, che include l' Occidente di Tolomeo, ma è molto più Occidentale. Et a quest' isola, che è tanto grande come l' Jngbilterra, vanno gl' Jnglesi con de loro mercatantie, specialmente quelli di Bristol. Et al tiempo, che io vi andai, non era congelato il mare, quantunque vi fossero si grosse maree, che in alcuni luoghi ascendeua ventisei braccia, et discendeua altre tanti in altezza. È bene il vero, che Tile, quella di cui Tolomeo fa mentione, giace doue egli dice; & questa da' moderni è chiamata Frislanda.'

of the Icelandic discovery through the English, and especially the Bristol trade with Iceland [1]. These theories do not require further consideration here, since they have no bearing on the primitive history of the Wineland discovery.

(2) Lǫgsǫgumenn [sing. lǫgsǫgumaðr], lit. law-saying men, publishers of the laws. The office was introduced into Iceland contemporaneously with the adoption of the law code of Ulfliot [Úlfljótr], and the establishment of the Althing [Popular Assembly] in the year 930, and was, probably, modelled after a similar Norwegian office. It was the duty of the 'law-sayer' to give judgment in all causes which were submitted to him, according to the common law established by the Althing. The 'law-sayer' appears to have presided at the Althing, where it was his custom to regularly announce the laws. From this last, his most important, function called 'law-saying' [lǫgsaga], the office received its name. From the time of its adoption, throughout the continuance of the Commonwealth, the office was elective, the incumbent holding office for a limited period [three years] although he was eligible for re-election [2]. [Vigfusson, Dict. s. v., states that during the first hundred years the law-speakers were elected for life.]

(3) Little is known of Rafn beyond his genealogy, which is given in Landnáma, Pt. II, ch. xxi, and again in Sturlunga Saga I, ch. vii [Vigfusson's ed. p. 5]. Rafn was distantly related to Ari Marsson and Leif Ericsson. His ancestor, Steinolf the Short [Steinólfr hinn lági], was the brother of Thorbiorg, Ari Marsson's grandmother, and through the same ancestor, Steinolf, Rafn was remotely connected with Thiodhild, Leif Ericsson's mother.

(4) By this Thorfinn, the second earl of that name, is probably meant, i. e. Thorfinn Sigurd's son. 'He was the most powerful of all the Orkney earls. * * * Thorfinn was five years old when the Scotch king, Malcolm, his maternal grandfather, gave him the title of earl, and he continued earl for seventy years. He died in the latter days of Harold Sigurdsson,' [ca. A.D. 1064] [3].

(5) It is recorded in Icelandic Annals [Annales regii, Skálholt, Gottskalk's, and Flatey Annals] that King Olaf Tryggvason effected the Christianization of Halogaland in the year 999. In this year, according to the Saga of Olaf Tryggvason in 'Heimskringla,' 'King Olaf came with his men the same autumn to Drontheim, and betook himself to Nidaros, where he established himself for the winter;' and in the same place we read, 'Leif, the son of Eric the Red, he who first settled Greenland, was come that summer from Greenland to Norway; he waited upon King Olaf, accepted Christianity, and spent the winter with King Olaf.' In the spring following, and hence in the spring of the year 1000, for Olaf was killed in the autumn of that year, 'King Olaf sent Leif Ericsson to Greenland to proclaim Christianity there, and he sailed that summer to Greenland. He rescued at sea a ship's crew of men who were in

[1] 'Bristol, wo die Gabotti [Cabots] ihre zweite Heimath gefunden hatten, unterhielt damals mit Island einen lebhaften Handelsverkehr, und da wir Sebastian Cabot auf seiner zweiten Fahrt Island berühren sehen, so hat man nicht ohne Grund vermuthet, dass die beiden Venetianer von den Entdeckungen der Normannen unterrichtet gewesen sind, deren Andenken auf jener Insel noch jetzt in aller Frische sich erhalten hat.' Peschel, Geschichte der Erdkunde, Munich, 1865, pp. 260-1.

[2] Cf. Maurer, Die Entstehung des Isländischen Staats und seiner Verfassung, Munich, 1852, pp. 147, 152-3, and the same author's, Island von seiner ersten Entdeckung bis zum Untergange des Freistaats, Munich, 1874. pp. 52-3.

[3] Orkneyinga Saga, ed. Vigfusson, in Icelandic Sagas, London, 1887, ch. xxxviii. p. 58.

desperate straits, and were clinging to a wreck, and he then found Wineland the Good.' [Heimskringla, ed. Unger, pp. 192, 196, 204.] The preponderance of evidence certainly points to the year 1000 as the year of Leif's discovery.

(6) Húsa-snotro-tré, lit. 'house-neat-wood.' The word húsa-snotra is of infrequent occurrence, and its exact significance has given rise to widely diverging opinions. Saxo Grammaticus renders it 'gubernaculum,' in an excerpt from Arrow-Odd's Saga [Book v, of Historia Danica, ed. P. E. Müller, Copenh. 1839, vol. ii. p. 251]. Torfæus, in his 'Historia Vinlandiæ' [p. 28], renders the word 'coronis;' 'vir quidam Bremensis coronidem ejus [husasnotra habetur] licitabat,' leaving us in doubt as to what he meant by 'coronis;' it may be conjectured, however, that he had in mind the same meaning which was subsequently given to the word by Biorn Haldorsen, in his dictionary, namely, 'coronis domus.' Werlauff [Symbolae ad geographiam medii ævi, ex monumentis Islandicis, p. 14] translated the word, as it occurs in this passage, 'scopæ.' 'Fertur Thorfinnum Karlsefni scopas ex ligno sibi aptasse.' Vigfusson [Dict. s. v.] defines the word, 'house-neat,' 'house-cleaner,' inclining evidently to Werlauff's interpretation, but quoting Finn Magnusen as having suggested the translation 'broom.' Fritzner [Dict. s. v.] defines the word 'a weather-vane, or other ornament, at the point of the gable of a house or upon a ship.' This interpretation of Fritzner's is confirmed by Dr. Valtýr Guðmundsson, in a critical study of the meaning of the word, wherein he shows the close relationship existing between the probable specific names for the parts connected with the ornamented point, occasionally vane-capped, both upon the peak of the house-gable and the peculiarly carved prow of the ship. That the names should have been used interchangeably for the similar object, in both house and ship, is the less remarkable, since we read of a portion of a ship's prow having been removed from a vessel and placed above the principal entrance of a house, that is, in some part of the gable-end of the dwelling[1].

(7) This passage is somewhat obscure. It may, perhaps, indicate that the 'house-neat-wood' was obtained at Stream-firth, although it is stated in general terms in Flatey Book that the 'house-neat-wood' came from Wineland. If the meaning is, as suggested in this passage, that the 'house-neat' was hewed to the northward of Hóp, the only intelligible interpretation of the following clause would seem to be that, although Karlsefni attained the region which corresponded with Leif's accounts of Wineland, he did not succeed, on account of the hostility of the natives which compelled him to beat a retreat, in accomplishing a thorough exploration of the country, nor was he able to carry back with him any of the products of the land. This author, it will be noted, records only the two voyages described in the Saga of Eric the Red, namely, Leif's voyage of discovery, and Karlsefni's voyage of exploration.

(8) Lit. the Uplanders, i.e. the people of the Norwegian Oplandene; a name given to a district in Norway comprising a part of the eastern inland counties.

(9) Olaf the White is called in the Eyrbyggja Saga 'the greatest warrior-king in the western sea,' [mestr herkonungr fyrir vestan haf]. This expedition, in which he effected the capture of Dublin, appears to have been made about the year 852. [Cf. Munch, Norske

[1] Cf. Guðmundsson, Privatboligen paa Island i Sagatiden, Copenhagen, 1889, pp. 154, 158-60.

Folks Historie, pt. i. vol. i. p. 441.] The title, which is assigned him, 'herkonungr,' signifies a king of troops, a warrior-king. Norway, prior to the reign of Harold Fairhair, was divided into numerous petty states, called 'fylki.' The rulers of these small kingdoms were called 'fylkiskonungar' [fylki-kings], as contradistinguished from those 'kings' who had command over a troop of warriors or a war-ship, but who were not necessarily rulers of the land. These warrior-kings were called 'herkonungar,' or occasionally 'sjókonungar [sea-kings]. [Cf. Keyser, Norges Stats- og Retsforfatning i Middelalderen, in his 'Efterladte Skrifter,' Chr'a, 1867, vol. ii. p. 20 et seq.] As the forays of these 'warrior-kings' were mainly directed against the people living in and about the British Isles, and hence to the westward of Norway, the expression, 'at herja í vestrvíking,' 'to engage in a westerly foray,' came to be a general term for a viking descent upon some part of the coast of Great Britain, Ireland, or the adjacent islands. These free-booting expeditions began on the Irish coasts, perhaps as early as 795. In 798, the Norsemen plundered the Hebrides, and in 807 obtained a lodgment upon the mainland of Ireland[1].

(10) Aud, or as she is also called Unnr, [cf. ante, note 4, p. 15], the Enormously-wealthy [hin djúpauðga] or Deep-minded [hin djúpúðga], was one of the most famous of the Icelandic colonists. Her genealogy is thus given in the first chapter of the Laxdœla Saga: 'There was a man named Ketil Flat-nose, a son of Biorn Buna; he was a mighty chieftain in Norway, and a man of noble lineage; he dwelt at Romsdal in the Romsdal-fylki, which is between South Mœr and North Mœr. Ketil Flat-nose married Ingvild, daughter of Ketil Wether, a famous man; they had five children. . . . Unn, the Enormously-wealthy, was Ketil's daughter, [she] who married Olaf the White, Ingiald's son, son of Frodi the Brave, who slew the Swertlings.' Aud was one of the few colonists who had accepted the Christian religion before their arrival in Iceland. Her relatives, however, seem to have lapsed into the old faith soon after her death, for on the same hill on which Aud had erected her cross, they built a heathen altar, and offered sacrifices, believing that, after death, they would pass into the hill. [Landnáma, Pt. ii. ch. xvi.] Earl Sigurd the Mighty, with whom Aud's son, Thorstein, formed his alliance, was the first earl of the Orkneys, and this league was formed ca. 880. [Orkneyinga Saga, ed. Vigfusson, l. c. p. 5.] Vigfusson makes the date of Thorstein the Red's fall, ca. 888, of Aud's arrival in Iceland, ca. 892, and of her death, ca. 908–10. [Tímatal l. c., p. 494]; Munch, on the other hand, gives the date of Aud's death as 900. [Norske Historie, pt i. p. 802.]

(11) Suðreyjar [Sodor], lit. the southern islands; a name applied specifically, as here, to the Hebrides.

(12) Knǫrr, a kind of trading-ship. It was in model, doubtless, somewhat similar to the modern Nordlands-jægter, the typical sailing craft of northern Norway. It was, probably, a clinker-built ship, pointed at both ends, half-decked, [fore?] and aft, and these half-decks were in the larger vessels connected by a gangway along the gunwale. The open space between the decks was reserved for the storage of the cargo, which, when the ship was laden, was protected by skins or some similar substitute for tarpaulins. The vessel was provided with a single mast, and was propelled by a rude square sail, and was also supplied with oars. The rudder

[1] Cf. Orkneyinga Saga, translated by Hjaltalin and Goudie, Edinburgh, 1873, p. xxi.

was attached to the side of the ship, upon the starboard quarter, and the anchor, originally of stone, was afterward supplanted by one of iron, somewhat similar in form to those now in use. When the vessel was in harbour a tent was spread over the ship at both ends. The vessel was supplied with a large boat, called the 'after-boat,' sometimes large enough to hold twenty persons [Egils Saga Skallagrímssonar, ch. 27], which was frequently towed behind the ship; in addition to this, a smaller boat often appears to have been carried upon the ship. [Cf. Egils Saga Skallagrímssonar, ch. 60, wherein we are told that three men enter the smaller boat, but eighteen the 'after-boat']. The knǫrr was swift and more easily controlled than the long-ship [langskip] or war-ship, as we may conclude from a passage in the Saga of Olaf Tryggvason, ch. 184, wherein Earl Hacon tells Sigmund Brestisson, when the latter is preparing to sail to the Færoes, to take vengeance for his father, 'the voyage is not so long as it is difficult, for long-ships cannot go thither on account of the storms and currents, which are oftentimes so severe there, that a merchant-ship [byrðingr] can scarcely cope with these, [wherefore] it seems to me best, that I should cause two "knerrir" to be equipped for your voyage.' Upon Queen Aud's vessel there were twenty freemen, and besides these there were probably as many more women and children, perhaps forty or fifty persons in all. As Aud was going to a new country to make it her permanent home, she took with her, no doubt, a considerable cargo of household utensils, timber, grain, live-stock, &c. In the Egils Saga mention is made of two vessels (knerrir, sing. knǫrr), presumably of about the same size as this 'knǫrr,' in which Aud and her people made the voyage to Iceland. We read there, that after the death of Thorolf Kveldulfsson, who received his death-wound from Harold Fairhair's own hand, because of his refusal to pay tribute to the king, that Kveldulf, Thorolf's father and Skallagrim, his brother, decided to go to Iceland. 'Early in the spring [878], Kveldulf and his son each made his ship ready. They had a considerable ship's company, and a goodly one. They made ready two large "knerrir," having upon each thirty able-bodied men, besides women and young persons. They took with them all of the property which they could.' [Egils Saga Skallagrímssonar, ed. Finnur Jónsson, Copenh. 1886, p. 81.] A recent writer, Tuxen, reasoning from this passage, concludes, that there could not have been less than forty persons on board each ship, there may well have been more, and to transport these, together with their probable cargo, would, he estimates, require a sloop of not less than forty tons burden, which would belong to the smallest class of vessels now making the voyage between Copenhagen and Iceland. Reasoning from a comparison of a vessel of this size with the ship unearthed at the farm of Gokstad, north of Sandefiord, Norway, in 1880, he concludes, that such a 'knǫrr' would have been somewhat over forty-two feet long, with a breadth of beam of from sixteen to eighteen feet, that is to say rather more than twenty feet shorter than the Gokstad ship, with about the same breadth of beam, but probably considerably deeper from gunwale to keel. It is not clear, however, why so small a size should be assigned to the 'knǫrr;' there seems excellent reason for the conclusion that these vessels were not only as large, but even decidedly larger, than the Gokstad ship. Sailing free, before the wind, these ships could doubtless attain a very creditable rate of speed, but the nature of the sail and its adjustment was apparently such that they could not make such favourable progress when beating into the wind, especially in land-locked waters, and hence the frequent recurrence in the sagas of the statement, that 'the ship waited for a fair wind' [byrr], before setting sail. It was, probably, in ships of a similar model to that of the 'knǫrr,' that Leif and Karlsefni made their voyages. These vessels, while they seem to have been constructed with little regard to the comfort of their crews, were well adapted to fulfill their duties in the more essential features of sea-worthiness and speed[1].

(13) Frjáls, a freedman, from frí-háls, i.e. having the neck free; a ring worn about the neck having been a badge of servitude. Slaves were called þrælar, thralls. The thrall was entirely under the control of his master, and could only obtain his freedom by purchase, with the master's approval. He was occasionally freed by his lord, as a reward for some especial act of devotion, for a long period of faithful service, or, in Christian times, as an act of atonement or propitiation on the part of the master. The early settlers of Iceland brought with them many of their thralls from Norway; others were captured in the westerly forays, or purchased in the British Isles,—indeed the ranks of the slaves would appear, both from actual record and from their names, to have been mainly recruited from the British Isles. The majority of these were, probably, not serfs by birth, but by conquest, as witness the case of Vifil in this saga. The freeing of thralls was very common in Iceland, and there are frequent references in the sagas to men who were themselves, or whose fathers had been, 'leysingjar,' freedmen. The master could kill his own thrall without punishment; if he killed the slave of another he was required to pay to the master the value of the slave, within three days, or he laid himself liable to condemnation to the lesser outlawry. The thralls were severely punished for their misdeeds, but if one man took into his own hands the punishment of the thralls of another, it was held to be an affront which could be, and usually was, promptly revenged by their master. It was this right of revenge for such an affront, which led Eric the Red to kill Eyiolf Saur, who had punished Eric's thralls for a crime committed against Eyiolf's kinsman, Valthiof. The master, however, was made liable for the misdeeds of his thrall, and could be prosecuted for these; the offence in Eyiolf's case was, that he took the execution of the law into his own hands[2].

(14) Dalalǫnd, lit. the Dale-lands. The region of which Aud took possession is in the western part of Iceland, contiguous to that arm of the Breidafirth [Broad-firth] which is known as Hvamms-firth. Hvammr is on the northern side of this firth at its head, and Krosshólar [Cross-hill] is hard by. Both Hvammr and Krosshólar still retain their ancient names.

(15) Vífilsdalr [Vifilsdale] unites with Laugardalr to form the Hörðadalr, through which the Hörda-dale river flows from the south into Hvamms-firth, at the south-eastern bight of that firth.

(16) Jæderen was a district in south-western Norway, in which the modern Stavanger is situated.

(17) Drangar on Horn-strands, where Eric and his father first established themselves,

[1] Cf. Tuxen, 'De Nordiske Langskibe,' in Aarbøger for Nord. Oldk. og Hist., 1888, pp. 47-134. For a description of the Gokstad ship see also, The Viking-ship discovered at Gokstad in Norway, described by N. Nicolaysen, Christiania, 1882.

[2] Cf. Maurer, Die Freigelassenen nach altnorwegischem Rechte, Munich, 1878; Kålund, Familielivet på Island i den første Saga Periode [indtil 1030], Copenh. 1870, pp. 354-364; Keyser, Stats- og Retsforfatning i Middelalderen, Chr'a., 1867, pp. 289-295.

is on the northern shore of the north-west peninsula of Iceland. Erics-stead, to which Eric removed after his father's death and his own marriage to Thorhild, was in Haukadalr, in western Iceland, in Queen Aud's 'claim;' through this valley the Haukadale river flows, from the east, into the south-easterly bight of Hvamms-firth.

(18) Brokey [Brok-island, which receives its name from a kind of grass called 'brok'] is the largest of the numerous islands at the mouth of Hvamms-firth, where it opens into Breida-firth. Eyxney, Öxney [Ox-island] is separated from Brokey by a narrow strait. Suðrey [South-island] is in the same archipelago, immediately south of Brokey. It is said that the first dwelling upon Brokey was built in the last half of the seventeenth century. Suðrey is no longer inhabited; the present dwelling on Öxney is situated on the southern side of the island, while Eric's home, it is claimed, was upon the northern side of the island, at the head of a small bay or creek, called Eiríksvágr, and it is stated that low mounds can still be seen on both Öxney and Suðrey, which are supposed to indicate the sites of Eric's dwellings[1].

(19) In the skáli, which was, perhaps, at the time of which this saga treats, used as a sleeping-room, there was a raised daïs or platform, called the 'set,' on either side of what may be called the nave of the apartment, extending about two-thirds the length of the room. This 'set' was used, as a sleeping-place by night, and the planks or timbers with which the 'set' was covered were called 'set-stokkar,' although this name seems to have been especially applied to those timbers, which formed the outer portion of the 'set[2].'

(20) Drangar [Monoliths] and Breiðabólstaðr [Broad-homestead] were both situated on the mainland, a short distance to the southward of the islands on which Eric had established himself.

(21) One of the famous 'settlers' of Iceland, named Thorolf Moster-beard [Mostrarskegg]; like many another 'settler' [landnámsmaðr], because he would not acknowledge the supremacy of king Harold Fairhair, left his home in the island of Moster, in south-western Norway, and sailed to Iceland, where he arrived about the year 884 [Vigfusson, Tímatal, l. c. p. 493]. He was a believer in the 'old' or heathen faith, and when he reached the land, he cast the pillars of the 'place of honour' of his Norwegian home into the sea; upon these the figure of the god Thor was carved, and where these penates were cast up by the sea, according to the custom of men of his belief, he established himself. The cape upon which the wooden image of the god drifted, Thorolf called Thorsness. This cape is on the southern side of Breidafirth, at the mouth of Hvamms-firth, and here Thorolf subsequently established a district court [héraðsþing] which received from his 'claim' the name of 'Thorsness-thing.' The exact site of this 'thing' is somewhat uncertain. Vigfusson [Eyrbyggja Saga, Vorrede, p. xix] suggests that it was, probably, somewhat to the westward of the mouth of Hvamms-firth. When the 'Quarter-courts' were established in the tenth century, Thorsness-thing was removed farther to the eastward [Eyrbyggja Saga, ed. Vigfusson, p. 12]—and there have been those, who claim to have been able to discover the

[1] Cf. Árni Thorlacius, 'Um Örnefni í þórnes þingi,' in Safn til Sögu Íslands, vol. ii. pp. 283, 293, 296; Kålund, Bidrag til en historisk-topografisk Beskrivelse af Island, Copenh. 1877, vol. i. pp. 455-6.

[2] Cf. Guðmundsson, Privatboligen på Island i Sagatiden, pp. 213-14.

true site of this ancient court. [Cf. Finn Magnusen, Grönlands historiske Mindesmærker, vol. i. pp. 520 et seq.; Thorlacius, Um Órnefni í Þórnes þingi., l. c. pp. 294–5.] Vigfusson says of Magnusen's supposed discovery, that it had in it more of 'poetry than truth' ['ist mehr Dichtung als Wahrheit'], and this opinion seems to be entirely confirmed by Dr. Kålund. [Cf. Vigfusson, Eyrbyggja Saga, Vorrede, p. xix; Kålund, Bidr. til en hist.-top. Beskr. af Island, vol. i. p. 443.] It was at this court that Eric the Red, despite the assistance which he received from his friends, was condemned to outlawry.

(22) Dímunarvágr [Dimun-inlet] was, probably, in that group of small islets called Dímun, situated north-east of Brokey at the mouth of Hvamms-firth.

(23) Very little information has been preserved concerning Gunnbiorn, or his discovery. His brother, Grimkell, was one of the early Icelandic colonists, and settled on the western coast of Snowfells-ness, his home being at Saxahóll. [Landnáma, pt. ii. ch. viii.] Gunnbiorn's sons, Gunnstein and Halldor, settled in the North-west peninsula, on arms of the outer Ice-firth [Ísafjarðardjúp] [Landnáma, pt. ii. ch. xxix]. It is not known whether Gunnbiorn ever lived in Iceland, but it would seem to be probable that it was upon a voyage to western Iceland, that he was driven westward across the sea between Iceland and Greenland, and discovered the islands, which received his name, and likewise saw the Greenland coast. Eric sailed westward from Snowfells-ness, the same cape upon which Gunnbiorn's brother had established himself, and it is, perhaps, not unlikely, that it was from somewhere in the region of Grimkell's 'claim' that Gunnbiorn was driven westward, and that the knowledge of this may have guided Eric in laying his course.

(24) Blacksark [Bláserkr] and Whitesark [Hvítserkr] may have been either on the eastern or the south-eastern coast of Greenland. It is not possible to determine from the description here given, whether Blacksark was directly west of Snæfellsjökull, nor is it clear whether Blacksark and Whitesark are the same mountain, or whether there has been a clerical error in one or the other of the manuscripts.

(25) An effort was made by the editors of 'Grönlands historiske Mindesmærker,' to determine the actual site of the different firths, islands and mountains here named. In the light of subsequent explorations, it may be said, this effort was crowned with rather dubious success. So much seems to be tolerably certain, from Captain Gustav Holm's explorations of the eastern coast of Greenland, accomplished in 1883–5, that there were no Icelandic settlements upon that coast; wherefore both the Eastern and Western Settlement must be sought upon the western coast of Greenland, that is, to the westward of Cape Farewell, and between that cape on the south and Disco Island on the north; for, according to Steenstrup, the only ruin in northern Greenland, not of Eskimo origin, of which we have any knowledge, is the so-called 'Bear-trap' on Nugsuak Cape[1], on the mainland, a short distance north of Disco Island. [Steenstrup, 'Undersøgelsesrejserne i nord-Grønland i Aarene 1878–80,' in Meddelelser om Grønland, Copenh. 1883, p. 51.] The principal Norse remains [i.e. remains from the Icelandic colony in Greenland] have been found in two considerable groups; one of these is in the vicinity of the modern Godthaab, and the other in the region about the modern Julianehaab [the famous Kakortok church ruin being in

[1] It is Captain Holm's opinion that this 'Bear-trap' is not of Icelandic but of Eskimo origin.

the latter group]. It may be, that the first or Godthaab ruins, are upon the site of the Western Settlement, and the second, or Julianehaab group, upon that of the Eastern Settlement. It is not apparent, however, whether the Western uninhabited region was between Godthaab and Julianehaab or beyond Godthaab to the north, but it seems clear, that Erics-firth, Hrafns-firth, Snowfell, Hvarfsgnipa, and Ericsey, were all situated upon the western coast of Greenland[1].

(26) This Ingolf was called Ingolf the Strong [hinn sterki]. There is some confusion in Landnáma concerning his genealogy; he was probably a son of one of the Icelandic colonists, named Thorolf Sparrow [spǫrr]. His home, Hólmslátr [Holm-litter], was on the southern side of Hvamms-firth.

(27) Thorbiorn's and Thorgeir's father was the same Vifil, who came out to Iceland with Queen Aud, and who received from her the land on which he settled, Vifilsdale, as has been narrated in this saga, and is thus told in Landnáma: 'Vifil was the name of a freedman of Aud's. . . She gave him Vifilsdale, where he dwelt. . . His son was Thorbiorn, father of Gudrid, who married Thorstein, the son of Eric the Red, and afterwards Thorfinn Karlsefni, from whom are descended Bishops Biorn, Thorlak, and Brand. Another son of Vifil's was Thorgeir, who married Arnora,' &c. [Landnáma, pt. ii. ch. xvii.] The estate which Thorbiorn received with his wife, and upon which he lived after his marriage, called Laugarbrekka [Warm-spring-slope] on Hellisvellir [Cave-fields], is situated on the southern side of Snowfells-ness, near the outer end of that cape. Arnarstapi [Eagle-crag], where Gudrid's foster-father lived, was a short distance to the north-east of Laugarbrekka.

(28) Thorgeirsfell was upon the southern side of Snowfells-ness, to the eastward of Arnarstapi.

(29) The simple fact, that Thorgeir was a freedman, would seem to have offered no valid reason for Thorbiorn's refusal to consider his son's offer for Gudrid's hand, since Thorbiorn was himself the son of a man who had been a thrall; the real ground for his objection was, perhaps, not so much the former thraldom of Einar's father, as the fact that he was a man of humble birth, which Thorbiorn's father, although a slave, evidently was not.

(30) Hraunhöfn [Lava-haven] was on the southern side of Snowfells-ness, nearly midway between Laugarbrekka and Thorgeirsfell. It was this harbour from which Biorn Broad-wickers'-champion set sail, as narrated in Eyrbyggja[2].

(31) Lítil-vǫlva. The word vǫlva signifies a prophetess, pythoness, sibyl, a woman gifted with the power of divination. The characterization of the prophetess, the minute description of her dress, the various articles of which would seem to have had a symbolic meaning, and the account of the manner of working the spell, whereby she was enabled to forecast future events, form one of the most complete pictures of a heathen ceremony which has been preserved in the sagas.

(32) The expression 'Leif had sailed' ['Leifr hafði sigit'], would seem to refer to an antecedent condition, possibly to the statement concerning the arrival of Thorbiorn and his daughter at Brattahlid; i.e. 'Leif had sailed,' when they arrived. If this be, indeed,

[1] An account of the explorations of the ruins in the vicinity of Godthaab will be found in Meddelelser om Grønland, Copenhagen, 1889, in Jensen's article entitled, 'Undersøgelse af Grønlands Vestkyst [1884–85] fra 64° til 67° N.' For a description of the ruins in the neighbourhood of Julianehaab, cf. Holm, 'Beskrivelse af Ruiner i Julianehaabs Distrikt, undersøgte i Aaret 1880,' in Meddelelser om Grønland, Copenh. 1883.

[2] Cf. ante, p. 84.

the fact, it follows that Thorbiorn and his daughter must have arrived at Brattahlid during Leif's absence in Norway, and obviously before his return to Greenland, in the autumn of the year 1000. Upon this hypothesis, it is clear, that Thorbiorn and Gudrid must have been converted to Christianity before its legal acceptance in Iceland, that is to say, before the year 1000; and further, that Thorstein Ericsson may have been married to Gudrid in the autumn after his return from his unsuccessful voyage, namely, in the autumn of the year 1001; accordingly Karlsefni may have arrived in the following year, have been wedded to Gudrid at the next Yule-tide, 1002–3, and have undertaken his voyage to Wineland in the year 1003. This chronology is suggested with the sole aim of fixing the earliest possible date for Karlsefni's voyage of exploration.

(33) The expression of ÞsK. 'margkunnig,' conveys the impression that Thorgunna was gifted with preternatural wisdom.

(34) It has been suggested, that this Thorgunna is the same woman of whom we read in the Eyrbyggja Saga: 'That summer, when Christianity was accepted by law in Iceland, a ship arrived out by Snowfells-ness; this was a Dublin ship . . . There was a woman of the Hebrides on board, whose name was Thorgunna; the ship's folk reported, that she had brought with her such precious articles as were very rare in Iceland. And when Thurid, the mistress of Fróðá, heard this, she was very curious to see these treasures; for she was fond of finery, and showy in her dress; she accordingly went to the ship, where she met Thorgunna, and enquired of her whether she had any woman's garb of surpassing beauty. She replied, that she had no precious things to sell, but that she had finery in which she felt it no disgrace to appear at feasts or other assemblies. Thurid asked to see these articles, and was well pleased with them, and thought them very becoming, but not of very great value. Thurid endeavoured to purchase these articles, but Thorgunna would not sell them. Thereupon Thurid invited her to make her home with her, for she knew that Thorgunna had many treasures, and she thought that, sooner or later, she might succeed in obtaining them. Thorgunna replies: "I am well content to make my home with thee, but thou shalt know that I am inclined to give but little for my maintenance, since I am well able to work; wherefore I will myself decide what I shall give for my support from such property as I possess." Thorgunna spoke about the matter somewhat harshly, but Thurid still insisted that she should accompany her. Thorgunna's belongings were then carried from the ship; they were contained in a large locked chest and a portable box; these were carried to Fróðá, and when Thorgunna came to her lodgings, she asked to be provided with a bed, and a place was assigned her in the innermost part of the sleeping-apartment. She then unlocked her chest, and took from it bed-clothes, which were all very elaborately wrought; she spread an English sheet and silk quilt over the bed; she took bed-curtains from the chest together with all the precious hangings of a bed; all of these were so fine that the folk thought they had never seen the like. Thereupon Mistress Thurid exclaimed: "Fix a price upon the bed-clothing." Thorgunna replies: "I shall not lie in straw for thee, even if thou art fine-mannered and carriest thyself proudly." Thurid was displeased at this, and did not again seek to obtain the precious articles. Thorgunna worked at weaving every day, when there was no hay-making; but when the weather was dry, she worked at hay-making in the in-fields, and she had a rake made especially for her, and would use no other. Thorgunna

was a large woman, tall, and very stout; with dark brown eyes set close together, and thick brown hair; she was for the most part pleasant in her bearing, attended church every morning before she went to her work, but was not, as a rule, easy of approach nor inclined to be talkative. It was the common opinion that Thorgunna must be in the sixties.' [Eyrbyggja Saga, ed. Vigfusson, pp. 92–3.] In the autumn after her arrival Thorgunna died, and the strange events accompanying her last illness, are recorded in the chapter following that above quoted. As she approached her end, she called the master of the house to her, and said: '"It is my last wish, if I die from this illness, that my body be conveyed to Skálholt, for I foresee that it is destined to be one of the most famous spots in this land, and I know that there must be priests there now to chant my funeral service. I would, therefore, request thee to have my body conveyed thither, for which thou shalt have suitable compensation from my possessions; while of my undivided property Thurid shall receive the scarlet cloak, and I thus direct, that she may be content, if I make such disposition of my other property as I see fit; moreover, I would have thee requite thyself for such expense as thou hast incurred in my behalf, with such articles as thou wishest, or she may choose, of that which I so appoint. I have a gold ring, which is to go with my body to the church, but my bed and hangings I wish to have burned, for these will not be of profit to any one; and this I say, not because I would deprive any one of the use of these things, if I believed that they would be useful; but I dwell so particularly upon this," says she, "because I should regret, that so great affliction should be visited upon any one, as I know must be, if my wishes should not be fulfilled."' [Eyrbyggja Saga, l. c. pp. 95–6.]

The age here assigned to Thorgunna hardly agrees with the probable age of the Hebridean Thorgunna of Leif's acquaintance. Indeed the description of this remarkable woman, as given in 'Eyrbyggja,' would seem to indicate that there may have been an error in the age there assigned her, possibly a clerical error; if this is not the fact, it is pretty clear, that the Hebridean Thorgunna of Leif's acquaintance and the Thorgunna of 'Eyrbyggja' cannot be the same person. We are given to understand in the Saga of Eric the Red, that the woman of Leif's intrigue was a woman out of the ordinary rank; we are also told, that Leif gave her many precious bits of finery, among the rest a gold ring, and a mantle of wadmal. The Thorgunna of 'Eyrbyggja' was certainly an extraordinary woman, and was distinguished also for the apparel and ornaments which she possessed. The parallelism is sufficiently striking to point to the possibility, that the Thorgunna of 'Eyrbyggja' was the Thorgunna of Eric's Saga, who had, perhaps, come to Iceland to seek a passage to Greenland, in pursuance of her intention as announced to Leif at their parting. It is stated in Eric's Saga to have been rumoured, that Thorgunna's son came to Iceland in the summer before the Fródá-wonder. The Thorgunna of the Eyrbyggja Saga arrived in Iceland the summer before this 'wonder,' which indeed, owed its origin to her coming, but there is no mention in this saga of her having had a son, a singular omission, truly, if it be an omission, in so minute a description as the saga has preserved of this remarkable woman. Finally, it is evident, if Leif's voyage to Norway was made in 999, and the Thorgunna of Leif's intrigue and she of 'Eyrbyggja' are the same, that Thorgunna's son must have been of a very tender age at the time of his mother's arrival in Iceland. In view of these, as well as certain chronological difficulties, which this narrative presents, it seems not improbable that the whole account of

Thorgunna and the Fróðá-wonder, as contained in 'Eyrbyggja,' was a popular tale interjected in the saga for a reason not now apparent. This tale may well have been builded upon a historical foundation, but the remains of this foundation are not sufficiently well-preserved to enable us to separate accurately the sound from the unsound material[1].

(35) The Fróðá-wonder is the name given to the extraordinary occurrences, which befell at the farmstead of Fróðá soon after Thorgunna's death. The 'wonder' began with the appearance of a 'weird-moon,' which was supposed to betoken the death of some member of the family. This baleful prophecy was followed by the death of eighteen members of the household, and subsequently by the nightly apparitions of the dead. The cause of this marvel was attributed to the fact, that the Mistress of Fróðá had prevailed upon her husband to disregard Thorgunna's injunction to burn the drapery of her bed; and not until these hangings were burned was the evil influence exorcised, and the ghostly apparitions laid, the complete restoration of the normal condition of affairs being further facilitated by the timely recommendations of a priest, whose services had been secured to that end[2].

(36) It is not certain what variety of wood is meant; the generally accepted view has been, that it was some species of maple. It has also been suggested that the word mausurr mǫsurr, may be allied to the modern Swedish Masbjörk, veined-birch, German, Maser-birke, and again [cf. Grönl. hist. Mindesm. vol. i. p. 280] to the German Meussdorn, a view which Arngrim Jonsson was the first to advance [Gronlandia, ch. x]. It was believed, that this last-named received its name, 'darumb das diser dorn den Meusen und ratten zu wider ist,' [Bock, Kreuter Buch, ch. cxliij]. The same author writes of this wood: 'ist man fro das man Meussdorn zu Besen bekommen kan, als zu Venedig vnd sunst auf den Meerstetten. Die Meuss vnd Ratten werden mit disen dornen verscheucht' [Hieronymus Bock [Tragus], Kreuter Buch, 1546, p. 347]. It may be, that this or a similar passage suggested to Finn Magnusen and Werlauff the interpretation, 'besom,' 'broom,' which they gave to húsasnotra [af mǫsurtré; cf. note 6]. That the tree called mǫsurr was also indigenous in Norway is in a manner confirmed by a passage in the Short Story of Helgi Thorisson [Þáttr Helga Þórissonar], contained in Flatey Book [vol. i. p. 359]: 'One summer these brothers engaged in a trading voyage to Finmark in the north, having butter and pork to sell to the Finns. They had a successful trading expedition, and returned when the summer was far-spent, and came by day to a cape called Vimund. There were very excellent woods here. They went ashore, and obtained some "mǫsurr" wood.' The character of this narrative, and the locality assigned to the 'mǫsurr' trees, affect the trustworthiness of the information. It is reasonably clear, however, that the wood was rare and, whether it grew in Finmark or not, it was evidently highly prized[3].

(37) Thiodhild is also called Thorhild, and similarly Gudrid is called Thurid. It has been conjectured, that Thorhild and Thurid were the earlier names, which were changed by their owners after their conversion to Christianity, because of the suggestion of the heathen god in the first syllable of their original names[4].

(38) Such a fall as this of Eric's does not seem to have been generally regarded as

[1] Cf. Vigfusson, Eyrbyggja Saga, Vorrede, p. xvii.

[2] Cf. Eyrbyggja Saga, ed. Vigfusson, pp. 98–102.

[3] Cf. Saga Haralds harðráða, Fornmannasögur, vol. vi. p. 184.

[4] Cf. Grønl. hist. Mindesm. vol. i. 256–7, 471.

an evil omen, if we may be guided by the proverb: 'Fall er farar heill' [Óláfs saga Tryggvasonar, Flateyjarbók. l. c. vol. i. p. 231]. The complete saying is given by Guðmundr Jónsson [Safn af Íslenzkum Orðskviðum, Copenh. 1830. p. 100]: 'Fall er fararheill, frá garði en ei í garð,' 'a fall bodes a lucky journey from the house but not toward it.'

(39) The display of an axe seems to have been peculiarly efficacious in laying such fetches. From among numerous similar instances the following incident may be cited: 'Thorgils heard a knocking outside upon the roof; and one night he arose, and taking an axe in his hand, went outside, where he saw a huge malignant spectre standing before the door. Thorgils raised his axe, but the spectre turned away, and directed itself toward the burial-mound, and when they reached it, the spectre turned against him, and they began to wrestle with each other, for Thorgils had dropped his axe[1].'

(40) Thorfinn Karlsefni's ancestral line was of rare excellence; it is given in Landnáma at rather greater length, but otherwise as here: 'Thord was the name of a famous man in Norway, he was a son of Biorn Byrdusmior,' &c. 'Thord went to Iceland and took possession of Höfdaströnd in Skaga-firth, . . and dwelt at Höfdi [Headland]. Headland-Thord married Fridgerd,' &c. 'They had nineteen children. Biorn was their son, . . Thorgeir was the second son . . Snorri was the third, he married Thorhild Ptarmigan, daughter of Thord the Yeller' [Landnáma, pt. iii. ch. x]. Karlsefni's mother is not named in Landnáma. His grandmother's father, Thord the Yeller, was one of the most famous men in the first century of Iceland's history; he it was who established the Quarter-courts.

(41) Álptafjörðr [Swan-firth] is on the southern side of Hvamms-firth, near its junction with Breida-firth, in western Iceland. It is not improbable that the two ships sailed from Breida-firth, the starting-point for so many of the Greenland colonists.

(42) It has been claimed that this Thorhall, Gamli's son, was no other than the Thorhall, Gamli's son, of Grettis Saga. [Cf. Vigfusson and Powell, Icelandic Reader, p. 381; Storm, Studier over Vinlandsreiserne, p. 305. The latter author calls attention, in his treatise, to Vigfusson's confusion of Thorhall the Huntsman with Thorhall, Gamli's son.] In the vellum manuscript AM. 152 fol., Grettis Saga, p. 6 *b*, col. 23. we read of a Thorvallr [sic] Vindlendingr, and in the same manuscript of a Thorhall, son of Gamli Vinlendingr [p. 17 *b*, col. 68]. In the Grettis Saga of the vellum AM. 551 *a*, 4to, in corresponding passages, we read first of a Thoralldr [sic] Vinlendingr, and subsequently of Thorhall, a son of Gamli Vidlendingr. Again, in the parchment manuscript AM. 556 *a*, 4to, we find mention [p. 11, ll. 6–7] of a Thorhalldr Vidlendingr, and in the same manuscript [p. 23, l. 11] of Thorhall, a son of Gamli Vidlendingr. From these passages it would appear that both Thorhall and his father Gamli are called Vindlendingr, Vidlendingr, and, once, Vinlendingr. This, in itself, would appear to preclude the conjecture that this Thorhall received the appellation, Vínlendingr [Winelander], because of his visit to Wineland, for his father had possessed the same title before him; moreover the Thorhall, Gamli's son, of the Saga of Eric the Red, is said to be an Eastfirth man, while the Thorhall of Grettis Saga belonged to a northern family living at Hrútafirth, in the Húnaflói. We find from the probable chronology of Grettis Saga that Thorhall's son was married, and living at Melar, in Hrútafirth, in 1014. [Cf. Tímatal í Islendinga Sögum, p. 473.] If the

[1] Flóamanna Saga, ch. 13, ed. Vigfusson and Möbius, in Fornsögur, Leipsic, 1860.

Thorhall who went to Wineland was a young man and unmarried, as is not improbable, it is manifest that he could not have had a married son living in Iceland in 1014, and chronologically it would then appear to be impossible to identify the Thorhall, Gamli's son of Grettis Saga, with the man of the same name in Eric's Saga; this is, of course, purely conjectural, but from the other data previously cited, it would appear to be pretty clearly established, that the Thorhall, Gamli's son of Grettis Saga, was called after his father Vindlendingr [Wendlander], and that he was an altogether different man from the Thorhall, Gamli's son, of the Saga of Eric the Red.

(43) The celebration of Yule was one of the most important festivals of the year, in the North, both in heathen and in Christian times. Before the introduction of Christianity, it was the central feast of three, which were annually held. Of the significance of these three heathen ceremonials, we read: 'Odin established in his realm those laws, which had obtained with the Ases . . . At the beginning of winter a sacrificial banquet was to be held for a good year [til árs], in mid-winter they should offer sacrifice for increase [til gróðrar], and the third [ceremonial], the sacrifice for victory, was to be held at the beginning of summer [at sumri].' [Ynglinga Saga, 'Lagasetning Óðins,' in Heimskringla, ed. Unger, Chr'a., 1868, p. 9.] As to the exact time of the holding of the Yule-feast, it is stated in the Saga of Hacon the Good: 'He established the law, that the keeping of Yule should be made to conform to the time fixed by Christians, and every one should then stand possessed of a measure of ale, or should pay the equivalent, and should hold the whole Yule-tide sacred. Before this Yule began with [lit. had been kept on] "hǫku" night, which was the mid-winter night, and Yule was kept for three nights.' [Saga Hákonar góða, in Heimskringla, ed. Unger, p. 92.] The heathen Yule seems not to have coincided exactly with the Christian Christmas festival, and hence the change adopted by Hacon, who was a Christian, and who hoped, no doubt, to aid the propagation of his faith by thus blending the two festivals. Of the manner in which the three heathen festivals were transformed into Christian holidays by those who had experienced a change of faith, we read: 'There was a man named Sigurd. . . . He was accustomed, while heathendom survived, to hold three sacrifices every winter; one at the beginning of winter [at vetrnóttum], a second at mid-winter, a third at the beginning of summer [at sumri]. But when he accepted Christianity, he still retained his old custom regarding the feasts. He gave a great banquet to his friends in the autumn; a Yule-feast in the winter, to which he also invited many persons; the third banquet he held at Easter, and to this also he invited many guests.' [Saga Óláfs hins helga, in Heimskringla, ed. Unger, p. 351–52.] We learn from the Saga of the Foster-brothers, that the celebration of the Yule-tide in this fashion, was of rare occurrence in Greenland, ['því at sjaldan var Jóladrykkja á Grœnlandi.' Fóstbrœðra Saga, Copenh. 1822, p. 138. Konrad Gislason's edition of the same saga has: 'því at hann vil jóladrykkju hafa, ok gera sér þat til ágætis—því at sjaldan voro drykkjur á Grœnlandi,' 'for he desired to give a Yule-wassail, and get himself fame thereby,—for they seldom had drinking-bouts in Greenland.' Fóstbrœðra Saga, Copenh. 1852, p. 84.]

(44) Freydis also accompanied the expedition, as appears further on in the saga.

(45) This passage is one of the most obscure in the saga. If the conjecture as to the probable site of the Western Settlement, in the vicinity of Godthaab is correct, it is not apparent why Karlsefni should have first directed his course to the north-west, when his

destination lay to the south-west. It is only possible to explain the passage by somewhat hazardous conjecture. Leif may have first reached the Western Settlement on his return from the voyage of discovery, and Karlsefni, reversing Leif's itinerary, may have been led to make the Western Settlement his point of departure; or there may have been some reason, not mentioned in the saga, which led the voyagers to touch first at the Western Settlement. [Prof. Storm would argue from the situation of Lýsu-firth, the home of Gudrid's first husband in that Settlement, that the expedition may have set sail from there. Cf. Storm, Studier over Vinlandsreiserne, pp. 326–8. In this place Storm calls attention to the fact, that Thorstein Ericsson's unsuccessful voyage was directed from Eric's-firth, which lay considerably farther to the eastward than the Western Settlement, and that he would therefore be less apt to hit the land, than Karlsefni who sailed from the Western Settlement.] The language of EsR. would admit of the conclusion, that the Bear Islands were not far removed from the Western Settlement ['til Vestri-bygdar ok til Biarmeyia' [sic]; the statement of ÞsK., however, which speaks of Bear Island [in the singular] seems to indicate that the point of departure was not immediately contiguous to that settlement ['til Vestri-bygðar ok þaðan til Biarneyiar'].

(46) Dœgr is thus defined in the ancient Icelandic work on chronometry called Rímbegla: 'In the day there are two "dœgr;" in the "dœgr" twelve hours.' This reckoning, as applied to a sea-voyage, is in at least one instance clearly confirmed, namely in the Saga of Olaf the Saint, wherein it is stated that King Olaf sent Thorarin Nefiolfsson to Iceland: 'Thorarin sailed out with his ship from Drontheim, when the King sailed, and accompanied him southward to Mœri. Thorarin then sailed out to sea, and he had a wind which was so powerful and so favourable [hraðbyrr], that he sailed in eight "dœgr" to Eyrar in Iceland, and went at once to the Althing.' [Saga Óláfs konungs ens helga, ed. Munch and Unger, Chr'a., 1853, pp. 125–6.] Thorarin's starting-point was, doubtless, not far from Stad, the westernmost point of Norway, the Eyrar, at which he arrived, probably, the modern Eyrar-bakki, in southern Iceland, the nearest harbour to the site of the Althing. The time which was consumed in this phenomenal voyage is confirmed by Thorarin's words on his arrival at the Althing: 'I parted with King Olaf, Harold's son, four nights ago' [Óláfs saga hins helga, l. c. p. 126]. It is tolerably clear from this passage, that this could not have been a normal voyage, and yet we are told in Landnáma, that from Stad, in Norway, to Horn, on the eastern side of Iceland, is seven 'dœgra-sigling' [a sail of seven 'dœgr']. In the same connection it is also stated, that from Snowfells-ness the shortest distance to Hvarf in Western Greenland, is a sail of four 'dœgr;' from Reykianess, on the southern coast of Iceland, southward to Jölduhlaup in Ireland is five [some MSS. have three] 'dœgr' of sea [Landnáma, pt. i. ch. i]. These and similar statements elsewhere, have led many writers to the conclusion, that the word 'dœgr' may also indicate a longer period than twelve hours, and possibly the same as that assigned to *dagr*, a day of twenty-four hours. The meaning of the word is not so important to enable us to intelligently interpret the saga, as is the determination of the distance, which was reckoned to an average 'dœgr's' sail; that is to say, the distance which, we may safely conclude, was traversed, under average conditions, in a single 'dœgr' by Icelandic sailing craft. It seems possible to obtain this information with little difficulty. The sailing distance, as given in Landnáma, from Reykianess to Ireland, may best be disregarded because of the confusion in the manuscripts; the sailing distance from Snowfells-ness to Hvarf in Greenland gives

rather better data, although it is only possible to determine approximately the site of Hvarf; but the distance from Stad in Norway to Cape Horn in Iceland, can be determined accurately, and as this was the voyage, with which Icelanders were most familiar, it affords us a trustworthy standard of measurement, from which it is possible to determine the distance which was traversed in a sail of one 'dœgr;' and the discussion of the mooted question, whether the 'dœgr' of Rímbegla, and of King Olaf the Saint's Saga is the same as that of Landnáma, is not material to this determination. Having regard to the probable course sailed from Norway to Iceland, it would appear that a 'dœgr's' sail was approximately one hundred and eight miles. This result precludes the possibility, that any point in Labrador could have been within a sailing distance of two 'dœgr' from the Western Settlement. It has been noted that there are variations in the different manuscripts touching the comparatively little known voyage from Iceland to Ireland; if, similarly, there may have been such a variation in EsR, for example, 'tvau' (two) having been written for the somewhat similar 'ſiau' (seven), of an elder text, it then becomes apparent that the distance could have been traversed in a sail of seven 'dœgr.' Such corruption might have taken place because of lack of accurate knowledge to correct the error at the time in which our MSS. were written. The winds appear to have been favourable to the explorers; the sail of seven 'dœgr' 'to the southward,' from Greenland with the needful westering, would have brought Karlsefni and his companions off the Labrador coast. Apart from this conjecture, it may be said that the distance sailed in a certain number of 'dœgr' (especially where such distances were probably not familiar to the scribes of the sagas), seem in many cases to be much greater than is reconcilable with our knowledge of the actual distances traversed, whether we regard the 'dœgra' sail as representing a distance of one hundred and eight miles or a period of twenty-four hours.

(47) This may well have been the keel of one of the lost ships belonging to the colonists who had sailed for Greenland with Eric the Red a few years before; the wreckage would naturally drift hither with the Polar current[1].

(48) MS. Skotzka, lit. Scotch. This word seems to have been applied to both the people of Scotland and Ireland. The names of the man and woman, as well as their dress, appear to have been Gaelic, they are, at least, not known as Icelandic; the minute description of the dress, indeed, points to the fact that it was strange to Icelanders.

(49) Enn rauðskeggjaði, i.e. Thor. It has been suggested, that Thorhall's persistent adherence to the heathen faith may have led to his being regarded with ill-concealed disfavour[2].

(50) There can be little doubt that this 'self-sown wheat' was wild rice. The habit of this plant, its growth in low ground as here described, and the head, which has a certain resemblance to that of cultivated small grain, especially oats, seem clearly to confirm this view. The explorers probably had very slight acquaintance with cultivated grain, and might on this account more readily confuse this wild rice with wheat. There is not, however, the slightest foundation for the theory, that this 'wild wheat' was Indian corn, a view which has been advanced by certain writers. Indian corn was a grain entirely unknown to the explorers, and they could not by any possibility have confused it with wheat, even if they had found this corn growing wild, a conjecture for which there is absolutely no support whatever. [Cf. Schübeler,

[1] Cf. Landnámabók, pt. ii. ch. xiv, see also the similar passage in the Flatey Book narrative, p. 61, ante.

[2] Cf. Icelandic Reader, Oxford, 1879, p. 381.

'Om den Hvede, som Nordmændene i Aaret 1000 fandt vildtvoxende i Vinland,' in Forhandlinger i Videnskabets-Selskab, Chr'a., 1859, pp. 21–30.] The same observation as that made by the Wineland discoverers was recorded by Jacques Cartier five hundred years later, concerning parts of the Canadian territory which he explored. Of the Isle de Bryon we have this description, 'Nous la trouuames plaine de beaulx arbres, champs de blé sauuaige,' &c., and in the same narrative, with reference to another portion of the discovery, we are informed that the explorers found 'blé sauuaige, comme seille, quel il semble y abuoir esté semé et labouré.' [Relation Originale du Voyage de Jacques Cartier au Canada en 1534, ed. Michelant and Ramé, Paris, 1867, pp. 19 and 25.] It is no less true that this same explorer found grapes growing wild, in a latitude as far north as that of Nova Scotia, and, as would appear from the record, in considerable abundance: 'Apres que nous feusmes arriuez auec noz barques ausdictz nauires & retournez de la riuyere saincte Croix, le cappitaine Hinanda apprester lesdictes barques pour aller à terre à la dicte ysle veoir les arbres qui sembloient fort beaulx a veoir, & la nature de la terre d'icelle ysle. Ce que fut faict, & nous estans à ladicte ysle la trouuasmes plaine de fors beaulx arbres de la sorte des nostres. Et pareillement y trouuasmes force vignes, ce que n'auyons veu par cy deuant a toute la terre, & par ce la nommasmes l'ysle de Bacchus.' [Bref recit, &c., de la Navigation faite en 1535–6 par le Capitaine Jacques Cartier aux Iles de Canada, Hochelaga, Saguenay et autres, ed. D'Avezac, Paris, 1863, p. 14 *b* and 15.] Again, in the following century, we have an account of an exploration of the coast of Nova Scotia, in which the following passage occurs: 'all the ground betweene the two Riuers was without Wood, and was good fat earth hauing seuerall sorts of Berries growing thereon, as Gooseberry, Straw-berry, Hyndberry, Rasberry, and a kinde of Red-wine-berry: As also some sorts of Graine, as Pease, some eares of Wheat, Barley, and Rye, growing there wild,' &c. [Purchas his Pilgrimes, London, 1625, vol. iv, Bk. x, ch. vi, p. 1873.]

(51) Helgir fiskar, lit. 'holy fish.' The origin of the name is not known. Prof. Maurer suggests that it may have been derived from some folk-tale concerning St. Peter, but adds that such a story, if it ever existed, has not been preserved[1].

(52) It is not clear what the exact nature of these staves may have been. Hauk's Book has for the word translated 'staves,' both 'triom' and 'trionum,' AM. 557 has 'trianum.' The word trjónum has the meaning of 'snout,' but the first form of the word, as given in Hauk's Book, 'triom,' i.e. trjóm [trjám], seems to be the correct form [from tré, tree]. These 'staves' may have had a certain likeness to the long oars of the inhabitants of Newfoundland, described in a notice of date July 29th, 1612: 'They haue two kinde of Oares, one is about foure foot long of one peece of Firre; the other is about ten foot long made of two peeces, one being as long, big and round as a halfe Pike made of Beech wood, which by likelihood they made of a Biskin Oare, the other is the blade of the Oare, which is let into the end of the long one slit, and whipped very strongly. The short one they use as a Paddle, and the other as an Oare.' [Purchas his Pilgrimes, London, 1625, vol. iv. p. 1880.]

(53) The white shield, called the 'peace-shield' [friðskjǫldr], was displayed by those who wished to indicate to others with whom they desired to meet that their intentions were not

[1] Cf. Maurer, Isländische Volkssagen der Gegenwart, Leipsic, 1860, p. 195. The fish, now so called, is halibut, and is described by Eggert Olafsen, Reise durch Island, Copenh. and Leipsic, 1774, Pt. I, p. 191.

hostile, as in Magnus Barefoot's Saga, 'the barons raised aloft a white peace-shield' [Saga Magnús berfœtts, in Codex Frisianus, ed. Unger, Chr'a., 1869, p. 267]. The red shield, on the other hand, was the war-shield, a signal of enmity, as Sinfiotli declares in the Helgi song, 'Quoth Sinfiotli, hoisting a red shield to the yard, . . . "tell it this evening, . . . that the Wolfings are come from the East, lusting for war."' [Cf. Helga kviþa Hundingsbana, in Edda-lieder, ed. Finnur Jónsson, Halle o. S. 1890, Pt. II, verses 34-5, pp. 4 and 5.] The use of a white flag-of-truce for a purpose similar to that for which Snorri recommended the white shield, is described in the passage quoted in note 52, 'Nouember the sixt two Canoas appeared, and one man alone coming towards vs with a Flag in his hand of a Wolfes skin, shaking it and making a loud noise, which we tooke to be for a parley, whereupon a white Flag was put out, and the Barke and Shallop rowed towards them.' [Purchas his Pilgrimes, l. c. vol. iv. p. 1880.]

(54) The natives of the country here described were called by the discoverers, as we read, Skrælingjar; since this was the name applied by the Greenland colonists to the Eskimo, it has generally been concluded that the Skrælingjar of Wineland were Eskimo. Prof. Storm has recently pointed out that there may be sufficient reason for caution in hastily accepting this conclusion, and he would identify the inhabitants of Wineland with the Indians [Beothuk or Micmac], adducing arguments philological and ethnographical to support his theory[1]. The description of the savages of Newfoundland, given in the passage in Purchas' 'Pilgrims,' already cited, offers certain details, which coincide with the description of the Skrellings, contained in the saga. These savages are said by the English explorers to be 'full-eyed, of a black colour; the colour of their hair was diuers, some blacke, some browne, and some yellow, and their faces something flat and broad.' Other details, which are given on the same authority, have not been noted by the Icelandic explorers, and one statement, at least, 'they haue no beards[2],' is directly at variance with the saga statement concerning the Skrellings seen by the Icelanders on their homeward journey. The similarity of description may be a mere accidental coincidence, and it by no means follows that the English writer and Karlsefni's people saw the same people, or even a kindred tribe.

(55) John Guy, in a letter to Master Slany, the Treasurer and 'Counsell' of the New-found-land Plantation, writes: 'the doubt that haue bin made of the extremity of the winter season in these parts of New-found-land are found by our experience causelesse; and that not onely men may safely inhabit here without any neede of stoue, but Nauigation may be made to and fro from England to these parts at any time of the yeare. . . . Our Goates haue liued here all this winter; and there is one lustie kidde, which was yeaned in the dead of winter.' [Purchas his Pilgrimes, vol. iv. p. 1878.] 'Captaine Winne' writes, on the seventeenth of August, 1622, concerning the climate of Newfoundland: 'the Winter [is] short & tolerable, continuing onely in Ianuary, February and part of March: the day in Winter longer then in England: . . . Neither was it so cold here the last Winter as in England the yeere before. I remember but three seuerall dayes of hard weather indeed, and they not extreame neither: for I haue knowne greater Frosts, and farre greater Snowes in our owne Countrey.' [Purchas his Pilgrimes, vol. iv. p. 1890.]

[1] Cf. Storm, Studier over Vinlandsreiserne, l. c. pp. 346-55.

[2] Cf. Purchas his Pilgrimes, vol. iv. p. 1881.

(56) Einfœtingr, i. e. a One-footer, a man with one leg or foot. In the Flatey Book Thorvald's death is less romantically described. The mediæval belief in a country in which there lived a race of one-legged men, was not unknown in Iceland, for mention is made in Rímbegla, of 'a people of Africa called One-footers, the soles of whose feet are so large, that they shade themselves with these against the heat of the sun when they sleep.' [Rímbegla, l. c. p. 344.] This fable seems to have been derived, originally, from Ctesias: ['Item hominum genus, qui Monosceli [Monocoli] vocarentur, singulis cruribus, miræ pernicitatis ad saltum: eosdemque Sciapodas vocari, quod in maiori aestu humi iacentes resupini, umbra se pedum protegant: non longe eos a Troglodytis abesse,' [Ctesiæ Cnidii quæ supersunt, ed. Lion, Göttingen, 1823, p. 264], and was very widely diffused [cf. C. Plinius Secundus, Naturalis Historia, lib. vii, ch. 2; Aulus Gellius, Noctes Atticæ, lib. ix, iv, 9; C. Jul. Solinus, Polyhistor, ch. lxv, &c.] It is apparent from the passages from certain Icelandic works already cited [pp. 15, 16, ante], that, at the time these works were written, Wineland was supposed to be in some way connected with Africa. Whether this notice of the finding of a Uniped in the Wineland region may have contributed to the adoption of such a theory, it is, of course, impossible to determine. The reports which the explorers brought back of their having seen a strange man, who, for some reason not now apparent, they believed to have but one leg, may, because Wineland was held to be contiguous to Africa, have given rise to the conclusion that this strange man was indeed a Uniped, and that the explorers had hit upon the African 'land of the Unipeds.' It has also been suggested[1] that the incident of the appearance of the 'One-footer' may have found its way into the saga to lend an additional adornment to the manner of Thorvald's taking-off. It is a singular fact that Jacques Cartier brought back from his Canadian explorations reports not only of a land peopled by a race of one-legged folk, but also of a region in those parts where the people were 'as white as those of France;' 'Car il (Taignoagny) nous a certiffié auoir esté à la terre de Saguenay, en laq̃lle y a infini or, rubis & aultres richesses. Et y sont les hoĩes blancs comme en France & accoutrez de dras de laynes. . . . Plus dict auoir esté en autre pais de Picquemyans & autres pais, ou les gens n'ont que vne iambe.' [Voyage de I. Cartier, ed. d'Avezac, Paris, 1863, p. 40 *b*.]

(57) These words, it has been supposed, might afford a clue to the language of the Skrellings, which would aid in determining their race. In view not only of the fact, that they probably passed through many strange mouths before they were committed to writing, but also that the names are not the same in the different manuscripts, they appear to afford very equivocal testimony. Prof. Storm with reference to these names, which he cites thus, Avalldamon, Avaldidida, Vætilldi and Uvæge, says, that, while the information they afford is very defective: 'So much seems to be clear, that in their recorded form, they [*these words*] cannot be Eskimo, for *d* is entirely wanting in Eskimo, and even *g* is rare except as a nasal sound [*he refers: Fr. v. Müller, Grundriss der Sprachwissenschaft, ii. 164*]; Avalldamon especially cannot be Eskimo, for Eskimo words must either end with a vowel, or one of the mute consonants b, k, [q], t, p. . . . Especially is the soft melody of these Skrelling-words altogether different from the harsh guttural sounds of the Eskimo language. We must therefore refer for the derivation of these words to the Indians, whom we know in this region

[1] Vigfusson and Powell, Icelandic Reader, l. c. p. 384.

in later times. The inhabitants, whom the discoverers of the sixteenth century found in Newfoundland, and who called themselves "Beothuk" [i.e. men], received from the Europeans the name of *Red Indians*, because they smeared themselves with ochre; they have now been exterminated, partly by the Europeans, partly by the Micmac Indians, who in the last century wandered into Newfoundland from New Brunswick. Of their language only a few remnants have been preserved, but still enough to enable us to form a tolerably good idea of it. This language lacks f, but possesses *b, d, g, l, m, n, v* as well as the vowels *a, e, i, o, u*, so that its sounds conform entirely to the requirements of the four Skrelling-words. Unfortunately no glossary for the words father, mother, king, has been preserved, so that a direct comparison is impossible; however, the female name Shanan*dithit* and the word adadimit [spoon] bear a remarkable resemblance to the ending -didida in Avilldidida, and the words buggishaman or bukashaman [man, boy] and anyemen [bow] may also be compared to the termination -amon in Avalldamon [Ref. Gatchet, two discourses before the Amer. Philos. Society, 19 June, 1885, and 7 May, 1886]. This is, of course, only suggested conjecturally; since the Beothuk seem now to have died out, we shall probably, never succeed in obtaining more accurate results. I must, however, not omit to mention, that the Micmac language [in Nova Scotia and New Brunswick] also has such sounds, as to render it possible that these words might have been derived from them; but the glossaries, which I have examined, and which are much more complete than that of the Beothuk tongue, afford no especial resemblance to the Skrelling-words under consideration.' [Storm, Studier over Vinlandsreiserne, l. c. pp. 349–51.]

Captain Gustav Holm, of the Danish Navy, whose explorations both upon the east and west coast of Greenland, and whose prolonged residence in that country entitle him to speak with authority, has, at my request, acquainted me with his conclusions respecting the possible resemblance between the Skrelling-words and the Eskimo language, and also with reference to the points of resemblance between the Skrellings of the saga and the present inhabitants of Greenland. These conclusions are as follows:

'1. Although the four names, Vætilldi, Uvœgi, Avalldamon and Valdidida have nothing in common with Eskimo words, it cannot be gainsaid that they may be of Eskimo origin, since

'(*a*) We do not know whether they have been properly understood and recorded.

'(*b*) The different manuscripts of the saga give the names in entirely different forms [e.g. Avalldania instead of Avalldamon].

'(*c*) Even if the names have been correctly understood and recorded, there is nothing to prevent their being Eskimo; as illustrative of this, the name-list of East-Greenlanders may be cited, [in 'Den østgrønlandske Expedition,' Copenh. 1888, pt. II. p. 183 et seq.], in which many names, although they are recorded by a Greenlander [my steersman, who was a remarkably intelligent and talented man] have quite as little appearance of being Eskimo as the four under consideration.

'(*d*) The Eskimo language has not always the harsh guttural sound which has hitherto been ascribed to it. The Angmagsalik language is, on the contrary, very soft; they use *d* instead of ts and t, *g* instead of k, &c. [Cf. Den østgrønlandske Expedition, I. p. 156; II. p. 213.]

'(*c*) It is not impossible, that the names may have been derived from Eskimo originals. I would mention Uvœgi, the father's name, for instance, which name, as recorded, follows that of the mother. "Uve" with the suffix "uvia," signifies in Danish, "hendes Ægtefælle" [i.e. her husband], [vide Kleinschmidt's Grønlandske Ordbog, p. 403]. That "Uvœgi" should have any connection with the Greenland word "uve"[1] is, as a matter of course, a mere guess, by which I have sought to point out, that the possibility of Eskimo origin may not be rashly rejected.

'2. The description of the Skrellings would apply to the Eskimo, with the exception, that their eyes cannot be called large, but neither can this be said of the eyes of the North American Indians.

'Even as there are on the north-western coast of North America races which seem to me to occupy a place between the Indian and the Eskimo, so it appears to me not sufficiently proven, that the now extinct race on America's east coast, the Beothuk, were Indians. Their mode of life and belief have many points of resemblance, by no means unimportant, with the Eskimo and especially with the Angmagsalik. It is not necessary to particularize these here, but I wish to direct attention to the possibility, that in the Beothuk we may perhaps have one of the transition links between the Indian and the Eskimo.'

It will be seen that Captain Holm, while he differs from Professor Storm in many of his views, still arrives at much the same conclusion.

(58) The sum of information which we possess concerning White-men's-land or Ireland the Great, is comprised in this passage and in the quotation from Landnáma (ante, p. 11). It does not seem possible from these very vague notices to arrive at any sound conclusions concerning the location of this country. Rafn [Grönlands historiske Mindesmærker, vol. iii. p. 886] concludes that it must have been the southern portion of the eastern coast of North America. Vigfusson and Powell [Icelandic Reader, p. 384] suggest that the inhabitants of this White-men's-land were 'Red Indians;' with these, they say, 'the Norsemen never came into actual contact, or we should have a far more vivid description than this, and their land would bear a more appropriate title.' Storm in his 'Studier over Vinlandsreiserne' (l. c. p. 355-363) would regard 'Greater Ireland' as a semi-fabulous land, tracing its quasi-historical origin to the Irish visitation of Iceland prior to the Norse settlement. No one of these theories is entirely satisfactory, and the single fact which seems to be reasonably well established is that 'Greater Ireland' was to the Icelandic scribes *terra incognita*.

(59) Staðr í Reynines, the modern Reynistaðr, is situated in Northern Iceland, a short distance to the southward of Skaga-firth. Glaumbœr, as it is still called, is somewhat farther south, but hard by.

(60) Thorlak Runolfsson was the third bishop of Skálholt. He was consecrated bishop in the year 1118, and died 1133 [Jón Sigurðsson, 'Biskupa tal á Íslandi,' in Safn til Sögu Íslands, vol. i. p. 30]. Biorn Gilsson was the third bishop of Hólar, the episcopal seat of northern Iceland; he became bishop in 1147, and died in the year 1162. Bishop Biorn's successor was Brand Sæmundsson, 'Bishop Brand the Elder,' who died in the year 1201 [Jón Sigurðsson, Biskupa tal á Íslandi, ubi sup. p. 4]. As AM. 557, 4to, refers to this

[1] Cf. in this connection, Rink, Tales and Traditions of the Eskimo, Edinb. and London, 1875, p. 13, where we find; 'uviga = my husband,' and again, p. 74: 'Uvœge, probably the Greenlandish *uvia*, signifying husband.'

Bishop Brand as 'Bishop Brand the Elder,' it is apparent that it, as well as Hauk's Book, must have been written after the second Bishop Brand's accession to his sacred office. Bishop Brand Jonsson, the second Bishop Brand, became Bishop of Hólar in the year 1263, and died in the following year [Biskupa tal, ubi sup. p. 4].

(61) We read concerning the introduction of Christianity into Iceland: 'Thorvald [Kodransson] travelled widely through the southern countries; in the Saxon-land [Germany] in the south, he met with a bishop named Frederick, and was by him converted to the true faith and baptised, and remained with him for a season. Thorvald bade the bishop accompany him to Iceland, to baptise his father and mother, and others of his kinsmen, who would abide by his advice; and the bishop consented.' ['Kristni Saga' in Biskupa Sögur, ed. Vigfusson, Copenh. 1858, vol. i. p. 3.] According to Icelandic annals, Bishop Frederick arrived in Iceland, on this missionary emprise, in the year 981; from the same authority we learn that he departed from Iceland in 985.

(62) Heriulf or Heriolf, who accompanied Eric the Red to Greenland, was not, of course, the same man to whom Ingolf allotted land between Vág and Reykianess, for Ingolf set about the colonization of Iceland in 874, more than a century before Eric the Red's voyage to Greenland. The statement of Flatey Book is, therefore, somewhat misleading, and seems to indicate either carelessness or a possible confusion on the part of the scribe. Heriulf, Eric the Red's companion, was a grandson of the 'settler' Heriulf, as is clearly set forth in two passages in Landnáma. In the first of these passages the Greenland colonist is called 'Heriulf the Younger' [Landnáma, pt. ii, ch. xiv]; the second passage is as follows: 'Heriolf, who has previously been mentioned, was Ingolf's kinsman and foster-brother, for which reason Ingolf gave him land between Vog and Reykianess; his son was Bard, father of that Heriolf, who went to Greenland and came into the "Sea-rollers."' [Landnáma, pt. iv, ch. xiv.] As has already been stated, there is no mention in Landnáma or other Icelandic saga, save that of the Flatey Book, of Heriulf's son, Biarni. Reykianess, the southern boundary of Heriulf's 'claim,' is at the south-western extremity of Iceland; Vág was, probably, situated a short distance to the north of this cape, on the western coast of the same peninsula.

(63) In the 'King's Mirror' [Konungs Skuggsjá], an interesting Norwegian work of the thirteenth century, wherein, in the form of a dialogue, a father is supposed to be imparting information to his son concerning the physical geography of Greenland, he says: 'Now there is another marvel in the Greenland Sea, concerning the nature of which I am not so thoroughly informed, this is that, which people call "Sea-rollers" [hafgerðingar]. This is likest all the sea-storm and all the billows, which are in that sea, gathered together in three places, from which three billows form; these three hedge in the whole sea, so that no break is to be seen, and they are higher than tall fells, are like steep peaks, and few instances are known of persons who, being upon the sea when this phenomenon befell, have escaped therefrom.' [Speculum regale, ed. Brenner, Munich, 1881, p. 47.] A Danish scholar, in a treatise upon this subject, concludes that the hafgerðingar were earth-quake waves, and that those here celebrated were such tidal-waves caused by an unusually severe earth-quake in the year 986. [Cf. Steenstrup, Hvad er Kongespeilets 'Havgjerdinger?' Copenh. 1871, esp. p. 49.] However this may be, there can be little question that Heriulf experienced a perilous

voyage, since out of the large number of ships, which set sail for Greenland at the same time, so few succeeded in reaching their destination.

(64) This has been assumed by many writers to have been Labrador, but the description does not accord with the appearance which that country now presents.

(65) Certainly a marvellous coincidence, but it is quite in character with the no less surprising accuracy with which the explorers, of this history, succeed in finding 'Leif's-booths' in a country which was as strange to them as Greenland to Biarni.

(66) This statement has attracted more attention, perhaps, than any other passage in the account of the Icelandic discovery of America, since it seems to afford data which, if they can be satisfactorily interpreted, enable us to determine approximately the site of the discovery. The observation must have been made within the limits of a region wherein, early in the eleventh century, the sun was visible upon the shortest day of the year between *dagmálastaðr* and *eyktarstaðr*; it is, therefore, apparent that if we can arrive at the exact meaning of either *dagmálastaðr* or *eyktarstaðr*, or the length of time intervening between these, it should not be difficult to obtain positive information concerning the location of the region in which the observation was made. We are informed by a treatise, inserted in the printed text of Rímbegla, written by Bishop John Arnason, that the method adopted by the ancient Icelanders for the determination of the various periods of the day, was to select certain so-called 'eykt-marks' [eyktamörk] about every dwelling, as, peaks, knolls, valleys, gorges, cairns, or the like, and to note the position of, and course of the sun by day, or the moon and stars by night, with relation to these 'eykt-marks [1].' The circle of the horizon having been thus artificially divided, in the absence of clocks or watches, certain names were assigned to the position which the sun occupied at, as we should say, certain 'hours' of the day; 'dagmálastaðr,' lit. 'day-meal-stead,' indicates the position of the sun at the 'day-meal,' which was the principal morning meal. We have, unfortunately, no accurate data which might enable us to determine the position of the sun at 'dagmálastaðr;' such information we have, however, concerning 'eykt,' for it is stated, in an ancient Icelandic law-code, that 'if the south-west octant be divided into thirds, it is "eykt" when the sun has traversed two divisions and one is left untraversed' ['þá er eykð er útsuðrsætt er deild í þriðjunga, ok hefir sól gengna tvá hluti, en einn ógenginn;' Kristinnréttr Þorláks ok Ketils, Copenh. 1775, p. 92. Cf. also Grágás, ed. Finsen, Copenh. 1852, Pt. I, p. 26]. There seems to be little room for question that the 'eykt' of 'Kristinnréttr' and the *eyktarstaðr* of the Flatey Book are the same, and the statement of 'Kristinnréttr' accordingly affords a clear and concise definition of the position of that point upon the horizon at which the sun set on the shortest day of the year in Wineland, and which the explorers called 'eyktarstaðr.' Nevertheless the rational and simple scientific application of this knowledge has been, until very recently, completely ignored, in the effort to reach, through this definition, the solution of the problem involving the exact *clock-time* of *dagmálastaðr* and *eyktarstaðr* and thus the *hour* at which the sun rose and set on the shortest Wineland day.

The widely divergent views of the leading writers upon this subject have been concisely summarized by Professor Gustav Storm, in a very able treatise wherein he points out the real value of the information, to be derived from the passage in 'Kristinnréttr.'

[1] Cf. Rímbegla, l. c. Eiktamörk Íslendsk, pp. 2, 4, and 22, recently reprinted in 'Kvæði eptir Stefán Ólafsson,' ed. Jón Þorkelsson, Copenh. 1886, vol. ii. pp. 358, 364–5.

With the addition of a few minor details as to authorities, cited by Professor Storm, which additions are here italicized, his summary is as follows:

'The first writer in modern times to seek to determine Wineland's geographical situation was Arngrim Jonsson in "Gronlandia;" he, as well as all subsequent investigators, has employed to this end the passage in the Grœnlendinga-þáttr of the Flatey Book, in which mention is made of the duration of the shortest day in Wineland [*the passage under consideration*]; but as to the significance of this passage many different opinions have been advanced, and, as far as I can see, there seem to be strong objections to them all. Arngrim Jonsson translated "sol in ipso solstitio hyberno, circiter 6 plus minus supra horizontem commorat;" he writes by way of caution "plus minus" [about], since he adds "sciotericiis enim destituebantur" [*Gronlandia, ch. ix, p. 55 of the Latin MS., gl. kgl. Saml.* [*Royal Library of Copenh.*] *No. 2876, 4to, but at p. 33, of the Icelandic printed text, heretofore cited, from which latter, however, all qualification is omitted, and the statement reads simply, "the sun could be seen fully six hours on the shortest day," "sva þar matte sol sia um skamdeigid sialft vel sex stunder"*]. This explanation was, doubtless, only known to the few Danish scholars of the seventeenth century, who had access to Arngrim's "Gronlandia;" it first became more widely disseminated in the Icelandic translation, which was published at Skálholt in 1688. Arngrim's explanation was also accepted by Torfæus in his "Vinlandia" [1705]: "Brumales diés ibi qvam vel in Islandia, vel Gronlandia longiores, ad horam nonam circa solstitia sol oriebatur, tertiam occidit" [Vinlandia, l. c. pp. 6 and 7], although Torfæus remarks that this observation must, on account of the fruitfulness of the country, be regarded as inaccurate, since it points to a latitude of 58° 26'. While his work was in the press Torfæus became acquainted with Peringskiöld's—or more correctly the Icelander, Gudmund Olafsson's—translation in the printed edition of Heimskringla[1], which he properly enough rejected, but which caused him to undertake a renewed consideration of the subject. With the passage from Grágás [*i. e. the passage defining "eykt"*] as a basis, he now arrived at the following interpretation of this: "spatium qvod sol à meridie in occidentem percurrit, sex horas reqvirit, ex qvibus singuli trientes duas constituunt, bes desinit in horam qvartam pomeridianam." [*Vinlandia, Addenda, pp. 6 and 7*]. Now if "eykt" be four o'clock, p.m.—and the shortest day accordingly eight hours—Wineland's latitude becomes 49°, i. e. Newfoundland, or the corresponding Canadian coast. This new interpretation became, by reason of the attention which Torfæus' writings attracted in the learned world, most widely disseminated in the last century; thus we find it accepted by the German investigator, J. R. Forster, who concludes that Wineland was either Gander Bay or the Bay of Exploits, in Newfoundland, or on the coast of the northern side of the Gulf of St. Lawrence [49°] [Joh. Reinh. Forster, Geschichte der Entdeckungen und Schifffahrten im Norden, Frankf. 1784, p. 112]; the same interpretation is also accepted by Malte Brun, Précis de la Géographie universelle, Paris, 1812, I. 394. Meanwhile, early in this century, Icelandic scholars began to advance a new view, which has gradually forced its way into general recognition. This view was first suggested by Vice-lawman Páll Vídalín in his unpublished Skýringar[2], subsequently adopted by Bishop Finnr Jónsson [1772] in his Hist.

[1] 'The day was longer there than in Greenland or Iceland, for the sun had there its hour of increase and the day-meal-stead or place of rising at breakfast-time [about six or seven o'clock] on the shortest day.' Heimskringla, ed. Peringskiöld, vol. i. p. 33. Suhm inclined to this opinion in Kjöbh. Selsk. Skrifter, viii. 80, and believed that Wineland was 'Pennsylvania, Maryland, or perhaps Carolina.'

[2] *Vidalin's work was written prior to 1727, but was not published until 1854, when it appeared in Reykjavík under the title, Skýringar yfir Fornyrði Lögbókar þeirrar, er Jónsbók kallast [Commentaries on ancient terms in the law-book called Jónsbók]. The subject under consideration is treated in this work, pp. 56–82.*

Eccl. Isl. 153 et seq. [*i. e. 153-56 note*], it was next approved by Schöning in a note to Heimskringla [*Heimskringla, Copenh. 1777, vol. i. p. 309*], and in his history of Norway [*Norges Riges Historie, Copenh. 1781, vol. iii. 419*], and in this century was more elaborately developed by Rafn and Finn Magnusen. The new point of departure in this theory is Snorri's expression in Edda concerning the seasons of the year, "Frá jafndœgri er haust til þess er sól sezt í eykðar stað" ["*Autumn lasts from the equinox until the sun sets in 'eyktarstaðr,'*" Edda Snorra Sturlusonar, Copenh. 1848, vol. i. p. 510]; since it was assumed that the beginning of winter, according to Snorri, coincided, as a matter of course, with the beginning of winter according to the Icelandic calendar [the week from the 11th to the 17th of October], it was found that the sun set at Reykholt [*Snorri's home*] on the 17th of October at four o'clock; to conform with this, "Eyktarstaðr" was interpreted to mean the end of "Eykt," and "Eykt" became the *period of* time from 3.30 to 4.30. Now if the sun was above the horizon in Wineland on the shortest day from Dagmál to Eyktarstaðr, a day nine hours in length was obtained, which Prof. Thomas Bugge computed gave a latitude of 40°22', or, according to Rafn and Finn Magnusen, more exactly, 41° 24'10". Rafn believed that it followed of a certainty that Wineland was identical with the southern coast of Rhode Island and Connecticut, directly to the westward of Cape Cod. But very serious objections to this theory suggest themselves. When Leif Ericsson—according to the Flatey Book—approached Wineland, he saw at first an island to the *northward* of the land; he then sailed to the *westward* into a sound between the island and the land's most *northerly* cape, and still *farther west*, they arrived at a river and lake, where they established themselves; the composer of the saga accordingly had in mind a country facing *toward the north*, and upon whose *northern* shore Leif and his people established themselves in "Leifsbúðir." Nevertheless Rafn renders this thus [Annaler for Nord. Oldkyndigh. Copenh. 1840-41, pp. 6 and 16]: "They came to an island, which lay to the *east* off the land, and sailed into a sound between this island and a cape, which projected toward the *east* [and north] from the land."' [Gustav Storm, Om Betydningen af 'Eyktarstaðr' i Flatøbogens Beretning om Vinlandsreiserne, foredraget i Christiania Videnskabsselskab 2den Nov. 1883, pp. 1-4. The article has since been published in Arkiv for Nordisk Filologi, November, 1885.]

Professor Storm, in this same treatise, points out the inaccuracy of Rafn's astronomical calculation, which corrected, would change the latitude to 42° 21', the vicinity of Boston, which region does not, however, correspond to the descriptions of the saga. He further shows the error in the interpretation of the passage in Snorri's Edda, upon which this theory is based. The cause of the confusion in these different theories is satisfactorily explained by the following paragraph in Professor Storm's article, the contribution of the astronomer, Mr. Geelmuyden, to whom Professor Storm had submitted the astronomical data for solution:

'For the correct understanding of the passages in the old sagas, wherein these day-marks [*i. e. the eyktamörk of Rimbegla*] are mentioned, it is of the utmost importance to bear in mind that they were in practical use; nor should it be forgotten that the sun's position above a certain day-mark only gives a certain horizontal projection, and especially it will not do to transfer the stroke of the clock corresponding to a certain day-mark—whether that corresponding to a certain season of the year be taken, or the mean for the entire year—to the similar day-mark at other places on the earth.

'When, therefore, the Greenlanders found, according to the statement in the Flatey

Book, that the sun upon the shortest day "had Dagmálastaðr and Eyktarstaðr," this does not mean that the sun was visible until a certain hour, for they lacked the means of determining the hour, according to our understanding of the word, but it does mean that the sun was visible in certain horizontal directions which they were experienced in determining.'

Applying the passage in Kristinnréttr to the determination of the position of the sun at sunset, on the shortest day of the year in Wineland, Mr. Geelmuyden concludes that:

'Since Útsuðrsætt is the octant, which has S. W. in its centre, therefore between 22·5° and 67·5° Azimuth, Eyktarstaðr must be in the direction 22·5° + ⅔ of 45° = 52·5° from the south toward the west. Solving the latitude in which the sun set in this direction on the shortest day [in the eleventh century] we find it to be 49°55′. Here, therefore, or farther to the south the observation must have been made.'

I am indebted to Capt. R. L. Phythian, U. S. N., Superintendent of the U. S. Naval Observatory, Washington, for the following detailed computation undertaken, at my request, from a brief statement of the problem:

'As the solution of the question you propose depends, of course, upon the interpretation of the data furnished, it is necessary that I should give in detail the process by which the amplitude of the sun is derived from the statement contained in your letter.

'"Eyktarstad" is assumed to be the position of the sun in the horizon when setting. The south-west octant you define to be the octant having S.W. as its centre; its limits, therefore, are S. 22½° W. and S. 67½° W.

'"It is eykt when, the south-west octant having been divided into thirds, the sun has traversed two of these and has one still to go." That is, it is eykt when the point of the horizon is 30° west of S. 22½ W., or S. 52½° W. From this the sun's amplitude when in this point of the horizon is W. 37° 30′ S.

'The sun's declination on the shortest day of the year 1015 was S. 23° 34′ 30″ [nearly].

'The simple formula for finding the sun's amplitude when in the true horizon is sufficiently accurate for the conditions of this case.

'It is $\sin A = \sin d \sec. L,$

from which $\sec L = \sin A \operatorname{cosec.} d.$

'Solving with the above data:

$$A = -37^\circ 30' \quad \ldots\ldots \quad \text{log. sin.} \quad -9{\cdot}78445$$
$$d = -23^\circ 34' 30'' \quad \ldots\ldots \quad \text{log. cosec.} \quad -0{\cdot}39799$$
$$L = +48^\circ 56 \quad \ldots\ldots \quad \text{log. sec.} \quad +0{\cdot}18244.$$

'If I have been in error in the process by which the amplitude has been arrived at, the substitution of its correct value in the above computation will give the proper latitude.'

This computation was undertaken independently of Mr. Geelmuyden's conclusions, and in reply to my query, evoked by the slight discrepancy in the two results, which was then first brought to his attention, Capt. Phythian writes, as follows:

'The formula by which I computed the latitude is the simplest form that can be employed for the purpose, but was, for reasons that will be mentioned later, deemed sufficiently accurate.

'It assumes that the bearing of the sun was taken when its centre was actually on the horizon, and the latitude is found by the solution of a spherical right-angled triangle. Manifestly the learned Professor has taken into account the effect of refraction, and solved an oblique triangle. By this method, calling the refraction 33′, we find the latitude to be 49° 50′·2. The slight difference between this result and that of the Professor [less than 5′] is accounted for by the supposition that he did not assume the same refraction.

'The conditions of this case do not seem to give additional value to a rigorous solution. Since the explorers were on the eastern coast of the continent they must have observed the setting of the sun over land, and probably recorded its bearing before it reached the horizon. In such a case, the introduction of refraction and semi-diameter would lead to a result more in error than the simpler solution.

'The data furnished are not sufficiently definite to warrant a more positive assertion than that the explorers could not have been, when the record was made, farther north than Lat. [say] 49°.'

The result, therefore, of the application of Professor Storm's simple and logical treatment to this passage in Flatey Book, 'the sun had there Eyktarstad,' &c., is summed up in Capt. Phythian's statement, 'the explorers could not have been, when the record was made, farther north than Lat. [say] 49°;' that is to say, Wineland may have been somewhat farther to the south than northern Newfoundland or the corresponding Canadian coast, but, if we may rely upon the accuracy of this astronomical observation, it is clear that *thus far south it must have been.*

(67) Kornhjálmr af tré, a wooden granary. The word 'hjálmr' appears to have a double significance. In the passage in the Saga of King Olaf the Saint: 'Wilt thou sell us grain, farmer? I see that there are large "hjálmar" here' [Heimskringla, ed. Unger, p. 353], the word 'hjálmar' may have the meaning of stacks of grain. The use of the word as indicating a house for the storage of grain is, however, clearly indicated in the Jydske Lov of 1241, wherein we read: 'But if one build upon the land of another either a "hialm" or any other house,' &c. ['æn byggær man annænds iord antugh mæth hialm æth mæth nokær andre hus,' &c. Danmarks gamle Provindslove, ed. Thorsen, Copenh. 1853, pp. 79–80]. As there is no suggestion in the saga of the finding of cultivated fields, it is not apparent for what uses a house for the storage of grain could have been intended.

(68) Vígflaki, lit. a war-hurdle. This was a protection against the missiles of the enemy raised above the sides of the vessel. In this instance, as perhaps generally on ship-board, this protecting screen would appear to have been formed of shields attached to the bulwarks, between these the arrow, which caused Thorvald's death, doubtless, found its way.

(69) The Landnámabók makes no mention of this Thori; its language would seem to preclude the probability of a marriage between such a man and Gudrid; the passage with reference to Gudrid being as follows: 'His son was Thorbiorn, father of Gudrid who married Thorstein, son of Eric the Red, and afterwards Thorfinn Karlsefni; from them are descended bishops Biorn, Thorlak and Brand.' Landnáma, pt. ii, ch. xvii.

(70) Námkyrtill [namkirtle] is thus explained by Dr. Valtýr Guðmundsson, in his unpublished treatise on ancient Icelandic dress: 'Different writers are not agreed upon the meaning of "námkyrtill;"' Sveinbjörn Egilsson [Lexicon poet.] interprets it as signifying a kirtle made from some kind of material called 'nám.' In this definition he

is followed by Keyser [Nordmændenes private Liv i Oldtiden], and Vigfusson [Dict.]. The Icelandic painter, Sigurðr Guðmundsson ['Um kvennabúninga á Íslandi að fornu og nýju,' in Ný fjelagsrit, vol. xvii], has, on the other hand, regarded the word as allied to the expression: 'at nema at beini' [i.e. fitting close to the leg, narrow], and concludes that 'námkyrtill' should be translated, 'narrow kirtle,' in which view Eiríkr Jónsson [Oldnordisk Ordbog] and K. Weinhold [Altnordisches Leben] coincide.

'I cannot agree with either of these interpretations. The mention in Flatey Book is so indefinite, that nothing can be determined from it. On the other hand, the meaning of this word becomes apparent from a passage in Laxdœla Saga, if this be compared with other references to female dress in ancient times, contained in the elder literature. This passage in Laxdœla Saga is as follows: "Gudrun wore a 'námkyrtill' and a close-fitting upper garment [vefjarupphlutr], with a large head-dress; she wore wrapped about her an apron with dark embroidery upon it and fringed at the ends" ["Guðrún var í námkyrtli, ok við vefjarupphlutr þrǫngr, en sveigr mikill á hǫfði; hon hafði knýtt um sik blæju ok váru í mǫrk blá ok trǫf fyrir enda."] "Námkyrtill" evidently means here half-kirtle or petticoat, for with it an "upphlutr" [waist] of different stuff is worn, which in Snorra Edda [ii. 494] is called "helfni" [i.e. half-kirtle]. The origin of the word seems to me to have been as follows: In the ordinary woman's gown [kirtle] the upper part, or "upphlutr," was, obviously, much narrower [i.e. closer-fitting] than the lower part of the garment, and was, in consequence, worn out sooner than the lower part. With the better class of people the kirtle was usually made from some foreign stuff of bright colour, especially red. Now when the upper part [upphlutr] was worn out, the wearers, indisposed to abandon the lower part of the garment, which was still serviceable, took [námu] or cut off the lower part, and wore it with an upper garment made from domestic stuff [homespun], the so-called wadmal [vefjarupphlutr]. The lower detached part of the garment or skirt then received the name of "nám" or "námkyrtill" [cf. landnám, órnám] because it had been taken [numið] from the entire kirtle. By the preservation of the serviceable lower part of the garment, with its foreign stuff of showy colour, the dress was rendered more ornamental than it would have been if both the lower and upper portion of the kirtle had been made from wadmal, which it was not easy to obtain, in Iceland, dyed in colours. Such I conclude to have been the origin of the word "nám" or "námkyrtill." The word subsequently continued in use, regardless of the fact whether the skirt or lower half-kirtle, to which it was applied, had been cut from an old kirtle or not[1].'

(71) A 'mǫrk' was equal to eight 'aurar' [cf. Laxdœla Saga, ch. 26. ed. Kålund, Copenh. 1889, p. 90]; an 'eyrir' [plur. 'aurar'] of silver was equal to 144 skillings [cf. Vídalín, Skýringar yfir Fornyrði Lögbókar, Reykjavík, 1854, p. 351]. An 'eyrir' would, therefore, have been equal to three crowns [kroner], modern Danish coinage, since sixteen skillings are equal to one-third of a crown [33⅓ øre], and a half 'mǫrk' of silver would accordingly have been equal to twelve crowns, Danish coinage. As the relative value of gold and silver at the time described is not clearly established, it is not possible to determine accurately the value of the half 'mǫrk' of gold. It was, doubtless, greater at that time, proportionately, than the value here assigned, while the purchasing power of both precious metals was very much greater then than now.

[1] Cf. also the same author's reference to 'námkyrtill' in Grundriss der Germ. Philol. XIII, Abschnitt, Sitte I, § 31.

(72) At the time of the 'settlement' of Iceland the homestead of the more prominent 'settler' became the nucleus of a little community. The head of this little community, who was the acknowledged leader in matters spiritual and temporal, was called the 'goði.' With the introduction of Christianity the 'goði' or 'goðorðsmaðr' lost his religious character though he still retained his place of importance in the Commonwealth.

(73) 'Þat var ofarliga á dögum Ólafs hins helga, at Guðleifr hafði kaupferð vestr til Dýflinnar; en er hann sigldi vestan, ætlaði hann til Íslands; hann sigldi fyrir vestan Írland, ok fékk austanveðr ok landnyrðinga, ok rak þá langt vestr í haf ok í útsuðr, svá at þeir vissu ekki til landa; en þá var mjök áliðit sumar, ok hétu þeir mörgu, at þá bæri ór hafinu, ok þá kom þar, at þeir urðu við land varir; þat var mikit land, en eigi vissu þeir hvert land þat var. Þat ráð tóku þeir Guðleifr, at þeir sigldu at landinu, því at þeim þótti illt at eiga lengr við hafsmegnit. Þeir fengu þar höfn góða; en er þeir höfðu þar litla stund við land verit, þá koma menn til fundar við þá; þeir kendu þar engan mann, en helzt þótti þeim, sem þeir mælti írsku; brátt kom til þeirra svá mikit fjölmenni, at þat skipti mörgum hundruðum. Þeir tóku þá höndum alla ok bundu, ok ráku þá síðan á land upp. Þá vóru þeir færðir á mót eitt, ok dæmt um þá. Þat skildu þeir, at sumir vildu at þeir væri drepnir, en sumir vildu at þeim væri skipt á vistir ok væri þeir þjáðir. Ok er þetta var kært, sjá þeir hvar reið flokkr manna, ok var þar borit merki í flokkinum; þóttust þeir þá vita, at höfðingi nökkurr mundi vera í flokkinum; ok er flokk þenna bar þangat at, sá þeir, at undir merkinu reið mikill maðr ok garpligr, ok var þó mjök á efra aldr ok hvítr fyrir hærum. Allir menn er þar vóru fyrir, hnigu þeim manni, ok fögnuðu sem herra sínum; fundu þeir þá brátt, at þangat var skotið öllum ráðum ok atkvæðum, sem hann var. Síðan sendi þessi maðr eptir þeim Guðleifi; ok er þeir kómu fyrir þenna mann, þá mælti hann til þeirra á norrænu, ok spyrr, hvaðan af löndum þeir vóru. Þeir sögðu, at þeir væri flestir íslenzkir. Þessi maðr spurði hverir þeir væri þessir íslenzku menn; gékk Guðleifr þá fyrir þenna mann ok kvaddi hann virðuliga, en hann tók því vel, ok spyrr hvaðan af Íslandi þeir væri, en Guðleifr segir at hann væri ór Borgarfirði; þá spurði hann hvaðan ór Borgarfirði hann var; en Gunnlaugr segir[þat]. Eptir þat spurði hann vandliga eptir sérhverjum hinna stærri manna í Borgarfirði ok Breiðafirði. Ok er þeir töluðu þetta, spyrr hann eptir Snorra goða ok Þuríði frá Fróðá, systur hans, ok hann spurði vandliga eptir öllum hlutum frá Fróðá ok mest at sveininum Kjartani, er þá var bóndi at Fróðá. Landsmenn kölluðu í öðrum stað, at nökkurt ráð skyldi gjöra fyrir skipshöfninni. Eptir þat gékk þessi mikli maðr brott frá þeim, ok nefndi með sér xij menn af sínum mönnum, ok sátu þeir langa hríð á tali. Eptir þat géngu þeir til mannfundarins. Þá mælti inn mikli maðr til þeirra Guðleifs: "Vér landsmenn höfum talat nökkut [mál] yðar, ok hafa landsmenn nú gefit yðvart mál á mitt vald, en ek vil nú gefa yðr fararleyfi þangat sem þér vilit fara; en þó yðr þykki nú mjök á liðit sumar, þá vil ek þó ráða yðr, at þér látið á brott héðan, því at hér er fólk útrútt ok illt viðreignar: en þeim þykkja áðr brotin lög á sér." Guðleifr mælti: "Hvat skulum vér til segja, ef oss verðr auðit at koma til ættjarða várra, hverr oss hafi frelsi gefit?" Hann svarar: "Þat mun ek yðr eigi segja, því at ek ann eigi þess frændum mínum ok fóstbræðrum, at þeir hafi híngat þvílíka ferð, sem þér mundut haft hafa, ef þér nytið eigi mín við; en nú er svá komit aldri mínum," sagði hann, "at þat er á öngri stundu örvænt, nær elli stígr yfir höfuð mér; en þóat ek lifa enn um stundar sakir, þá eru hér á landi ríkari menn en ek, þeir at lítinn frið munu gefa útlendum mönnum, þóat þeir sé eigi híngat nálægir, sem þér erut at komnir. Síðan lét þessi maðr búa

skipit með þeim, ok var þar við til þess er byrr kom, sá er þeim var hagstæðr út at taka. En áðr þeir Guðleifr skildu, tók þessi maðr gullhring af hendi sér, ok fær í hendr Guðleifi, ok þar með gott sverð; en síðan mælti hann við Guðleif: "Ef þér verðr auðit at koma til fóstr-jarðar þinnar, þá skaltú færa sverð þetta Kjartani, bóndanum at Fróðá, en hringinn Þuríði móður hans." Guðleifr mælti: "Hvat skal ek til segja, hverr þeim sendi þessa gripi?" Hann svarar: "Seg, at sá sendi, at meiri vin var húsfreyjunnar at Fróðá en goðans at Helgafelli, bróður hennar. En ef nökkurr þykkist vita þar af, hverr þessa gripi hefir átta, þá seg þau mín orð, at ek banna hverjum manni á minn fund at fara, þvíat þat er en mesta úfæra, nema þeim takist þann veg giptusamliga um landtökuna, sem yðr hefir tekizt; er hér ok land [vítt ok] illt til hafna, en ráðinn ófriðr allstaðar útlendum mönnum, nema svá beri til sem nú hefir orðit." Eptir þetta skildu þeir. [Þeir] Guðleifr létu í haf, ok tóku Írland síð um haustið, ok vóru í Dýflinni um vetrinn; en um sumarit sigldu þeir til Íslands, ok færði Guðleifr þá af höndum gripina, ok höfðu allir þat fyrir satt, at þessi maðr hafi verit Björn Breiðvíkingakappi; en engi önnur sannyndi hafa menn til þess, nema þau sem nú vóru sögð.' Eyrbyggja Saga, ed. Vigfusson, pp. 119-22.

(74) The paper manuscripts founded upon the text of the saga presented in Hauk's Book are as follows:

IN THE ARNA-MAGNÆAN COLLECTION, COPENHAGEN.

No. 118, 8vo. The first page of this manuscript bears the following title: 'Hier hefur Grænlan[ds Ann]ál. Er fyrst Saga *edr* [His]toria Þorfin*ns* K*ar*lsef[nis] Þordar sonar.' The saga, which fills twenty-four sheets, was written in the seventeenth century by Björn á Skarðsá. There are certain interpolations in the text, as on p. 15 *b*, concerning 'Helluland hið mikla,' p. 16, on the origin of the name 'Markland,' and on p. 19 *b*, concerning the Skrelling boats. With the exception of these inserted passages, and a few minor verbal changes, the text follows closely that of ÞsK.

No. 281, 4to. On the back of p. 83 [modern pagination] of this book is the title: 'Hier hef*ur* sǫgu Þorfins Kallsefnis Þord*ar*son*ar*.' It is a neatly written manuscript, in a hand somewhat resembling the elder vellum hands. On the back of p. 84 the passage from Landnáma: 'So s*egir* Ari Þorgylsson ad þ*at* sum*ar* fóru XXII skip,' &c., together with the list of colonists as given in the Flatey Book text, have been inserted by the scribe, and the fact noted at the bottom of the page. On p. 93 the saga concludes with the words: 'Vere Gud med oss,' as in Hauk's Book, which words are usually omitted from the paper transcripts of ÞsK. It is a good clear copy of the Hauk's Book text, one of the most accurate and useful. It was made by Sigurður Jónsson of Knör toward the close of the seventeenth century. [Cf. AM. Katalog.]

No. 597 *b*, 4to. In the centre of p. 32 [modern pagination] is the title: 'Hier hefur Sǫgu Þorfins Kallsefnes Þord*ar*son*ar*.' This text, like that of 281, 4to, has the interpolated passage from Landnáma, above noted; unlike 281, 4to, however, it is a careless copy, and contains many errors, as: 'kirtel' for 'kistil,' 'fuller vonn' for 'fulltrúann,' &c. It contains numerous marginal notes in an old hand, ends on the back of p. 41, and was written [cf. AM. Katalog] in the latter half of the seventeenth century.

No. 768, 4to. At the head of the first page of text of this manuscript is the title: 'Hier hefur Grænlands Annal, er fyrst Saga edur Historia Þorfins Kalls efnis Þordar Sonar.' The saga contains thirty-eight pages, based upon the text of Hauk's Book, although with numerous additions from the narrative of the Flatey Book, as also concerning Helluland it mikla, &c. It is written in German script, dates from the seventeenth century, having belonged, according to Arni Magnusson's conjecture, in 1669, to Bishop Thord, from whom Thormod Torfæus received it. It would appear from a passage on p. 5 of this manuscript, that the scribe had access to Hauk's Book, for he writes: 'Þesser efterfarandi Capituli er einfalldliga efter Hauks Bök skrifadir,' &c.

No. 770 *b*, 4to. This manuscript contains two sagas written about 1770. The first of these, covering thirty-six pages, bears the title: 'Hier hefur Sögu Þorfinns Karlsefnis Þórdarsonar.' It is an almost literal transcript of the text of ÞsK.

No. 1008, 4to. Near the middle of this book is the saga bearing the title: 'Her hefr vpp sogu þeirra Þorfinnz Karlsefnis oc Snorra Þorbrandz sonar.' In the margin, in an old hand, are the words 'Fordret Mag. Joon Arnesen af AM,' and upon the same page Dr. Gudbrand Vigfusson has written 'eptir Hauksbók.' It is a fair copy of ÞsK, written ca. 1700.

IN THE ROYAL LIBRARY, COPENHAGEN.

No. 1692, 4to [Ny kgl. Saml.]. This copy, written in cursive hand, in the last century, fills one hundred pages, and is entitled: 'Sagan af Þorfinni Karlsefni Þórðar syni.' According to an inserted note, the copy was made by J. Johnsen [Jón Jónsson] from AM. 281, 4to.

No. 1698, 4to [Ny kgl. Saml.]. This saga, which follows closely ÞsK, under the title: 'Her hefur upp Søgu þeirra Þorfin*ns* Karls-Efnis og Snorra Þorbrandssonar,' fills twenty-seven pages of the manuscript, and was written, in German script, probably in the last century. This text is peculiarly interesting because of the variant it has from the words of the original in the passage describing the distance from Bjarneyjar to Helluland, which is thus given in this text: 'þaðan sigldu [þeir] iii dægur,' &c. [Cf. Note 46, p. 174.]

No. 1734, 4to [Ny kgl. Saml.]. This manuscript, while it does not contain ÞsK, does contain certain notabilia concerning Eric the Red, Greenland, the situation of Wineland, Albania [Hvítramannaland], &c., and on pp. 21 et seq. has an account of Þorbjörn, [sic] Kallz Efni. It was written in the last half of the last century by J. Johnson [Jónsson] after AM. 770 *b*, 4to.

No. 1754, 4to [Thott. Saml.]. This text of the saga, with the title: 'Her hefr upp sogu þeirra Þorfinnz Karlsefnis oc Snorra Þorbrandzsonar,' contains seventy-two pages, copied 'Ex codice vetusto membraneo in Bibl. Acad. Hafn. inter MSS. Arnæ Magnæi, No. 544 in 4to.' As the scribe states, 'there are certain lacunæ here and there in the Codex illegible by reason of smoke and age, which have caused certain lacunæ in this copy;' it is otherwise a good clear copy, in running hand, of ÞsK, made at a time when Hauk's Book was in no better state than at present, as the lacunæ of the copy indicate.

The paper manuscripts founded upon the text [EsR] of AM. 557, 4to, are as follows:

IN THE ARNA-MAGNÆAN COLLECTION.

No. 563 *b*, 4to. This is an inferior copy from the latter half of the seventeenth century. It is in running hand and contains nineteen pages. According to a slip, in Arni Magnusson's hand, inserted in the manuscript, it has been compared with a copy in quarto 'written by the Rev. Vigfus Gudbrandsson,' and is filled with interlineations and corrections, which bring it to a fair likeness with the text of 557, 4to.

No. 770 *b*, 4to. The second saga in this manuscript has the title: 'Hier hefst Saga af Eiríki Rauda,' beside which title Arni Magnusson has written 'er miǫg o correct' ['is very incorrect']. It is an inferior transcript of EsR, in the same hand as that of the text of ÞsK which precedes it.

No. 931, 4to. At the foot of p. 13 of this manuscript is the title 'Her Byriar Sauguna Af Eyrcke Rauda Þorvaldss.' This text covers twenty-two pages, completed, as is stated at the end of the saga, in the year 1734 ['oc likr her þessare sǫgu þann 3. Januarij Anno 1734']. It is a good clear copy of the text of EsR, omitting, however, the verses of Þorw. [sic] the Huntsman, and the Einfœting ditty.

No. 932, 4to. This collection of sagas was written, as is stated on the title-page, in the year 1821. On p. 268 of the manuscript the 'Saga fra Eyreci Rauda' begins, and is concluded on p. 297. While it follows the text of EsR, certain of the minor errors of that text have been corrected in conformity with the language of ÞsK.

No. 401, fol. This transcript of the 'Saga Eiríks Rauða' contains forty-four pages in cursive hand, with notes at the foot and in the margin of the text. Originally a close copy of AM. 557, 4to, it has been corrected in many places apparently to conform to the text of ÞsK. According to the 'Katalog' this copy was made in the latter half of the last century.

No. 30 Rask Coll. The text here presented under the title 'Sagann af Eireke Rauda,' is a rather inexact copy of EsR, written ca. 1770. This text makes Thorvald Ericsson shoot the Uniped, and has such minor variants from the original as 'Þorvalldr var kall*a*dr veidimadr,' 'samtymnis lanþar' in the second line of the second verse, &c.

No. 36 Rask Coll. On p. 116 of this collection of sagas this copy of 'Sagann af Eyríke enum Rauda' begins, and is brought to a conclusion on p. 129. It was written, as is stated at the end of the saga, by Olaf Sigurdsson, and by him completed in January 1810. While it is founded upon EsR, it is rather a paraphrase than a literal copy of that text.

In the Royal Library, Copenhagen.

No. 1697, 4to [Ny kgl. Saml.]. This text, which fills 115 pages, was copied [probably late in the last century], as is stated in the manuscript, from AM. 563 *b*, 4to, by J. Johnsson. The scribe has followed the corrected text of the manuscript from which his copy was made.

No. 1714, 4to [Ny kgl. Saml.]. This 'Saga af Eyrcke Rauda' contains eighteen pages, written in 1715. While it follows in the main EsR, it is not without minor changes due apparently to the influence of ÞsK.

No. 1173, fol. [Ny kgl. Saml.]. This manuscript, from the early part of the present century (?), contains both the Icelandic text and a Latin translation of the 'Saga af Eircke Rauda,' derived, as is stated, from AM. 557, 4to, compared with AM. 281 and 563, 4to, and Hauk's Book, together with an excerpt from AM. 770, 8vo.

No. 616, 4to [Kall. Saml.]. The 'Saga Eireks Rauda,' which occupies the ninth place in this collection, fills twelve pages. It is written in a good hand of the early part of the last century, or the end of the seventeenth century, and follows the text of AM. 557, 4to, closely.

No. 1776, 4to [Thott. Saml.]. In this bundle of sagas the text of 'Sagan af Eyreke Rauda' forms a separate tractate. This is a copy of EsR made, probably, in the latter part of the last century, with unimportant variants of the original text as 'Þorvallþr veiþimadr;' in Thorhall's second ditty 'knarrar skurd,' instead of 'knarrar skeið,' &c.

No. 984 *a*, fol. [Thott. Saml.]. In this collection of folios there are two texts of EsR; one has the title 'Saga Eyreks Rauda,' the other 'Saga af Eyreke Rauda.' The first contains twenty-six pages, following closely the text of AM. 557, 4to, except in the omission of the stanzas of Þorvald [sic] the Huntsman, and that which refers to the Uniped. The second text contains twenty-eight pages, and, like the first, is a close copy of the text of AM. 557, 4to, except, in this case, in the orthography. Both transcripts appear to have been made in the latter half of the last century.

In the British Museum Library.

No. 11,123. At the end of this quarto manuscript are fifty-three pages, in running hand, containing 'Sagan af Eirike Rauða.' This saga is a fairly literal transcript of the text of EsR. It is preceded by a woodcut of Eric the Red, being the same as that contained in Arngrim Jonsson's 'Gronlandia,' and is followed by a few pages of 'Annals' and notes, the concluding notice bearing the title 'Af Þorbirni Karlsefni,' with the entry, at the end, written at Borgartún, 1775, by Oddr Jónsson.

No. 11,126. This is a folio manuscript of thirty-seven pages. On an inserted fly-leaf is the note 'Saga Eiriks Rauda ex membrana in Arnæ Magnæi Bibliotheca in 4to, Num. 557.' There are a few marginal corrections of the clerical errors of AM. 557, 4to, as 'skridu' for 'skylldu,' 'fundu kiol' for 'fengu skiol,' &c., and a few lacunæ in the transcript where the scribe has not been able to read the words of the vellum. According to the Manuscript Catalogue, this copy was made in Copenhagen in 1768 by Odd Jónsson. Both 11,123, and 11,126 are from the collection of Finn Magnusen.

No. 4,867 [Banks Coll.]. A manuscript in folio containing many sagas, of which the third in the collection is 'Sagann af Eyreke Ravda,' which fills sixteen pages, and is a fairly accurate copy of the text of AM. 557, 4to, written, as would appear from an entry at the end of the saga, in 1691.

In addition to these paper manuscripts of the text of EsR there are others in the National Library of Reykjavík [143, 4to, 150, 4to, and 151, 4to], and one in the Royal Library of Stockholm, which I have not found it possible to examine. The text of the Stockholm manuscript, No. 35, fol., conforms to that of AM. 557, 4to [cf. Arwidsson, Förteckning öfver Kongl. Bibliothekets i Stockholm Isländska Handskrifter, Stockholm, 1848, pp. 66–7], and it is not probable that the Reykjavík manuscripts offer any peculiarities differing from those exhibited by the paper transcripts above mentioned.

Of the Wineland history of the Flatey Book there is in the Arna-Magnæan Collection a paper copy of the Saga of Olaf Tryggvason, being No. 57, fol., which contains the Þáttr Eireks Rauda' [pp. 1064–73, new pagination 533 *b*–38], as well as the 'Grænlendingha þáttr' [pp. 1361–94, new pagination 682–98 *b*]. This is a literal transcript of the narrative of the Flatey Book.

It seems safe to conclude that the texts of all these paper manuscripts are derived, directly or indirectly, from the vellum manuscripts which have been preserved, and of which facsimiles are here given. In the numerous transcripts of the texts of EsR and ÞsK there are no passages which indicate an origin other than the two vellum manuscripts, AM. 544 and 557, 4to, and the numerous variants from these originals have, in all likelihood, arisen either through the editorial care or clerical carelessness of the scribes of these transcripts.

INDEX.

NAMES OF PERSONS.

NAMES OF PLACES.

THE END.

www.ingramcontent.com/pod-product-compliance
Lightning Source LLC
Chambersburg PA
CBHW030731280326
41926CB00086B/1104